HEART FAILURE

HEART FAILURE

EDITOR
Alfred P. Fishman
Hospital of the University of Pennsylvania

HEMISPHERE PUBLISHING CORPORATION

Washington   London

McGRAW–HILL BOOK COMPANY

New York   St. Louis   San Francisco   Auckland   Bogotá
Düsseldorf   Johannesburg   London   Madrid   Mexico
Montreal   New Delhi   Panama   Paris   São Paulo
Singapore   Sydney   Tokyo   Toronto

NOTICE

Medicine is an ever-changing science. As new research and clinical experience broaden our knowledge, changes in treatment and drug therapy are required. The editors and the publisher of this work have made every effort to ensure that the drug dosage schedules herein are accurate and in accord with the standards accepted at the time of publication. Readers are advised, however, to check the product information sheet included in the package of each drug they plan to administer to be certain that changes have not been made in the recommended dose or in the contraindications for administration. This recommendation is of particular importance in regard to new or infrequently used drugs.

HEART FAILURE

Copyright © 1978 by Hemisphere Publishing Corporation. All rights reserved. Printed in the United States of America. No part of this publication may be reproduced, stored in a retrieval system, or transmitted, in any form or by any means, electronic, mechanical, photocopying, recording, or otherwise, without the prior written permission of the publisher.

1 2 3 4 5 6 7 8 9 0   H D H D   7 8 3 2 1 0 9 8

This book was set in Press Roman by Hemisphere Publishing Corporation. The editors were Mary Dorfman and Judith B. Gandy; the designer was Myung H. K. Bae; the production supervisor was Rebekah McKinney; and the typesetter was Wayne Hutchins.
Halliday Lithograph Corporation was printer and binder.

Library of Congress Cataloging in Publication Data

Main entry under title:

Heart failure.

   Papers presented at a symposium in honor of Dr. Isaac Starr, held at the University of Pennsylvania.
   Includes index.
   1. Congestive heart failure—Congresses. 2. Starr, Isaac, date. I. Fishman, Alfred P. II. Starr, Isaac, date. III. Pennsylvania. University.
[DNLM: 1. Heart failure, Congestive—Diagnosis— Congresses. 2. Heart failure, Congestive—Therapy— Congresses. WG370 H436 1977]
RC685.C53H4   616.1'2   78-59673
ISBN 0-07-021118-3

CONTENTS

7052399

FOREWORD

Many years of physiological and clinical study have confirmed that the heart is not anxious to disclose its innermost workings. Even in the normal heart, particularly at the ultrastructural level, large conceptual jumps have to be made in order to relate structure and function. The bridges of hypotheses become longer and more tenuous when one or both ventricles begin to fail.

Recently there has been a renaissance of research into heart failure. As a result, much has been learned about the assessment of ventricular performance, the effects of different types of loads on the behavior of the affected ventricle, the energetics of the normal and failing heart, the determination of contractility, and the contributions of autonomic control to the function of the cardiac pump. But many enigmas remain. How do the anatomic and biochemical transformations that are operative in the normal heart operate in hearts that are hypertrophied or dilated or failing? Indeed, are the same mechanisms operative? What are the ultrastructural bases for heart failure? What are the biochemical and physiological consequences of unloading a failing ventricle? How does failure of one ventricle affect the behavior of the other? How do pharmacological agents exert their distinctive inotropic effects on the failing heart?

For the symposium to honor Dr. Isaac Starr, experts were drawn from near and far to review the current understanding of heart failure. In the essays that follow these experts have drawn clear pictures of the scientific bases for clinical practice. In doing so they have made a sharp distinction between empirical and scientific practice, identified pathogenetic gulfs that separate fundamental science from bedside diagnosis and treatment, and highlighted the exciting new frontiers in concept and technology. It is difficult to escape the impression that we are on the brink of important new discoveries in heart failure and that fresh approaches are destined to be important bridgeheads on the way to new understanding.

The major purpose of this foreword is to acknowledge indebtedness to those who have paved the way for this book: Dr. Starr for allowing us to dedicate this volume in his honor, the University of Pennsylvania and School of Medicine for encouraging this exchange of ideas, and the Steering Committee (Alfred P. Fishman, M.D., James J. Ferguson, Jr., M.D., Lee D. Peachey, M.D., Karl T. Weber, M.D., and Francis C. Wood, M.D.) for attracting the distinguished participants. A special word of thanks is also due to Ms. Susanna Doyle for the painstaking editorial assistance that made this publication possible.

Alfred P. Fishman, M.D.

WELCOMING REMARKS
FROM THE PRESIDENT
OF THE UNIVERSITY

Five or six years ago I was at a dinner party at the Athenaeum in London. I was there as the guest of friends—professors of medicine in the United Kingdom and other parts of the British Commonwealth. On that occasion, I remember, I received a very special accolade from them. They said, "Oh, you are from the University of Pennsylvania, the place where that great man, Isaac Starr, is."

Isaac Starr is very much part of the University of Pennsylvania. Ever since he graduated from the School of Medicine in 1920 he has been part of our Medical School. He has been professor of therapeutics and therapeutic research and dean of the medical school. And he is very much a part of things now. He is active in the laboratory, he is active publishing—and he is an active participant in this seminar in his honor, on the failing heart. Isaac Starr is, indeed, a name to conjure with.

Starr has been described as a major planet in the solar system of Alfred Newton Richards, and it was Richards who offered him his first position as instructor of pharmacology at the University of Pennsylvania. On that occasion Richards wrote to Starr promising him little but hard work. That was the nature of Richards, who never even bothered to learn to drive an automobile because it would be too much of a diversion.

I have been doing some writing on Richards, and I have read what Starr has written about Richards. At one point, he recalled the definition of genius as the capacity to take infinite pains and, of course, he applied this definition to Richards. It is also a hallmark of Starr's career, one which we are celebrating today. He has been devoted to hard work, but hard work accompanied by the most extraordinary intellectual and professional accomplishments.

As you know, according to Starling's law of the heart, when the heart is stretched it does more work. I would like to suggest that there is another law: Starr's law of life. And according to Starr's law of life, when you stretch yourself, you get more out of yourself and out of life.

It is thus with great pleasure and pride that I greet here today, in honor of Isaac Starr, some of the great contributors to cardiology. Warmest welcome to the University of Pennsylvania.

Martin Meyerson

OPENING REMARKS
FROM THE DEAN
OF THE MEDICAL SCHOOL

I, too, would like to extend my greetings in behalf of our faculty and students, Dr. Starr. Your constituents are delighted to see this seminar assembled.

It was about a year ago that we conceived the idea of honoring Dr. Starr. Dr. Fishman translated that idea into the planning, then the structure, and finally the implementation of this symposium. I certainly cannot think of a better way to honor Dr. Starr than by assembling a group of individuals interested in science and the heart so that they might share knowledge in his behalf.

I would like to speak to only a few points. President Meyerson addressed a different perspective. But first I would like to comment about Dr. Starr's retirement.

As you may or may not know, Dr. Starr retired in 1961. In this era in which the federal government is attempting to write laws to organize the lives of all of us—and, of course, one such law under consideration is the extension of the retirement age—I think we can point to Dr. Starr as an example of an individual who retired voluntarily and yet continued productively for many years; in fact, it has been almost 17 years.

During those 17 years of leisure Dr. Starr has published 46 papers. I emphasize this in an advisory way to our young people in the audience who are just beginning their careers. I know another individual in this audience who has addressed this same point in terms of my own career development, and that is Dr. Francis C. Wood, who always made me focus on how much time there was left, and not on how much time has gone by. Dr. Starr, we certainly are very appreciative of the standards you have set for us.

I also want to comment on another aspect of Dr. Starr's career. You know, even great people occasionally deviate from their career trajectory. There was a period from 1945 until 1948 in which Dr. Starr assumed the deanship of this great School of Medicine. But, in his wisdom, he rapidly shed that responsibility and headed back into science.

Finally, I came across an article that was written by Dr. Starr in 1948. I will read it to you as testimony of his wisdom and his prophetic nature. Dr. Starr, if I may, and I am quoting now:

> *Medical care is in a state of rapid transition. Never in history has the advance of medical knowledge been as rapid as it is at this minute. The*

increasing benefit to the public is so striking that those elements of the population who have not had the best in medical services now are demanding it. This is right and proper; to secure an ideal medical service for all is a noble goal, and to find the best means of reaching it is one of the burning problems of our time.

Therefore, let us now consider by what means the advance of medical knowledge was brought about, how a further advance can be accomplished and how the rapidly increasing knowledge can be brought to bear effectively on all problems of sick people. Let us first consider the ways and means of continuing the medical advance in an undiminished pace. This advance has depended chiefly on five needs, and I think this is the message: brains, training, teamwork, time *and* tools.

The determinants of our current scientific advances still derive from these factors. I am delighted that this session is being held because it has assembled the brains, addresses itself to training, and illustrates a serious commitment to time.

Dr. Starr, there is nothing else that I can say in testimony that could be better than the program that is to follow. My greetings, sir.

Edward J. Stemmler

DEDICATION OF THE STARR SYMPOSIUM

When Dr. Fishman asked me to take part in this program and gave me as a subject the "Dedication of the Symposium," I looked up "dedication" in the large Webster's dictionary and found, "to devote exclusively to the service or worship of a divine being," so at that point I terminated my hunt for a definition of my function.

Dr. Isaac Starr, although not a divine being, is such a remarkable man that, when I was asked to introduce this symposium, I began to wonder how he got that way. I wondered if he had followed Oliver Wendell Holmes' prescription and chosen his great-grandfather wisely. So one day I asked him to tell me about all the great physicians and scientists on his genealogical tree. There weren't any!

An ancestor, a captain of infantry in Cromwell's army, was given land in County Meath, Ireland. Subsequently his son was converted to the Quaker faith and gave up his share of the spoils of war. The Starrs came to America in 1702 and bought land near Kennett Square from William Penn. One of Dr. Starr's ancestors called a son "Isaac," for no reason one can discern, and there has been one in every generation since. Our Dr. Isaac Starr is the seventh one in direct line. The fourth Isaac Starr became a prosperous shipowner, moved to Philadelphia, and also had a summer home "in the country" in Chestnut Hill, and that gives you a brief excursion into the genealogical and geographic history of the Starrs.

Where, then, can we find the origin of the inspiration to a career in medicine and medical science? Dr. Starr's mother had paroxysmal tachycardia for years, and there were doctors around the house; that made him think about medicine. When he was at Princeton Dr. Starr's admiration was captured by two professors, who similarly captured my admiration a few years later. They were Edwin Grant Conklin, professor of biology—of sea urchin egg fame, the gastrula and the blastula. There was also Dr. E. Newton Harvey, professor of physiology—of "cold light" fame. Incidently, these two Princeton professors also stimulated George Berry and Philip Bard. When you think of the inspiration and admiration that has been stimulated by Dr. Starr in his time—well, I will not go further with this arithmetic.

After medical school at Pennsylvania and internship at Massachusetts General Hospital, Dr. Starr returned here, to our Department of Pharmacology, and came under the influence of Dr. Alfred Newton Richards. Those of you who knew A.N.R. know what that meant.

At that time Sir Henry Dale said that pharmacology was a science that studied the effects, in animals, of various drugs that clinicians believed to be effective in their patients, in the hope of finding some plausible explanation for that belief. Of course, Dr. Richards took it further. He was interested in the effects of drugs on sick *people.* He made Dr. Starr the first assistant professor of clinical pharmacology in the world. Dr. Starr and Joseph Hayman developed a course in clinical pharmacology—one of the best courses I have ever had. Dr. Starr was a superb teacher. He had the knack of explaining almost anything better than anyone else. I have enjoyed his teaching ever since I heard him tell us how to cure a cold by the "hat method."

How did he get into investigation? He tells me that when he came to Dr. Richards' department, insulin had just been discovered, and he had a supply before anyone else in the vicinity, and had the responsibility of a lot of very sick diabetic patients with much vascular disease and angina. One of his early and important innovations in therapy came as a result of putting his hand on the leg of a diabetic patient with threatened gangrene, whose leg was covered by a cradle with an electric light bulb in it. He says the leg was so hot he could hardly keep his hand on it. He was the originator of the idea of putting a thermostat in those cradles. How many legs he has saved no one can calculate.

About that time Dr. Starr says he wanted to measure something, and used Yandell Henderson's ethyl iodide method for measuring cardiac output. It did not work, because Henderson (a brilliant conceiver and sometimes a careless experimenter) did not know that the rubber in the breathing bag absorbed ethyl iodide. Dr. Starr made a metal breathing bag and then became successful in measuring cardiac output.

He later became interested in acetyl-β-methylcholine chloride, and I took part in observing what happened to Dr. Starr when he himself took the first dose any human being had received. Several of us were watching his electrocardiogram, pulse, respiration, etc. The blood pressures were being taken by Kendall Elson and recorded by Carl Schmidt, and went something like this: 120/80, 110/70, 95/60, 75/40, . . . , 70/30, 90/40, 110/80—at which moment Dr. Starr, who had been perspiring profusely, commented "Please record: 'Patient smiles for the first time.' "

At one time Dr. Starr made observations on the effect of counterirritation on pain in his own arm, produced by the subcutaneous injection of hypertonic saline. He demonstrated that a pain in the left forearm is mitigated by putting an ice bag on the right foot. Acupuncture in China had, of course, preceded his experiments, but what he recorded might well throw light on some of its puzzling phenomena.

He was one of the first, I believe, to observe that the high venous pressure in the neck of a patient with congestive heart failure does not drop when the patient dies.

I will not enlarge on his unselfishness in taking on the deanship of the medical school during World War II, or on how well he did it. I will not try to mention all the important national and international committees on which he has served. Probably relatively few of you knew that he was, for 20 years, a member of the committee to revise the *U.S. Pharmacopeia.*

He has one habit I have always admired. He will listen to a young person detailing an investigation, and when the talk is over Dr. Starr will ask, "How did you happen to start doing these experiments in the first place?"

Of course, the accomplishment for which he is best known is the development and use of the ballistocardiograph (the name first appeared in his bibliography in 1939). The idea was actually thought of by an Englishman by the name of Gordon in the late nineteenth century. Also, Yandell Henderson, when standing on a spring scale one day, noted movement of the indicator with each heart beat; he constructed a table for a person to lie on, and recorded its movements on a smoked drum. Yet neither of these early episodes ever came to anything, and it was Dr. Starr's meticulous, intelligent observations and experiments that led to the present state of our knowledge.

Well, I have watched Dr. Starr for 50 years, listened to him, worked with him, objected to some of his statements and conclusions now and then—and usually have been wrong. You know, when someone is a close friend, it is almost a shock when you suddenly wake up and find he has amounted to something. But there it is. When it finally dawns on you it gives you a very pleasant sensation.

Francis C. Wood

CONTRIBUTORS

Francois M. Abboud, M.D.   Cardiovascular Division, Department of Internal Medicine, Cardiovascular Center, College of Medicine, University of Iowa, Iowa City, IA 52242

Gary Bailin   Department of Biochemistry, New Jersey School of Osteopathic Medicine, Piscataway, NJ 08854

Eugene Braunwald, M.D.   Department of Medicine, Harvard Medical School and Peter Bent Brigham Hospital, Boston, MA 02115

Robert A. Bruce, M.D.   Professor of Medicine & Co-Director, Division of Cardiology, University of Washington, Seattle, WA 98195

Mortimer J. Buckley, M.D.   Department of Surgery, Massachusetts General Hospital and Harvard Medical School, Boston, MA 02114

L. John Clarke, M.D.   Senior Fellow, Division of Cardiology, University of Washington, Seattle, WA 98195

Jay N. Cohn, M.D.   Department of Medicine, University of Minnesota Medical School, Minneapolis, MN 55455

Anthony N. DeMaria, M.D.   Section of Cardiovascular Medicine, Departments of Medicine & Physiology, University of California at Davis and Sacramento Medical Center, Davis, CA 95616

Harold T. Dodge, M.D.   Department of Medicine, Division of Cardiology, University of Washington, Seattle, WA 98195

Alfred P. Fishman, M.D.   Director, Cardiovascular-Pulmonary Division, Hospital of the University of Pennsylvania, 3600 Spruce Street, Philadelphia, PA 19104

Stephen F. Flaim, Ph.D.   Division of Cardiology, The Milton S. Hershey Medical Center, Pennsylvania State University, College of Medicine, Hershey, PA 17033

Nicholas J. Fortuin, M.D.   Associate Professor of Medicine, Division of Cardiology, The Johns Hopkins University, School of Medicine, Baltimore, MD 21205

Morris Frimer, M.S.   Department of Medicine, Division of Cardiology, University of Washington, Seattle, WA 98195

Martin Goldberg, M.D.   Renal-Electrolyte Section, Department of Medicine, Hospital of the University of Pennsylvania, 3600 Spruce Street, Philadelphia, PA 19104

Richard Gorlin, M.D.   Chairman, Department of Medicine, Mount Sinai School of Medicine, New York, NY 10029

Edgar Haber, M.D.   Cardiac Unit, Massachusetts General Hospital and Department of Medicine, Harvard University, Boston, MA 02114

Tatsuo Iwazumi   Department of Anesthesiology and Division of Bioengineering, University of Washington, Seattle, WA 98195

Joseph S. Janicki, Ph.D.   Cardiovascular-Pulmonary Division, Hospital of the University of Pennsylvania, 3600 Spruce Street, Philadelphia, PA 19104

James A. Joye, M.D.   Section of Cardiovascular Medicine, Departments of Medicine & Physiology, University of California at Davis and Sacramento Medical Center, Davis, CA 95616

Arnold M. Katz   Division of Cardiology, Department of Medicine, University of Connecticut Health Center, Farmington, CT 06032

Madeleine A. Kirchberger   Departments of Physiology & Biophysics, Mount Sinai School of Medicine, New York, NY 10029

Nicholas T. Kouchoukos, M.D.   Division of Cardiovascular and Thoracic Surgery, Department of Surgery, University of Alabama Medical Center, Birmingham, AL 35294

Garrett Lee, M.D.   Section of Cardiovascular Medicine, Departments of Medicine & Physiology, University of California at Davis and Sacramento Medical Center, Davis, CA 95616

John Longhurst, M.D.   Division of Cardiology, University of Texas, Southwestern School of Medicine, Dallas, TX 75235

Dean T. Mason, M.D.   Professor and Chief, Section of Cardiovascular Medicine, Departments of Medicine & Physiology, University of California at Davis and Sacramento Medical Center, Davis, CA 95616

Ralph Moskowitz, M.D.   Division of Cardiology, The Milton S. Hershey Medical Center, Pennsylvania State University, College of Medicine, Hershey, PA 17033

Stephen Nellis, Ph.D.   Division of Cardiology, The Milton S. Hershey Medical Center, Pennsylvania State University, College of Medicine, Hershey, PA 17033

John C. Norman, M.D.   Section of Surgery and Cardiovascular Surgical Research Laboratories, Texas Heart Institute of St. Luke's Episcopal & Texas Children's Hospitals and University of Texas Health Sciences Center, Houston, Texas 77025

William W. Parmley, M.D.   Chief, Cardiovascular Division, University of California, 1186 Moffitt Hospital, Third & Parnassus Avenue, San Francisco, CA 94143

Kirk L. Peterson, M.D.   Cardiology Section, University of California, School of Medicine, San Diego, CA 92103

Giuseppe G. Pietra, M.D.   Cardiovascular-Pulmonary Division, Hospital of the University of Pennsylvania, 3600 Spruce Street, Philadelphia, PA 19104

Bertram Pitt, M.D.   Cardiology Division, University of Michigan, Medical School, Ann Arbor, MI 48109

Gerald H. Pollack, Ph.D.   Department of Anesthesiology and Division of Bio-engineering, University of Washington, Seattle, WA 98195

Martin Reivich, M.D.   Cerebrovascular Research Center, Department of Neurology, University of Pennsylvania, Philadelphia, PA 19104

David Schaffer   Department of Medicine, Wayne State University, School of Medicine and Harper Hospital, Detroit, MI 48201

Phillip G. Schmid   Cardiovascular Division, Department of Internal Medicine, Cardiovascular Center, College of Medicine, University of Iowa, Iowa City, IA 52242

Louis C. Sheppard, Ph.D.   Division of Cardiovascular and Thoracic Surgery, Department of Surgery, University of Alabama Medical Center, Birmingham, AL 35294

Young H. Sohn, M.D.   Department of Medicine, Wayne State University, School of Medicine and Harper Hospital, Detroit, MI 48201

Richard S. Stack, M.D.   Department of Medicine, Wayne State University, School of Medicine and Harper Hospital, Detroit, MI 48201

Isaac Starr, M.D.   Emeritus Professor of Therapeutic Research, University of Pennsylvania, School of Medicine, Department of Medicine, Philadelphia, PA 19104

Douglas K. Stewart, M.D.   Department of Medicine, Division of Cardiology, University of Washington, Seattle, WA 98195

Edward B. Stinson, M.D.   Department of Cardiovascular Surgery, Stanford University Medical Center, Stanford, CA 94305

Michihiko Tada   First Department of Medicine, Osaka University Medical School, Fukushima-ku, Osaka 553, Japan

Henk E. D. J. ter Keurs   Division of Cardiology, University of Leiden, Leiden, Nederland

Karl T. Weber, M.D.   Cardiovascular-Pulmonary Division, Hospital of the University of Pennsylvania, 3600 Spruce Street, Philadelphia, PA 19104

Arnold M. Weissler, M.D.   Department of Medicine, Wayne State University, School of Medicine and Harper Hospital, Detroit, MI 48201

Robert Zelis, M.D.   Chief, Division of Cardiology, The Milton S. Hershey Medical Center, Pennsylvania State University, College of Medicine, Hershey, PA 17033

PART I

BASIC ASPECTS OF MYOCARDIAL CONTRACTION

CHAPTER I

CONTRACTILE MECHANISMS IN CARDIAC MUSCLE

GERALD H. POLLACK
TATSUO IWAZUMI
HENK E. D. J. TER KEURS

The state of cardiac mechanics is one of disequilibrium. The disequilibrium stems from a number of recent observations that have had a substantial impact on the field. These observations have raised important questions about the validity both of the established principles of cardiac mechanics and of the underlying mechanisms that many of us have been using as a theoretical framework for interpreting the mechanics. We take this as a salutary indication.

The quest to unravel the principles of cardiac mechanics was the motivating force behind our recent experiments. Having been intensively involved in the field for several years, we found ourselves confused by the bewildering array of results, interpretations, and conclusions, some of which appeared to be mutually exclusive. We felt that the isolated papillary muscle preparation we and others had been using might be the source of the confusion, and therefore decided to look directly at the sarcomeres. Krueger and Pollack then began dissecting papillary muscles thin enough for measuring the dynamics optically; that is, we could measure not only the length and tension but the time course of sarcomere length changes as well.

We were shocked by our findings. When we measured the time course of sarcomere length during isometric contraction, we found that it did not remain constant, or even approximately constant, even though the contraction was ostensibly isometric. It decreased by 0.2–0.3 μm, an amount that was appreciable relative to the limited range of sarcomere lengths encompassing the entire length-tension curve. At first we were puzzled by this large internal shortening and considered various types of sarcomere rearrangements that might give rise to an apparent reduction of overall sarcomere length. In retrospect, we wonder why it took us so long to discover the simple explanation: the end regions of the preparation were damaged by clamping and acted as a large series compliance. The viable muscle in the center of the preparation contracted and stretched these anomalous compliant regions at the ends of the specimen (13).

We wondered at first whether this clamping artifact was a consequence of the particular way we grasped our specimens, and although we found that similar results could be obtained with several different types of clamp, it was not yet clear that this finding might be a general one. Just after we published our observations, Julian and Sollins (11) also reported internal shortening on the order of 15% in rat papillary muscle, and more recently Huntsman and Stewart (7) have reported comparable results in larger cat papillary muscles. In addition to these published reports, preliminary observations of other colleagues who have begun studies of cardiac muscle at the sarcomere level have confirmed these findings. It appears that the clamping artifact is probably a common feature of many, if not all, preparations of isolated cardiac muscle.

The implication of this finding is far-reaching. Beginning with the pioneering work of Sonnenblick and colleagues, followed by Brady, Hefner, Noble, and others, a set of "principles" of cardiac mechanics gradually evolved, although never into great lucidity. These principles evolved from results obtained with preparations that were not exclusively muscle, but almost certainly a series combination of muscle, a gray zone of partially contractile tissue (H. E. D. J. ter Keurs and G. H. Pollack, unpublished results), and noncontractile tissue immediately adjacent to the clamps. Properties interpreted to be those of *muscle* were almost certainly properties of an inhomogeneous mix of contractile and noncontractile tissues. This raises the question of whether *all* of the many experiments performed on isolated papillary muscle need be repeated at the sarcomere level or, at the very least, reinterpreted. Thus, the present disequilibrium.

We have begun such studies (16), as have several others. As these studies are in their infancy, it may be more interesting at this stage to describe the techniques rather than the results.

The most direct approach, photographing the striation pattern during contraction, has been employed by Julian and Sollins (11) in rat papillary muscle. With this technique, they have been able to measure the length-tension relation at the sarcomere level. This technique has the inherent disadvantage of allowing no on-line analysis or feedback control of sarcomere length.

Another approach used by the same group is that of surface markers (12). Two markers on the surface of the muscle are used to delineate a segment of muscle and are assumed to reflect the spacing of the striations within the specimen. The segment length signal can be fed back to control the segment length. The validity of this approach depends on the precision with which surface markers can reflect internal motion.

Muscle segments can also be defined through the use of microsphere markers lodged in the vasculature. The distance between markers is assumed to reflect the striation spacing in the tissue between the microsphere pairs (13).

An ingenious technique for measuring segment length has been devised by Huntsman (6). It is based on the principle of constant volume during contraction, in that sarcomere shortening can be sensed indirectly by measuring the increased cross-sectional area. This is achieved with a lightweight coil mounted around the specimen. When a magnetic field is applied normal to the plane of the coil, the voltage induced in the coil is proportional to its instantaneous cross-sectional area.

In our laboratory the optical diffraction technique is being used. Because the muscle consists of repeating bands of alternating refractive index, it acts as a diffraction grating. When a beam of collimated, monochromatic light (as from a laser) impinges on the muscle in a direction normal to the muscle axis, the light transmitted through the muscle emerges in a series of bands. The spacing between bands is uniquely related to the sarcomere length. On-line analysis of sarcomere length is straightforward, and one can feed the signal back to control the sarcomere length of the preparation.

These five techniques (and we may have missed some others) have just begun to be exploited. The results are sketchy, and we cite a recent review (10) rather than catalog them here, for the pieces of the puzzle have yet to fit together. We trust that these techniques will soon lead to an elucidation of the principles of cardiac mechanics (and possibly to an understanding of cardiac arrhythmias as well).

We now turn to the second aspect of the problem—the molecular mechanism underlying cardiac contraction. We presume, to begin with, that this mechanism is similar in principle to that in skeletal muscle, so that one may consider the contractile mechanism of striated muscle in more general terms. Current ideas arose almost a quarter century ago. Without going into detail, since the evidence has been adequately reviewed, it is now generally accepted that 1) thick and thin filaments do not change their length, and passive stretch or active shortening is achieved by a relative sliding motion of the thick and thin filaments, and 2) active shortening is mediated by cyclic attachment and detachment of cross-bridges. These two theories have become dogma and only rarely have they been seriously questioned or challenged during the past decade.

On the other hand, a growing number of observations do not readily fit into the sliding filament and cross-bridge framework. Some of them have been reviewed (14), and we will deal here with recent experiments we have done that we believe raise even more serious questions about the validity of the cross-bridge mechanisms.

The first observation deals with the time course of sarcomere shortening in cardiac and skeletal muscle. Before describing the finding, consider the kind of shortening time course predicted by the cross-bridge theory. A rowboat with a crew of a hundred or so is a simple but useful analogy for the thick filament and its constituent cross-bridges. In such a rowboat, there is no coxswain calling the strokes; the crew members row asynchronously. This follows from the theory, as attachment of each bridge is a stochastic process, in which the probability of attachment depends on the proximity of an attachment site, the biochemical conditions, the relative velocity of sliding of the filaments, and other factors. If only one oar were in the water at a time, the motion of the boat (ignoring inertia) would be irregular, with periods of motion alternating with periods of standstill. With an increasing number of the crew rowing asynchronously, there will be fewer periods of zero velocity. With more than half the crew rowing at any time (consistent with X-ray and stiffness data), one would expect the motion to be fairly smooth, allowing perhaps some irregularity.

Measuring the velocity of a single boat is akin to measuring the relative velocity of a single pair of thick and thin filaments; we know of no way to achieve this. More realistically, one measures the *average* velocity of a large ensemble of thick and thin filaments, on the order of 10^9 in a representative microscopic field. If we consider the average velocity of 10^9 rowboats in series and parallel, the action of *each* of the 10^{11} rowers being uncoordinated with the action of any other rower, we certainly ought to observe motion that is steady; periods in which the average velocity is zero would be difficult to envision.

Figure 1 shows the time course of sarcomere shortening in a single fiber of skeletal muscle. This fiber was held isometrically, so we are measuring the "internal" shortening in a localized region under the microscope objective. The field dimensions are on the order of $(100 \ \mu m)^3$, a tissue volume containing on the order of 10^{11} bridges. The pattern of Fig. 1 is striking in that the shortening pattern is not at all smooth. There are periods of zero velocity interspersed with periods of steady shortening. Such periods of zero velocity, if they are not artifacts, signify that if the motion were indeed brought about by the action of bridges, the motion of each bridge would have to be cooperatively linked to the motion of other bridges. (A coxswain must be synchronizing the actions of the crew.) However, this conclusion conflicts with the stochastic nature of cross-bridge activity, which is central to the theory.

Figure 1 is representative of many such records we have obtained, in both cardiac and skeletal muscle. After our first excitement over having identified so striking and unexpected a phenomenon, we began to develop some skepticism. Early

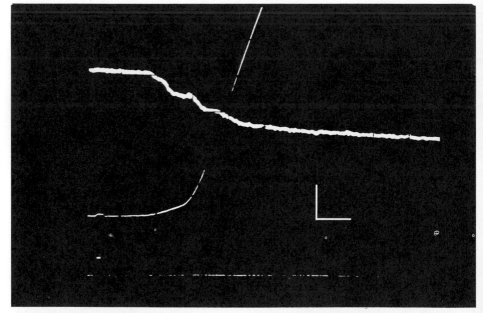

FIGURE 1 Time course of sarcomere shortening in a single fiber of skeletal muscle. The traces, from top to bottom, are sarcomere length, tension, and stimulus pulse. Ordinate scale: sarcomere length, 0.1 μm; tension, 20 mg; stimulus, 10 V. Abscissa time scale: 5 msec. Initial sarcomere length, 2.23 μm.

patterns were obtained by using a photodiode array to detect the spacing of the orders (plus circuitry to convert the spacing into units of sarcomere length). As this sensor contained discrete elements, we were concerned about the possibility that the steps might be a sensor artifact. We therefore obtained simultaneous registrations of sarcomere length by using both a photokymographic technique and a continuous electronic sensor (Schottky barrier photodiode). The records obtained with these diverse devices were similar (15), which ruled out the possibility of sensor artifact.

The implication of stepwise shortening in the molecular mechanism is not yet clear; however, one can be fairly confident that the contractile mechanism, whatever its nature, contains a high degree of temporal and spatial coherence.

A second finding that engenders some concern over the cross-bridge theory is the length-tension relation. According to the theory, the amount of tension developed when the contractile apparatus is fully activated should depend on the number of attached cross-bridges. This, in turn, should depend on the relative overlap of thick and thin filaments.

We have done a series of experiments using single fibers of frog semitendinosus muscle to test whether tension was directly proportional to the degree of overlap of thick and thin filaments. We measured the steady tetanic tension developed at each of a series of sarcomere lengths. Because the fibers we used were highly uniform from tendon to tendon, it was not necessary to length-clamp a uniform segment of the fiber, as was required in the experiments of Gordon et al. (4, 5).

We found that steady-state tension was constant at sarcomere lengths ranging between 1.9 and 2.6 μm and then fell off relatively slowly at higher degrees of stretch (Fig. 2). At 3.4 μm, where there is theoretically 10% maximal overlap, we obtained 50% maximal tension (17). This finding is at odds with the prediction of the cross-bridge theory. A priori, it would also seem to be at odds with the results obtained by Gordon et al. (5). However, the significant difference between the two sets of results was that we plotted *steady-state* tensions, while Gordon et al. plotted *transient* values of tension, obtained before the steady-state tension had been attained.

In isometric tetanus at sarcomere lengths exceeding 2.2 μm, tension normally develops in three phases: 1) a rapid rise phase, 2) a slow rise or "creep" phase, and 3) a plateau. Gordon et al. plotted the tension extrapolated back to the beginning of phase 2, while we plotted the tension during phase 3. The rationale used by Gordon et al. to plot the extrapolated values of tension was that the tension developed beyond phase 1 was probably artifactual. They assumed that the creep of tension (phase 2) arose from the progressive development of inhomogeneity of striation spacing along the fiber. This seemed a reasonable possibility if one assumed that the descending limb of the length-tension relation, because of its negative slope, was unstable. However, the assumption of progressive dispersion was not tested in that study.

We tested the assumption and found it to be invalid (H. E. D. J. ter Keurs et al., unpublished observations). The inhomogeneity of striation spacing increased by only several percent during contraction, far less than would be required to account for the large increase in tension during phase 2. These measurements were carried out three

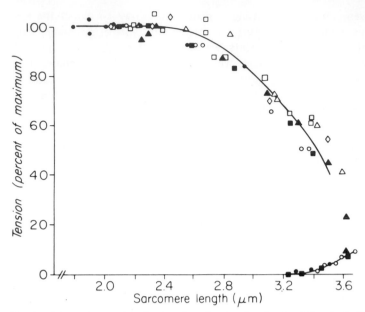

FIGURE 2 Steady-state active tension (top) and resting tension (bottom) for single fibers of frog semitendinosus muscle contracting in isometric tetani. The temperature was 8°C. Each symbol refers to an individual fiber.

ways. First, we scanned the laser beam along the muscle from tendon to tendon before contraction and then during the plateau of contraction. Second, we photographed the diffraction pattern at 0.5-sec intervals during the tetanus (broadening of the orders indicates increased dispersion). Third, we continuously measured (using fast electronics) the breadth of the first order of the diffraction pattern. There was excellent concurrence between all three methods.

We therefore concluded that the assumption of Gordon et al. was incorrect. This does not mean that one cannot plot extrapolated tensions and arrive at a length-tension relation. One has to decide whether the length-tension relation based on such extrapolated tensions or the one based on steady-state tensions better describes the force-generating characteristics of the contractile machinery.

These two sets of results have raised additional questions about the validity of the cross-bridge theory. They underline the need for additional tests, and also suggest that it might be prudent to go beyond testing the cross-bridge theory per se and consider some of the "axioms" of muscle contraction on which the cross-bridge theory rests. The sliding filament theory is an obvious and important candidate for such reexamination.

Do the filaments slide by one another during passive stretch or active shortening *without* any alteration of filament length? To question such a dogma at this late stage may seem to transcend heresy, but there are some unsettling observations that lead one to wonder.

The accepted position up to the early 1950s was that the muscle proteins folded, or shortened. These findings were discounted as artifactual by A. F. Huxley and Niedergerke (8) and by H. E. Huxley and Hanson (9). Although these two papers are now widely quoted as reporting no filament length changes during stretch or contraction, there is some room left for doubt. Huxley and Niedergerke, using interference microscopy, found an increase in the A band width of about 10% when the fiber was stretched between 2.0 and 2.5 μm. This change was claimed to be within the accuracy of their measurement technique. They also observed that the A band decreased a small amount (no values were given) when the fiber shortened actively from a sarcomere length of 2.5 μm, and particularly from 2.0 μm. These changes of A band width were interpreted as due to the limited resolution of the optical microscope.

These observed variations of A band width were not accorded much attention at the time they were reported. More recently, sufficient additional data have appeared on thick filament length changes in other species to raise the question of whether the findings of Huxley and Niedergerke merit reconsideration. Most appropriate here are the data of Winegrad (18), who found that when frog atrial trabeculae were stretched from 1.9 to 2.9 μm the measured width of the A band varied from 1.1 to 1.7 μm. These findings in cardiac muscle parallel the findings by Huxley and Niedergerke in skeletal muscle. Winegrad attributed these variations in A band width to the limited resolution of the optical microscope and possibly to variations of thick filament alignment.

Do all these measured changes in A band width represent real changes of thick filament length? One clue comes from measurements of specimens with sarcomere lengths on the order of 5–10 μm, where the resolution of the light microscope is not a limiting factor in the interpretation. In these specimens (*Limulus* and insect muscle) it has been shown by both light microscopy and electron microscopy that thick filaments undergo substantial length changes similar in nature to the A band changes reported by Huxley and Niedergerke and by Winegrad in vertebrate muscle (1, 2, 3, 8, 18). The thick filaments in these fibers differ in protein content and dimension from those in vertebrate muscle, so the observations may be irrelevant to contraction in vertebrate muscle; on the other hand, the existence of thick filament length changes in any contractile system is provocative and indicates that a careful reexamination of possible filament length changes in vertebrate muscle may not prove fruitless.

Thus, the state of disequilibrium in the field is, in our view, a healthy sign. We will reexamine not only the basic mechanical properties of cardiac muscle, but the validity of the dogmas that we have all held to tenaciously. Some surprises may loom on the horizon.

REFERENCES

1. DeVillafranca, G. W. and Marschhaus, C. E. Contraction of the A band. J Ultrastruct Res 9:156–165, 1963.
2. Dewey, M. M., Levine, R. J. C., and Colflesh, D. E. Structure of *Limulus* striated muscle. The contractile apparatus at various sarcomere lengths. J Cell Biol 58:574–593, 1973.
3. Gilmour, D. and Robinson, P. M. Contraction in glycerinated myofibrils of an insect (Orthoptera Acrididae). J Cell Biol 21:385–396, 1964.

4. Gordon, A. M., Huxley, A. F., and Julian, F. J. Tension development in highly stretched vertebrate muscle fibers. J Physiol (Lond) 184:143–169, 1966.
5. Gordon, A. M., Huxley, A. F., and Julian, F. J. The variation in isometric tension with sarcomere length in vertebrate muscle fibres. J Physiol (Lond) 184:170–192, 1966.
6. Huntsman, L. L. Segment length measurements in papillary muscle. Biophys J 17:175a, 1977.
7. Huntsman, L. L., Day, S. R., and Stewart, D. K. Nonuniform contraction in isolated cat papillary muscle. Am J Physiol 233:H613–H616, 1977.
8. Huxley, A. F. and Niedergerke, R. Structural changes in muscle during contraction. Nature (Lond) 173:971–976, 1954.
9. Huxley, H. E. and Hanson, J. Changes in the cross-striations of muscle during contraction and stretch and their structural interpretation. Nature 173:973–976, 1954.
10. Jewell, B. R. A reexamination of the influence of muscle length on myocardial performance. Circ Res 40:221–230, 1977.
11. Julian, F. J. and Sollins, M. R. Sarcomere length-tension relations in living rat papillary muscle. Circ Res 37:299–308, 1975.
12. Julian, F. J., Sollins, M. R., and Moss, R. L. Absence of a plateau in length-tension relationship of rabbit papillary muscle when internal shortening is prevented. Nature (Lond) 260:340–342, 1976.
13. Krueger, J. W. and Pollack, G. H. Myocardial sarcomere dynamics during isometric contraction. J Physiol (Lond) 251:627–643, 1975.
14. Noble, M. I. M. and Pollack, G. H. Molecular mechanisms of contraction. Circ Res 40:333–342, 1977.
15. Pollack, G. H., Iwazumi, T., ter Keurs, H. E. D. J., and Shibata, E. F. Sarcomere shortening in striated muscle occurs in stepwise fashion. Nature (Lond) 768:757–759, 1977.
16. Pollack, G. H. and Krueger, J. W. Sarcomere dynamics in intact cardiac muscle. Proceedings of the Third Workshop on Cardiac Contractility (Antwerp). Eur J Cardiol 4(Suppl):53–65, 1976.
17. ter Keurs, H. E. D. J., Iwazumi, T., and Pollack, G. H. Is muscle force independent of sarcomere length between 2 and 3 μm? Biophys J 17:199a, 1977.
18. Winegrad, S. Functional implications of the resting sarcomere length-tension curve in living heart muscle. Ciba Found Symp 24:43–56, 1974.

CHAPTER 2

REGULATION OF MYOCARDIAL CELL FUNCTION BY AGENTS THAT INCREASE CYCLIC AMP PRODUCTION IN THE HEART

ARNOLD M. KATZ
GARY BAILIN
MADELEINE A. KIRCHBERGER
MICHIHIKO TADA

Modulation of the electric and mechanical properties of the myocardial cell underlies virtually every important physiological, pharmacological, and pathological change in the performance of the heart. This muscular pump, which requires neither somatic nor autonomic innervation to initiate its contractile activity, responds to the changing needs of the circulation primarily by varying the complex cellular processes responsible for excitation and contraction. Unlike most skeletal muscles, the heart is unable to modulate tension through tetanic contraction or by the summation of the mechanical responses to individual nerve impulses because the cardiac action potential lasts throughout the phase of systole. In addition, the mechanical performance of the heart cannot be varied by utilization of a variable fraction of its muscular units because these are linked electrically in a functional syncytium. Thus, the heart meets the constantly changing demands placed on it by varying the properties of its individual muscle cells (16).

Utilization of cardiac muscle for studies of cellular control systems is especially rewarding because of the ease with which cardiac mechanical and electric function can be quantified and related to specific events occurring within the cell. Each myocardial cell is capable of varying the amount of tension during contraction, and the rates at which tension rises and falls are also graded. In view of abundant evidence that the tension in a contracting cardiac muscle fiber reflects the amount of calcium that is bound to a regulatory site on the troponin complex of the myofilaments (5, 15), changes in the rate of tension increase at the onset of systole, the total tension, and the rate of tension decline during relaxation can be related to changes in the rate of Ca^{2+} delivery to the myofilaments, the total amount of Ca^{2+} made available for binding to troponin, and the rate of Ca^{2+} removal from the contractile proteins, respectively. All of these processes are stimulated by catecholamines and other agents that increase cyclic AMP production in the heart.

The electric behavior of the heart is also modulated by agents that increase cyclic AMP production. From a physiological standpoint, the most important of these electrophysiological changes is an accelerated rate of pacemaker activity. As will become apparent during the subsequent discussion, this acceleration of pacemaker activity arises from changes in specific ionic channels in the sarcolemma (plasma membrane) of the cells in the *sinoatrial (SA) node* that normally initiate the heartbeat. In addition, there are important effects of beta adrenergic agonists on ionic channels in the membranes of cells in other regions of the heart. For example, agents that elevate cyclic AMP levels influence ionic currents in the sarcolemma of cells that do not normally control the rate of beating. These changes are intimately involved in the modulation of the electric behavior of the heart and, in some cases, of the contractile processes as well.

Our discussion begins with a description of the cardiac response to catecholamines that, by binding to the beta receptors on the cardiac sarcolemma, promote cyclic AMP production in the heart. Both the electric and mechanical responses of the heart to catecholamines are discussed, but the reader is referred elsewhere (16, 31) for a description of accompanying changes in intermediary metabolism. After this introduction to the effects of catecholamines on the heart, we turn our attention to the mechanism by which relaxation is accelerated by catecholamines. A cascade of chemical events is described that is initiated when cyclic AMP activates a class of enzymes, the cyclic AMP-dependent protein kinases. Other responses of cardiac muscle to catecholamines, and possible mechanisms underlying these alterations in electric and mechanical behavior, are also reviewed.

CARDIAC RESPONSE TO AGENTS THAT INCREASE CYCLIC AMP PRODUCTION

General features of the cardiac response to agents that increase cyclic AMP production in the heart are listed below.

Electric responses
  Accelerated pacemaker activity
  Alterations in action potential conformation
Mechanical responses
  Increased tension
  Increased rate of tension rise
  Increased rate of fall in tension

The circulatory response to exercise provides a useful illustration of the changes in cardiac function that are initiated by such agents. While all but the most sedentary readers of this article will be familiar with the tachycardia that accompanies physical exertion, more subtle changes in the shape of the action potential also occur in cells that do not participate in the initiation of the heartbeat. The most obvious mechanical response of the heart to exercise is a more forceful contraction, but careful observation also demonstrates that the pulse rises and falls more rapidly during exercise. These changes reflect increases in both the rise and fall of tension generated by the myocardium.

ELECTRIC EFFECTS

Acceleration of Pacemaker Activity in the Sinoatrial Node

The accelerated pacemaker activity described above results from an increased rate of spontaneous diastolic depolarization in the cells of the SA node that normally initiate each heartbeat. Figure 1 shows diagrammatically the action potentials in a cell of the SA node in the control state and under the influence of catecholamines. The increased rate of discharge in the latter state can be seen to result from an increased upward slope of the spontaneous diastolic depolarization that precedes the more rapid upstroke of the action potential. This effect is believed to result from an increase in membrane conductance to Ca^{2+} (4), which allows this cation to carry positive charge into the cell at a more rapid rate (Table 1). Catecholamines also shorten the action potential and cause hyperpolarization in the SA node (Table 1).

Changes in the Action Potential in Other Myocardial Cells

Catecholamines shorten the duration of the *atrial* action potential (Table 1). As in the SA node, this effect appears to be due to the enhancement of a repolarizing, outward, potassium current. Catecholamines also promote Ca^{2+} influx during depolarization by increasing a Ca^{2+}-selective ionic current that flows during the systolic phase of the action potential, the slow inward current (49). This enhancement of the slow inward current, which modifies both the electric and mechanical properties of the heart, is discussed more extensively when the effects of catecholamines on the cells of the ventricle are examined below.

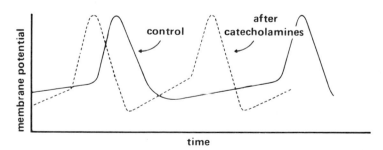

FIGURE 1   Effects of catecholamines, or sympathetic stimulation, on the action potential in the SA node. Even though there is hyperpolarization early in diastole, the rate of diastolic depolarization is increased sufficiently to accelerate pacemaker activity. Accelerated diastolic depolarization in the SA node is due to an increased inward current, possibly one carried by Ca^{2+}. Modified from Katz (16).

TABLE 1 Effects of catecholamines on the electrophysiological properties of the heart[a]

Region	Physiological response	Effects on action potential
SA node	Acceleration of pacemaker	Accelerated diastolic depolarization[b]
	Shortened refractory period	Accelerated repolarization[c] (hyperpolarization[c])
Atrial myocardium	Shortened refractory period (enhanced contractility[b])	Accelerated repolarization[c]
AV node	Accelerated conduction	Increased amplitude[b] Increased rate of depolarization[b]
His-Purkinje system	Promotion of pacemaker activity	Accelerated diastolic depolarization[d]
	Shortened refractory period	Accelerated repolarization[c] (hyperpolarization[c])
Ventricular myocardium	Shortened refractory period (enhanced contractility[b])	Accelerated repolarization[c] (hyperpolarization[c])

[a]Reproduced from A. M. Katz, Physiology of the Heart, p. 369, 1977, Raven Press.
[b]Possibly or probably due to increased calcium conductance.
[c]Probably due to increased potassium conductance.
[d]Probably due to accelerated decrease in a diastolic potassium conductance.

The ability of catecholamines to accelerate conduction in the *atrioventricular (AV) node* (Table 1) probably reflects the ability of beta adrenergic agonists to increase membrane conductance to Ca^{2+} (4). The resulting enhancement of an inward current that is carried by Ca^{2+} increases both the amplitude and rate of depolarization in the cells of the AV node and so speeds conduction through this structure.

Effects of catecholamines and cyclic AMP have been studied most extensively in the *Purkinje fiber*. These fibers can exhibit a low rate of pacemaker activity (Fig. 2) that is normally obscured by the more rapid impingement on these cells of the train of electric impulses that originates in, and is conducted from, the SA node pacemaker. Pacemaker activity in the Purkinje fiber is mediated by a mechanism that differs fundamentally from the mechanism of pacemaker discharge in the SA node. The diastolic depolarization that causes membrane potential to decrease toward threshold is not related to the opening of an ionic channel that carries inward current, but to the slow closing of a channel that allows K^+ to flow out of the cell. The resulting decrease in this outward potassium current allows a "background" inward current, which is probably carried by Na^+, to depolarize the membrane. The ability of catecholamines to promote diastolic depolarization in the Purkinje fiber has been shown to result from accelerated closing of this potassium channel in the sarcolemma (Table 1) (32, 47). A similar effect can also be initiated by cyclic AMP and its derivatives (46, 48). Accelerated opening of a different potassium channel, which is similar to that already described in the atria, shortens both action potential duration (Fig. 2) and refractory period (Table 1) in the Purkinje fiber.

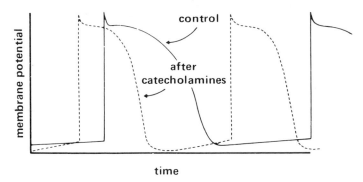

FIGURE 2 Effects of catecholamines, or sympathetic stimulation, on the action potential of the Purkinje fiber. Even though catecholamines cause hyperpolarization early in diastole, the rate of diastolic depolarization is increased sufficiently by accelerated closure of a potassium channel to speed pacemaker activity. The action potential is shortened because the outward potassium currents that cause repolarization are increased by a shift in the voltage dependence of their opening. Modified from Katz (16).

The major electrophysiological effects of catecholamines in the *ventricles* are to accelerate repolarization (Fig. 3) and to increase the slow inward current that allows Ca^{2+} to flow into the myocardial cell. The first effect is due to enhancement of an outward potassium current, and resembles the effect that causes the action potential to shorten in the atria and Purkinje fibers. Promotion of the slow inward current

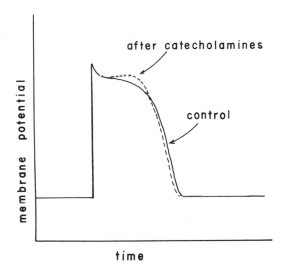

FIGURE 3 Effects of catecholamines, or sympathetic stimulation, on the action potential of the ventricles. The major effect, an upward (depolarizing) shift in the plateau, reflects the depolarizing effect of the increased slow inward current that augments calcium influx during systole.

that carries Ca^{2+} into the cell, which resembles the enhancement of Ca^{2+} influx in the SA and AV nodes and in the atria, increases the extent of depolarization during the plateau phase of the ventricular action potential (Fig. 3). This latter effect, which increases calcium entry into the ventricular cell (see below), is probably mediated by cyclic AMP (35).

The increased slow inward current in ventricular myocardial cells that is caused by catecholamines cannot be explained by changes in either the kinetics of activation of the slow channel or its cation selectivity, such as might occur if this ionic channel increased in size (36). Instead, it has been attributed to a cyclic AMP-induced increase in the number of channels that open during the plateau phase of the action potential (36).

Conclusions

Catecholamines effect a variety of changes in the electric properties of the myocardial cell, most likely by elevating intracellular cyclic AMP levels. As shown in Table 1, these changes can be attributed to three general effects on sarcolemmal ionic channels: 1) increased calcium conductance, 2) increased potassium conductance, and 3) changes in the rate of reduction of potassium conductance. We will return to the first of these effects when we discuss the biochemical mechanisms by which cyclic AMP modulates calcium fluxes across another cardiac membrane, the sarcoplasmic reticulum.

MECHANICAL EFFECTS

The final step in excitation-contraction coupling, which causes tension to appear in the myocardium, occurs when calcium binds to troponin, a regulatory protein complex that is present along with actin in the thin filaments of muscle (5, 15). For this reason, changes in total tension and the rates of tension development and decline (Fig. 4) can be attributed to changes in the amount of calcium released into the cytosol for binding to the contractile proteins and in the rates at which this cation is released into and removed from the cytosol.

Increased Rate of Tension Rise
and Rate of Calcium Release
at Onset of Systole

In most adult mammalian hearts, as in skeletal muscle, the calcium that mediates the final step in excitation-contraction coupling is derived from stores within the sarcoplasmic reticulum. The mechanism by which the action potential at the sarcolemma causes release of calcium from stores within the sarcoplasmic reticulum remains controversial (see below), but it is generally agreed that increased Ca^{2+} permeability of this intracellular membrane system allows Ca^{2+} to flow down an electrochemical gradient from within the sarcoplasmic reticulum into the cytosol. Thus, it can be postulated that the increased rate of tension rise that characterizes the cardiac response to catecholamines results in part from an increase in the calcium permeability of the sarcoplasmic reticulum at the onset of systole. Whether this putative effect is caused by a direct action on these membranes, a change in the system

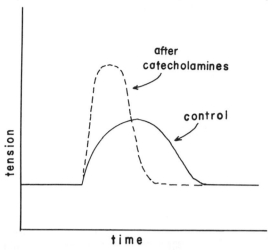

FIGURE 4   Effects of catecholamines, or sympathetic stimulation, on the tension response in cardiac muscle.

that links depolarization of the sarcolemma to the proposed increase in the Ca^{2+} permeability of the sarcoplasmic reticulum, or both, is discussed later.

Two hypotheses have been advanced to explain the link between the passage of an action potential across the sarcolemma and the initiation of calcium release by the sarcoplasmic reticulum. The first of these is based on studies of "skinned" muscle fibers, in which the sarcolemma is mechanically removed (6), and purified sarcoplasmic reticulum vesicles (14). Evidence obtained in both types of preparation suggests that changes in an electric potential across the membrane of the calcium-filled sarcoplasmic reticulum induce calcium release. The second hypothesis is based on the observations that an increase in the level of Ca^{2+} outside the sarcoplasmic reticulum of a skinned fiber that, itself, is too small to initiate tension causes both a twitchlike tension response (6, 8) and a transient calcium release (11). Evidence that elevated Ca^{2+} outside the sarcoplasmic reticulum can induce calcium release has been provided by Katz et al. (18, 20), who found that increasing Ca^{2+} in the medium surrounding calcium-filled sarcoplasmic reticulum vesicles increases their calcium permeability. On the basis of our current knowledge it is not possible to state with certainty which, if either, of these two hypotheses correctly explains this critical step in excitation-contraction coupling.

Increased Tension and the Amount of Calcium Released by the Sarcoplasmic Reticulum

In view of the proposed relationship between calcium release from the sarcoplasmic reticulum and tension development, the ability of catecholamines to increase tension in cardiac muscle could arise from an increase in the maximum calcium permeability of these membranes during systole. This hypothesis, if correct, provides a mechanism that would supplement the well-documented effect of catecholamines to promote calcium entry into the cell by way of the slow inward current (see above).

Although the amount of calcium that enters the cell during each action potential by way of the slow inward current is too small to contribute significantly to the tension developed in a given contraction (2), this calcium influx probably increases the total calcium content of the sarcoplasmic reticulum during a series of contractions under the influence of catecholamines.

Perhaps the strongest evidence that cyclic AMP exerts a direct effect on the sarcoplasmic reticulum that contributes to the enhancement of tension developed in the heart comes from the experiments of Fabiato and Fabiato (9). These investigators found that skinned cardiac muscle fibers responded to a calcium-triggered contraction (see above) in the presence of cyclic AMP with marked increases in the amount of tension developed and in the rate of tension rise and fall. Thus, cyclic AMP can produce a change in mechanical response in the absence of the sarcolemma that is, in all essentials, similar to the response of the intact myocardium to catecholamines (Fig. 4). That both the rate of rise of tension and the total tension are increased by cyclic AMP in the absence of the sarcolemma provides strong evidence that the sarcoplasmic reticulum plays a role in mediating these mechanical responses.

Increased Rate of Fall in Tension and the Calcium Pump of the Sarcoplasmic Reticulum

The sarcoplasmic reticulum plays a major role in reducing the cytosolic Ca^{2+} concentration to levels sufficiently low to cause this cation to dissociate from its binding sites in the troponin complex (5). This is accomplished by an ATP-dependent calcium pump in these membranes. The function of this calcium pump is at least twofold: 1) it provides a mechanism that removes calcium from the cytosol, thereby causing muscle to relax, and 2) it leads to calcium accumulation within the sarcoplasmic reticulum and thereby contributes to the intracellular calcium stores that initiate contraction. Recently, it has been proposed that the proteins of the calcium pump also participate in controlling calcium efflux from the sarcoplasmic reticulum (19). The following discussion focuses on the mechanism by which the cyclic AMP-protein kinase system acts on the sarcoplasmic reticulum to accelerate relaxation in the heart.

In view of the proposed causal link between the rate of calcium transport by the calcium pump of the sarcoplasmic reticulum and the rate at which a muscle relaxes, we (26) and others (27, 52) examined the properties of cardiac sarcoplasmic reticulum vesicles *in vitro* to determine whether the cyclic AMP-protein kinase system, previously shown in other reactions to mediate effects of catecholamines, was able to stimulate the calcium pump. The results summarized in the following section are presented in some detail, as studies of the mechanism responsible for the increased rate of relaxation have proved most fruitful in elucidating, at a biochemical level, one of the reactions responsible for the cardiac response to catecholamines.

MECHANISM BY WHICH AGENTS THAT INCREASE MYOCARDIAL CYCLIC AMP ACCELERATE RELAXATION

We have seen that relaxation can be accelerated by any intervention that facilitates the removal of calcium from troponin. Such an effect can occur through either or both of two fundamentally different mechanisms: 1) an increased rate of calcium transport into the sarcoplasmic reticulum, and 2) a decreased Ca^{2+} affinity of troponin that facilitates the dissociation of this cation from the troponin complex. At this time, both mechanisms appear to mediate the increased rate of cardiac relaxation in response to catecholamines.

A number of early studies suggested that catecholamines or cyclic AMP could exert a direct effect to stimulate the calcium pump of the sarcoplasmic reticulum (7, 13, 39), but several other groups, including our own (17), were unable to confirm these findings. The key to these discrepancies, and to the mechanism by which catecholamines stimulate this calcium pump, was provided by the discovery of the cyclic AMP-dependent protein kinases. These enzymes respond to the presence of cyclic AMP by transferring the terminal phosphate of ATP to form phosphoesters with serine and threonine residues of proteins. We found that inclusions of a cyclic AMP-dependent protein kinase along with cyclic AMP led to a twofold to threefold stimulation of the rate of calcium transport by cardiac sarcoplasmic reticulum (26). This finding led us to propose that the cascade of reactions shown in Fig. 5 explains two of the mechanical responses to catecholamines: increased tension and increased rate of fall in tension. Some of the findings that support this hypothesis are described in the following paragraphs, where our discussion focuses on the later reactions in the cascade.

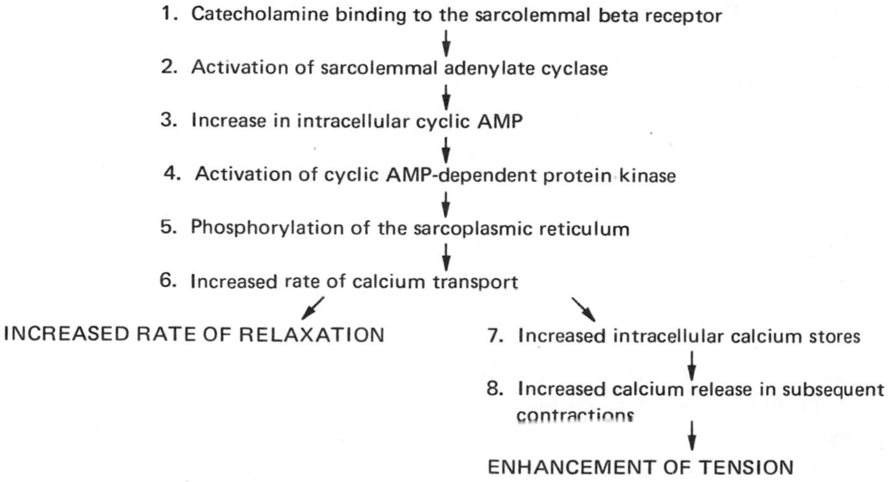

1. Catecholamine binding to the sarcolemmal beta receptor
   ↓
2. Activation of sarcolemmal adenylate cyclase
   ↓
3. Increase in intracellular cyclic AMP
   ↓
4. Activation of cyclic AMP-dependent protein kinase
   ↓
5. Phosphorylation of the sarcoplasmic reticulum
   ↓
6. Increased rate of calcium transport
   ↙ ↘

INCREASED RATE OF RELAXATION

7. Increased intracellular calcium stores
   ↓
8. Increased calcium release in subsequent contractions
   ↓

ENHANCEMENT OF TENSION

FIGURE 5 Proposed mechanism by which catecholamines modify the amount and rate of fall in tension in the myocardium. Modified from Katz et al. (21).

Phosphorylation of the Cardiac
Sarcoplasmic Reticulum

Cardiac sarcoplasmic reticulum vesicles, purified from the "heavy" microsomal fraction of canine ventricles, serve as a substrate for both intrinsic and extrinsic cyclic AMP-dependent protein kinases (26, 27, 52). The phosphoprotein formed in these reactions has the chemical characteristics of a phosphoester in which the phosphate is bound primarily as phosphoserine (25). The amount of phosphoester formed, approximately 1.5 nmol/mg protein, is the same as the amount of phosphate incorporated into the calcium pump in a different chemical form, namely the acyl phosphate of the ATPase intermediate (38). This finding suggests that there is a 1:1 molar ratio of these two phosphorylation sites, which differ both functionally and chemically.

The phosphoester formed by the action of cyclic AMP-dependent protein kinases in cardiac sarcoplasmic reticulum is dephosphorylated by phosphoprotein phosphatase (23, 27, 44), indicating the potential physiological reversibility of this reaction.

The protein that is phosphorylated by the cyclic AMP-dependent protein kinase can be readily separated from the ATPase protein by polyacrylamide gel electrophoresis. The latter protein has a molecular weight of 90,000–100,000 (10, 41), whereas the protein kinase substrate, which has been tentatively named *phospholamban*, has an apparent molecular weight of approximately 22,000 (27, 43). The inability to demonstrate phosphorylation of a protein corresponding to phospholamban in sarcoplasmic reticulum vesicles from rabbit fast skeletal muscle (24) is in accord with the inability of catecholamines to stimulate relaxation in this type of muscle (21).

Stimulation of Calcium Transport in
the Cardiac Sarcoplasmic Reticulum

The ability of the cyclic AMP-protein kinase system to stimulate calcium transport in cardiac sarcoplasmic reticulum vesicles (26, 27, 45, 50) is consistent with the view that phosphorylation by this enzyme accelerates calcium transport by this membrane pump. Evidence for a causal link between membrane phosphorylation and stimulation of calcium transport has been provided by Tada et al. (43), who found that brief, controlled, tryptic digestion of the sarcoplasmic reticulum caused a proportionate fall in the ability of the protein kinase to catalyze phosphate incorporation and to stimulate calcium transport. These studies also indicate that at least a portion of the phospholamban molecule is located on the external surface of the vesicles. This protein was found by Louis and Katz (29) to not be iodinated by peroxidase in the presence and absence of Triton X-100, which suggests that most of the protein is located within the membrane, where it is tightly bound to membrane lipids.

Further evidence that phosphorylation of phospholamban causes stimulation of calcium transport was obtained by Tada et al. (43) and Kirchberger and Chu (22), who found a close parallel between phosphoester formation and the degree to which calcium transport was stimulated by skeletal protein kinases. Recently, Kirchberger and Raffo (23) documented a parallel decrease in phospholamban phosphorylation and calcium transport stimulation when the phosphorylated cardiac sarcoplasmic reticulum was dephosphorylated by a phosphoprotein phosphatase associated with these membranes.

The experimental findings reviewed in the preceding paragraphs provide strong evidence that phosphorylation of phospholamban is causally linked to stimulation of the calcium pump of the cardiac sarcoplasmic reticulum. Present evidence cannot distinguish between two explanations for these findings: 1) that phosphorylated phospholamban is an activator of the calcium pump, and 2) that, when dephosphorylated, this protein inhibits calcium transport. Evidence bearing on this question has been reported by Tada et al. (45), who found that the apparent Ca^{2+} sensitivity of oxalate-supported calcium uptake velocity was increased after phospholamban was phosphorylated. Although these results could not be interpreted with precision because of the complex Ca^{2+} kinetics (28) of reactions carried out in the presence of oxalate (which is employed to stabilize the Ca^{2+} concentration inside the vesicles). Tada's original hypothesis is supported by a recent study by Hicks, Shigekawa, and Katz (unpublished observations) indicating that the Ca^{2+} sensitivity of the calcium pump is increased when phospholamban is phosphorylated. In view of the approximately threefold lower Ca^{2+} affinity of the calcium pump in cardiac sarcoplasmic reticulum vesicles, compared to those obtained from fast white skeletal muscle (38), it appears that phosphorylation of phospholamban converts a low-affinity "cardiac-type" calcium pump enzyme to one with the high-affinity characteristics of the skeletal sarcoplasmic reticulum. As will be discussed later, an analogous reaction involving the contractile proteins may have the opposite effect.

Relationship between Stimulation of Calcium Transport in Cardiac Sarcoplasmic Reticulum Vesicles and Increased Rate of Relaxation in Heart Exposed to Catecholamines

The causal relationships shown by the arrows linking the first six steps in the cascade shown in Fig. 5 rest on a solid body of experimental evidence. Similarly, there is substantial evidence that the increased rate of relaxation seen in the myocardium under the influence of catecholamines can be attributed in part to the stimulation of the sarcoplasmic reticulum calcium pump described above. A causal relationship between phosphorylation of phospholamban, stimulation of calcium transport by the sarcoplasmic reticulum, and accelerated relaxation has already been proposed because of the role of this intracellular membrane structure in terminating the contractile process. Additional and more direct evidence for this view is the finding of a strong correlation between the physiological ability of a muscle to respond to catecholamines with an increased rate of tension fall and the existence in the muscle of the phospholamban regulatory system.

The mechanical response of fast skeletal muscle is relatively insensitive to catecholamines, and is characterized by slight prolongation of the active state without acceleration of relaxation (3, 12). Thus, our findings that cyclic

AMP-dependent protein kinases from cardiac and skeletal muscle are unable either to phosphorylate a 22,000-dalton protein (phospholamban) or to stimulate calcium transport in rabbit fast skeletal muscle (21, 24) are in accord with the proposed causal link between accelerated calcium transport by the sarcoplasmic reticulum and the acceleration of relaxation shown in Fig. 5. There remains, however, some dispute about these findings. Schwartz et al. (37) confirmed our observations that a 22,000-dalton substrate for protein kinase does not exist in fast skeletal muscle, but found significant stimulation of calcium transport by protein kinase in this type of muscle. This discrepancy may reflect the fact that most of the calcium transport measurements of Schwartz et al. (37) were carried out at Ca^{2+} concentrations greater than 10 μM, well above those in the physiological range, where the change in Ca^{2+} affinity described by Tada et al. (45) would have no effect on calcium transport. The potential significance of the reported stimulation of calcium transport in fast skeletal muscle sarcoplasmic reticulum vesicles thus remains unclear.

A careful study of several slow skeletal muscles, in which relaxation is slightly enhanced by catecholamines (3), provided further evidence that phosphorylation of phospholamban causes both stimulation of calcium transport and acceleration of relaxation (24). This study documented both slight stimulation of calcium transport and phosphorylation of a 22,000-dalton protein in the sarcoplasmic reticulum of slow skeletal muscle. It thus appears highly probable that phosphorylation of the sarcoplasmic reticulum explains, at least in part, the ability of catecholamines to accelerate relaxation. The following section, which describes yet another biochemical explanation for this physiological response, illustrates the complexity of the regulatory systems within the cardiac cell.

Reduction in the Calcium Sensitivity of Cardiac Troponin

As was true in studies of the response of the cardiac sarcoplasmic reticulum to catecholamines and cyclic AMP, a number of early studies yielded conflicting results concerning a possible role for changes in cardiac troponin in mediating the response of the heart to catecholamines. These discrepancies now appear to have been resolved by the finding by four groups (1, 33, 34, 40) that phosphorylation of troponin I, the inhibitory component of the troponin complex, by cyclic AMP-dependent protein kinases reduces the calcium sensitivity of the troponin complex. This shift in calcium sensitivity, which is opposite to that caused by phosphorylation of the sarcoplasmic reticulum (Fig. 6), would facilitate relaxation by making it easier for Ca^{2+} to dissociate from the troponin complex when the cystolic Ca^{2+} concentration is reduced. As is true of the response of the sarcoplasmic reticulum, this effect of the cyclic AMP-protein kinase system appears to be absent in fast skeletal muscle.

The preceding paragraphs have described two opposing effects on the Ca^{2+}-dependent processes involved in excitation-contraction coupling. Cyclic AMP increases calcium delivery to the contractile proteins, whereas it also decreases the Ca^{2+} sensitivity of the calcium receptor of the contractile proteins. In view of the slow onset of the catecholamine effects in the intact heart, it appears unlikely that

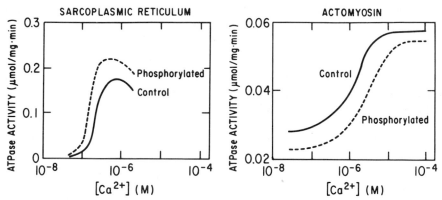

FIGURE 6 Effects of phosphorylation of the sarcoplasmic reticulum and troponin I on the Ca^{2+}-dependent ATPase activities of the sarcoplasmic reticulum and actomyosin. The curves on the left are based on data obtained by Tada et al. (43) during oxalate-supported calcium uptake by cardiac sarcoplasmic reticulum; those on the right are from the studies of Bailin (1) on cardiac actomyosin.

significantly different time courses could allow one or the other reaction to predominate during the response to catecholamines. Why, then, has the cell chosen to make it easier for calcium to be removed from troponin, instead of facilitating the binding of this cation to the contractile proteins? One interpretation of these findings (P. Greengard, personal communication) is based on the fact that calcium is dissociated from troponin when the cytosolic Ca^{2+} concentration is lowered by the ATP-dependent calcium pump of the sarcoplasmic reticulum, whereas association of Ca^{2+} and troponin occurs when this ion is released into the cytosol as the result of membrane permeability changes that allow it to move passively from regions of high activity (the extracellular space and the interior of the sarcoplasmic reticulum) to one of low activity (the cytosol). The apparent ability of troponin phosphorylation to reduce the extent to which cytosolic Ca^{2+} must be lowered to dissociate the Ca^{2+}-troponin complex would allow relaxation to occur at higher levels of cytosolic Ca^{2+}, where a larger proportion of the calcium pump sites in the sarcoplasmic reticulum would remain bound to Ca^{2+}. This has two advantages for the cell. The rate of calcium transport, which is highly dependent on the cytosolic Ca^{2+} concentration would be more rapid at the higher levels of Ca^{2+}, and the reduced Ca^{2+} sensitivity of troponin would have an energy-sparing effect during relaxation, as the amounts of ATP hydrolyzed per mole of calcium transported into the sarcoplasmic reticulum increase when the calcium pump operates at very low Ca^{2+} levels (30). While these advantages require that more calcium be released to initiate systole, the latter process involves passive, energy-independent Ca^{2+} fluxes whose rates are limited by diffusion, which is several orders of magnitude faster than calcium transport by the sarcoplasmic reticulum.

   It is apparent that the ability of cyclic AMP-dependent protein kinases to reduce the Ca^{2+} sensitivity of the cardiac troponin complex would, if this were the only response of the myocardial cell to an increased level of cyclic AMP, lead to a reduction in tension. The finding that more tension is developed by the heart under the influence of catecholamines, therefore, must mean that stimulated calcium delivery to the contractile proteins provides enough of this activator to exceed the need for higher cytosolic Ca^{2+} levels to promote contraction.

MECHANISM BY WHICH AGENTS THAT INCREASE MYOCARDIAL CYCLIC AMP ENHANCE TENSION AND THE RATE OF TENSION RISE

At least two membrane systems appear to participate in the augmentation of calcium delivery to the contractile proteins in the heart after its cyclic AMP levels are raised. The first is the sarcolemma, in which the ability of both catecholamines and cyclic AMP to augment calcium influx via the slow channel has been extensively documented (see above). While this sarcolemmal response might, by itself, account for the ability of catecholamines to increase the amount of calcium bound to troponin during systole, the finding that tension is also enhanced when skinned cardiac fibers are exposed to cyclic AMP (9) demonstrates that this response is not wholly dependent on an intact sarcolemma. Evidence that an increased release of calcium from stores within the sarcoplasmic reticulum contributes to this augmentation of tension was obtained by Katz et al. (21), who found that calcium efflux from cardiac sarcoplasmic reticulum vesicles was increased after pretreatment with a cyclic AMP-dependent protein kinase. The ability of phospholamban phosphorylation to increase calcium efflux across the cardiac sarcoplasmic reticulum, as well as to promote active calcium transport, is in accord with recent evidence that the calcium pump ATPase protein can participate in the release of calcium from within the sarcoplasmic reticulum into the cytosol (18, 19). Thus, similarities between the ability of phospholamban phosphorylation to promote calcium efflux across these membranes and its ability to stimulate the calcium pump are not wholly unexpected.

Aside from the evidence, cited above, that the effect of catecholamines to increase the slow inward current is mediated by cyclic AMP, little is known of the biochemical mechanism underlying this effect. Wollenberger (51) and Sulakhe et al. (42) have obtained data indicating that the cardiac sarcolemma is a substrate for cyclic AMP-dependent protein kinase, and that phosphorylation of a 24,000-dalton protein in this membrane is associated with increased calcium binding and transport in sarcolemmal vesicles. However, a causal relationship between these findings and the enchanced slow inward current remains to be documented.

The increased passive calcium fluxes across the membranes of both the sarcoplasmic reticulum and the sarcolemma described above may also account for the increased rate of tension rise in the heart under the influence of catecholamines. In the case of the sarcolemma, these agents do not appear to increase the rate of opening of the slow channel (36), but there are no studies of their effects on the rate at which calcium permeability increases in the sarcoplasmic reticulum. Thus, there is currently no evidence that catecholamines and cyclic AMP affect the *rate* at which calcium channels open, although it is clear that they increase the *extent* to which they open.

MECHANISMS BY WHICH AGENTS THAT INCREASE MYOCARDIAL CYCLIC AMP ALTER IONIC CONDUCTANCES IN THE SARCOLEMMA

As described in Table 1, catecholamines (and presumably cyclic AMP) have different actions on the sarcolemmal conductances for various ions in specific regions of the heart. These can be grouped into three general actions: increase in calcium conductance, increase in potassium conductance, and modification of certain time-dependent characteristics that accelerate the rate at which calcium conductance increases in the SA node and potassium conductance decreases in the Purkinje fiber. Possible mechanisms for the increased calcium conductance have already been described. In the case of the increases in potassium conductance, little is known of the mechanism at the molecular level. Tsien (47) pointed out that a modification of surface charge, which could result from phosphorylation of the sarcolemma by a cyclic AMP-dependent protein kinase, can explain many, but not all, of the characteristics of the increased rate of closure of potassium channels in the Purkinje fiber caused by catecholamines. A more elaborate explanation of the effect of catecholamines to promote pacemaker activity in the SA node was recently suggested by Pollack (32a). The explanation is based on a proposed feedback loop in which catecholamines reaching the outside of the cell membrane promote calcium influx, which, in addition to its depolarizing action, enhances the release of endogenous catecholamines. The resulting further increase in calcium influx leads to more catecholamine release, with this positive feedback process continuing until a threshold is reached and the cell generates a propagated action potential. This theory does not, however, depend on a specific model by which catecholamines promote the inward calcium current.

Unfortunately, biochemical studies of the actions of catecholamines, cyclic AMP, and cyclic AMP-dependent protein kinases on the sarcolemma are severely limited by the existing methodology. Purification of cardiac sarcolemmal membranes is difficult, as attested to by the large number of published methods, each of which appears to have its own limitations. More important, perhaps, is the inherent complexity of the sarcolemma, which mediates virtually all communication between the cell interior and the surrounding world. For this reason, it is likely that the concentration of any specific receptor or functional site would be extremely low, even in the purest of sarcolemmal preparations. In contrast, the membrane of the sarcoplasmic reticulum is highly specialized for calcium transport and release, as shown by the fact that the calcium transport ATPase protein makes up 15-20% of the protein in cardiac preparations and up to 80% in skeletal muscle preparations. This is why studies of the biochemical actions of the cyclic AMP-dependent protein kinase on the sarcoplasmic reticulum have proved so fruitful. Future studies of the mechanisms by which catecholamines modulate sarcolemmal function will demonstrate the extent to which the knowledge gained from work on the simpler membrane can be applied to the more complex ionic channels that control the properties of pacemaker activity, excitability, and conduction.

REFERENCES

1. Bailin, G. Adenosine $3':5'$-monophosphate-dependent protein kinase phosphorylation of a bovine cardiac actin complex. Biophys J 17:159a, 1977.
2. Bassingthwaite, J. B. and Reuter, H. Calcium movements and excitation-contraction coupling in cardiac cells. In: Electrical Phenomena in the Heart, W. C. DeMello, ed. New York: Academic Press, 1972, pp. 393–395.
3. Bowman, W. C. and Raper, C. Adrenotropic receptors in skeletal muscle. Ann NY Acad Sci 139:741–753, 1967.
4. Cranefield, P. The Conduction of the Cardiac Impulse and the Slow Response and Cardiac Arrhythmias. Mount Kisco, N.Y.: Futura, 1975.
5. Ebashi, S. Excitation-contraction coupling. Annu Rev Physiol 38:293–313, 1976.
6. Endo, M. Calcium release from the sarcoplasmic reticulum. Physiol Rev 57:71–108, 1977.
7. Entman, M. L., Levey, G. S., and Epstein, S. E. Mechanism of action of epinephrine and glucagon on the canine heart. Evidence of increase in sarcotubular calcium stores mediated by cyclic $3',5'$-AMP. Circ Res 25:429–438, 1969.
8. Fabiato, A. and Fabiato, F. Calcium release from the sarcoplasmic reticulum. Circ Res 40:119–129, 1977.
9. Fabiato, A. and Fabiato, F. Relaxing and inotropic effects of cyclic AMP in skinned cardiac cells. Nature (Lond) 253:556–558, 1975.
10. Fanburg, B. L. and Matsushita, S. Phosphorylated intermediate of ATPase of isolated cardiac sarcoplasmic reticulum. J Mol Cell Cardiol 5:111–115, 1973.
11. Ford, R. E. and Podolsky, R. J. Intracellular calcium movements in skinned muscle fibres. J Physiol (Lond) 223:21–33, 1972.
12. Goffart, M. and Ritchie, J. M. The effect of adrenaline on the contraction of mammalian skeletal muscle. J Physiol (Lond) 116:357–371, 1952.
13. Hess, M. L., Briggs, F. N., Shinebourne, E., and White, R. Effect of adrenergic blocking agents on the calcium pump of the fragmented cardiac sarcoplasmic reticulum. Nature (Lond) 220:79–80, 1968.
14. Kasai, M. and Miyamoto, H. Depolarization-induced calcium release from sarcoplasmic reticulum membrane fragments. FEBS Lett 34:299–301, 1973.
15. Katz, A. M. Contractile proteins of the heart. Physiol Rev 50:58–163, 1970.
16. Katz, A. M. Physiology of the Heart. New York: Raven, 1977.
17. Katz, A. M. and Repke, D. I. Calcium-membrane interactions in the myocardium: Effects of ouabain, epinephrine and $3',5'$-cyclic adenosine monophosphate. Am J Cardiol 31:193–201, 1973.
18. Katz, A. M., Repke, D. I., Dunnett, J., and Hasselbach, W. Dependence of calcium permeability of sarcoplasmic reticulum vesicles on external and internal calcium ion concentrations. J Biol Chem 252:1950–1956, 1977.
19. Katz, A. M., Repke, D. I., Fudyma, G., and Shigekawa, M. Control of calcium

efflux from sarcoplasmic reticulum vesicles by external calcium. J Biol Chem 252:4210–4214, 1977.

20. Katz, A. M., Repke, D. I., and Hasselbach, W. Dependence of ionophore and calcium-induced calcium release from sarcoplasmic reticulum vesicles on external and internal calcium ion concentration. J Biol Chem 252: 1938–1949, 1977.

21. Katz, A. M., Tada, M., and Kirchberger, M. A. Control of calcium transport in the myocardium by the cyclic AMP-protein kinase system. Adv Cyclic Nucleotide Res 5:453–472, 1975.

22. Kirchberger, M. A. and Chu, G. Correlation between protein kinase-mediated stimulation of calcium transport by cardiac sarcoplasmic reticulum and phosphorylation of a 22,000 dalton protein. Biochim Biophys Acta 419:559–562, 1976.

23. Kirchberger, M. A. and Raffo, A. Decrease in calcium transport associated with phosphoprotein phosphatase-catalyzed dephosphorylation of cardiac sarcoplasmic reticulum. J Cyclic Nucleotide Res 3:45–53, 1977.

24. Kirchberger, M. A. and Tada, M. Effects of adenosine $3':5'$-monophosphate dependent protein kinase on sarcoplasmic reticulum isolated from cardiac and slow and fast contracting skeletal muscles. J Biol Chem 251:725–729, 1976.

25. Kirchberger, M. A., Tada, M., and Katz, A. M. Adenosine $3':5'$-monophosphate-dependent protein kinase-catalyzed phosphorylation reaction and its relationship to calcium transport in cardiac sarcoplasmic reticulum. J Biol Chem 249:6166–6173, 1974.

26. Kirchberger, M. A., Tada, M., Repke, D. I., and Katz, A. M. Cyclic adenosine $3',5'$-monophosphate-dependent protein kinase stimulation of calcium uptake by canine cardiac microsomes. J Mol Cell Cardiol 4:673–680, 1972.

27. LaRaia, P. J. and Morkin, E. Adenosine $3',5'$-monophosphate dependent membrane phosphorylation; a possible mechanism for the control of microsomal calcium transport in heart muscle. Circ Res 25:298–306, 1974.

28. Li, H. C., Katz, A. M., Repke, D. I., and Failor, A. Oxalate dependence of calcium uptake kinetics of rabbit skeletal muscle microsomes (fragmented sarcoplasmic reticulum). Biochim Biophys Acta 367:385–389, 1974.

29. Louis, C. F. and Katz, A. M. Lactoperoxidase coupled iodination of cardiac sarcoplasmic reticulum proteins. Biochim Biophys Acta 494:255–265, 1977.

30. Makinose, M. and The, R. Calcium-Akkumulation und Nucleosidtriphosphatspaltung durch die Vesikel des Sarkoplasmatischen Reticulum. Biochem Z 373:383–393, 1965.

31. Neely, J. R. and Morgan, H. E. Relationship between carbohydrate and lipid metabolism and the energy balance of heart muscle. Annu Rev Physiol 31:413–459, 1974.

32. Noble, D. The Initiation of the Heartbeat. Oxford: Claredon, 1975.

32a. Pollack, G. H. Cardiac pacemaking: An obligatory role of catecholamines. Science 198:731–738, 1977.

33. Ray, K. P. and England, P. Phosphorylation of the inhibitory component of troponin and its effect on Ca^{2+} dependence of cardiac myofibril ATPase. FEBS Lett 70:11–16, 1976.

34. Reddy, Y. S. and Wyborny, L. E. Phosphorylation of guinea pig actomyosin and its effect on ATPase activity. Biochem Biophys Res Commun 73:703–709, 1976.

35. Reuter, H. Localization of beta adrenergic receptors and effects of noradrenaline and cyclic nucleotides on action potentials, ionic currents and tension in mammalian cardiac muscle. J Physiol (Lond) 242:429–451, 1974.

36. Reuter, H. and Scholz, H. The regulation of the calcium conductance of cardiac muscle by adrenaline. J Physiol (Lond) 264:49–62, 1977.

37. Schwartz, A., Entman, M. L., Kaniike, K., Lane, L. K., van Winkle, W. B., and Bornet, E. P. The rate of calcium uptake in sarcoplasmic reticulum of cardiac muscle and skeletal muscle. Effects of cyclic AMP-dependent protein kinase and phosphorylase b kinase. Biochim Biophys Acta 426:57–72, 1976.

38. Shigekawa, M., Finegan, J.-A. M., and Katz, A. M. Calcium transport ATPase of canine-cardiac sarcoplasmic reticulum: A comparison with that of rabbit fast skeletal muscle sarcoplasmic reticulum. J Biol Chem 251:6894–6900, 1976.

39. Shinebourne, E. and White, R. Cyclic AMP and calcium uptake of the sarcoplasmic reticulum in relation to increased rate of relaxation under the influence of catecholamines. Cardiovasc Res 4:194–200, 1970.

40. Solaro, R. J., Moir, A. J. G., and Perry, S. V. Phosphorylation of the inhibitory component of troponin and the inotropic effect of adrenaline in perfused rabbit heart. Nature (Lond) 262:615–616, 1976.

41. Suko, J. and Hasselbach, W. Characterization of cardiac sarcoplasmic reticulum ATP-ADP exchange and phosphorylation of the calcium transport adenosine triphosphatase. Eur J Biochem 64:123–130, 1976.

42. Sulakhe, P. V., Leung, N. L. K., and St. Louis, P. Stimulation of calcium accumulation in cardiac sarcolemma by protein kinase. Can J Biochem 54:438–445, 1976.

43. Tada, M., Kirchberger, M. A., and Katz, A. M. Phosphorylation of a 22,000-dalton component of the cardiac sarcoplasmic reticulum by adenosine 3′,5′-monophosphate dependent protein kinase. J Biol Chem 250:2640–2647, 1975.

44. Tada, M., Kirchberger, M. A., and Li, H. C. Phosphoprotein phosphatase catalyzed dephosphorylation of the 22,000 dalton phosphoprotein of cardiac sarcoplasmic reticulum. J Cyclic Nucleotide Res 1:329–338, 1975.

45. Tada, M., Kirchberger, M. A., Repke, D. I., and Katz, A. M. The stimulation of calcium transport in cardiac sarcoplasmic reticulum by adenosine 3′,5′-monophosphate-dependent protein kinase. J Biol Chem 249:385–389, 1974.

46. Tsien, R. W. Adrenaline-like effects of intracellular iontophoresis of cyclic AMP in cardiac Purkinje fibers. Nature New Biol 245:120–122, 1973.

47. Tsien, R. W. Effects of epinephrine on the pacemaker potassium current of cardiac Purkinje fibers. J Gen Physiol 64:293–319, 1974.

48. Tsien, R. W., Giles, W., and Greengard, P. Cyclic AMP mediates the effects of adrenaline on cardiac Purkinje fibers. Nature New Biol 240:181–183, 1972.

49. Vassort, G., Rougier, O., Garnier, O., Sanvait, M. P., Coraboeuf, E., and Gargouil, Y. M. Effects of adrenaline on membrane inward currents during the cardiac action potential. Pfluegers Arch 309:70–81, 1969.

50. Will, H., Blanck, J., Smettar, G., and Wollenberger, A. A quench-flow kinetic investigation of calcium ion accumulation by isolated cardiac sarcoplasmic reticulum. Dependence of initial velocity on free calcium ion concentration and influence of preincubation with a protein kinase, MgATP and cyclic AMP. Biochim Biophys Acta 449:297–303, 1976.

51. Wollenberger, A. The role of cyclic AMP in the adrenergic control of the heart. In: Contraction and Relaxation in the Myocardium, W. G. Nayler, ed. New York: Academic Press, 1975, pp. 113–190.

52. Wray, H. L., Gray, R. R., and Olsson, R. A. Cyclic adenosine 3′,5′-monophosphate-stimulated protein kinase and a substrate associated with cardiac sarcoplasmic reticulum. J Biol Chem 248:1496–1498, 1973.

CHAPTER 3

MUSCLE-PUMP FUNCTION OF THE INTACT HEART

KARL T. WEBER
JOSEPH S. JANICKI

To me the evidence shows clearly that when Newtonian concepts of motion are applied to heart disease a new window is opened.

Dr. Isaac Starr, *Proceedings of the Royal Society of Medicine*, 1967

Over the years, few subjects have captured the imagination and attention of physicians and physiologists as has the description of cardiac performance, and in particular the evaluation of the failing heart. At the turn of the century and from the laboratories of Frank and Starling emerged the view of the heart as a compression pump. This concept, which likened the heart to a piston-cylinder arrangement, focused on its pressure-volume relations and employed such displacement terms as stroke volume, cardiac output, and stroke work. These parameters have served as useful descriptors of ventricular failure. In more recent years, others (1, 5) have approached this subject from a different vantage point. They have emphasized the mechanical properties of cardiac muscle and in particular the behavior of its contractile element. The application of fundamental muscle concepts to the diseased heart, which was greeted with much enthusiasm initially, has not been without controversy. Lack of confidence in the applicability of these concepts focused on the muscle models and simplifying assumptions that were necessary to characterize the contractile element of the intact ventricle. Particularly unsettling was the fact that pertinent experimental data were limited because of technical difficulties in controlling and monitoring ventricular loading (i.e., its two major determinants, chamber volume and pressure).

To circumvent these problems, we undertook in 1972 to develop and apply a mechanical servo system to an isolated canine heart preparation (2). With this system, it has been possible to examine in detail the shortening characteristics of the intact ventricle, including the influence of instantaneous wall force and length and myocardial contractile state (7-11). The purpose of this review is to elucidate these shortening characteristics and thereby describe the heart as an integrated muscle-pump system. That is, it will be shown that the determinants of wall shortening regulate chamber volume displacement. Finally, the relevance of these behavioral characteristics of the myocardium is discussed with respect to the failing heart.

THE CONCEPT OF FORCE AND LENGTH

The pressure and volume events of cardiac contraction are an integral part of standard physiology textbooks. In systole, the ventricle develops pressure that leads to the ejection of blood. The generation of pressure occurs as a result of the force developed by the myocardium; the shortening of myocardial fibers accounts for the stroke volume. Chamber pressure and myocardial force, however, are by no means synonymous.

To determine the force and length for any particular fiber composing the muscular wall of the ventricle requires a detailed understanding of fiber distribution and orientation. This problem is compounded by the sequence of fiber contraction, which varies topographically according to the time course of electric depolarization. However, a detailed analysis of the distribution of mural force and individual fiber length is beyond the current state of the art. But more importantly, the broad description of ventricular function in terms of an integrated muscle-pump system depends neither on correlating the structure-function relationship at the individual fiber level nor on knowing the force on any particular fiber. It is the summated contraction of all fibers that determines chamber volume displacement. Hence, we have chosen to confine our estimate of length to the circumferential direction that represents the predominant orientation of fibers (6). This circumferential length, located in the equatorial plane, has been calculated for the mid-wall of a thick-walled sphere.

The net force in the wall of the myocardium may be described as follows: envision the ventricle as spherical in shape and divided into two parts by an imaginary plane passing through a cross-sectional area of its chamber and a rim of myocardium (Fig. 1). In accordance with Newton's law of motion, the force that exists in this rim (and is perpendicular to the plane) must be equal and opposite in direction to the force created by the pressure of blood in the chamber times the area of the chamber included in the plane. Importantly, it is independent of 1) the shape, area, or thickness of the subtended rim, 2) the orientation of individual fibers, or the distribution of forces that they generate, and 3) interfascicular tension or shearing forces. Thus, net wall force, in grams, is calculated as the product of chamber pressure and the cross-sectional area (πr_i^2) of the chamber in the plane, where r_i is the internal chamber radius determined from the measured volume of the ventricle and the volume equation for a sphere. The circumferential fiber length for the mid-wall of the ventricle $(2\pi r_m)$, as indicated in Fig. 1, has been determined from $\pi(r_o + r_i)$, where r_o is the external radius of the heart calculated from the volume of heart muscle, knowing the weight of the heart and the specific gravity of muscle. A further description of the assumptions and rationale implicit in the derivation of these calculations may be found elsewhere (10).

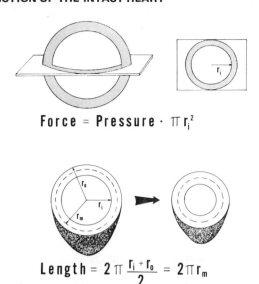

$$\text{Force} = \text{Pressure} \cdot \pi r_i^2$$

$$\text{Length} = 2\pi \frac{r_i + r_o}{2} = 2\pi r_m$$

FIGURE 1 Determination of net wall force and mid-wall circumferential fiber lengths outlined for a thick-walled sphere. The dimensions shown include internal, external, and mid-wall radii (r_i, r_o, and r_m, respectively).

It would seem prudent at the outset to define the force and length terms that we will use throughout this review. *Instantaneous force* refers to the net wall force that exists at any instant during the cardiac cycle and is dependent on chamber pressure and area at that instant; the term *load*, which is used throughout the text, denotes this force. *Instantaneous length* is the time-varying dimension of the mid-wall circumferential fiber. *Instantaneous shortening load* refers to the force that exists at any instant during ventricular ejection (i.e., from aortic valve opening to closure).

MAXIMAL DEVELOPED FORCE–LENGTH RELATION

The maximal wall force that can be developed for any degree of fiber stretch is found in the isovolumetrically beating heart (9). Under this condition the contraction of the myocardium does not result in a change in chamber volume. An isovolumetric beat, however, does not represent an isometric contraction, since the ventricle undergoes a change in shape, and thus fiber length is not constant. The relation between maximal developed force and fiber length is represented in Fig. 2A for the physiological range of left ventricular filling pressures (i.e., ≤ 25 mmHg). It is apparent that as end-diastolic volume and fiber length are increased there is an associated augmentation in developed force, as well as in the resting, or end-diastolic, force. The developed force-length relation provides an expression of the fundamental length-dependent property of cardiac muscle. In this connection, and unlike the case of isolated muscle, a length at which force peaked and subsequently declined could not be demonstrated for the intact left ventricle (9).

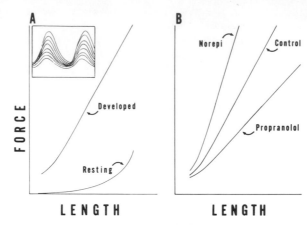

FIGURE 2   Maximal force-length relation of the isovolumetrically beating heart. (A) Oscillo-
graphic display of ventricular pressure for a series of isovolumetric beats, and
resulting relations of developed and resting (or end-diastolic) force to end-diastolic
fiber length. (B) Representative responses in the developed force-length relation
induced by the pharmacological manipulation of contractile state obtained with
norepinephrine (Norepi) or propranolol.

Thus, the left ventricle normally functions on the ascending limb of this maximal
force-length relation.

Variations in contractile state (Fig. 2B) create nonparallel shifts in the
developed force-length relation; positive and negative inotropic interventions raise
and reduce the slope of this relation, respectively. For example, after the
administration of norepinephrine, the ventricle is able to develop a greater force
from any equivalent fiber length examined under control conditions. The augmentation in slope of the maximal force-length relation depends on the rate of
norepinephrine infusion (9, 10). Propranolol, on the other hand, attenuates the
slope of the force-length relation. Thus, the isovolumetric, developed force-length
relation that is dependent on contractile state represents the maximal force that can
be generated for any particular fiber length.

LIMITS OF WALL SHORTENING

The extent of wall shortening is determined by the isovolumetric force-length
relation of that contractile state (9). That is, the wall force that exists at any
end-systolic length equals the maximal force that that length can sustain. To
illustrate this further, two force-length loops representing two ejecting contractions
during variable loading are shown in Fig. 3A together with the corresponding
isovolumetric force-length relation. From an initial or end-diastolic length denoted
as point a the ventricle generates an isovolumic force before ejection. Fiber
shortening (i.e., ventricular ejection) commences at point b and continues until
point c is reached. The course of this contraction is described as abc. From the
opening of the aortic valve to its closure the ventricle must shorten against a force
whose magnitude is determined by the response in chamber pressure and dimension.

The other contraction represented is given as *def*. In each case the end-systolic (points *c* and *f*) and isovolumetric (dashed line) force-length relations are equivalent.

The equivalence of these relations can also be shown by varying the time course of the ejection force (Fig. 3B) from the same onset force (point *e*) while initial length (point *d*) is held constant (7). As the instantaneous force opposing shortening (i.e., the shortening load) is varied, the extent of shortening, and thereby the end-systolic length, is also altered (see below). Consequently, from a particular end-diastolic length, three different end-systolic lengths (points *f, g,* and *h*) are obtained. In each case, shortening ends when the ejecting force-length relation corresponds to a point on the isovolumetric force-length curve (dashed line). Thus, shortening ceases when a force is reached that is maximal for the accompanying instantaneous length.

Although the isovolumetric force-length relation defines the limits of shortening, the extent to which the ventricle will shorten (i.e., its end-systolic length) is determined by the instantaneous course of systolic force and length (see below). For example, contraction *deg*, which has an ever decreasing shortening load, has the greatest degree of shortening, while the least shortening is observed for contraction *deh*, in which this load is ever increasing. In contrast, end-systolic length is independent of initial length and onset ejection force, which only serve to determine the starting points of the contraction.

Finally, the equivalence of the isovolumetric and end-systolic force-length relations has been verified for either positive (e.g., norepinephrine, as shown in Fig.

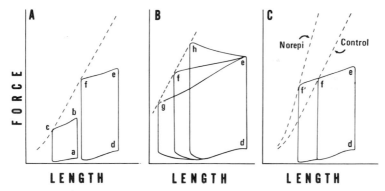

FIGURE 3 Interrelationship of ejecting and isovolumetric force-length relations. (A) Two ejecting beats (*abc* and *def*) of variable length and force are given along with the isovolumetric relation (dashed line). Note that despite the differences in initial length and onset systolic force, the end-systolic points fall on the isovolumetric force-length relation. (B) Three contractions of equivalent initial length and onset ejection force in which the trajectory of instantaneous force was varied. Again, the end-systolic and isovolumetric (dashed line) force-length relations are equivalent. (C) For two contractions that have an equivalent initial length and ejection force, the extent of shortening is determined by contractile state. The control condition (beat *def*) and the condition following norepinephrine (Norepi; beat *def'*) are shown. The positive inotropic agent permits a greater degree of fiber shortening. Despite these differences in shortening, however, the ventricle continues to shorten to its maximal force-length relation.

3C) or negative (e.g., propranolol) variations in contractile state (9). Therefore, regardless of its particular contractile state, the ejecting ventricle contracts within the confines of its isovolumetric, developed force-length relation.

ROLE OF INSTANTANEOUS FORCE, LENGTH, AND CONTRACTILE STATE

The importance of instantaneous force and length on the extent (and velocity) of mid-wall circumferential fiber shortening has been alluded to above. To examine this further, a series of variably loaded contractions and the respective trajectories of force, velocity, and length have been illustrated in Fig. 4. Each contraction originates from the same resting length. For simplicity, differences in resting force, which are the result of changes in ventricular distensibility accompanying variations in systolic pressure (3), have not been included. Three counterclockwise force-length loops are shown in Fig. 4A together with the isovolumetric relation (dashed line). In each case the extent of shortening (i.e., the change in length, ΔL) is determined by the *instantaneous force* opposing that shortening. The value of ΔL will be greater for beat a, which has the smallest shortening load, than for beats b and c. In Fig. 4B the corresponding velocity-length relations indicate that the maximum velocity of shortening is not attained instantaneously. Instead a finite time is required, and the maximum velocity that is achieved occurs at a fiber length less than the end-diastolic length. For contractions that have equivalent instantaneous ejection lengths, it is clear that the maximum and instantaneous velocities of shortening, as well as the extent of shortening, are determined by the instantaneous shortening

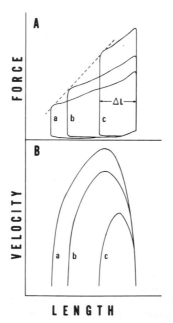

FIGURE 4 Importance of instantaneous force on the extent (ΔL) and velocity of shortening demonstrated for three variably afterloaded beats. See text for details.

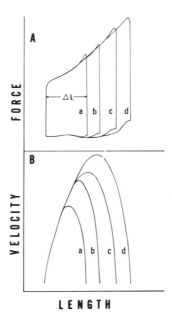

LENGTH

FIGURE 5 Effect of instantaneous length on the extent (ΔL) and velocity of shortening. See text for details.

load (7). This load-dependent aspect of fiber shortening is a fundamental property of cardiac muscle.

A second property of cardiac muscle is related to fiber length. The importance of *instantaneous length* in determining the extent and rate of shortening is illustrated in Fig. 5. Here, beginning with beat *a*, end-diastolic fiber length was progressively raised by increasing end-diastolic pressure from 2 to 10 mmHg (beat *d*). For each increment in initial or onset contraction length a greater resting force, instantaneous length, maximal velocity, and ΔL were observed. The systolic force trajectory followed a common path, so that each contraction terminated at a constant end-systolic length. Consequently, the shortening response for beats that traverse a path of equivalent instantaneous force indicates that the rate and extent of shortening are a function of instantaneous length. This is another expression of the length-dependent (Frank-Starling) property of cardiac muscle. The augmentation in shortening that accompanies increments in initial (and instantaneous) length may be viewed as representing the *diastolic reserve* of the ventricle. Finally, the velocity and extent of shortening are also independent of contraction time (7). For example, beat *d* reached the common force trajectory much later in its contraction than beats *c* and *b*.

Thus, the instantaneous velocity and extent of shortening for any particular contractile state are determined by both instantaneous force and instantaneous length. In addition to these two fundamental properties of muscle, the role of myocardial *contractile state* must be considered. The response in shortening during pharmacological depression of the contractile state by propranolol (0.5 mg/min) is illustrated in Fig. 6, where control (beat *c*) and beta blockade (beat *c'*) data are

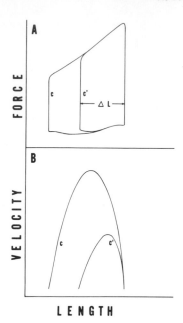

FIGURE 6   Response of the extent (ΔL) and velocity of shortening to the pharmacological depression of contractile state with propranolol. The instantaneous force-length and velocity-length relations for the control state (beat c) and the state following the infusion of propranolol (0.5 mg/min; beat c') are shown.

given. As expected, the end-systolic force-length relation after propranolol (not shown) is shifted to the right: for comparable conditions of instantaneous length and force, the instantaneous velocity and extent of shortening for beat c' are reduced. These alterations in shortening following propranolol are analogous to those observed for the failing heart (see below). A positive inotropic agent, such as norepinephrine, causes a shift in the opposite direction; that is, the end-systolic force-length relation moves to the left, and a greater rate and greater extent of shortening are observed for any particular length or load. The degree to which the slope of the isovolumetric relation can be raised determines the increment in shortening and consequently reflects the *systolic reserve* of the ventricle.

By utilizing the previous phase plane trajectories of instantaneous force, length, and shortening velocity, a geometric solid representing the limits of shortening and the mechanical behavior of the ventricle during shortening may be constructed. An example of such a solid is shown in Fig. 7. The course of a single contraction (indicated by the arrows) from end-diastole to onset ejection, end ejection, and onset filling (represented by a, b, c, and d, respectively) may be traced within this surface. Shortening ceases when the isovolumetric force-length relation (point c) is reached. Intrinsic or pharmacological shifts in myocardial contractile state either increase (toward the reader) or decrease (away from the reader) the dimensions of this solid. Thus, the consideration of these variables also provides a unique relation that will describe the contractile state of the underlying myocardium.

THE HEART AS A MUSCLE–PUMP SYSTEM

As a pump, the ventricle generates pressure and displaces volume. These properties of the heart as a pump may be expressed in terms of the development of muscle force and shortening, respectively. In this context the pumping characteristics of the heart are an expression of the behavior of the muscle fibers that comprise its wall. The time course of mechanical contraction may be viewed as follows: at end-diastole the fibers have a particular stretch or length, which is determined by the resting force. This distending force, which is a function of chamber pressure and myocardial compliance, is analogous to the preload of the isolated muscle preparation. After depolarization, the ventricle generates pressure, which leads to the opening of the aortic valve and the ejection of blood. Up to this point the course of systolic pressure is related to the force created by the myocardium. The magnitude of this wall force is a function of chamber pressure and volume. Consequently, the larger heart must develop more force to generate the same pressure.

During ejection the myocardium must also sustain a particular force. As chamber volume decreases during the ejection of blood into the aorta, instantaneous force will normally decrease. This shortening load is analogous to the afterload of the isolated muscle preparation. However, unlike the constant weight that the muscle lifts after its contraction (i.e., an isotonic load), the force on the ventricle has a changing, albeit ever declining, value (i.e., an allassotonic contraction). Thus, it may be prudent to delete the term afterload from clinical parlance in favor of instantaneous shortening load (i.e., instantaneous ejection force). The magnitude of

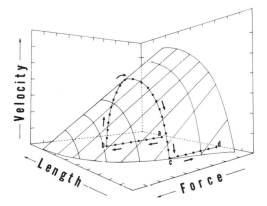

FIGURE 7 Schematic representation of the three-dimensional plane describing the instantaneous trajectory of force, velocity, and length for a particular contractile state. The course of a single contraction is indicated by the arrows, and points corresponding to end-diastole, onset ejection, end ejection, and onset filling are identified as *a, b, c,* and *d,* respectively. A positive inotropic agent such as norepinephrine would augment the dimensions of this solid (toward the reader), while a depression in contractility with propranolol would reduce its dimensions (away from the reader).

this shortening load is a function of the instantaneous change in chamber size, shape, and pressure, with the viscoelastic properties of the circulatory system dictating the time course of pressure. Consequently, the impedance characteristics of the vascular bed will influence ventricular loading. This includes both the resistance and capacitance of the vasculature, with each element imposing an additional force on the contracting fibers. The force resulting from the resistive component is a function of the velocity of fiber shortening (i.e., ejection rate), whereas that attributable to the capacitive portion is related to the extent of fiber shortening or the volume ejected.

This heart-blood vessel interaction may also be viewed as feedback control of myocardial contraction (4). For example, an increment in stroke volume (and ejection rate) leads to an increase in aortic impedance and, subsequently, in wall force. As a result of this increased load, subsequent contractions have an attenuated stroke volume (11). Contrariwise, if an increment in aortic impedance is the initial event, the accompanying reduction in stroke volume should lead to a greater end ejection and end-diastolic chamber volume. As a consequence of this increase in fiber length, stroke volume would be restored to original levels. This coupling between the heart and the vascular bed necessitates not only that cardiac fibers be able to react to beat-to-beat variations in filling volume and arterial impedance, but also that they adjust instantaneously to differences in length and load. That this is indeed possible was shown in the preceding section.

In addition to the influence of pressure on ventricular loading, the change in ventricular dimension represents an important determinant of shortening load. The alteration in dimension for any particular load will be a function of the geometric configuration of the chamber as well as the myocardial contractile state. In the normal heart the reduction in radius throughout ejection permits wall force to decline despite the fact that chamber pressure increases. As the heart enlarges it loses this advantage. For example, the extent of shortening by fibers comprising the wall of a large spherical ventricle is less than that associated with an equivalent stroke volume from a smaller chamber. Thus the marked abbreviation of shortening in the enlarged and failing ventricle will contribute significantly to instantaneous load for any particular condition of arterial pressure. This important aspect of the failing heart will be discussed further below.

According to the traditional pump concept, the performance of the ventricle may be gauged from the relation between stroke volume and end-diastolic volume. Stroke volume may be raised by the augmentation in filling volume (Frank-Starling response) or myocardial contractile state (e.g., catecholamines or digitalis). Stroke volume, however, is also dependent on arterial pressure (11). Elevations in systolic pressure and, concomitantly, in wall force serve to reduce the ejected fraction or stroke volume from any particular diastolic volume. Alternatively, a reduction in impedance, as with aortic or mitral regurgitation, allows for greater ventricular emptying.

The product of stroke volume and aortic pressure, which approximates stroke work, has also been utilized to assess pump function. The relation of work to end-diastolic volume (or end-diastolic pressure) has been termed the *ventricular function curve*. The origins of this relation, which are critical to understanding its

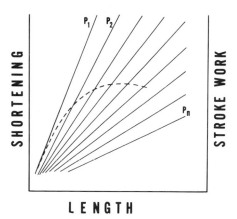

FIGURE 8 Derivation of the ventricular function curve based on the shortening-length relation of the myocardium. The linear shortening-length relations obtained for a series of constant ejection pressures ($P_1 < P_2 < \cdots < P_n$) are plotted along with the theoretical function curve (dashed line).

meaning, require comment. For any particular contractile state the extent to which a fiber will shorten will depend on its instantaneous length and force. Taking the instantaneous force trajectory shown in Fig. 4A for example, increments in end-diastolic and instantaneous length result in progressive elevations in stroke volume (or shortening), thereby describing the shortening-length relation. This force trajectory was experimentally obtained by keeping the ejection pressure term of the shortening load constant (10). A number of such linear shortening-length relations derived for a series of constant ejection pressures (P), where $P_1 < P_2 < \cdots < P_n$, are given in Fig. 8. The slope of the shortening-length relation decreases as ejection pressure increases. However, in the intact animal, or in humans, it is obviously not possible to maintain these rigidly controlled conditions of loading when deriving a function curve. For example, when the circulating volume is expanded by using dextran, both the intracardiac space and the intravascular (capacitance) space are expanded. Consequently, arterial pressure, chamber dimension, and instantaneous force increase continuously. The resulting relation between work and diastolic volume (or fiber length) therefore traverses these shortening-length relations, as indicated by the dashed line in Fig. 8. Alterations in myocardial contractile state for a particular heart or differences in contractility between hearts produce a series or family of function curves.

THE FAILING HEART

As we use the term here, heart failure refers specifically to a compromised contractile state of the left ventricle that is accompanied by forward flow inadequate to accommodate the needs of the peripheral circulation. Because ventricular emptying is less, signs and symptoms of pulmonary venous hypertension may also be present. The reduction in contractile state or the decreased slope of the isovolumetric force-length relation accounts for the decline in both the extent and rate of fiber shortening for any condition of length or load. The force-length loop given in Fig. 6 for propranolol would be illustrative of this circumstance. This attenuation in shortening implies that the slope of the shortening-length relation is also reduced. Translated into terms of the heart's function as a pump, stroke volume, ejection fraction, and ejection rate will be reduced.

Each decrement in the developed force-length relation attenuates the ability of the heart's diastolic reserve to restore stroke volume; that is, as this curve shifts to the right, the increment in shortening that is possible with chamber dilation (i.e., greater fiber length) becomes less. The depression in the maximal force-length relation also represents a reduction in the heart's systolic reserve. In other words, the ability of positive inotropic agents, such as digitalis, to shift this relation to the left and permit greater shortening becomes impaired. A critical reduction in systolic reserve exists when the failing ventricle becomes refractory to such agents. At this point increments in shortening may be achieved only by manipulating instantaneous force (i.e., the concept of unloading), as with vasodilators (8).

In this connection, one other point deserves comment. The reduction in chamber dimension or radius during ejection is abbreviated in the enlarged, failing ventricle. That is, the change in ventricular size from end-diastole to end ejection is less than under normal conditions. This circumstance may be accounted for by 1) the reduced stroke volume of the failing heart, and 2) the fact that its end-diastolic chamber size is enlarged. Recall that for any particular stroke volume the extent of shortening of fibers is less for those encompassing a large ventricle than for those of a smaller chamber. When wall motion becomes severely restricted, creating an essentially invariant chamber dimension, the absolute level of systolic force remains high (i.e., essentially unchanged from its onset value or even increasing throughout the ejection period). This sustained shortening load further decreases the degree of wall shortening (8). Reducing chamber size and thereby instantaneous force in such a heart with a diuretic, by venesection, or with a vasodilator permits an increase in shortening without influencing contractility. From the traditional viewpoint, this increment in stroke volume represents an ascent from a depressed position on the ventricular function curve.

CONCLUSION

The heart functions as an integrated muscle-pump system so that the determinants of fiber shortening regulate the volume displaced from the chamber. In this review we have attempted to unite these two concepts of ventricular performance by first examining the behavioral characteristics of the myocardium viewed as a muscle compromised of circumferentially oriented fibers. The isovolumetric force-length relation of these fibers, which depends on the contractile state, describes the maximal force attainable for any degree of fiber stretch. It further establishes the limits to fiber shortening. During ejection, the extent and rate of fiber shortening are determined by the instantaneous trajectories of force (i.e., a function of chamber pressure and dimension) and fiber length, as well as by the contractile state of the myocardium. These properties of the myocardial fiber may be utilized to describe the heart as a pump, including the derivation of the ventricular function curve. Finally, the relevance of these relations for characterizing the failing heart is emphasized. Specifically, the attenuation in slope of the maximal force-length relation and the sustained shortening load of the enlarged chamber account for the reduced output of the compromised ventricle.

REFERENCES

1. Fry, D. L., Griggs, D. M., and Greenfield, J. C. Myocardial mechanics: Tension-velocity-length relationships in heart muscle. Circ Res 14:73–85, 1964.
2. Janicki, J. S., Reeves, R. C., Weber, K. T., Donald, T. C., and Walker, A. A. The application of pressure-servo system developed to study ventricular dynamics. J Appl Physiol 37:736–741, 1974.
3. Janicki, J. S. and Weber, K. T. Ejection pressure and the diastolic left ventricular pressure-volume relation. Am J Physiol 232:H545–H552, 1977.
4. Milnor, W. R. Arterial impedance as ventricular afterload. Circ Res 36:565–570, 1975.
5. Sonnenblick, E. H. Implications of muscle mechanics in the heart. Fed Proc 21:975–990, 1962.
6. Streeter, D. D., Spotnitz, M. H., Patel, D. P., Ross, J., Jr., and Sonnenblick, E. H. Fiber orientation in the canine left ventricle during diastole and systole. Circ Res 24:339–347, 1969.
7. Weber, K. T. and Janicki, J. S. Instantaneous force-velocity-length relations in isolated dog heart. Am J Physiol 232:H241–H249, 1977.
8. Weber, K. T. and Janicki, J. S. Instantaneous force-velocity-length relations: Experimental findings and clinical correlates. Am J Cardiol 40:740–741, 1977.
9. Weber, K. T., Janicki, J. S., and Hefner, L. L. Left ventricular force-length relations of isovolumic and ejecting contractions. Am J Physiol 231:337–343, 1976.
10. Weber, K. T., Janicki, J. S., Reeves, R. C., and Hefner, L. L. Factors influencing left ventricular shortening in isolated canine heart. Am J Physiol 230:419–426, 1976.
11. Weber, K. T., Janicki, J. S., Reeves, R. C., Hefner, L. L., and Reeves, T. J. Determinants of stroke volume in isolated canine heart. J Appl Physiol 37:742–747, 1974.

CHAPTER 4

IMPLICATIONS OF SHAPE, STRESS, AND WALL DYNAMICS IN CLINICAL HEART DISEASE

HAROLD T. DODGE
DOUGLAS K. STEWART
MORRIS FRIMER

Angiographic imaging of the left ventricle has made it possible to determine the volume, dimensions, wall thickness, and regional wall motion of this chamber throughout the cardiac cycle in normal humans and in humans with heart disease.

The normal left ventricle is ellipsoidal with a long axis at end-diastole that is approximately twice the minor, or transverse, axes (7). The minor axes, as determined from biplane angiograms filmed in the anteroposterior and lateral projections, are nearly equal in most ventricles, normal or with heart disease (11). Therefore, the left ventricle can usually be considered as an ellipsoid of revolution for computing chamber volumes from ventriculograms taken in a single projection and for computing wall forces (10).

The effect of left ventricular dilation, hypertrophy, and abnormal function on the shape of the left ventricle at end-diastole and end-systole is illustrated in the engineering drawings in Fig. 1, which show a normal left ventricle (Fig. 1a) a dilated, hypertrophied left ventricle from a patient with volume overload from valvular insufficiency and relatively normal ventricular function (Fig. 1b), and a dilated, hypertrophied left ventricle with depressed function (ejection fraction, 0.12) from a patient with cardiomyopathy (Fig. 1c). The shape of the ventricle is expressed as the ratio of the radii of curvature, R_1 and R_2 being the radii of curvature in the meridional (longitudinal) and equatorial (latitudinal) directions, respectively. As ventricles become more spherical, R_2/R_1 becomes larger. As shown in Fig. 1, each of the left ventricles is relatively more spherical and its walls are thinner at end-diastole than at end-systole. The dilated, hypertrophied ventricles are also somewhat more spherical than the normal ventricles at end-diastole. The ventricle with depressed function, shown in Fig. 1c, is much more spherical at end-systole than are the ventricles illustrated in Fig. 1, a and b.

These relations at end-systole and end-diastole are further illustrated for groups of patients in Fig. 2, in which classification is on the basis of the end-diastolic volume and ejection fraction. The ventricles in group I have normal, or slightly

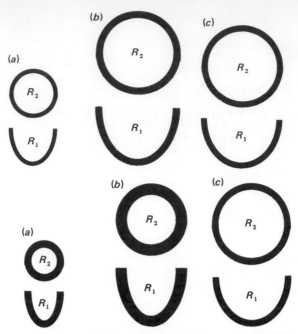

FIGURE 1 Schematic drawing of three left ventricles at end-systole (lower half) and end-diastole (upper half): (a) normal; (b) volume overload; and (c) cardiomyopathy. Upper half: (a) patient: I.D., EDV = 130 ml, $R_1 = 7.34$ cm, $R_2 = 2.77$ cm, $R_1/R_2 = 0.37$; (b) patient: J.J., EDV = 616 ml, $R_1 = 10.11$ cm, $R_2 = 4.79$ cm, $R_1/R_2 = 0.47$; (c) patient: L.C., EDV = 533 ml, $R_1 = 7.15$ cm, $R_2 = 4.85$ cm, $R_1/R_2 = 0.67$. Lower half: (a) ESV = 42 ml, EF = 0.67, $R_1 = 8.73$ cm, $R_2 = 1.75$ cm, $R_2/R_1 = 0.20$; (b) ESV = 262 ml, EF = 0.57, $R_1 = 12.29$ cm, $R_2 = 3.29$ cm, $R_2/R_1 = 0.26$; (c) ESV = 467 ml, EF = 0.12, $R_1 = 7.38$ cm, $R_2 = 4.57$ cm, $R_2/R_1 = 0.61$. From Dodge et al. (1), with permission of the American Heart Association, Inc.

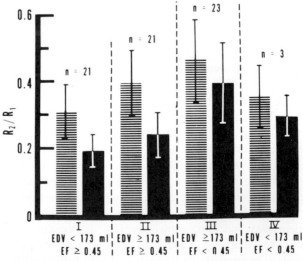

FIGURE 2 Ratio of radii of curvature R_2/R_1 for patients divided into four groups on the basis of end-diastolic volume and ejection fraction. (Cross-hatched bars) diastole; (solid bars) systole. From Dodge et al. (1), with permission of the American Heart Association, Inc.

enlarged, end-diastolic volumes and normal, or only slightly depressed, ejection fractions. Those in group II are dilated and hypertrophied from volume overload and have essentially normal ejection fractions. They are slightly more spherical at both end-diastole and end-systole than those in group I, which is also illustrated in Fig. 1b. In groups III and IV of Fig. 2, the ventricles have depressed ejection fractions and are somewhat more spherical than those in group I at end-diastole, and much more spherical at end-systole. These changes in volume and shape of the left ventricle are associated with changes in the magnitude and distribution of wall forces, as discussed below.

LEFT VENTRICULAR WALL STRESSES

From a knowledge of the chamber pressure, dimensions, and wall thickness, the forces acting within the walls of the left ventricle have, in previous studies, been computed by applying thin-wall theory (law of Laplace) and thick-wall theory (9, 10). Values obtained by these two methods generally agree within 10–15% (6, 9). The equation for these calculations, using the Laplace expression, is

$$\frac{T_1}{R_1} + \frac{T_2}{R_2} = P$$

where P is chamber pressure, T_1 and R_1 are the tension and radius of curvature, respectively, in the meridional direction; and T_2 and R_2 are the tension and radius of curvature, respectively, in the equatorial direction. Tension is usually expressed as force per centimeter and can be considered as the force acting on a slit of unit length through the entire thickness of the wall in a direction perpendicular to the direction of the force. Tension can be normalized for wall thickness (h) to compute wall stress, or force per unit area within the wall, as follows:

$$\frac{S_1}{R_1} + \frac{S_2}{R_2} = \frac{P}{h}$$

where S_1 and S_2 are wall stresses in the meridional and equatorial directions, respectively. Accordingly, wall stress equals wall tension divided by wall thickness. Wall stress is usually calculated for the ventricular mid-wall at the equator and expressed as force per square centimeter, or in the same units as chamber pressure. According to the equations above, wall stress is directly proportional to chamber pressure and radii of curvature and inversely proportional to wall thickness.

Figure 3 illustrates the results of applying these equations to compute wall stresses in four ventricles: 1) normal, 2) volume overloaded from mitral valve regurgitation, 3) pressure overloaded from aortic valve stenosis, and 4) dilated and functionally depressed from cardiomyopathy. In the normal ventricle, the mid-wall peak systolic stress in the equatorial direction, approximately 300 g/cm², is more than twice the peak systolic stress in the meridional direction, greatly exceeds the peak chamber systolic pressure, and, because of increasing wall thickness during systole, drops rapidly as systole progresses. In the ventricle with dilation and

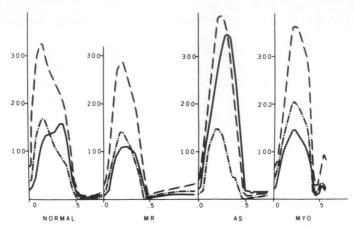

FIGURE 3 Chamber pressure and wall stress in the meridional and equatorial directions in four left ventricles: normal; mitral regurgitation (MR); aortic stenosis (AS); and cardiomyopathy (MYO). (Solid lines) Pressure; (dashed-dotted lines) meridional stress; and (dashed lines) equatorial stress.

hypertrophy from volume overloading as a consequence of mitral regurgitation, the peak values for wall stress are essentially normal despite the larger chamber dimensions. This is because of the increased wall thickness that occurs in compensated volume overload ventricles. In the subject with aortic valve stenosis, the ventricular systolic pressure is greatly elevated, but this is not accompanied by a proportionate increase of peak wall stress. Peak systolic wall stress in compensated aortic stenosis is usually normal or only slightly increased because of ventricular wall thickening (5). In the dilated ventricle with cardiomyopathy, peak systolic wall stress is somewhat higher than normal, although peak systolic chamber pressure is somewhat lower. Wall stress in the meridional direction is larger relative to peak equatorial stress than in the normal ventricle. Furthermore, wall stress remains elevated throughout ventricular systole. Accordingly, the dilated, relatively thin-walled, poorly contracting left ventricle has high wall stress values that remain elevated throughout systole.

Figure 2 showed that the dilated left ventricle tends to become more round and R_2/R_1 becomes larger. The increasing roundness of the left ventricle also occurs with depression of the ejection fraction, as shown by the relation between R_2/R_1 and ejection fraction in Fig. 4. This is associated with an increase in the ratio of the peak stress values in the equatorial and meridional directions, as shown in Fig. 5, with meridional stress becoming relatively larger. The ventricle with cardiomyopathy in Fig. 3 illustrates this relative increase of meridional stress. Therefore, as the ventricle dilates and fails there is a change in both the magnitude and the distribution of wall forces.

In the ventricle with cardiomyopathy in Fig. 3, end-diastolic wall stress is greatly elevated relative to chamber pressure. Figure 6 shows values for end-diastolic chamber pressure and wall stress in a group of patients with chronic heart disease and a wide range of diastolic volumes and chamber pressures. These data demonstrate that diastolic wall stress is elevated considerably more than diastolic

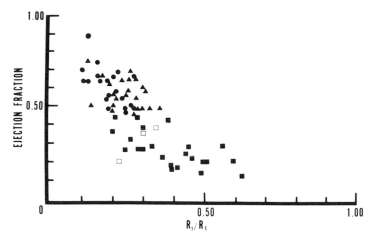

FIGURE 4 Shape of the left ventricle expressed as the ratio of radii of curvature and related to the ejection fraction. The groups are the same as in Fig. 2. (●) Group I; (▲) group II; (■) group III; and (□) group IV ($n = 68$; $r = 0.78$).

pressure in subjects with dilated left ventricles, and that it may be elevated in the absence of an elevated diastolic pressure. Accordingly, during diastole the ventricular preload, or the wall force acting to stretch the myocardium, is also a function of the chamber pressure, dimensions, and wall thickness. The influence of chamber dimensions and wall thickness on preload has not usually been considered in hemodynamic studies, but as we have illustrated, wall stress can vary widely relative to diastolic pressure among subjects with different kinds of chronic heart disease.

The contributions of longitudinal shortening, circumferential shortening, and

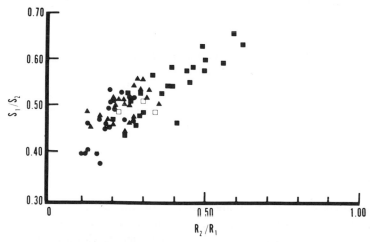

FIGURE 5 Ratio of stresses in the meridional and equatorial directions (S_1/S_2) related to the ratio of the radii of curvature (R_2/R_1). The groups are the same as in Fig. 2. (●) Group I; (▲) group II; (■) group III; and (□) group IV ($n = 68$; $r = 0.81$). From Dodge et al. (1), with permission of the American Heart Association, Inc.

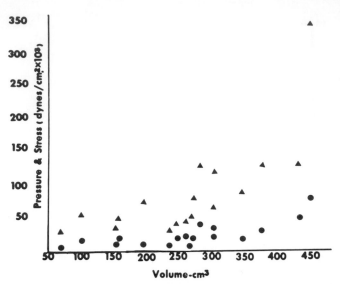

FIGURE 6 Left ventricular end-diastolic pressure and stress related to chamber volume in different subjects with heart disease. Normal end-diastolic volume (EDV), 100 ± 25 cc. (▲) End-diastolic stress, and (●) end-diastolic pressure.

systolic wall thickening to overall and segmental myocardial performance have been determined and have been related to the respective wall stress values to compute myocardial force-velocity relations and segmental work and rate of doing work, or power (3). These studies demonstrated that segmental performance is reduced in patients with depressed overall myocardial performance, and provided an increased understanding of the mechanics of ventricular performance. Such analyses are tedious, however, and have not yet been shown to be of sufficient value to warrant general clinical use.

CINEANGIOGRAPHIC ANALYSIS OF LEFT VENTRICULAR ABNORMALITIES

Measurements of overall or global ventricular performance do not adequately describe the kind of regional wall motion abnormalities that occur in patients with coronary artery disease (12) and that have been termed hypokinesis, akinesis, dyskinesis, or paradoxical focal systolic expansion (4). In addition, focal abnormalities of timing of contraction, or asynergy, have been recognized (4).

In our laboratory, we developed a quantitative method for better recognizing and characterizing the abnormalities of extent and timing of contraction. This method is based on frame-by-frame analysis of the motion of the endocardial surface of the left ventricle as determined from cineangiograms of the left ventricle taken at 60 frames per second in biplane or single-plane projections, with the timing of cine exposure recorded with respect to the electrocardiogram (12). For analysis, the cine frames are projected on the face of an X-Y digitizer, which is interfaced to a computer. The endocardial margins in each frame are manually traced and digitized for each frame throughout systole and diastole of an entire cardiac cycle, and the data are stored. The images of the chamber margin from each digitized frame are then displayed, superimposed on the face of a persistence scope, as in Fig. 7, for images taken in the anteroposterior and lateral projections. We developed a computer program to realign the images along the long axis constructed from the midaortic valve to apex in the anteroposterior projection. For analysis, the aortic valve during systole is permitted to move toward the apex along the long axis by a distance equal to the minimum distance between the midaortic valve of each frame to the line of the aortic valve at end-diastole. This is also illustrated in Fig. 7. For the lateral projection, images are realigned along an axis constructed from the apex to the junction of the posterior wall of the aorta and ventricle.

The long axis of the end-systolic image is divided into 10 equal segments by chords, which are perpendicular to the long axis and intersect the endocardial surface at 18 points (Fig. 7). The chords drawn from the long axis to the endocardial outline on the anterolateral surface are designated segments 1-9; those drawn to the outline on the posteromedial surface, segments 11-19; the chord at the apex, segment 10; and that at the aortic valve, segment 20.

Wall motion is determined along each of the 20 chords and displayed as shown in Fig. 8, which is constructed from data from a normal left ventricle. The time from the QRS in the electrocardiogram is shown on the horizontal axis, and motion normalized for segment length is shown on the vertical axis. From these curves, the extent, timing, and rate of motion of each segment during systole and diastole can be determined.

Using these methods, we analyzed the cineangiograms of the left ventricles of 25 subjects with no demonstrable heart disease to establish normal values for various measurements of regional wall motion. Figure 9 illustrates normalized extent

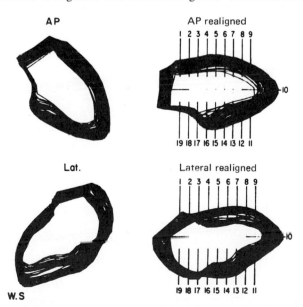

FIGURE 7 Display of the superimposed images of the left ventricular chamber with the chords.

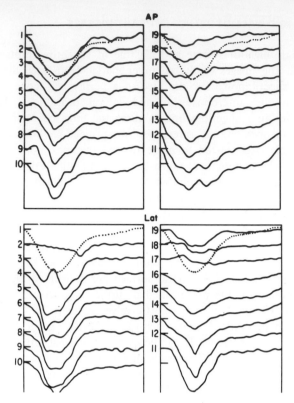

FIGURE 8 Normalized chord length versus time. Wall motion on the vertical axis with respect to time after the QRS on the horizontal axis for each of the chords shown in Fig. 7. The chamber volume curve is illustrated by dotted lines.

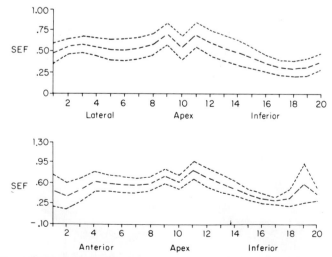

FIGURE 9 Normalized regional wall motion: segmental ejection fraction (SEF) for controls. From Stewart et al. (12).

of motion, or segmental ejection fraction, with the mean ± 1 SD in the anteroposterior and lateral projections. Similarly, Fig. 10 shows the mean ± 1 SD for time to maximum inward movement of the individual segments. This time, even in normal subjects, is not the same for all segments. The anterolateral endocardial surface usually reaches maximum inward motion before the inferior and medial surfaces. The individual segments may differ from one another in their time to maximum inward movement by several frames (at 60 frames per second) so that no single systolic frame will represent maximum motion for all regions of the ventricle. This can also be seen in Fig. 8, which shows the superior lateral surface reaching maximum inward motion before the lateral surface near the apex.

In patients with coronary artery disease, many abnormalities have been recognized. In Fig. 11, the extent of wall motion in a patient with coronary artery disease is shown as the solid line. For comparison, the normal mean and plus and minus 1 SD for wall motion are shown by the dashed and dotted lines, respectively. There is a region of hypokinesis on the lateral surface. The hypokinetic segments can be readily identified from this display. There is also compensatory hyper-contraction of the opposite inferior surface. Such regions of focal hypercontraction are common in ventricles with regional hypokinesis, which in part accounts for the observation that overall ventricular ejection fraction may be normal in the presence of regional hypokinesis.

Abnormalities of timing of contraction, or asynchrony, are also common. In Fig. 12 there is an area of lateral hypokinesis that reaches maximum inward excursion early and then expands during the later part of systole, making overall systolic performance of the left ventricle less effective. This, in all likelihood, is a consequence of local myocardial weakness from scarring or ischemia.

Delayed segmental contraction, and therefore relaxation, is also a common abnormality, as shown in Fig. 13 and by the delayed time to midsystole in Fig. 14.

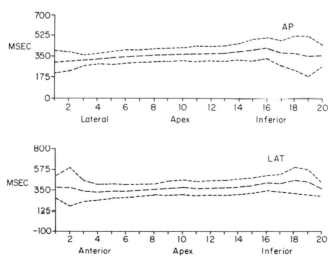

FIGURE 10 Time to minimum segment length for controls: time from the QRS to maximum inward segmental motion. From Stewart et al. (12).

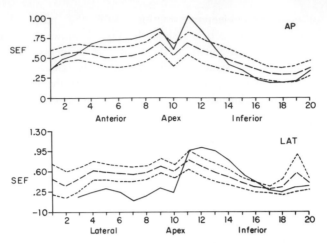

FIGURE 11 Compensation for lateral hypokinesis. (Solid lines) Segmental wall motion of the ventricle of a patient with coronary artery disease, showing lateral hypokinesis with compensatory inferior and anterior hyperkinesis. (Broken lines) Normal values, previously shown in Fig. 9.

Regional time delays in reaching maximum inward motion of as much as 200 msec are occasionally observed. This is more than 10 cine frames at 60 frames per second. With such differences in local timing of contraction, which are common in patients with coronary disease, it is clear that the extent of contraction of all myocardial segments cannot be properly assessed by comparing one so-called

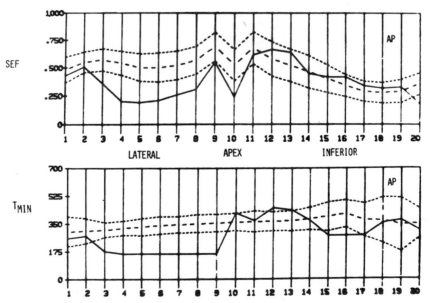

FIGURE 12 Lateral hypokinesis with abbreviated time to maximum inward segment motion. From Stewart et al. (12).

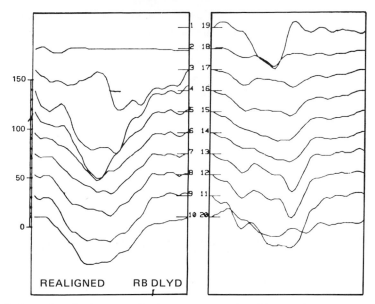

FIGURE 13 Lateral projection normalized segmental motion. Motion of individual segments of a left ventricle, with hypokinesis and delayed time to minimum of segments 14–17 and hyperkinesis of segments 4–9.

end-systolic image with one end-diastolic image, which has been a common practice in wall motion analysis.

The mechanism of this delayed segmental contraction and relaxation is unknown. It may be related to ischemia, which is known to be associated with delayed contraction and relaxation. However, this delay is commonly observed in

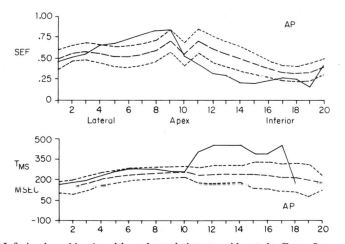

FIGURE 14 Inferior hypokinesis with prolonged time to mid-systole. From Stewart et al. (12).

resting, stable patients with coronary artery disease and is usually associated with some hypokinesis. It seems possible that activation is delayed in regions of delayed contraction, which is known to occur with ischemia and myocardial scarring from ischemia and infarction (2). If delayed activation is the basis for the delayed mechanical events, then identifying the presence and location of delayed mechanical activity by techniques such as the one described here could provide a means of identifying areas of delayed activation, which could be foci for reentrant arrhythmias (2). It is also possible that delayed focal contraction could, in itself, induce arrhythmias through the mechanical stretching of adjacent muscle cells.

Regional abnormalities of extent and timing of contraction interfere with the symmetrical relative synchronous contraction and relaxation of the left ventricle. The segmental delays in contraction and relaxation may in part explain the reduced rate of fall of left ventricular pressure in diastole and the increased myocardial diastolic stiffness that have been observed in coronary artery disease (8). Furthermore, these abnormalities may help to explain some of the abnormalities in the ballistocardiogram as recorded and described by Dr. Isaac Starr in patients with coronary artery disease.

REFERENCES

1. Dodge, H. T., Frimer, M., and Stewart, D. K. Functional evaluation of the hypertrophied heart in man. Circ Res Suppl II 34 and 35:122–127, 1974.
2. El-Sherif, N., Sherlag, B. J., Larrara, R., and Hope, R. R. Re-entrant ventricular arrhythmias in the late myocardial infarction period. 1. Conduction characteristics in the infarction zone. Circulation 55:686–702, 1977.
3. Gould, K. L., Kennedy, J. W., Frimer, M., Pollack, G. H., and Dodge, H. T. Analysis of wall dynamics and directional components of ventricular contraction in man. Am J Cardiol 38:322–331, 1976.
4. Herman, M. V., Heinle, R. A., Klein, M. D., and Garlin, R. Localized disorders in myocardial contraction. N Engl J Med 277:222–232, 1967.
5. Hood, W. P., Jr., Rackley, C. E., and Rolett, E. L. Wall stress in the normal and hypertrophied human left ventricle. Am J Cardiol 22:550–558, 1968.
6. Hood, W. P., Jr., Thomson, W. J., Rackley, C. E., and Rolett, E. L. Comparison of calculations of left ventricular wall stress in man from thin-walled and thick-walled ellipsoidal models. Circ Res 24:575–582, 1969.
7. Lewis, R. P. and Sandler, H. Relationship between changes in left ventricular dimensions and the ejection fraction in man. Circulation 44:548–557, 1971.
8. McLaurin, L. P., Rolett, E. L., and Grossman, W. Impaired left ventricular relaxation during pacing-induced ischemia. Am J Cardiol 32:751–757, 1973.
9. Mirsky, I. Left ventricular stresses in the intact human heart. Biophys J 9:189–208, 1969.
10. Sandler, H. and Dodge, H. T. Left ventricular tension and stress in man. Circ Res 13:91–104, 1963.
11. Sandler, H. and Dodge, H. T. The use of single plane angiograms for the calculation of left ventricular volume in man. Am Heart J 75:325–334, 1968.
12. Stewart, D. K., Dodge, H. T., and Frimer, M. Quantitative analysis of regional myocardial performance in coronary artery disease. In: Cardiovascular Imaging and Image Processing, Theory and Practice 1975. Palo Verdes Estates, Calif.: Society of Photo-Optical Instrumentation Engineers, 1976, pp. 217–224.

CHAPTER 5

HEART FAILURE: AN OVERVIEW

EUGENE BRAUNWALD

Heart failure is the pathophysiological state in which an abnormality of *cardiac* function is responsible for the failure of the heart to pump blood at a rate commensurate with the requirements of the metabolizing tissues. Heart failure is frequently, but not always, caused by a defect in myocardial contraction. Under these circumstances it may be termed *myocardial failure.*

In the presence of a defect in myocardial contraction and/or an excessive hemodynamic burden placed on the ventricle, the heart is dependent on three principal compensatory mechanisms in order to maintain its function as a pump: 1) the Frank-Starling mechanism, in which an increased preload—i.e., lengthening of sarcomeres to provide optimal overlap between thick and thin myofilaments—acts to sustain cardiac performance; 2) myocardial hypertrophy with or without cardiac chamber dilation, in which the mass of contractile tissue is augmented; and 3) increased release of catecholamines by adrenergic cardiac nerves and the adrenal medulla, which act on myocardial beta receptors and augment myocardial contractility. Initially, these three compensatory mechanisms may be adequate to restore relatively normal pumping performance of the heart, although intrinsic myocardial contractility may be substantially reduced. However, the potential of each of these compensatory mechanisms is limited, and the clinical syndrome of heart failure occurs as a consequence of these limitations.

The cardiac output is often depressed in the basal state in patients with the common forms of heart failure secondary to coronary artery disease, hypertension, primary myocardial disease, valvular disease, and pericardial disease (so-called low-output heart failure), but tends to be elevated in patients with heart failure and conditions in which there is reduced afterload and/or hypermetabolism, such as hyperthyroidism, anemia, arteriovenous fistula, beriberi, and Paget's disease (so-called high-output heart failure). The mechanisms responsible for the development of heart failure in patients whose cardiac output is initially high are complex and depend on the specific underlying disease process and its effect on the myocardium. In most of these conditions the heart is called on to pump an abnormally large volume of blood in order to deliver an adequate quantity of oxygen to the metabolizing tissues. This increased volume load exerts an effect on the myocardium resembling that produced by regurgitant valvular lesions. The inadequate delivery of oxygen to the metabolizing tissues, characteristic of heart failure, is reflected in an abnormally widened arterial-mixed venous oxygen difference. In mild cases, this abnormality may not be present in the basal state and may become evident only during the stress of increased activity.

When the volume of blood delivered into the systemic vascular bed is chronically reduced, and when one (or both) ventricle(s) fails to expel the normal fraction of its end-diastolic volume, a complex sequence of adjustments occurs that ultimately results in the abnormal accumulation of fluid. Although many of the clinical manifestations of heart failure are secondary to this excessive retention of fluid, hypervolemia also constitutes an important compensatory mechanism that tends to maintain cardiac output by elevating ventricular preload, since the myocardium operates on an ascending, albeit depressed, function curve (11, 15) and the augmented ventricular end-diastolic volume must be regarded as aiding the maintenance of cardiac output, except in the terminal stages of heart failure. The elevation of ventricular end-diastolic volume and pressure, in accordance with the Frank-Starling mechanism, raises ventricular performance, but at the same time causes pulmonary or systemic venous congestion and promotes the formation of pulmonary or peripheral edema.

A number of peripheral mechanisms are brought into play to conserve the limited cardiac output in heart failure. Among these are the redistribution of left ventricular output; vasoconstriction, mediated largely by the adrenergic nervous system, is primarily responsible for this redistribution of peripheral blood flow, which occurs when an additional burden (such as exercise, fever, or anemia) is imposed on the circulation in the presence of impaired myocardial function, and cardiac output cannot rise normally. As heart failure advances, there is a redistribution of left ventricular output, even in the basal state. This redistribution maintains the delivery of oxygen to vital organs such as the heart and brain, while blood flow to less critical areas such as the skin is reduced.

A progressive decline in the affinity of hemoglobin for oxygen resulting from an increase in 2,3-diphosphoglycerate (DPG) also occurs in heart failure. This rightward shift in the oxygen-hemoglobin dissociation curve represents an additional compensatory mechanism to facilitate oxygen transport; increased DPG, tissue acidosis that produces a similar shift in the oxygen-hemoglobin dissociation curve, and the slow circulation time characteristic of heart failure all act synergistically to maintain the delivery of oxygen to the metabolizing tissues in the face of a reduced cardiac output.

CONTRACTILITY OF HYPERTROPHIED AND FAILING MYOCARDIUM

There is general agreement that when an excessive load is imposed on a ventricle, the development of myocardial hypertrophy provides a fundamental compensatory mechanism that permits it to sustain this burden. There has been substantial interest in analyzing the behavior of isolated muscle removed from animals whose hearts had been subjected to a controlled major stress. A convenient experimental model is the cat with pulmonary artery constriction. Papillary muscles are removed from the right ventricles, in which either hypertrophy or overt failure had developed, and the excised muscles are then studied *in vitro*. Right ventricular hypertrophy and failure both reduce the maximum velocity of unloaded shortening (V_{max}) below the values observed in muscles obtained from normal cats; the changes are more marked in muscles obtained from animals with heart failure than in those with hypertrophy alone (Fig. 1). Heart failure clearly depresses the maximum isometric tension, but hypertrophy without failure produces only a borderline depression of this variable (14).

Electron microscopic studies of myocardium removed from overloaded, dilated hearts fixed at the elevated failing pressures existing in life have revealed sarcomere lengths averaging 2.2 μm—i.e., no longer than those at the apex of the length-active tension curve of normal cardiac muscle (12). These observations suggest that the depressed contractility of failing heart muscle is *not* a result of the disengagement of actin and myosin filaments. Thus, it appears to be related to an *intrinsic* defect of the muscle rather than to its operation at an abnormal position on a basically normal length-tension curve; also, these findings are *not* consistent with the hypothesis that the depressed contractility of failing heart muscle results from its operation on the descending limb of the Frank-Starling curve.

The findings summarized above are, in general, consonant with results obtained for cardiac muscle isolated from animals with experimentally produced pressure overload, left ventricular papillary muscles from Syrian hamsters with hereditary cardiomyopathy, and papillary muscles removed from the left ventricles of patients with heart failure due to chronic valvular disease (2). The contractile performance of the intact right ventricles of cats with pulmonary artery constriction also reveals a marked depression that parallels that observed in the isolated papillary muscles

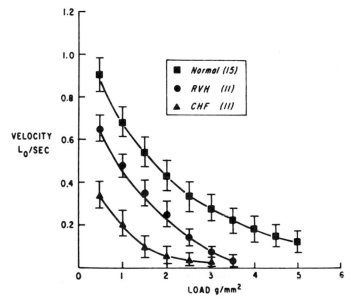

FIGURE 1 Force-velocity relations of the three groups of cat papillary muscles. Each point is the mean ± SEM. Velocity has been corrected to muscle lengths per second (L_0/sec). Numbers of animals are given in parentheses. From Spann et al. (14), by permission of the American Heart Association, Inc.

removed from these ventricles. The active tension developed by the right ventricle at
equivalent end-diastolic fiber lengths is markedly reduced in cats with heart failure
compared with normal cats (15) (Fig. 2).

It may be concluded that the depression of the cardiac contractile state
observed in the hypertrophied and failing ventricle represents an *intrinsic* property
of the muscle. This depression is evident *in vitro* when the physical and chemical
milieu of the muscle is controlled, and it is therefore not dependent on any altered
humoral or other environmental factors existing *in vivo*. Although contractile state
is uniformly depressed in the intact ventricle and in isolated muscles of cats with
heart failure, the cardiac index and stroke volume are often maintained. It appears
that when the ventricle is chronically stressed by an increase in the impedance to
emptying, the initial response is an increase in the total muscle mass. Initially, and
if the pressure overload is not too extreme, this adaptation can allow maintenance
of a high systolic pressure without depression of contractility in the intact heart.
Later, as the intrinsic contractile state of each unit of myocardium becomes
depressed, increased muscle mass, in conjunction with increased sympathetic
stimulation and perhaps the Frank-Starling mechanism, maintains overall circulatory
compensation. The depression of contractility is manifest, in the mildest form, by a
reduction in the V_{max} of each myocardial fiber, but with little, if any, decrease in
the development of maximal isometric force. As the intrinsic contractile state of
each unit of myocardium becomes further depressed, a more extensive reduction in
V_{max} occurs, and this is now accompanied by a reduction in maximal isometric

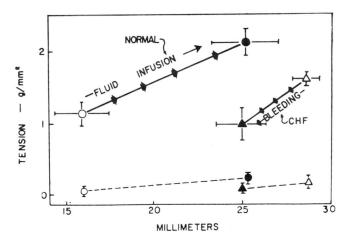

FIGURE 2   Length-tension relations in the intact ventricle. Acute manipulation of end-diastolic
volume to obtain ventricular Frank-Starling curves. Lines represent segments of
active and resting length-tension curves (Frank-Starling relationship) of five normal
(circles) and five failing ventricles (triangles). Solid lines represent active tension and
dashed lines resting or diastolic tension. Open symbols refer to values obtained at
spontaneously occurring end-diastolic volume, solid symbols to values obtained after
volume infusion in normal cats and bleeding of cats with heart failure. Average
values ± SEM are shown. Active and resting tension are given on the ordinate and
end-diastolic circumference on the abscissa. From Spann et al. (15).

force. At this point, circulatory compensation is provided by an increase in muscle mass and cardiac dilation. As contractility declines further, congestive heart failure becomes overt. Furthermore, while an improvement in function in response to positive inotropic stimuli, such as digitalis, can occur in failing muscle, the degree of augmentation falls, and at a late state the contractility of even the stimulated heart is subnormal.

The character of the stress responsible for inciting the hypertrophy also appears to play a critical role in determining whether it is detrimental to myocardial contractility. When a volume overload is produced by the creation of an aortocaval fistula, resulting in progressive left ventricular dilation and moderate left ventricular hypertrophy without clinical evidence of heart failure, the length-active tension relations of the dilated, hypertrophied ventricle remain essentially normal (8); within 1 wk of the creation of the fistula the left ventricular end-diastolic pressure rises and then remains constant, while the left ventricular end-diastolic diameter continues to increase progressively. Following chronic adjustment to the shunt, the end-diastolic volume increases at any particular end-diastolic pressure, but myocardial function, as reflected in the velocity of circumferential fiber shortening, usually remains normal. Also, in papillary muscles removed from animals with a volume overload resulting from an experimentally produced atrial septal defect, contractility is entirely normal, without the changes in the force-velocity or length-tension curves noted in muscles obtained from animals with pressure-induced hypertrophy. However, in the presence of a very large shunt and clinical evidence of congestive heart failure, myocardial contractility does become markedly reduced.

In the presence of volume overload, the development of eccentric ventricular hypertrophy, which presumably is associated primarily with an increase in the number of sarcomeres laid down in series, allows the chronically dilated heart to deliver an increased stroke volume at a normal level of contractility and a normal extent of shortening of each individual sarcomere. Some increase in wall thickness and a change to a more spherical ventricular shape tend to maintain wall stress relatively constant and sarcomere length remains maximal. Thus, the ventricle compensates for a volume overload with both a change in ventricular geometry and an increase in the number of sarcomeres, resulting in an augmentation of stroke volume. In the compensated state the combination of ventricular dilation and hypertrophy associated with chronic volume overloading allows enhancement of overall cardiac performance, with normal performance of each unit of an enlarged ventricle operating at an optimal sarcomere length.

In conditions of pressure overloading, the principal hemodynamic adjustment results from concentric ventricular hypertrophy, expressed as increases in the wall thickness and the mass of ventricular muscle; additional sarcomeres are laid down, primarily in parallel. Hypertrophy progresses until the stress on each unit of myocardium is restored to normal. The ejection fraction and end-diastolic volume remain normal, or almost so, until late in the course of the disease, when progressive ventricular dilation occurs.

Myocardial Energy Production

Considerable effort has been directed toward elucidating the fundamental mechanism responsible for the relative decrease in useful external work delivered by the myocardium in the common forms of low-output heart failure. Recent observations on the relation between left ventricular performance and myocardial oxygen consumption have shown that when contractility becomes depressed acutely, myocardial oxygen consumption also declines. Patients with chronic impairment of left ventricular performance and reduction of the velocity of myocardial fiber shortening also exhibit reduction of coronary blood flow and myocardial oxygen consumption per unit of muscle (5).

To determine whether energy supplies are adequate in cardiac hypertrophy and failure, the contents of high-energy phosphate were compared in the papillary muscles of normal cats, cats with hypertrophy without failure, and cats with overt right ventricular failure induced by pulmonary artery constriction. Concentrations of adenosine triphosphate (ATP) and creatine phosphate (CP) were normal in the papillary muscles removed from failing hearts and nonfailing, hypertrophied hearts studied *in vitro* (10). Since, as already pointed out, the mechanical performance of these isolated muscles was impaired (14), this depression of contractility could not be attributed to a reduction of total myocardial high-energy stores. In addition, there appear to be no reductions of ATP and CP concentrations in papillary muscles removed from failing human hearts. Thus, it would appear that energy production and the total reserve of high-energy phosphate compounds are not *primarily* responsible for the reduced contractility of the hypertrophied or failing heart, regardless of any changes in mitochondrial function. However, the possibility that reduction of a small compartment of ATP vital for muscular contraction plays a key role in the depression of contractility characteristic of heart failure has certainly not been excluded.

Myocardial Energy Utilizatior.

Analysis of the contractile proteins obtained from hypertrophied or failing hearts has, in general, failed to show significant qualitative or quantitative abnormalities, despite early evidence to the contrary. However, the activity of myofibrillar adenosine triphosphatase (ATPase) was found to be reduced in the hearts of patients who had died of heart failure and in dogs with naturally occurring heart failure (2). Furthermore, there is evidence that reductions in the activities of both myofibrillar and actomyosin ATPase occur in heart failure induced by pulmonary artery constriction in cats and by constriction of the ascending aorta in guinea pigs. These depressions of enzymatic activity could occur if an altered low-molecular-weight subunit of the myosin molecule—i.e., the portion of the molecule responsible for the ATPase activity—were produced in the overloaded heart, and if it reduced contractility by lowering the rate of interaction between actin and myosin filaments (2). Synthesis of a myosin with an abnormally low intrinsic ATPase activity could explain many of the functional changes in failing heart muscle, such as depression of the force-velocity curve.

Excitation-Contraction Coupling

Studies in a number of *in vitro* systems indicate that there is impairment of the delivery of Ca^{2+} for activation of the contractile process in heart failure. A variety of cellular structures, including the sarcolemma, the sarcoplasmic reticulum (SR), and the mitochondria, affect the myoplasmic concentration of Ca^{2+}. It has been proposed that structural damage to these organelles or changes in the intracellular concentrations of other cations, adenine nucleotides, or free fatty acids may interfere with mechanisms regulating the myoplasmic concentration of Ca^{2+} and may thus participate in the production of heart failure. Uptake of Ca^{2+} by these structures is dependent on a Ca^{2+}-activated ATPase, and depression of the activity of this enzyme or defects in Ca^{2+} accumulation sites could play a role in the development of myocardial failure, in that a reduction in Ca^{2+} pumping could be responsible for a reduction of Ca^{2+} bound to the SR and eventually for a reduction of Ca^{2+} available for the contractile process.

The reduction in contractility of papillary muscle from cats with constriction of the pulmonary artery is accompanied by a reduction in the muscle's resting membrane potential, maximum rate of rise, and overshoot, as well as in the duration of the action potential (4). Although the precise mechanism responsible for these changes in electric properties is unknown, they may be related to elevations of intracellular $[Na^+]$ and depressions of intracellular $[K^+]$, and could be associated with diminished entry of Ca^{2+} into myocardial cells, which in turn could impair myocardial contraction. The ATPase isolated from the SR obtained from the right ventricles of dogs with heart failure has been found to be depressed (9), and in failing calf hearts the rate of Ca^{2+} uptake by the SR and the activity of microsomal Ca^{2+}-activated ATPase are reduced to about 50% of normal (16). A disturbance in the uptake of Ca^{2+} by the SR could interfere with cardiac performance, since inadequate reduction of the intracellular $[Ca^{2+}]$ at the end of systole could result in delayed or incomplete relaxation. In studies employing murexide, a dye that rapidly binds Ca^{2+} in solution, it has been demonstrated that the rate of Ca^{2+} uptake by the SR obtained from failing heart muscle in humans, rabbits, and hamsters is slowed and that the total binding of Ca^{2+} is reduced (2).

Experimental heart failure produced in the rabbit by aortic regurgitation, in which there is depression of myocardial contractile performance *in vitro*, appears to be associated with a significant alteration of the intracellular distribution of Ca^{2+}. Although total intracellular $[Ca^{2+}]$ is normal, mitochondrial $[Ca^{2+}]$ has been found to be greatly increased. The rates of uptake and binding of Ca^{2+} to the SR are reduced. With greater quantities of Ca^{2+} accumulated in the mitochondria, contractility might then be reduced by limiting the quantity of Ca^{2+} available to initiate contraction; moreover, if enough Ca^{2+} enters the mitochondria, uncoupling of oxidative phosphorylation can occur. Interestingly, uptake of Ca^{2+} by the SR was found to be significantly reduced in rabbits that were sacrificed before objective signs of heart failure had developed. This finding very early in the course of failure suggests that this reduction of Ca^{2+} uptake is responsible for, rather than a consequence of, the impairment of contractility (6).

The hamster with hereditary cardiomyopathy offers the opportunity for study of the function of the SR in a naturally occurring form of myocardial failure. There is a depression of the rate of Ca^{2+} binding by the SR, and this depression becomes more severe as the heart failure progresses (17); abnormalities of phospholipid and cholesterol composition, which have been described in the SR of the cardiomyopathic hamster, might explain these changes. Also, both the rate and the extent of energy-linked Ca^{2+} binding by mitochondria have been reported to be greatly reduced in these failing hearts (17). Abnormalities in the accumulation of Ca^{2+} by the SR have been demonstrated in other forms of heart failure as well (2), including the spontaneously failing dog heart-lung preparation, ischemic failing heart muscle, the substrate-depleted failing rat heart, the heart with isoproterenol-induced necrosis, the failing heart with potassium deficiency, and cardiac muscle removed from patients with cardiomyopathy who were recipients of cardiac transplants. However, while disturbances of Ca^{2+} transport frequently accompany heart failure, the nature of the abnormality of Ca^{2+} transport differs in various forms of heart failure.

Function of the Autonomic Nervous System

In view of the importance of the adrenergic nervous system in normal regulation of the circulation, considerable attention has been directed to the activity of this system in heart failure. A crude index of the activity of this system, at rest and during exercise, is provided by the concentration of norepinephrine (NE) in arterial blood. No change or very small increases were noted during exercise in normal subjects, whereas much larger elevations occurred in patients with heart failure, presumably reflecting the greater activity of their adrenergic nervous systems during exercise. Measurement of 24-hr urinary NE excretion revealed marked elevations in patients with heart failure, indicating that the activity of the adrenergic nervous system and, presumably, secretion of catecholamines by the adrenal medulla are also augmented at rest in these patients; abnormality of adrenergic nervous activity is also reflected in the very low concentrations of NE in the atrial tissue of these patients, which are sometimes less than 10% of normal (Fig. 3). The NE

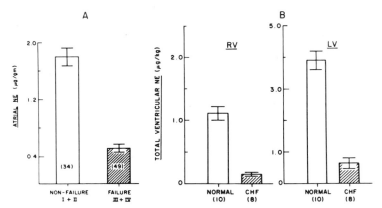

FIGURE 3   Effects of heart failure on the cardiac stores of norepinephrine. (A) Concentration of NE in atrial appendage biopsies taken during cardiac operations from 34 patients without heart failure (classes I and II) and 49 patients with heart failure (classes III and IV). Average values ± SEM are shown. (B) Total ventricular NE content in normal dogs and in dogs with pulmonary stenosis, tricuspid insufficiency, and congestive heart failure (CHF). Average values ± SEM are given. RV, right ventricle; LV, left ventricle. From Braunwald et al. (2), with permission from Little, Brown & Co.

concentrations have also been shown to be markedly depressed in papillary muscles removed from the left ventricles of patients with severe left ventricular failure who underwent mitral valve replacement (1).

Since the changes in cardiac NE concentration that occurred in some patients with heart failure appeared to be severe enough to impair adrenergic function, an attempt was made to define the mechanism of this depletion. In dogs with right ventricular failure produced by creation of pulmonary stenosis and tricuspid insufficiency, the reduction of cardiac NE concentration was shown *not* to be the result of a simple dilution of sympathetic nerve endings in a hypertrophied muscle mass, since the total ventricular NE contents were lower in both the hypertrophied right and the nonhypertrophied left ventricle (Fig. 3).

After the production of heart failure in the guinea pig by constriction of the aorta, the left ventricular NE concentration immediately fell to approximately 30% of normal. Infusion of a large dose of NE raised cardiac NE stores much less in guinea pigs with heart failure than in normal animals. This impaired capacity to retain administered NE might result from a reduction of either the total number of neurons in the myocardium or the number of intraneuronal binding sites. The rate of NE synthesis, estimated by measuring the turnover of radiolabeled amine in the guinea pig heart, is diminished roughly in proportion to the change in pool size (2).

The cardiomyopathic Syrian hamster also exhibits cardiac NE depletion terminally (13). This is accompanied by a marked increase in the NE turnover rate to a level that approaches the maximum achievable under stress, leaving little, if any, reserve. These findings are compatible with the concept that heart failure is accompanied by a progressive increase in tone in the adrenergic cardiac nerves, which leads to a concomitant reduction in cardiac NE stores. Marked reductions in the activity of tyrosine hydroxylase accompany cardiac NE depletion in dogs with experimental heart failure, while no alterations in enzyme activity occur in the hearts of animals in which NE depletion is produced with reserpine (2). These findings suggest that the reduction in the activity of this enzyme is responsible for the depletion of NE in the heart in cardiac failure. An absence of fluorescence in the terminal varicosities of sympathetic fibers in close association with cardiac muscle cells in the NE-depleted, failing heart has been noted. Recovery from heart failure is associated with virtual restoration both of the NE concentration and of the histochemical appearance of adrenergic nerve distribution, suggesting that a rapidly reversible abnormality, presumably of neurotransmitter synthesis, occurs in the terminal portion of the cardiac adrenergic innervation in heart failure.

NE exerts a strongly positive inotropic effect, even in the failing heart, and the adrenergic nervous system may be considered to provide important potential support to the failing myocardium. However, with supramaximal stimulation of the cardiac adrenergic nerves, the increments of heart rate and contractile force that occur in animals with heart failure and cardiac NE depletion are abolished or are much smaller than in normal dogs (2) (Fig. 4). Thus, it is likely that when heart failure is accompanied by depletion of cardiac NE stores, the quantity of NE released by the adrenergic nerve endings in the heart is deficient in relation to the impulse traffic along these nerves. However, the contractile state is normal in isolated right ventricular papillary muscles obtained from cats with cardiac NE

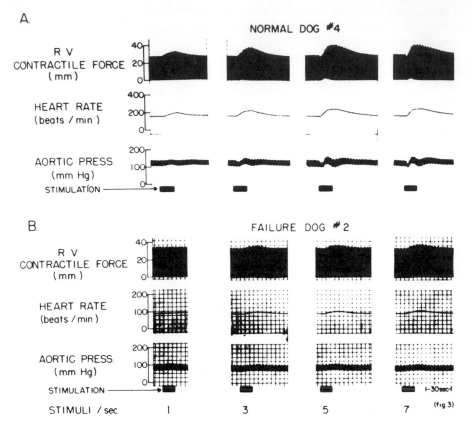

FIGURE 4 Records showing the effect of right cardioaccelerator stimulation (A) in a normal dog and (B) in a dog with congestive failure. From Covell et al. (2a), by permission of the American Heart Association, Inc.

depletion produced surgically or pharmacologically. Therefore, it may be concluded that the stores of NE in the heart are *not* fundamental for maintenance of its intrinsic contractile state. However, since the reduction of stores of cardiac NE in heart failure is associated with a diminished release of the neurotransmitter, this depletion of NE may be responsible for loss of the much needed adrenergic support and reflex control of the failing heart, and in this manner it could intensify the severity of heart failure.

Evidence indicating that the NE-depleted, failing heart is increasingly dependent on circulating catecholamines for the maintenance of basal hemodynamic function has been obtained from experiments in calves with experimentally produced heart failure and cardiac NE depletion (19). In the later stages of heart failure, when levels of circulating catecholamines are elevated and the cardiac NE stores are depleted, the myocardium is largely dependent on a more generalized adrenergic stimulation derived from extracardiac sources. In patients with heart failure, interference with the adrenergic nervous system by propranolol or guanethidine, in doses that do not lower arterial pressure, frequently causes sodium and water retention as well as intensification of heart failure.

The possibility of defective adrenergic control of heart rate in patients with heart failure has been studied by observing the reflex chronotropic responses to both upright tilt and nitroglycerin-induced hypotension. An attenuation of the normal increase in heart rate, both before and after atropine, confirms that a defect exists in the adrenergic component of baroreceptor-mediated reflex heart rate control in patients with cardiac dysfunction; the severity of this defect is, in general, proportional to the impairment of cardiac reserve. Similar observations have been made in dogs with experimental heart failure. A reduction in responsiveness of the beta receptors as a cause of impaired sympathetic influence could be excluded by noting a normal response of heart rate to isoproterenol, suggesting that the adrenergically mediated heart rate response results from NE depletion rather than from a defect in the beta adrenergic receptor mechanism in the sinoatrial node. In addition, the heart rate at maximal exercise is reduced in patients with cardiac dysfunction, suggesting that the ability of the adrenergic nervous system to speed the heart is impaired in these subjects. Thus, cardiac dysfunction appears to be associated with a marked impairment of autonomically mediated changes in heart rate.

Heart failure is associated with disturbances of parasympathetic function as well. The degree of parasympathetic restraint on the automaticity of the sinoatrial node is reduced in patients with heart disease; after pharmacological blockade of the adrenergic system with propranolol, heart rate is similar in normal subjects and in patients with heart disease. However, when resting parasympathetic tone is then inhibited with atropine in these adrenergically blocked subjects, the degree of cardiac acceleration is reduced in patients with heart failure compared to normal subjects. Patients with heart disease also exhibit a reduction in heart rate slowing for any particular elevation of systemic arterial pressure compared to normal subjects. Since this slowing can normally be virtually abolished by parasympathetic blockade, these findings suggest an abnormality of heart rate control by the parasympathetic nervous system in patients with heart failure (3). The sensitivity of the baroreceptor reflex to transient hypertension has also been shown to be significantly reduced in dogs with hypertrophy alone and reduced further in dogs with heart failure.

Although the precise mechanism responsible for the demonstrated impairment of parasympathetic function in heart failure is not clear, this disturbance may be of considerable functional importance, since the ability to alter heart rate constitutes an extremely important mechanism by which the cardiac output is adjusted; indeed, under normal circumstances changes in heart rate account in large measure for changes in cardiac output. Patients with heart failure are unable to elevate stroke volume normally during exercise, and when this limitation occurs together with defective control of heart rate as a consequence of abnormalities of both the sympathetic and parasympathetic limbs of the autonomic nervous system, the inability of these patients to raise cardiac output appropriately is readily appreciated.

Heart Failure in Anoxia
and Ischemia

The depression of myocardial contractility that occurs in acute myocardial anoxia or ischemia is associated with an abbreviation of the plateau of the action potential, suggesting an abnormality in the Ca^{2+} current and therefore in the movement of Ca^{2+} into the cell. The latter, in turn, may reduce the quantity of Ca^{2+} released by the SR and thereby impair contractility. Furthermore, a reduction of intracellular pH, such as occurs in anoxia and particularly in ischemia, augments the affinity of the SR for Ca^{2+} and thereby perhaps reduces its ability to release Ca^{2+} to the contractile sites. Studies of the binding and release of Ca^{2+} by isolated SR have, in fact, shown that there is an impairment in the release of Ca^{2+} early in the course of ischemia at a time when other membrane-associated functions are still normal. With more prolonged ischemia there is also marked binding of Ca^{2+} by the SR at a time when both mitochondrial and sarcolemmal Na, K-ATPase activities are severely impaired. It has been proposed that even when a normal quantity of Ca^{2+} is made available for activating the contractile mechanism, the development of intracellular acidosis can impair contractility by displacing this ion from its binding side on troponin, thus reducing contractility (7).

More than 40 yr ago, Tennant and Wiggers (18) demonstrated that after ligation of a coronary artery, the contraction of cardiac muscle ceases and the affected area appears cyanotic, dilated, and bulging. While patients with coronary artery disease usually do *not* show impaired left ventricular function in the absence of angina and of a previous myocardial infarction, transient episodes of myocardial ischemia produce transient episodes of left ventricular failure. Myocardial ischemia generally eliminates the normal contractile performance in a *localized area* of myocardium, resulting in an asynergic contraction. During brief periods of myocardial ischemia, manifest clinically as angina pectoris, ventricular wall motion becomes abnormal, and with the subsidence of ischemia these mechanical changes revert to control.

Regional loss of myocardial contractile activity, whether sustained or transient, may depress overall left ventricular function, producing reductions of stroke volume, stroke work, cardiac output, and ejection fraction and elevations of end-diastolic volume and pressure. Clinical evidence of heart failure occurs when regional asynergy is so severe and extensive that the uninvolved myocardium cannot compensate adequately. Hemodynamic evidence of left ventricular failure develops when contraction ceases or becomes seriously impaired in 20-25% of the left ventricle; with a loss of 40% or more of left ventricular myocardium, severe pump failure and the clinical picture of cardiogenic shock usually occur. Clinical evidence of impaired left ventricular function in most patients with acute myocardial infarction ranges from the barely detectable to the most severe forms of pump failure; the severity of heart failure is directly related to the extent of acute myocardial damage, whether the latter has occurred in a previously normal heart or is superimposed on previously damaged myocardium. Pulmonary rales, one of the principal clinical manifestations of heart failure, are secondary to a compensatory mechanism—cardiac dilation—and possibly to increased stiffness of the left ventricle as well.

The abnormality in circulatory regulation that is present in ischemic heart disease is shown in Fig. 5. The process begins with an obstruction in the coronary vascular bed that results in regional myocardial ischemia. If it is widespread, myocardial ischemia depresses overall left ventricular function so that left ventricular stroke volume falls. A marked depression of left ventricular stroke volume ultimately lowers aortic pressure and reduces coronary perfusion pressure. This situation may intensify myocardial ischemia and thereby initiate a vicious cycle. The reduction of left ventricular stroke volume also leads to an increased preload—i.e., it dilates the well-perfused, normally functioning portion of the left ventricle. Although this compensatory mechanism tends to restore stroke volume to normal, the dilation of the left ventricle also elevates ventricular afterload, because at any particular arterial pressure the dilated ventricle must develop greater tension. The increased afterload not only depresses left ventricular stroke volume but elevates myocardial oxygen consumption, which in turn exaggerates regional myocardial ischemia. The outcome of the coronary obstruction, then, depends on the balance attained between these processes. When regional myocardial ischemia is limited and the function of the remainder of the left ventricle is normal, the compensatory mechanisms will sustain overall left ventricular function. If a large portion of the left ventricle becomes ischemic, as occurs in massive coronary occlusion, overall left ventricular function becomes so depressed that the circulation cannot be sustained despite the dilation of the remaining viable portion of the ventricle.

CONCLUSIONS

It may be useful to consider normal and impaired myocardial function, whatever the etiology and pathogenesis, within the framework of the familiar Frank-Starling mechanism (2). The normal relation between ventricular end-diastolic

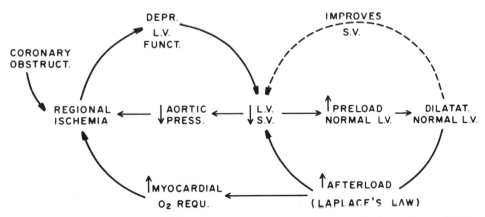

FIGURE 5 Schema showing changes in circulatory regulation in ischemic heart disease. DEPR. L.V. FUNCT., depressed left ventricular function; S.V., stroke volume; DILATAT., dilatation; O_2 REQU., oxygen requirements. Solid lines indicate that the effect is produced or intensified, dashed lines that it is diminished. Reprinted by permission from the New England Journal of Medicine (290:1420–1425, 1974).

volume and performance is shown in Fig. 6, curve 1. Normally, assumption of the upright posture tends to reduce venous return, and as a consequence, at any particular level of exercise, the cardiac output is lower in the upright than in the recumbent position. On the other hand, the hyperventilation of exercise, the pumping action of the exercising muscles, and the venoconstriction that occur all tend to augment ventricular filling. Simultaneously, the increase in sympathetic nerve impulses to the myocardium and in the concentration of circulating catecholamines and the tachycardia that occur during exercise all result in augmentation of the contractile state of the myocardium and elevation of stroke volume, with either no change or even a decrease of end-diastolic pressure and volume. This state is represented by a shift from point *A* to point *B* in Fig. 6. Vasodilation occurs in the exercising muscles, reducing peripheral vascular resistance and aortic impedance. This ultimately allows the achievement of a greatly elevated cardiac output during exercise, at an arterial pressure not greatly different from that occurring in the resting state. During intense exercise, cardiac output can rise to a maximal level only if use is made of the Frank-Starling mechanism, as reflected in increases in the left ventricular end-diastolic volume and pressure (Fig. 6, point *C*).

In heart failure, the fundamental abnormality resides in depressions of the

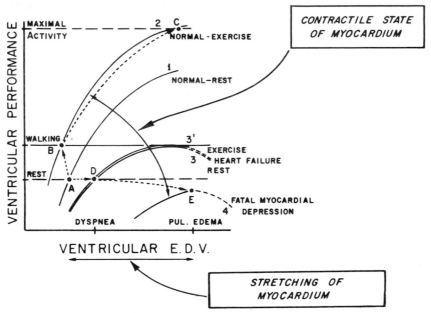

FIGURE 6 Diagram showing the interrelations between influences on ventricular end-diastolic volume (E.D.V.) through stretching of the myocardium and the contractile state of the myocardium. Levels of ventricular E.D.V. associated with filling pressures that result in dyspnea and pulmonary edema are shown on the abscissa. Levels of ventricular performance required during rest, walking, and maximal activity are designated on the ordinate. The dotted lines are the descending limbs of the ventricular performance curves, which are rarely seen during life but show the level of ventricular performance if end-diastolic volume could be elevated to very high levels. From Braunwald et al. (1a), with permission from Little, Brown & Co.

myocardial force-velocity relation and of the length-active tension curve, reflecting reductions in the contractile state of the myocardium. In many cases, such as those represented by Fig. 6, curve 3, cardiac output and external ventricular performance at rest are within normal limits, but are maintained at these levels only because the end-diastolic fiber length and ventricular end-diastolic volume are above normal—i.e., through the operation of the Frank-Starling mechanism. The elevations of left ventricular end-diastolic volume and pressure are associated with greater than normal levels of the pulmonary capillary pressure, contributing to the dyspnea experienced by patients with heart failure (Fig. 6, point D).

Since heart failure is frequently accompanied by a depletion of cardiac NE stores and a reduction of the inotropic response to impulses in the cardiac adrenergic nerves, ventricular performance curves cannot be elevated to normal levels by the adrenergic nervous system, and the normal improvement of contractility that takes place during exercise is attenuated or even prevented (Fig. 6, curves 3-3'). The factors that tend to augment ventricular filling during exercise in the normal subject push the failing myocardium even farther along its flattened length-active tension curve, and although left ventricular performance may be augmented somewhat, this occurs only as a consequence of an inordinate elevation of ventricular end-diastolic volume and pressure and therefore of pulmonary capillary pressure. The elevation of the latter intensifies dyspnea and therefore has an important role in limiting the intensity of exercise that the patient can perform. According to this concept, left ventricular failure becomes fatal when the myocardial length-active tension curve becomes depressed (Fig. 6, curve 4) to the point at which either cardiac performance fails to satisfy the requirements of the peripheral tissues even at rest or the left ventricular end-diastolic and pulmonary capillary pressures are elevated to levels that result in pulmonary edema, or both (Fig. 6, point E).

REFERENCES

1. Braunwald, E. and Chidsey, C. A. The adrenergic nervous system in the control of the normal and failing heart. Proc R Soc Med 58:1062–1066, 1965.
1a. Braunwald, E., Ross, J., Jr., and Sonnenblick, E. H. Mechanisms of Contraction of the Normal and Failing Heart, ed. 1. Boston: Little, Brown, 1968.
2. Braunwald, E., Ross, J., Jr., and Sonnenblick, E. H. Mechanisms of Contraction of the Normal and Failing Heart, ed. 2. Boston: Little, Brown, 1976.
2a. Covell, J. W., Chidsey, C. A., and Braunwald, E. Reduction of the cardiac response to postganglionic sympathetic nerve stimulation in experimental heart failure. Circ Res 19:51–56, 1966.
3. Eckberg, D. L., Drabinsky, M., and Braunwald, E. Defective cardiac para-sympathetic control in patients with heart disease. N Engl J Med 285:877–883, 1971.
4. Gelband, H. and Bassett, A. L. Depressed transmembrane potentials during experimentally induced ventricular failure in cats. Circ Res 32:625–634, 1973.
5. Henry, P. D., Eckberg, D., Gault, J. H., and Ross, J., Jr. Depressed inotropic state and reduced myocardial oxygen consumption in the human heart. Am J Cardiol 31:300–306, 1973.

6. Ito, Y., Suko, J., and Chidsey, C. A. Intracellular calcium and myocardial contractility. V. Calcium uptake of sarcoplasmic reticulum fractions in hypertrophied and failing rabbit hearts. J Mol Cell Cardiol 6:237-247, 1974.

7. Katz, A. M. Congestive heart failure. Role of altered myocardial cellular control. N Engl J Med 293:1184-1191, 1976.

8. McCullagh, W. H., Covell, J. W., and Ross, J., Jr. Left ventricular dilatation and diastolic compliance changes during chronic volume overloading. Circulation 45:943-951, 1972.

9. Mead, R. J., Peterson, M. B., and Welty, J. D. Sarcolemmal and sarcoplasmic reticular ATPase activities in the failing canine heart. Circ Res 29:14-20, 1971.

10. Pool, P. E., Spann, J. F., Jr., Buccino, R. A., Sonnenblick, E. H., and Braunwald, E. Myocardial high energy phosphate stores in cardiac hypertrophy and heart failure. Circ Res 21:365-373, 1967.

11. Ross, J., Jr. and Braunwald, E. Studies on Starling's law of the heart. IX. The effects of impeding venous return on performance of the normal and failing human left ventricle. Circulation 30:719-727, 1974.

12. Ross, J., Jr., Sonnenblick, E. H., Taylor, R. R., and Covell, J. H. Diastolic geometry and sarcomere length in the chronically dilated canine left ventricle. Circ Res 28:49-61, 1971.

13. Sole, M. J., Chi-Man, L. O., Laird, C. W., Sonnenblick, E. H., and Wurtman, R. J. Norepinephrine turnover in the heart and spleen of the cardiomyopathic Syrian hamster. Circ Res 37:855-862, 1975.

14. Spann, J. F., Jr., Buccino, R. A., Sonnenblick, E. H., and Braunwald, E. Contractile state of cardiac muscle obtained from cats with experimentally produced ventricular hypertrophy and heart failure. Circ Res 21:341-354, 1967.

15. Spann, J. F., Jr., Covell, J. W., Eckberg, D. L., Sonnenblick, E. H., Ross, J., Jr., and Braunwald, E. Contractile performance of the hypertrophied and chronically failing cat ventricle. Am J Physiol 223:1150-1157, 1972.

16. Suko, J., Vogel, J. H. K., and Chidsey, C. A. Intracellular calcium and myocardial contractility. III. Reduced calcium uptake and ATPase of the sarcoplasmic reticular fraction prepared from chronically failing calf hearts. Circ Res 27:235-247, 1970.

17. Sulakhe, P. V. and Dhalla, N. S. Excitation-contraction coupling in heart. VII. Calcium accumulation in subcellular particles in congestive heart failure. J Clin Invest 50:1019-1027, 1971.

18. Tennant, R. and Wiggers, C. J. The effect of coronary occlusion on myocardial contraction. Am J Physiol 112:351-361, 1935.

19. Vogel, J. H. K. and Chidsey, C. A. Cardiac adrenergic activity in experimental heart failure assessed by beta receptor blockade. Am J Cardiol 24:198-208, 1969.

PART II

DIRECT (INVASIVE) ASSESSMENT OF CARDIAC PERFORMANCE

VENTRICULAR PERFORMANCE IN THE CARDIOMYOPATHIES AND VALVULAR HEART DISEASE: DIRECT QUANTIFICATION

DEAN T. MASON
GARRETT LEE
JAMES A. JOYE
ANTHONY N. DeMARIA

Congestive heart failure is the pathological condition in which severely impaired cardiac performance is responsible for the inability of the heart to deliver blood at a rate commensurate with the basal metabolic requirements of the organs throughout the body (11, 13). The concept delineated in this review is that the fundamental physiological abnormality leading to decompensation in heart failure resides in depression of myocardial contractility in disorders characterized by chronic ventricular hemodynamic overloading, as well as in the cardiac diseases caused primarily by inotropic defects (12).

PATHOPHYSIOLOGICAL TYPES OF HEART DISEASE

Clinical heart disease can be broadly classified on a pathophysiological basis according to three general types of cardiac functional abnormalities: 1) primary disturbance in contractility, as in idiopathic or ischemic myocardial disease; 2) mechanical inhibition of cardiac performance during diastole (ventricular underloading), as in restricted ventricular filling in mitral stenosis or cardiac tamponade; and 3) mechanical ventricular overloading during systole, characterized by excessive pressure loading, as in aortic stenosis or essential hypertension; or increased volume loading, as in mitral or aortic regurgitation (10). Congestive heart failure in chronic systolic ventricular overloading and in primary inotropic disorders occurs when myocardial contractility is substantially depressed; heart failure ensues when this impairment of contractile state becomes particularly severe.

REGULATION OF CARDIAC PERFORMANCE IN HEART DISEASE

The function of the intact heart is governed by intimate integration of four principal determinants that regulate stroke volume and cardiac output: 1) preload (ventricular end-diastolic volume), 2) contractility (variable force of ventricular contraction independent of loading), 3) afterload (intraventricular systolic tension during ejection), and 4) heart rate (18). The first two determinants are fundamental mechanisms inherent in the contractile machinery of the myocardium, whereas the last two are largely under extrinsic autonomic modulation. When considering cardiac function in coronary heart disease, it is important to add a fifth determinant, one that adversely affects ventricular performance: 5) dyssynergy, or abnormal temporal sequence of segmental ventricular contraction.

The terms *cardiac performance* and *ventricular function* are used in the general sense to refer to the combined action of these determinants of cardiac output, and not necessarily to the single determinant contractility (inotropism) itself. The disturbed mechanisms operative in all types of clinical heart disease can be evaluated and accurately characterized within the framework of isolated or composite disorders of these five major determinants of cardiac performance. The recent development of improved techniques and concepts for the assessment of cardiac function in patients by both hemodynamic methods and myocardial mechanics (15) has provided the means for differential analyses of the nature and degree of importance of each of these fundamental determinants and their interrelations with cardiac compensatory mechanisms governing stroke output in heart disease.

ASSESSMENT OF CARDIAC PERFORMANCE AND CONTRACTILITY

In the evaluation of the principal determinants of cardiac performance in heart disease, it has been possible to measure precisely ventricular preload (end-diastolic pressure, volume, and tension) and afterload (Laplace relation, in which systolic tension is directly equated with the product of ventricular systolic pressure and radius) and to characterize the nature and extent of dyssynergy. However, it has been considerably more difficult to assess accurately the contractile state of the intact human heart. There are two general approaches (20) to the evaluation of contractility and function of the heart, in terms of the characteristics of its performance as 1) a pump (hemodynamics), and 2) a muscle (mechanics).

Hemodynamic Evaluation

In the traditional approach of pump analysis, contractile state can be estimated qualitatively by resting values of the standard hemodynamic variables of cardiac output, stroke volume, systolic ejection rate, and left ventricular end-diastolic pressure, and by the more complex measurements of ventricular end-diastolic volume, ejection fraction, stroke work, stroke power, and ventricular mass. Besides being influenced by contractility, these measurements of pump performance are dependent on ventricular loading. Although these hemodynamic indices provide considerable useful information concerning cardiac function and directional inotropic differences, they are indirect and often relatively insensitive indicators of cardiac contractility. The sensitivity of cardiac pump measurements in the evaluation of contractility is increased by determining the hemodynamic response to certain interventions, such as exercise and alterations in ventricular loading. Further, inotropic specificity is improved by evaluating hemodynamic responses, using the Frank-Starling principle (ventricular function curve), which relates pump performance characteristics such as cardiac output to ventricular preload.

Mechanical Evaluation

It has also become possible to quantify contractility clinically by the second approach, in terms of muscle mechanics that describe the properties of force, velocity, and length of the ventricular myocardium. In the numerical assessment of contractile state, the mechanical events occurring during both the isovolumetric and ejection phases of systole have been characterized. Thus, measures of the inotropic state have been developed along two general lines: 1) isovolumetric indices utilizing dP/dt (rate of rise of ventricular pressure) (14), and 2) ejection indices employing V_{CF} (circumferential fiber-shortening rate).

At present there is considerable discussion concerning the advantages and limitations of derived variables in the examination of the contractile state. Because it has been difficult to evaluate the validity and sensitivity of various indices of contractility in the intact heart, since there is no standard measure of this property of the myocardium with which they can be compared, much of the discussion has consisted of circular reasoning. Nevertheless, certain isovolumetric and ejection mechanical indices appear to provide quantitative data that permit estimation and comparison of basal contractile state among different patients. The ejection measures (20) include V_{CF} at peak tension and mean V_{CF} determined angiographically and by echocardiography.

The isovolumetric indices applicable in interpatient studies include: 1) $(dP/dt_{CPIP})/LVEDVI$, in which $CPIP$ is developed isovolumetric pressure common to each ventricle (usually 50 mmHg) and $LVEDVI$ is left ventricular end-diastolic volume index (16); 2) extrapolated V_{max} (maximal V_{CE}) from total pressure-velocity curves, using V_{CE} (contractile element velocity) calculated as $(dP/dt)/K\,IP$, in which K is the series elastic stiffness constant and IP is total isovolumetric pressure (17); 3) peak measured V_{CE} (V_{pm}) also calculated as $(dP/dt)/K\,IP$; and 4) extrapolated V_{max} (or V_{CE} at 10 mmHg of developed pressure) from developed pressure-velocity curves (11), using developed pressure for IP in the V_{CE} equation.

Although changes in preload, compliance variations, dyssynergy, nonisovolumetric systole (mitral regurgitation), and segmental necrosis may considerably affect loaded V_{CE} before aortic valve opening, the accompanying alterations of the slope of the total and developed pressure-V_{CE} curves are such that extrapolated V_{max} is undisturbed or minimally influenced (11). Thus, it now appears that these problems largely represent "biologic noise" concerning the clinical application of V_{max} from isovolumetric pressure-velocity curves as an index estimating contractile state. On the other hand, the use of peak measured V_{CE} (V_{pm}) in these situations is limited, since loaded V_{CE} is substantially affected (11). Also, in these particular conditions there may appropriately be a marked disparity between ventricular hemodynamic performance and contractility estimated as V_{max} (11).

CARDIAC COMPENSATORY MECHANISMS

When systolic hemodynamic overloading or a primary defect in contractility is imposed on the heart, three principal compensatory mechanisms are available to it that provide a limited amount of ventricular reserve for the direct support of cardiac function and its fundamental goal of maintaining a normal resting level of cardiac output; these involve 1) the Frank-Starling principle, 2) ventricular hypertrophy, and 3) the sympathetic nervous system (18). Untoward symptoms necessarily accompany the operation of these compensatory mechanisms in their primary role of sustaining basal stroke volume, and these symptoms restrict the extent to which the adaptive systems can be used.

Ventricular Dilation

The Frank-Starling preload mechanism of ventricular dilation is immediately utilized to aid the ventricle in maintaining cardiac output in the presence of an excessive systolic hemodynamic (particularly volume) overload or primary inotropic disturbance. The increased end-diastolic volume permits more forceful contraction, and the greater ventricular size allows ejection of a larger stroke volume with less shortening of the circumferential fibers. On the other hand, the effectiveness and the reserve capacity of the Frank-Starling system are encroached on when contractile state is diminished, since its ascending limb becomes less steep and flattened, with its apex decreased in amplitude, so that the reduced maximal stroke volume possible must be delivered at an abnormally high level of end-diastolic pressure. Thus, the failing ventricle in patients has a lowered and depressed function curve and exhibits decreased systolic response to preload increments. Furthermore, operation of the Frank-Starling preload mechanism by the ventricles for maintaining cardiac output is obligatorily associated with pulmonary and systemic congestion and increased myocardial systolic tension; therefore the price for using this reserve system is dyspnea, peripheral edema, and increased cardiac oxygen needs.

The clinically dysfunctioning left ventricle does not usually perform for long periods on the descending limb of the Frank-Starling curve, although the descending portion can be demonstrated in severe failure by interventions that transiently augment preload. Importantly, in chronic left ventricular dilation, excessive muscle fiber stretch does not result in disengagement of the actin-myosin overlap region in the sarcomere, but rather causes slippage among myofibrils, thereby aiding the preload mechanism in developing systolic tension without reducing the number of cyclic interactive force-generating sites among the contractile proteins. Furthermore, hypertrophy occurring concomitantly in the chronically dilated ventricle results in longer myofibrils with more sarcomeres in series; therefore at increased end-diastolic volumes there is a greater total extent of ventricular thick and thin filament interface as well as retention of some preload reserve within the sarcomeres.

Ventricular Hypertrophy

An increase in the number of contractile units by the development of ventricular hypertrophy provides a relatively quickly responsive second compensatory system in support of cardiac output in systolic mechanical (particularly pressure) overloading and in contractile state impairment. Thus, protein synthesis is stimulated by excessive intramyocardial tension, which appears to serve as the mechanical-biochemical transducer or coupling mechanism responsible for accelerated production of ventricular mass. Since extensive ventricular hypertrophy results in relative myocardial ischemia because of cardiac oxygen demands in excess of the delivery capacity of even the normal coronary circulation, angina pectoris may attend marked use of the reserve mechanism of hypertrophy. In addition to the increase in oxygen requirements because of greater muscle mass, myocardial oxygen utilization is enhanced by the Frank-Starling and adrenergic adaptive mechanisms. Thus at a particular ventricular mass, myocardial oxygen consumption is principally determined directly by three hemodynamic variables (11): 1) intramyocardial systolic tension (governed by systolic pressure and cardiac size), 2) heart rate, and 3) contractile state. Ventricular dilation and increased sympathetic activity raise the first two of these factors above normal levels in heart disease.

In adult patients with compensated primary and secondary ventricular hypertrophy, it has been shown that even before the onset of circulatory congestion, the contractile state is moderately reduced as estimated by the indices V_{max} (obtained from total isovolumetric pressure), peak measured V_{CE}, and $(dP/dt_{CPIP})/LVEDVI$ (19). In comparison, contractility is markedly decreased in patients with ventricular hypertrophy and congestive heart failure. Thus, clinically as well as experimentally, there is a spectrum of decreasing contractile states between ventricular hypertrophy without failure and hypertrophy with decompensated failure, the latter condition being manifested by a low basal level of cardiac output despite a marked increase in end-diastolic pressure. Although the adaptive system of hypertrophy is associated with some decline in contractility per muscle unit, cardiac compensation with normal cardiac output at rest is supported by generation of additional myocardial contractile units, so that stroke volume is maintained with moderately increased end-diastolic pressure. The concept has been developed that inotropic integrity is the crucial determinant of congestive heart failure; when this fundamental property (contractility) becomes too severely depressed in systolic mechanical overloading or primary myocardial disease, cardiac decompensation results (low basal cardiac output with poor organ perfusion and resting fatigue) despite the maximal use of all three compensatory mechanisms with their consequent effects of marked circulatory congestion and additional associated symptoms.

Increased Adrenergic Activity

Besides ventricular dilation and hypertrophy reserves, the dysfunctioning heart has immediately available some inotropic support provided by adrenergic activity. Thus, the ventricles are richly innervated by sympathetic fibers in which an increased impulse traffic, through release of its endogenous neurotransmitter norepinephrine, and consequent myocardial beta receptor stimulation, is capable of improving contractility and increasing frequency of contraction. There is abundant evidence that sympathetic activity is augmented in congestive heart failure. Paradoxically, however, norepinephrine is reduced in the hypertrophied myocardium because of its defective synthesis, and the chronically dysfunctioning ventricle is largely deprived of this rapidly responsive compensatory mechanism. Thus the abnormally performing ventricle clinically shows increased impairment of contractile state during cardiac sympathetic stimulation accompanying leg exercise and forearm isometric exercise. On the other hand, adrenergic support is partially restored to the failing heart as the result of increased circulating norepinephrine because of its increased synthesis in the peripheral vasculature and adrenal medulla. The symptoms accompanying utilization of sympathetic assistance include tachycardia and tachyarrhythmias and those caused by redistribution of peripheral blood flow, such as excessive sweating, cool skin, and oliguria.

VENTRICULAR PRESSURE PULSES

In conditions in which ventricular diastolic distensibility is markedly diminished, such as constrictive pericarditis, cardiac tamponade, restrictive cardiomyopathy, endocardial fibroelastosis, amyloid disease, and severe concentric hypertrophy of any etiology, a characteristic modification of the ventricular pressure pulse takes place. The early rapid phase of ventricular filling is abruptly terminated as ventricular filling is slowed by the restriction to ventricular expansion. Ventricular pressure remains elevated during mid- and late diastole. The ventricular pressure pulse during diastole thus exhibits an early dip followed by a plateau.

An early response to depressed myocardial contractility and to systolic mechanical ventricular overloading is dilation of the ventricle during diastole, a compensatory mechanism that tends to maintain the force of ventricular contraction through operation of the Frank-Starling mechanism. Since the elevation of ventricular end-diastolic volume is often accompanied by an elevation of ventricular end-diastolic pressure, the level of the ventricular end-diastolic pressure may serve as an index of ventricular function in the absence of pericardial or endocardial disease. An elevated ventricular end-diastolic pressure in turn increases the corresponding atrial and venous pressures, which ultimately may be responsible for many of the symptoms of congestive heart failure.

VENTRICULAR END-DIASTOLIC PRESSURE

Inadequate systolic emptying of the ventricle leads to an increased end-systolic residual volume in this chamber and thereby to an augmentation of ventricular end-diastolic volume. Since the elevation of ventricular end-diastolic volume is usually accompanied by an elevation of ventricular end-diastolic pressure, the level of ventricular end-diastolic pressure may serve as a measure of ventricular function (20). The upper limit of normal left ventricular end-diastolic pressure (LVEDP) is 12 mmHg (15). However, LVEDP may be elevated without increased end-diastolic volume because of diminished ventricular compliance in hypertrophy, fibrosis, and infiltrative disease of the ventricle and in pericardial disease. Conversely, ventricular end-diastolic volume may be increased without elevation of LVEDP when ventricular compliance is increased, such as in some instances of ventricular systolic volume overloading.

Although acute hypervolemia resulting from fluid accumulation in the absence of heart disease results in an increase in LVEDP, this variable should remain within normal limits in the absence of an abnormality of myocardial compliance or contractility. Thus, although acute systolic mechanical overloading of the left ventricle may cause LVEDP elevation because of increased left ventricular end-diastolic volume, an LVEDP above 12–15 mmHg indicates at least a certain component of depressed ventricular contractility when the compliance of this chamber is normal (18).

Elevation of LVEDP in turn increases mean left atrial and pulmonary venous pressures and, consequently, pulmonary and right ventricular systolic and diastolic pressures. In the absence of mitral valve obstruction or increased left atrial contraction with diminished left ventricular compliance, mean left atrial pressure and pulmonary capillary wedge pressure closely reflect LVEDP (18). Similarly, without increased pulmonary vascular resistance and mitral obstruction, the pulmonary arterial diastolic pressure provides an estimation of LVEDP. The pulmonary arterial diastolic pressure is more closely correlated with the left atrial mean pressure and the left ventricular diastolic pressure immediately before the onset of atrial contraction. The recent development of catheters that can be placed easily in the pulmonary artery has allowed monitoring of pulmonary arterial diastolic pressure as an indicator of left ventricular function in patients with acute myocardial infarction (10). Although central venous pressure provides a useful estimation of total blood volume and an evaluation of right ventricular function, this variable does not necessarily reflect the level of left ventricular function (10).

CARDIAC OUTPUT

Determination of the cardiac output by the Fick principle or indicator dilution technique provides a useful measure of overall cardiac performance. The lower limit of normal of this variable is 2.50 liters/min $\cdot$ m^2 of body surface area, and the upper limit usually is not above 3.60 liters/min $\cdot$ m^2 (15). However, the cardiac index may not be diminished except with advanced abnormalities of ventricular contractility or with severe mechanical overloading or underloading of the ventricle (19). Thus, in lesser degrees of heart disease, operation of the ventricular compensatory mechanisms of elevation of LVEDP, ventricular hypertrophy, and enhanced activity of the sympathetic nervous system usually maintain the basal cardiac index at a normal level, despite impaired contractility and excessive loading of the ventricle (18).

LEFT VENTRICULAR VOLUME, EJECTION FRACTION, WORK, POWER, STRESS, AND MASS

Angiographic techniques allow determination of the chamber dimensions, volume, wall thickness, and mass of the left ventricle (4, 22), which, when combined with measurements of intraventricular pressure and cardiac output, provide a detailed assessment of the function of the heart as a pump (2, 3, 5-9, 21, 23). By analysis of these complex variables and their interrelationships, it is possible to evaluate qualitatively the contractile state separately from abnormalities of ventricular loading.

Ejection Fraction

The relation of stroke volume to left ventricular end-diastolic volume provides important information concerning ventricular contractility. From angiographic measurements, the normal left ventricular end-diastolic volume index is 70 ± 20 (SD) cc/m^2, and the normal systolic ejection fraction is 0.56–0.78 (9). Although the systolic ejection fraction is dependent on acute variations of systemic arterial resistance, the ventricle utilizes the development of hypertrophy rather than an increase of end-diastolic volume in its adjustment to chronic elevation of resistance to ejection. Thus, the ejection fraction is little influenced by chronic alterations of afterload per se. A reduced ejection fraction suggests relatively more ventricular dilation than can be accounted for by excessive preload alone and thereby indicates the presence of reduced myocardial contractility.

Ventricular Work and Power

The instantaneous relation of left ventricular pressure and volume throughout the cardiac cycle constitutes the pressure-volume loop of the ventricle (2, 21) (Fig. 1).

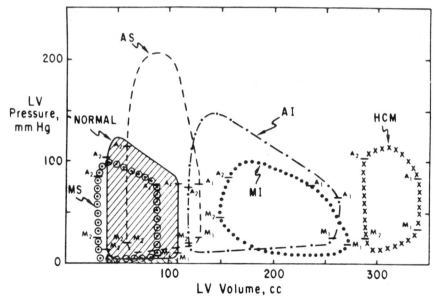

FIGURE 1 Representative comparison of pressure-volume (work) curves of the left ventricle (LV) in mitral stenosis (MS), normal subject, aortic stenosis (AS), aortic regurgitation (AI), mitral regurgitation (MI), and hypertrophic cardiomyopathy (HCM). Systolic pressure-volume work is determined from the systolic pressure-volume relations, and work expended in distending the diastolic left ventricle is obtained from pressure-volume relations during diastole. Net systolic work in the normal subject is shown by the area containing the right upward diagonal lines, diastolic work by the right downward diagonal lines abutting on the abcissa, and total systolic work by net systolic work plus diastolic work. The height of each pressure-volume loop is determined by systolic pressure, and the width is determined principally by the stroke volume of the LV. The smallest curves occur in MS, resulting from diminished preload, and in HCM, resulting from depressed contractility with cardiac output supported in part by end-diastolic dilation. Wide loops caused by volume overloading are observed in MI and AI, and the tall curve of pressure overloading is seen in AS. Other abbreviations: A_1, aortic valve opening; A_2, aortic valve closure; M_1, mitral valve closure; and M_2, mitral valve opening. From Mason et al. (20).

Analysis of the shape and position of these pressure-volume curves provides a qualitative evaluation of depressed myocardial contractility and loading abnormalities due to valvular heart disease. Integration of the pressure-volume loop during contraction—including the diastolic portion above the base line—yields total systolic work. The diastolic area below the curve is diastolic work and represents the energy expended in distending the ventricle during the resting stage of the cardiac cycle. When contractility is reduced, increased diastolic work is necessary to distend the ventricle. Net systolic work is the difference between total systolic and diastolic work, and net systolic work decreases with reduced left ventricular contractility.

The rate at which ventricular systolic work is performed is ventricular power, calculated as the product of instantaneous intraventricular pressure and the rate of ventricular ejection, which in turn is determined from the rate of change of ventricular volume during systole (23). The left ventricular power curve can be constructed during the cardiac cycle and peak systolic power can be determined; this variable normally ranges between 450 and 550 g · m/sec, and it is substantially reduced with depressed myocardial contractile state.

Ventricular Mass

Knowing the left ventricular wall thickness, chamber dimensions, and volume, one can calculate left ventricular mass, which is normally found to be 92 ± 16 (SD) g/m^2 by this method (22). In chronic systolic pressure overloading of the left ventricle, hypertrophy often occurs with little or no increase in chamber volume. Conversely, in chronic systolic volume overloading of the left ventricle, ventricular dilation occurs to a proportionally greater degree than does hypertrophy. However, in both chronic systolic pressure and volume overloading the extent of left ventricular mass is correlated with stroke work (2, 3).

Ventricular Wall Stress

End-diastolic stress and peak systolic wall stress, normally 327 ± 24 (SD) $\times 10^3$ dyn/cm^2 (7), have been evaluated in chronic mitral and aortic valve disease and in cardiomyopathies (5, 7, 8). The degree of hypertrophy is correlated with peak systolic stress in chronic hemodynamic overloading caused by valvular disease, whereas in cardiomyopathies the increase in left ventricular muscle mass is inadequate (congestive myopathies with markedly increased end-diastolic volumes) or excessive (hypertrophic myopathies with normal end-diastolic volumes) relative to peak systolic stress (7). Markedly elevated peak systolic stress indicates decreased contractility, but normal peak systolic stress may occur with impaired cardiac performance in mitral stenosis (7).

Ejection Fraction, Work, and Power Related to End-Diastolic Volume and Mass

Reductions in the ratio of ejection fraction to ventricular end-diastolic volume and of ventricular power to end-diastolic volume indicate depressed left ventricular contractility (3, 6, 23). Ventricular stroke work and power are maintained at a normal level at the expense of ventricular dilation by the Frank-Starling mechanism

and at the expense of diminished cardiac reserve in terms of the capacity for further
ventricular dilation. Since left ventricular mass is correlated with diastolic volume in
chronic systolic volume overloading when the contractile state is maintained at a
normal level, the relation of ventricular mass to diastolic work is inappropriately
large with diminished myocardial contractility and increased preloading. Also,
inappropriately increased ventricular dilation and elevated end-diastolic volume per
unit of stroke work (Frank-Starling principle) indicate depressed ventricular
contractility (3, 6).

Since there is a positive correlation between left ventricular mass and stroke
work in patients with chronic valvular heart disease resulting in pressure or volume
overloading of the ventricle, excessive development of ventricular hypertrophy or
mass relative to stroke work indicates an associated decrease in myocardial
contractility in these conditions, as well as in primary cardiomyopathies. Patients
with depressed left ventricular contractility and loading abnormalities have low
values of stroke work per unit mass, diminished values of peak power per unit mass,
and reduced ejection fraction relative to end-diastolic volume (2, 3, 6, 23). Thus,
the assessment of cardiac performance in terms of the heart as a pump provides a
qualitative evaluation of contractility by relating stroke volume, rate of ejection,
systolic and diastolic work, stroke work, and stroke power to left ventricular
end-diastolic volume and left ventricular mass.

PRIMARY VERSUS SECONDARY HYPERTROPHY

The inotropic state and compensatory mechanisms in primary cardiomyopathy
have recently been compared to those in ventricular hypertrophy secondary to
chronic pressure overloading in aortic stenosis (19). It was considered that
there might be quantitative differences in contractility and utilization of reserve
mechanisms between the primarily and secondarily hypertrophied ventricles. The
results of this investigation are shown in Fig. 2, where the contractile state and
compensatory systems for cardiac output maintenance are compared in patients
with these two lesions. In response to pressure overloading in compensated aortic
stenosis, the ventricle principally employs the hypertrophy mechanism for supporting cardiac output. Although the inotropic state of this secondarily hyper-

	V_{max}	LVEDV	LVH
CARDIOMYOPATHY (primary LV inotropic defect)	↓↓↓	↑	↑
MITRAL REGURGITATION (primary LV volume overload)	↓↓	↑↑	↑
AORTIC STENOSIS (primary LV pressure overload)	↓	0	↑↑↑

FIGURE 2   Compensatory mechanism for maintaining normal cardiac output in chronic primary
and secondary left ventricular hypertrophy (LVH). Abbreviations: LV, left
ventricle; LVEDV, left ventricular end-diastolic volume; and V_{max}, contractile
state index. From Mason (12).

trophied muscle is somewhat diminished, cardiac output is sustained in chronic excessive pressure loading by the development of more contractile units without increasing end-diastolic volume.

In contrast, in patients with compensated cardiomyopathy who have depressed inotropism as the basic derangement, cardiac output is maintained by operation of both the Frank-Starling and hypertrophy compensatory mechanisms (12) (Fig. 2). In these patients, normal cardiac output and thereby compensation are accomplished, although the contractile state is more depressed than in aortic stenosis, since in cardiomyopathy the ventricle does not eject against a severe mechanical abnormality opposing the velocity and extent of fiber shortening.

In decompensated congestive heart failure caused by primary myocardial disease, cardiac output is reduced when the contractile state becomes further depressed to a very low level, despite additional maximal utilization of dilation and hypertrophy compensation. In aortic stenosis there is decompensation with decline of cardiac output when the adverse effects of chronic left ventricular outflow obstruction on the myocardium reduce contractility more than in the compensated state, despite further marked hypertrophy and, with the onset of decompensated heart failure, the development of ventricular dilation.

Thus, compensation is maintained in cardiomyopathy and in aortic stenosis by relatively dissimilar degrees of use of preload and hypertrophy reserve mechanisms. Decompensation occurs when the normal basal cardiac output cannot be delivered because the contractile state has fallen below a certain critical level in both primary hypertrophy and hypertrophy secondary to chronic pressure overloading; this critical level is lower in primary cardiomyopathy.

PRESSURE VERSUS VOLUME OVERLOADING

In further clinical studies, contractility and compensatory mechanisms were compared in adult patients with chronic ventricular pressure and volume overloading (12). In compensated volume overload resulting from long-standing mitral or aortic regurgitation, contractility is more depressed than in chronic aortic stenosis (Fig. 2). Also, in long-term volume overloading, cardiac output is maintained by both dilation and hypertrophy, whereas compensation is obtained by marked use of the hypertrophy reserve alone in aortic stenosis. However, preload remains highly important for maintenance of cardiac output in the hypertrophied nondilated ventricle, as evidenced in this condition by the function of atrial systole as a booster pump for enhancement of ventricular filling in late diastole (1). The finding that, in chronic left ventricular dilation, conversion of atrial fibrillation to normal sinus rhythm usually does not substantially increase cardiac output represents poor atrial contraction and reduced Frank-Starling reserve in this setting.

In both chronic volume overloading and primary cardiomyopathy, Frank-Starling and hypertrophy reserves are used to maintain cardiac output (Fig. 2). Decompensated congestive heart failure occurs when there is a further reduction in contractility, but to a lesser degree in volume overloading than in cardiomyopathy. Thus, resting cardiac output cannot be maintained at a normal level when the contractile state declines to a precarious value. This crucial inotropic level is lowest in primary cardiomyopathy, intermediate in chronic volume overloading, and least reduced (but considerably diminished compared to normal) in chronic excessive ventricular pressure overloading.

COMPARISON OF VOLUME OVERLOADS

The recent recognition that alterations in instantaneous impedance to ejection and ventricular fiber tension during ejection (afterload) are important determinants of the dynamics of cardiac contraction has led to an appreciation of the differences in cardiac performance in conditions of systolic mechanical volume overloading. Thus, in mitral compared to aortic regurgitation with equivalent total and effective stroke volumes, left ventricular function is more disturbed with greater end-diastolic pressure and volume in aortic regurgitation (25). In the latter, the entire stroke volume must be delivered into the physiologically high-pressure ascending aorta, whereas the regurgitant volume in mitral insufficiency is immediately ejected into the low-pressure left atrium. These findings concerning the greater afterload burden on the left ventricle in aortic incompetence emphasize the clinical observation of poorer cardiac tolerance chronically present in this condition with marked extent of utilization of preload and hypertrophy reserves, in contrast to chronic mitral insufficiency, in which similar systolic volume overload is accompanied by considerably less ventricular mass and systolic tension or afterload.

In additional studies of differences in cardiac performance in systolic volume overloading, it has been shown that left ventricular function is substantially less compromised in ventricular septal defect than in patent ductus arteriosus at the same level of abnormally increased pulmonary blood flow (12). Thus in ventricular septal defect, the shunted flow is ejected directly into the low-pressure right ventricle, whereas in patent ductus arteriosus the entire left ventricular stroke output must be ejected into the high-pressure aorta before shunting. Therefore, at identically elevated ratios of pulmonary to systemic flow, the left ventricular end-diastolic pressure and volume are greater; the duration of ejection is prolonged and the ventricular ejection rate and fraction are less increased; and there are greater ventricular mid-wall systolic tension, contractile element work, and power in patent ductus arteriosus than in ventricular septal defect. In ventricular septal defect, the lesser increase in end-diastolic pressure and volume, greater increase in ejection rate and fraction, lesser increase in tension early in systole and in contractile element work and power throughout systole, in contrast to patent ductus arteriosus, and the shorter ejection period with a more rapid fall in tension than normal are all the result of a greater reduction in instantaneous impedance to left ventricular emptying.

From these observations concerning the dynamics of ventricular contraction, ventricular septal defect is similar to mitral regurgitation, and patent ductus arteriosus is similar to aortic regurgitation. Thus, although each of these four conditions of systolic volume overloading encroaches on ventricular performance, cardiac function is more disturbed in aortic insufficiency and patent ductus arteriosus. Furthermore, since resistance to ejection is more reduced in mitral regurgitation and ventricular septal defect, their integrated ventricular systolic tension is similar to the normal value, whereas left ventricular afterload is substantially increased above normal in aortic regurgitation and patent ductus. In regard to myocardial oxygen consumption, cardiac energy costs are considerably greater in pressure overloading, in which ventricular systolic tension and afterload are more increased, than in volume overloading. Furthermore, comparing different types of systolic volume overloads, there is a smaller increase in cardiac oxygen requirements in the conditions in which the impedance offered to ejection is considerably reduced, such as mitral regurgitation and ventricular septal defect, than in the conditions in which systemic resistance is decreased to a smaller degree, such as patent ductus and aortic regurgitation.

COMPARISON OF PRESSURE OVERLOADS

There are probably also important differences in ventricular dynamics in various types of systolic pressure overloading. Thus, quantitative dissimilarities in ventricular mechanics, loading, contractility, oxygen consumption, and utilization of compensatory mechanisms are suggested in different types of aortic stenosis, coarctation of the aorta, and systolic and diastolic hypertension. Although pure systolic hypertension due to diminished aortic compliance has been generally regarded as unimportant in the development of ventricular dysfunction, recent evidence indicates that this condition increases cardiac outflow impedance and systolic tension during ejection, thereby raising ventricular afterload (24). Whereas the response to acute pressure overload includes ventricular dilation, in chronic conditions of increased pressure loading compensation is maintained with delivery of normal stroke output principally by the utilization of hypertrophy reserve.

REFERENCES

1. DeMaria, A. N., Lies, J. E., King, J. F., Miller, R. R., Amsterdam, E. A., and Mason, D. T. Echographic assessment of atrial transport, mitral movement and ventricular performance following electroversion of supraventricular arrhythmias. Circulation 51:273–282, 1975.
2. Dodge, H. T. and Baxley, W. A. Hemodynamic aspects of heart failure. Am J Cardiol 22:24–34, 1968.
3. Dodge, H. T. and Baxley, W. A. Left ventricular volume and mass and their significance in heart disease. Am J Cardiol 23:528–537, 1969.
4. Dodge, H. T., Sandler, H., Baxley, W. A., and Hawley, R. R. Usefulness and limitations of radiographic methods for determining left ventricular volume. Am J Cardiol 18:10–24, 1966.
5. Gaasch, W. H., Battle, W. E., Oboler, A. A., Banas, J. S., Jr., and Levine, H. J. Left ventricular stress and compliance in man with special reference to normalized ventricular function curves. Circulation 45:746–762, 1972.
6. Greene, D. G. and Bunnell, I. L. Quantitative left ventriculography: Structure and function of the adult human left ventricle in health and disease. In: Progress in Cardiology, P. Yu and J. Goodwin, eds. Philadelphia: Lea & Febiger, 1975, vol. 4, pp. 71–98.
7. Hood, W. P., Jr., Rackley, C. E., and Rolett, E. L. Wall stress in the normal and hypertrophied human left ventricle. Am J Cardiol 22:550–558, 1968.

8. Hood, W. P., Jr., Thomson, W. J., Rackley, C. E., and Rolett, E. L. Comparison of calculations of left ventricular wall stress in man from thin-walled and thick-walled ellipsoidal models. Circ Res 24:575–582, 1969.

9. Kennedy, J. W., Baxley, W. A., Figley, M. M., Dodge, H. T., and Blackmon, J. R. Quantitative angiocardiography: The normal left ventricle in man. Circulation 34:272–278, 1966.

10. Mason, D. T. Congestive Heart Failure: Mechanisms, Evaluation and Treatment. New York: Yorke, 1976.

11. Mason, D. T. Mechanisms of cardiac contraction: Structural, biochemical, and functional relations in the normal and diseased heart. In: Pathologic Physiology: Mechanisms of Disease, ed. 5, W. A. Sodeman and W. A. Sodeman, Jr., eds. Philadelphia: Saunders, 1974, pp. 206–234.

12. Mason, D. T. Regulation of cardiac performance in clinical heart disease: Interactions between contractile state, mechanical abnormalities and ventricular compensatory mechanisms. Am J Cardiol 32:437–448, 1973.

13. Mason, D. T. The Failing Heart. Chicago: Year Book Medical Publishers, 1977.

14. Mason, D. T. Usefulness and limitations of the rate of rise of intraventricular pressure (dp/dt) in the evaluation of myocardial contractility in man. Am J Cardiol 23:516–527, 1969.

15. Mason, D. T. and Braunwald, E. Hemodynamic techniques in the investigation of cardiovascular function in man. In: Clinical Cardiopulmonary Physiology, ed. 3, B. Gordon, ed. New York: Grune & Stratton, 1969, pp. 153–170.

16. Mason, D. T., Braunwald, E., Covell, J. W., Sonnenblick, E. H., and Ross, J., Jr. Assessment of cardiac contractility: The relation between the rate of pressure rise and ventricular pressure during isovolumic systole. Circulation 44:47–58, 1971.

17. Mason, D. T., Spann, J. F., Jr., and Zelis, R. Quantification of the contractile state of the intact human heart: Maximum velocity of contractile element shortening determined from the relation between the rate of pressure rise and pressure in the ventricle during isovolumic systole. Am J Cardiol 26:248–257, 1970.

18. Mason, D. T., Spann, J. F., Jr., Zelis, R., and Amsterdam, E. A. Alterations of hemodynamics and myocardial mechanics in patients with congestive heart failure: Pathophysiologic mechanisms and assessment of cardiac function and ventricular contractility. Progr Cardiovasc Dis 12:507–557, 1970.

19. Mason, D. T., Spann, J. F., Jr., Zelis, R., and Amsterdam, E. A. Comparison of the contractile state of the normal, hypertrophied, and failing heart in man. In: Cardiac Hypertrophy, N. R. Alpert, ed. New York: Academic Press, 1971, pp. 443–444.

20. Mason, D. T., Zelis, R., Amsterdam, E. A., and Massumi, R. Clinical determination of left ventricular contractility by hemodynamics and myocardial mechanics. In: Progress in Cardiology, P. Yu and J. Goodwin, eds. Philadelphia: Lea & Febiger, 1972, pp. 121–153.

21. Rackley, C. E., Behar, V. S., Whalen, R. E., and McIntosh, H. D. Biplane cineangiographic determinations of left ventricular function: Pressure-volume relationships. Am Heart J 74:766–779, 1967.

22. Rackley, C. E., Dodge, H. T., Coble, Y. D., Jr., and Hay, R. E. A method for determining left ventricular mass in man. Circulation 29:666–671, 1964.

23. Russell, R. O., Jr., Porter, C. M., Frimer, M., and Dodge, H. T. Left ventricular power in man. Am Heart J 81:799–808, 1971.

24. Urschel, C. W., Covell, J. W., Sonnenblick, E. H., Ross, J., Jr., and Braunwald, E. Effects of decreased aortic compliance on performance of the left ventricle. Am J Physiol 214:298–304, 1968.
25. Urschel, C. W., Covell, J. W., Sonnenblick, E. H., Ross, J., Jr., and Braunwald, E. Myocardial mechanics in aortic and mitral valvular regurgitation: The concept of instantaneous impedance as a determinant of the performance of the intact heart. J Clin Invest 47:867–883, 1968.

CHAPTER 7

QUANTITATIVE ANGIOGRAPHY: CHRONIC ISCHEMIC HEART DISEASE

RICHARD GORLIN

Meaningful quantitative studies of ventricular dynamic morphology and performance required the advent of cineventriculography. Thus, it has only been within the last decade that the unique findings of the effects of ischemic heart disease on the left ventricle have been delineated.

Historically, in relation to this symposium in honor of Dr. Isaac Starr, we should note his early studies utilizing the ballistocardiogram. These ballistocardiographic studies performed more than 30 yr ago demonstrated a disordered ballistic or projectile action of the left ventricle in patients who had coronary artery disease (18). At the time it was not known which type of abnormality accounted for this unique pattern. Starr believed this provided a diagnostic clue to the presence of ischemic disease far in advance of the recognition of any other functional or performance abnormalities. In the same era, other workers had described how either focal ischemia of the myocardium (20) or postinfarctional damage (19) could give rise to segmental dysfunction. Harrison (9a), in 1965, coined the term asynergy to describe abnormalities recorded at the precordial area generated by a disordered cardiac impulse in patients with ischemic heart disease. In 1967, our own group applied the technique of cineventriculography to quantify ventricular performance and to dissect and describe in detail the localized disorders of cardiac contraction now commonly recognized as part of the picture of dysfunction in ischemic heart disease. These studies have been extended by groups at the University of Alabama and the University of Washington, Seattle, among others.

CURRENT STATUS

Methodology

The cine camera, providing time-motion records, was the single major advance in indicating the variety as well as the extent of disturbances in the contractile pattern of the chronically ischemic left ventricle. The static cut film, or serialogram, which provides a somewhat more easily resolved and accurate image of the ventricle, does not convey the same sense of disordered motion. For a time the latter was the only available technique, which probably accounts for the lack of appreciation of the problem of asynergy. Many of the earlier studies were performed with single-plane cine methods. It has now been accepted that two planes of the ventricular silhouette should be imaged to map completely the quantitative contractile effort of the chronically ischemic left ventricle. The preferred views are the right and left anterior obliques. The former provides definition of the anterior apical and true inferior surfaces of the left ventricle, while the latter indicates motion of the septum and the posterolateral portions of the ventricle (Fig. 1).

It has been demonstrated that the impact of power injection of contrast into the ventricle affects its function very little if the volume of dye is in the vicinity of 30–40 ml delivered at a rate of 15 ml/sec. The problems inherent in injecting dye include depression of the ventricle from the dye itself, followed by a Starling effect from its hyperosmolar, hypervolemic actions. However, the first few cycles during the initial injection seem to be free of these later depressant and hypervolemic effects. At least 30 min must be allowed to pass between the introduction of any volume of contrast medium and a ventriculogram to obviate these effects. Problems may arise in recording sinus beats when the injection is made selectively into the left ventricle, and for this reason there are theoretical advantages to injecting into the left atrium or into the inflow tract of the mitral valve. In practice, however,

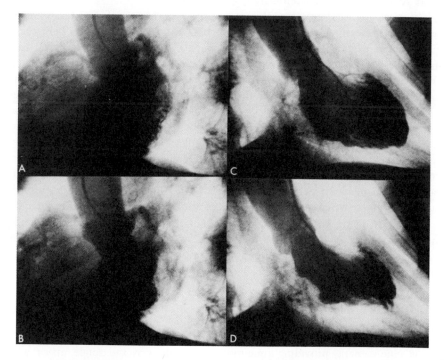

FIGURE 1   Small ventricular aneurysm of the inferior surface; biplane left anterior oblique (LAO) and right anterior oblique (RAO) views. (A) In the LAO projection, a slight bulge is noted in end-diastole. (B) The bulge becomes more pronounced at end-systole in the lower right quadrant of the ventriculographic silhouette. (C) In the RAO projection, an extension of this aneurysm is seen on the true inferior surface as a double bulge in the posterior half of the inferior segment. (D) At end-systole the bulge is accentuated. From Gorlin (8).

injection directly into the left ventricle is the most commonly used technique. There have been discrepancies between the measures of ventricular contraction derived by using the levophase of the right-sided contrast injection and those derived by using direct injection into the left ventricle. Occasionally, dysrhythmias are provoked either by the catheter or by direct impingement of a jet of dye against the ventricular wall. As will be mentioned later, this is not altogether a disadvantage because the analysis of a postextrasystolic contractile effort provides information in addition to that obtained during a sinus beat.

Ventricular volume is usually determined by the methods of Dodge et al. (5) or modifications thereof (14). The ejection fraction, a dimensionless number, can be derived without calibration of the cine record.

Asynergy may be quantified in a variety of ways. The ventricular silhouettes can be subdivided by transecting the ventricle longitudinally from midaortic valve to apex. A series of minor hemiaxes may then be drawn perpendicular to this line and motion along each line recorded (Fig. 2). Because there have been objections to artifacts introduced by rotatory motion of the heart, some investigators have analyzed asynergy without longitudinally bisecting the ventricle, instead drawing a series of minor axes and analyzing the percentage change in axis irrespective of the wall believed to be contributing to the dysfunction (16).

Measures of Quantitative Dynamic Morphology

Left Ventricle Diastolic Volume and Mass

The volume of the left ventricle has been shown to vary widely, with values as low as 55 and as high as 350 ml/m^2 (12, 17). Volumes associated with frank aneurysms have usually been large enough to be estimated in their own right. Patients show mitral regurgitation, considered particularly common in severe coronary artery disease by Rackley et al. (17), as another associated factor, while a very small group of patients exhibit what, for want of a better term, might be called an ischemic cardiomyopathy in which there is generalized cardiac dilation.

Cardiac mass in general tended to increase at an equal rate with end-diastolic volume, as might be expected from the known stress as well as the method of calculation. On the other hand, no relations could be shown between end-diastolic volume and end-diastolic pressure; in many instances the highest end-diastolic pressures were seen with only moderate increases in volume and normal ventricular mass. Our group found that patients with asynergy had significantly larger volumes than did patients without it (12). Baxley et al. (2), however, could not confirm this finding, nor did they find any greater prevalence of asynergy in patients with either reduced cardiac output or increased end-diastolic pressure, or both.

Shape

With progressive damage and increase in volume, the ventricle assumes a more globular shape. However, in contrast, to the ventricle in patients having a generalized disorder of cardiac muscle, such as that secondary to valvular regurgitation or nonischemic cardiomyopathy, the ischemic left ventricle will often have an irregular configuration due to segmental damage.

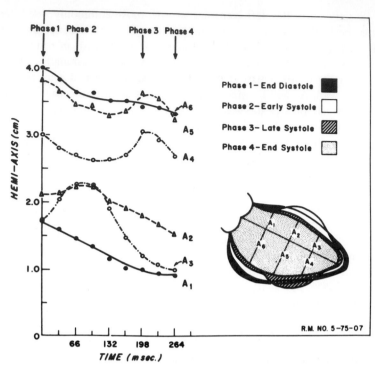

FIGURE 2 Left ventricular asynchronism. Three minor axes as well as a long axis are employed in the right anterior oblique projection. Asynchronous contraction of the heart could be expressed only by analysis of multiple axes. Note the early systolic bulge of the anterior wall (A_2 and A_3) and the late systolic bulge of the inferior wall (A_4 and A_5). Effective ejection of stroke volume is markedly vitiated by this uncoordinated contraction; it can be expressed quantitatively only by references to multiple axes. From Herman et al. (12). Reprinted, by permission, from the New England Journal of Medicine (277:222–232, 1967).

Ejection

Cardiac ejection is highly variable in ischemic heart disease. Stroke volume and minute output may be completely normal in one patient (perhaps in the presence of a large end-diastolic volume), and substantially reduced in another with a very small end-diastolic volume (Fig. 3). The latter are usually patients with extensive asynergy (12). The ejection fraction varies, in general, independently of ventricular diastolic volume, although there is little doubt that when the volume is markedly increased, the ejection fraction is proportionately reduced (17). The not infrequent reduction in ejection fraction in the presence of a ventricle of normal or nearly normal size reflects the inadequate and disordered contractile pattern present in a ventricle with an apparently limited ability to distend—that is, a secondary Starling effect. No relationship has been found, however, to the degree or distribution of coronary artery disease. The reduction in ejection fraction that is seen in many patients is also accompanied by decreases in other indices of contractile effort. For example, average circumferential shortening rate is reduced and the rate of development of pressure is decreased, particularly in patients who have asynergy.

Asynergy

Asynergy is best defined as a disturbance of either the configuration or the temporal sequence of contraction of the cardiac muscle. Such disturbances result from local abnormalities in the contractile pattern. These abnormalities have been classified as follows: *akinesis*, or total lack of motion of a portion of the ventricular wall; *dyskinesis*, or paradoxical systolic expansion of part of the wall; *hypokinesis*, or diminished motion of part of the wall; and *asynchronism*, or a disturbed temporal sequence of contraction of the several segments of myocardium (Fig. 4). The importance of this classification will become apparent in the discussion of reversible and irreversible asynergy.

Causes

In ischemic heart disease, asynergy is usually correlated with severe local obstructive coronary disease, abnormalities of lactate metabolism (80% of cases), and electrocardiographic evidences of either old infarct or inducible myocardial ischemia (ECG change during exercise). It must be emphasized, however, that there are notable exceptions in that obstructive disease can be present, Q waves can be present, and the ventriculographic segment can be completely normal. Conversely, asynergy can be seen when there is no corresponding ECG abnormality.

Asynergy may result from old scar that has replaced myocardium. This may be either full thickness or partial thickness (interspersed scar and muscle), or there may be frank thinning of the wall with true aneurysm formation. Asynergy can occur in otherwise normal-looking muscle (10, 12) and may be the result of altered electric activation, functional damage such that tension development is perturbed in both intensity and sequence, or a state of ischemia that transiently alters function.

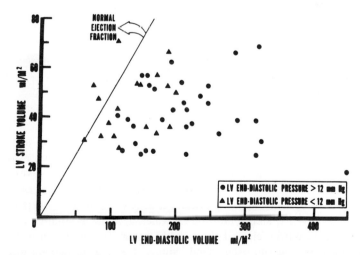

FIGURE 3   Relationship of left ventricular (LV) stroke volume and end-diastolic volume for 50 patients. The diagonal line defines the lower limit of normal ejection fraction. From Baxley et al. (2).

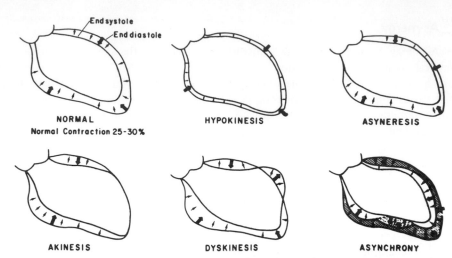

FIGURE 4 Localized and generalized abnormalities in cardiac, contraction: a schematic representation. Motion from end-diastole to end-systole is represented by arrows. From Herman et al. (12). Reprinted, by permission, from the New England Journal of Medicine (277:222–232, 1967).

Effects

The effects of asynergy are variable. This is because there are variations not only in topographical site and extent, but also in the type of asynergy that is present; thus, a particular degree of shortening results in normalization of ejection volume. Some of the factors in the ventricular response to asynergy are listed below.

Afflicted area
    Site: anterior, inferior
    Extent
    Type: dyskinesis, etc.
Normal area
    Hyperdynamic response
    Development of hypertrophy
    Acute and chronic dilation (Starling effect)

Evidence is accumulating that the zone of asynergy may have some effect on total left ventricular function. Anterior zone asynergy is more often associated with disturbance of the total ventricular response than is inferior wall involvement. It is not clear, however, whether this is a result of the site or the extent of involvement.

Each type of asynergy appears to have a different effect on overall function. A dyskinetic area, by expanding during systole, accepts a volume of blood that otherwise might have been ejected through the aorta. This is shown in Fig. 5, A and B. An akinetic zone, on the other hand, simply does not participate in contraction, although its shape may alter the requirements for developed stress elsewhere in the ventricle. Hypokinesis, again a milder form of disturbance, simply limits the overall contractile effort. Asynchronism, on the other hand, can vary in its extent. In its more extensive forms this can seriously disturb the ultimate ejection of blood by translocation of volume from contracting areas to simultaneously expanding areas and back again.

The end result is also dependent on the response of the normal myocardium. For reasons that are not clear, there may or may not be a compensatory increase in contractile effort by the unaffected myocardium. Thus, the combination of a

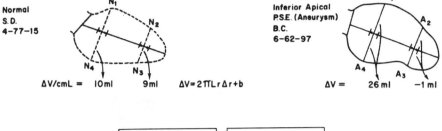

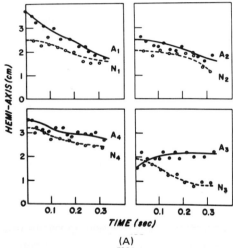

(A)

FIGURE 5 Effects of dyskinesis on ventricular function. (A) Regional contribution to stroke output. For this demonstration a cylinder was assumed and base-to-apex shortening was ignored. This relation was expressed as $\Delta V = 2\pi L r \, \Delta r + b$, where ΔV is the change in volume per centimeter in length of the long axis, L is the long axis, r is the minor hemiaxis, Δr is the change in minor axis, and $b = 2\pi L (\Delta r)^2$. The end-diastolic left ventricular silhouette is shown for a normal subject (N) and for a patient with apical dyskinesis (A). The major axis runs from the bisected base of the aortic valve to the apex. The length of the minor hemiaxis (i.e., $N_{1,2,3,4}$) was measured from calibrated consecutive cine frames and plotted as length (ordinate) against time in systole (abscissa). Note the relatively uniform emptying in the normal subject. In the subject with apical dyskinesis, all ejection occurs from an augmented contraction of the base of the heart, whereas the apical portion makes a negative contribution with the paradoxical expansion during systole (PSE). From Herman et al. (12). Reprinted, by permission, from the New England Journal of Medicine (277:222–232, 1967).

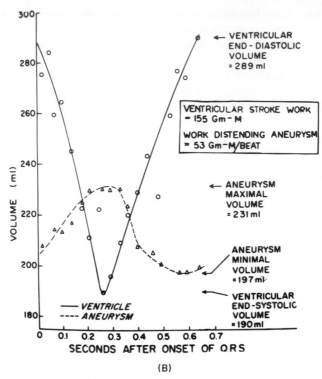

FIGURE 5   Effects of dyskinesis on ventricular function (*Continued*). (B) Volume curves of left ventricular aneurysm and of the more normal portion of the left ventricle for one heart cycle in patient J.B. From Baxley et al. (2).

hyperdynamic contraction in the face of akinetic or dyskinetic response in certain segments of myocardium may result in an *overall* normal ejection fraction with a normal stroke volume and cardiac index.

Hypertrophy does occur in patients with coronary heart disease irrespective of the presence of preexisting hypertension. It would appear to occur in the unaffected portions of cardiac muscle that are called on for an excessive contractile effort to compensate for asynergy elsewhere. It may well be that the development of hypertrophy determines whether the overall ventricular response can compensate for existing areas of asynergy.

In this regard, it is worth noting that as more of the ventricular surface fails to participate in the contractile effort, there comes a point at which compensation is no longer possible elsewhere in the ventricle through excessive shortening of sarcomeres. The "break point" is at approximately 25% involvement of the surface area (Fig. 6). From this point on either there must be a sharp reduction in ejection (and therefore stroke volume) or the ventricle must dilate in order to maintain stroke volume.

Dilation is a highly variable response on the part of the heart with ischemic disease. Thus, the effect of the Starling mechanism, through both a geometric increase in size and an increase in intrinsic developed force, can also normalize the ultimate ventricular response and therefore the volume of blood delivered to the body.

To recapitulate, then, the extent and type of asynergy only partially affect ultimate ventricular performance. They can be compensated for in whole or in part by hyperdynamic contraction of normal or hypertrophied myocardium and by invocation of the Starling effect through expanded end-diastolic volume (see p. 94).

RECENT ADVANCES

Perhaps the most interesting aspect of our new knowledge on this topic has been the dynamic nature of asynergy in many patients. The use of intervention

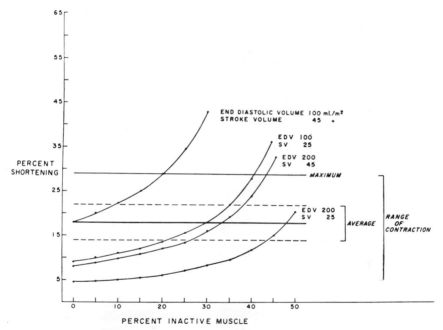

FIGURE 6 Relationship between percentage of circumferential shortening and percentage of inactive muscle (expressed in terms of left ventricular surface area). The horizontal lines define average range and maximal degree of fiber shortening. The curve to the left defines the degree of shortening necessary in a normal-sized left ventricle expelling 45 ml/m². Note that 17% shortening is required if all muscle is active (zero on the abscissa). As progressively more muscle is inactivated, the degree of shortening finally exceeds the physiological limit, which is reached when inactive muscle constitutes about 20% of surface area. Stroke volume can no longer be maintained. The second curve indicates that a normal degree of shortening can deliver only a small stroke volume from this ventricle with 20% limitation. A normal stroke volume at this degree of muscle inactivation can be maintained only by an increase in end-diastolic volume (EDV), as shown in the third curve (EDV = 200 ml/m²). Finally, as shown in the last curve, even such an increase in volume does not permit delivery of a normal stroke volume as shortening is impaired; this state was commonly observed in this series. From Klein et al. (13), by permission of the American Heart Association, Inc.

ventriculograms has been particularly revealing. Interventions have been used that are intended to compromise ventricular function, such as the induction of ischemia by atrial pacing tachycardia and exercise and by the increase in afterload (impedance to ejection) by such stimuli as isometric hand grip, exercise, and atrial pacing (Fig. 7). Abnormalities in contractile pattern can also be induced through acute myocardial depression, as with beta adrenergic blockade. These methods have been useful in demonstrating sites of ischemia or areas of potentially compromised segmental dysfunction that are not apparent under conditions of resting hemodynamics.

Perhaps even more useful have been interventions that elicit improvement in ventricular contraction and thereby aid in determining whether overall dysfunction or a zone of asynergy is potentially reversible by an alteration in either hemodynamics or local blood supply. The interventions that have been utilized most successfully in this regard have been postextrasystolic potentiation (6) (Fig. 8) and nitroglycerin (1, 11) (Fig. 9). The first of these interventions serves to elicit a strong positive inotropic response, which is only weakly related to the preceding postextrasystolic coupling interval. The latter, nitroglycerin, was shown by Starr to improve the ballistocardiographic record in most patients with coronary artery disease. This agent not only reduces afterload but also redistributes the blood supply in favor of ischemic segments. As a result of a variety of studies, primarily by Helfant, Mason, and our own group, it has been demonstrated that virtually

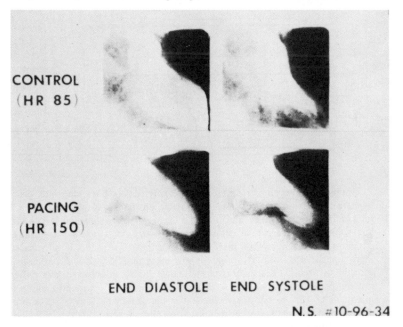

FIGURE 7 Induction of apical asynergy by atrial pacing tachycardia. This patient had a subtotal obstruction of the left anterior descending coronary artery. In the control state the ventriculogram exhibited normal contraction. When ischemia was induced by pacing tachycardia, apical asynergy ensued. Abbreviation: HR, heart rate. From Pasternac et al. (15), by permission of the American Heart Association, Inc.

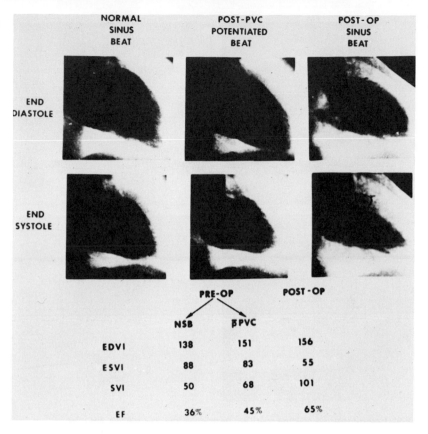

FIGURE 8 Example of ventriculographic analysis in a single patient. Abbreviations: EDVI, end-diastolic volume index (ml/m²); EF, ejection fraction; ESVI, end-systolic volume index (ml/m²); NSB, normal sinus beat; pPVC, after (post) premature ventricular contraction; POST-OP, postoperative; PRE-OP, preoperative; PVC, premature ventricular contraction; and SVI, stroke volume (ml/m²). From Popio et al. (16).

all types of asynergy may be reversible, although dyskinesis is the least and hypokinesis is the most responsive to intervention (Table 1). Helfant and co-workers (10) have shown that there is a high incidence of Q waves in the ECG correlating with zones of asynergy that are fixed (or irreversible), although they have cautioned that some patients exhibiting Q waves do have the potential for improved contraction (Table 2). They have also demonstrated that in patients whose asynergy is reversible on intervention, both the histopathologic examination and electrophysiological studies at the time of revascularization surgery are characteristic of normal myocardium.

Perhaps the most important aspect of the study of reversible asynergy has been its predictive value in demonstrating zones of dysfunctioning myocardium that are likely to be improved by successful revascularization surgery. This has been reported by Helfant et al. (10) (Table 3), Hamby et al. (9), and Popio et al. (16). Thus, it is incumbent on the angiographer not only to determine the resting or basal status of

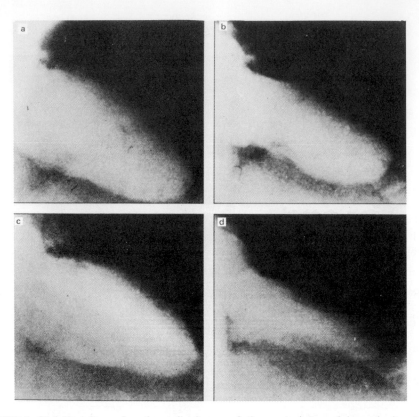

FIGURE 9   End-diastolic and end-systolic frames of the control (a and b) and nitroglycerin angiographic ventriculogram (c and d) in a patient with 90% proximal stenosis of the left anterior descending coronary artery. The control ventriculogram reveals frank dyskinesis of the anteroapical region, while the ventriculogram after nitroglycerin shows normalization of the contractile pattern. From Helfant et al. (10).

myocardium in ischemic heart disease but to subject that myocardium to an intervention that is capable of eliciting the reserve functional or potential functional capacity of muscle. Both postextrasystolic potentiation (which requires only a single ventriculogram) and sublingual nitroglycerin (and a second ventriculogram) have been shown to be effective in obtaining the necessary information. Both have been well correlated with the subsequent response of segments to myocardial revasculari-

TABLE 1   Severity of asynergy and response to nitroglycerin

Type	Total segments	Responsive segments	Unresponsive segments
Hypokinesis	56	42 (75%)	14 (25%)
Akinesis	54	9 (17%)	45 (83%)
Dyskinesis	22	1 (5%)	21 (95%)

TABLE 2 Relationship of pathological Q waves to reversible asynergy[a]

| | No. of segments | |
Type	With Q waves	Without Q waves
Nitroglycerin-responsive	11	30
Nitroglycerin-unresponsive	14	6

[a]$p < 0.005$.

zation (Fig. 7). The response has been demonstrated not only with respect to segmental motion but also to prognosis. This is best illustrated when overall left ventricular dysfunction improves with intervention. Cohn et al. (4) and Popio et al. (16) have shown that improved ventricular contraction, as studied by the ejection fraction, is well correlated with both good postoperative survival and good medical survival (4).

Right Ventricle

Space does not permit a discussion of right ventricular findings in coronary artery disease. Suffice it to say that when the right coronary artery was severely obstructed, the ejection fraction and the diastolic volume-pressure relationship were abnormal. Asynergy of the right ventricle was usually seen in association with an adjacent zone of left ventricular asynergy (6).

FUTURE DIRECTIONS

The most important investigative effort at present is devoted to developing means of recording a dynamic image of the left ventricle with respect to time, utilizing noninvasive techniques. This is possible to a limited extent through ultrasound, but delimited portals of viewing of the heart may confine and restrict its extensive use. Radionuclide angiography, on the other hand, either through first pass or through the gated scan technique, does permit imaging of the heart in multiple planes as a function of time.

These methods, which are virtually free of effects detrimental to the patient and capable of being reproduced at will and as frequently as needed, are now being combined with interventions so that it will be possible not only to determine volume and ejection and local asynergy, but also to study the effects of the

TABLE 3 Number of asynergic zones

Type	Responsive to nitroglycerin	Improved with bypass graft
Hypokinesis	11	10
Akinesis	7	5
Dyskinesis	1	1

previously mentioned interventions. By these means, it should be possible to determine the overall potential for contraction and therefore prognosis or selection for surgery, as well as the potential for the restoration of ischemic segments to a normal contractile state.

In the latter goal we see a return to some of the original aims of Isaac Starr's work, namely to develop methods that are relatively simple and harmless for the patient and that will provide critical information concerning the dynamic functions of the heart.

REFERENCES

1. Banka, V. S., Bodenheimer, M. M., Shah, R., and Helfant, R. H. Intervention ventriculography: Comparative value of nitroglycerin, post-extrasystolic potentiation and nitroglycerin plus post-extrasystolic potentiation. Circulation 53:632–637, 1976.
2. Baxley, W. A., Jones, W. B., and Dodge, H. T. Left ventricular anatomical and functional abnormalities in chronic postinfarction heart failure. Ann Intern Med 74:499–508, 1971.
3. Baxley, W. A. and Reeves, T. J. Abnormal regional myocardial performance in coronary artery disease. Progr Cardiovasc Dis 13:405–421, 1971.
4. Cohn, P. F., Gorlin, R., Herman, M. V., Sonnenblick, E. H., Horn, H. R., Cohn, L. H., and Collins, J. J., Jr. Relation between contractile reserve and prognosis in patients with coronary artery disease and a depressed ejection fraction. Circulation 51:414–420, 1975.
5. Dodge, H. T., Sandler, H., Baxley, W. A., and Hawley, R. Usefulness and limitations of radiographic methods for determining left ventricular volume. Am J Cardiol 18:10–24, 1966.
6. Dyke, S. H., Cohn, P. F., Gorlin, R., and Sonnenblick, E. H. Detection of residual myocardial function in coronary artery disease using postextrasystolic potentiation. Circulation 50:694–699, 1974.
7. Ferlinz, J., Delvicario, M., and Gorlin, R. Incidence of right ventricular asynergy in patients with coronary artery disease. Am J Cardiol 38:557–563, 1976.
8. Gorlin, R. Coronary Artery Disease. Philadelphia: Saunders, 1976, pp. 132–133.
9. Hamby, R. I., Aintablian, A. Wisoff, B. G., and Hartstein, M. L. Response of the left ventricle in coronary artery disease to postextrasystolic potentiation. Circulation 51:428–435, 1975.
9a. Harrison, T. R. Some unanswered questions concerning enlargement and failure of the heart. Am Heart J 69:100–115, 1965.
10. Helfant, R. H., Banka, V. S., and Bodenheimer, M. M. Left ventricular dysfunction in coronary heart disease: A dynamic problem. Cardiovasc Med 2:557–571, 1977.
11. Helfant, R. H., Pine, R., Meister, S., Feldman, M. S., Trout, R. G., and Banka, V. S. Nitroglycerin to unmask reversible asynergy: Correlation with post coronary bypass ventriculography. Circulation 50:108–113, 1974.
12. Herman, M. V., Heinle, R. A., Klein, M. D., and Gorlin, R. Localized disorders in myocardial contraction: Asynergy and its role in congestive heart failure. N Engl J Med 277:222–232, 1967.
13. Klein, M. D., Herman, M. V., and Gorlin, R. A hemodynamic study of left ventricular aneurysm. Circulation 35:614–630, 1967.

14. Kreulen, T., Gorlin, R., and Herman, M. V. Ventricular patterns and hemodynamics in primary myocardial disease. Circulation 47:299–308, 1973.
15. Pasternac, A., Gorlin, R., Sonnenblick, E. H., Haft, J. I., and Kemp, H. G. Abnormalities of ventricular motion induced by atrial pacing in coronary artery disease. Circulation 45:1195, 1972.
16. Popio, K. A., Gorlin, R., Bechtel, D., and Levine, J. Postextrasystolic potentiation as a predictor of potential myocardial viability: Preoperative analyses compared with studies after coronary bypass surgery. Am J Cardiol 39:944–953, 1977.
17. Rackley, C. E., Dear, H. D., Baxley, W., Jones, W. B., and Dodge, H. T. Left ventricular chamber volume, mass, and function in severe coronary artery disease. Circulation 41:605–613, 1970.
18. Starr, I. and Ogawa, S. Incoordination of the cardiac contraction in clinical conditions, as judged by the ballistocardiogram and the pulse derivatives. Am J Med Sci 35:663–679, 1962.
19. Sussman, M. L., Dack, S., and Master, A. M. The roentgenokymogram in myocardial infarction. I. The abnormalities in left ventricular contraction. Am Heart J 19:453–463, 1940.
20. Tennant, R. and Wiggers, C. J. Effect of coronary occlusion on myocardial contraction. Am J Physiol 112:351–361, 1935.

CHAPTER 8

HEMODYNAMIC MONITORING IN ACUTE ISCHEMIC DISEASE

WILLIAM W. PARMLEY

The benefits of continuous electrocardiographic monitoring in the coronary care unit have been established, and have resulted in a reduction of mortality from serious arrhythmias (12). A natural extension of this concept over the past several years has been continuous bedside monitoring of hemodynamic parameters in critically ill patients. The ability to measure hemodynamics invasively at the bedside has been greatly facilitated by the development of a new generation of balloon-tip flotation catheters (22), which are relatively easily inserted into the pulmonary artery without fluoroscopy. Such techniques have helped greatly in characterizing the hemodynamic status of patients with acute ischemic disease and, in particular, monitoring their response to specific therapeutic interventions. In this chapter, I will briefly discuss the pathophysiology of ischemic myocardium, the various techniques available for hemodynamic monitoring, and how such information helps in placing patients in subsets and individualizing their therapy.

Overall, the three major goals considered in treating the infarction are:

1. Prevention and/or treatment of serious arrhythmias
2. Correction of hemodynamic abnormalities
3. Preservation of ischemic myocardium

In this chapter I will focus on goal 2, although I will also briefly discuss goal 3 as it is related to hemodynamic monitoring and therapy. I will concentrate on four primary hemodynamic measurements:

1. Heart rate
2. Arterial pressure
3. Left ventricular filling pressure (pulmonary capillary wedge pressure)
4. Cardic output

Derived parameters include stroke volume and stroke work. These parameters are normalized by dividing by the body surface area (m^2) to obtain stroke volume index (cc/m^2) and stroke work index ($g \cdot m/m^2$).

The concept of left ventricular stroke work and its calculation are illustrated in Fig. 1. The pressure-volume loop of the left ventricle has four phases: 1) filling of

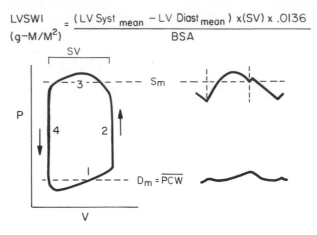

$$\underset{(g-M/M^2)}{LVSWI} = \frac{(LV\ Syst_{mean} - LV\ Diast_{mean}) \times (SV) \times .0136}{BSA}$$

$$Sm \sim SYSTOLIC\ BP - {}^1/_3 (SYSTOLIC - DIASTOLIC\ BP)$$
$$SV = CO/HR$$

FIGURE 1 Calculation of left ventricular stroke work index. On the left is the pressure-volume loop of the left ventricle with each contraction. Phase 1 is diastole; phase 2, isovolumetric contraction; phase 3, ejection; and phase 4, isovolumetric relaxation. The area inside this loop represents the stroke work of the ventricle, which is estimated by converting the loop into a rectangle. The vertical length of the rectangle equals systolic mean pressure (S_m) minus diastolic mean pressure (D_m). The latter can be approximated by mean pulmonary capillary wedge pressure $(\overline{PCW})$. The horizontal limb of the rectangle is the difference between end-diastolic volume and end-systolic volume, which by definition is stroke volume (SV). The 0.0136 is the conversion factor from mmHg to the gram-centimeter system. Patient normalization is accomplished by dividing by the body surface area (BSA) to give left ventricular stroke work index $(LVSWI)$ in gram-meters per square meter.

the left ventricle during diastole along the passive pressure-volume relation, 2) the isovolumetric phase of pressure development, 3) the ejection phase, while the aortic valve is open, and 4) the relaxation phase, where pressure declines until the mitral valve opens again. The area inside this counterclockwise loop represents the work done by the left ventricle with each contraction (stroke work). It is calculated by approximating the loop with a rectangle. The width of the rectangle is stroke volume (SV). The height of the rectangle is approximated by the difference between systolic mean pressure (S_m) and left ventricular mean diastolic pressure (D_m). The latter is approximated by mean pulmonary capillary wedge pressure $(\overline{PCW})$. Systolic mean pressure can be estimated as systolic arterial pressure minus one-third of the pulse pressure. The constant 0.0136 is a conversion factor.

EFFECTS OF ISCHEMIA ON MECHANICAL PERFORMANCE

If one abruptly occludes a coronary artery in an experimental animal, the myocardium supplied by that artery becomes noncontractile in about 1 min. Shortly thereafter it undergoes paradoxical expansion with each systole. In the course of acute myocardial infarction in humans, it is probable that the same sequence of events occurs. Shortly after reduction in blood supply or increase in myocardial oxygen demand, the affected area becomes ischemic and noncontractile. If this state persists for a sufficient time, the area is no longer viable, becomes necrotic, and ultimately goes through a reparative phase with subsequent fibrosis. It is apparent that the paradoxical expansion associated with the acute phase of infarction puts the rest of the ventricle at a mechanical disadvantage, since some of the blood is pumped backward into the expanding zone rather than into the aorta.

A simple conceptual representation of this phenomenon is seen in Fig. 2, where the ejection fraction of the ventricle is plotted as a function of the size (percentage of the left ventricle) of the infarct. If the infarcted myocardium were noncontractile but also rigid and nonexpansile, one might expect that the ejection fraction would go down approximately in proportion to the percentage of the left ventricle that was infarcted. This assumes that the uninvolved normal myocardium remains normally contractile but is neither hypo- nor hypercontractile. These assumptions are inconsistent with clinical and pathological data from patients in cardiogenic shock. An infarction that leads to cardiogenic shock usually involves about 40-50% of the left ventricle (15). Figure 2, however, suggests that the ejection fraction would be reduced to only approximately 0.33 (upper line), which should be

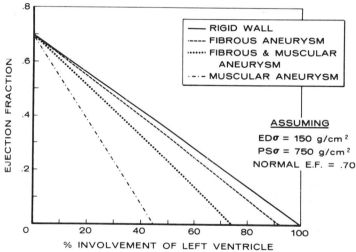

FIGURE 2 Conceptual plot of ejection fraction as the percentage of the left ventricle involved with either acute myocardial infarction or an aneurysm. If the noncontractile portion of the heart were rigid and did not paradoxically expand with systole, the ejection fraction would fall approximately in proportion to the percentage involvement of the left ventricle (upper line). If the involved portion of the ventricle underwent some degree of paradoxical systolic expansion, however, the ejection fraction and forward stroke volume would be reduced below the upper line in proportion to the compliance of the aneurysm. Data from patients following acute myocardial infarction are illustrated by the three lines. The lowest line, which represents patients with acute myocardial infarction and acute paradoxical systolic expansion, indicates that by the time 40% of the ventricle is involved with the acute infarct, the ejection fraction has been reduced to nonsurvival levels. From Parmley et al. (16).

compatible with life. Calculations made with data from tissues removed from patients with acute infarction and chronic aneurysms (16) have made it clear that the paradoxical expansion associated with the acute phase produces a severe mechanical disadvantage, as illustrated by the lower line in Fig. 2. Thus, with paradoxical expansion of the involved segment, there is a further reduction of *forward* ejected volume, with the result that by the time 40–50% of the ventricle is involved, ejection fraction has been reduced to nonsurvival levels. This conceptual scheme suggests the important deleterious effects of paradoxical expansion. Paradoxical expansion will be reduced by the natural process of edema formation and ultimately fibrous tissue formation, which stiffens this segment of infarcted myocardium. Stiff ventricular aneurysms are not very expansile, and thus do not produce the same mechanical disadvantage as acutely ischemic tissues (Fig. 2).

Variable amounts of ischemia represent another important factor influencing the course of patients with acute myocardial infarction. In association with infarcted tissue, there is a surrounding ischemic area whose function depends on the severity of the ischemia. With minimal ischemia it may only be hypokinetic, but with more severe ischemia it may become akinetic or even expand paradoxically. Since the function of the heart is extremely sensitive to changes in ischemia, it is apparent that alterations that disturb the balance between myocardial oxygen supply and demand may also have profound effects on cardiac function.

Normal myocardium remote from an infarction presumably would be contracting normally if there were no additional coronary stenoses. Although there is some evidence that at times this normal tissue may be slightly hypokinetic, it is apparent that with increased sympathetic stimulation and increased levels of circulating catecholamines, the normal area is probably stimulated to become hypercontractile (23). From the discussion above it is apparent that if one could carefully measure ventricular volume and segmental wall motion, it might be possible to quantitate some of the changes in function that have been described.

Although there are some obvious difficulties in doing this at the bedside, there are some newer techniques that promise to make this possible. The first technique utilizes a radionuclide marker of the intravascular pool (^{99}Tc-labeled albumin or pertechnetate). Gated electrocardiogram studies at end-diastole or end-systole help determine end-diastolic and end-systolic volumes and wall motion (1). As the resolution of the images obtained improves, it may be possible to define subtle changes in ischemia and local function. Since portable gamma cameras are available for use in critically ill patients, this technique has the capability for wide application in a number of settings.

Standard M mode echocardiography has a major disadvantage in patients with coronary artery disease in that it can provide only a single "ice pick" view of the heart; thus it is difficult to delineate the various areas of hypokinesis, akinesis, or dyskinesis. Two-dimensional echocardiography promises to be a major factor in providing this kind of information at the bedside. The use of apical views of the heart, which can provide an estimate of biplane volume and wall motion, promises to revolutionize the ability of the physician to obtain such information at the bedside (18).

Since the two new methods are still in their developmental phase, hemodynamic function is currently evaluated at the bedside by invasive hemodynamic monitoring. In the following I will briefly outline the various measurements that are made and discuss their relative usefulness. In some instances, the most important bedside measurement is the arterial pressure, obtained with an indwelling arterial catheter. In patients with severe power failure who have a low cardiac output and are extremely hypotensive and vasoconstricted, it is impossible to measure arterial pressure accurately with a standard arm cuff. Not only are the Korotkoff sounds indistinct or absent, but they often underestimate true intravascular pressure because of the associated vasoconstriction and low flow (5). It is not uncommon, therefore, to find that blood pressure determined indirectly by Korotkoff sounds is considerably below direct intravascular pressure. Furthermore, it is impossible to follow cuff blood pressure on a beat-to-beat and minute-by-minute basis, which is required when one is trying to monitor the unstable course of such patients and their response to a variety of therapeutic interventions. In patients who are not in power failure and who have a good cardiac output and reasonable blood pressure, indirect pressure recordings with a sphgymomanometer are satisfactory.

The newest and most important advance in hemodynamic monitoring has been the introduction of balloon-tip catheters by Swan et al. (22). These catheters have several major advantages over those previously used for the measurement of right-side pressures. First, they can generally be inserted at the bedside without fluoroscopy. Inflation of the balloon when the tip of the catheter is in the right atrium allows the blood flow to help propel the catheter into the pulmonary artery, as it is pushed by the physician. Once the catheter is in the pulmonary artery, the balloon is deflated. Transient reinflation of the balloon to occlude the branch of the pulmonary artery in which the catheter sits will provide a measurement of pulmonary artery occluded pressure (pulmonary capillary wedge pressure), which is an indirect measure of left atrial pressure. Thus, this catheter has the capability of measuring left-side filling pressure as a guide to the diagnosis and management of left heart failure.

Several newer versions of the balloon-tip catheter are now available that can be used for a number of other critical measurements, listed below.

1. Pulmonary artery systolic and diastolic pressure
2. Pulmonary capillary wedge pressure
3. Central venous (right atrial) pressure
4. Cardiac output by thermodilution
5. V waves of mitral regurgitation
6. Mixed venous blood for oxygen saturation
7. Pullback measurements of oxygen saturation to detect left to right shunts (ruptured interventricular septum)
8. Right atrial and right ventricular electrograms
9. Capability for right ventricular pacing
10. Capability for right atrial or atrioventricular sequential pacing

The standard triple-lumen balloon-tip catheter measures right atrial pressure in addition to pulmonary artery pressure. It can also be used to measure cardiac output by the thermodilution technique (10). An indicator (10 cc of cold D5W) is injected into the right atrium and mixes with blood as it passes through the right ventricle. A thermistor at the tip of the catheter in the pulmonary artery senses the temperature change as the wave of colder blood passes, and cardiac output can be calculated by the dilution principle. Tabletop cardiac output computers now allow this information to be processed and automatically presented as a digital readout. The technique is relatively simple and reproducible so that triplicate measurements of outputs obtained within a very short time are relatively accurate measurements of cardiac output.

Pulmonary artery diastolic pressure is frequently quite similar to pulmonary capillary wedge pressure. In the presence of pulmonary hypertension and elevated pulmonary vascular resistance, however, pulmonary artery diastolic pressure may be considerably higher than wedge pressure. When a catheter is first passed, it is useful to calibrate one against the other. Since the balloon at the tip of the catheter sometimes breaks with time, one can follow pulmonary artery diastolic pressure, which can be used as a reasonable estimate of wedge pressure, based on the original calibration.

This catheter can also be helpful in confirming the diagnosis of mitral regurgitation (4). The syndrome of moderate to severe acute mitral regurgitation is not uncommon in patients with acute coronary artery disease. In most cases, it is caused by some degree of papillary muscle dysfunction or infarction, although occasionally one may have ruptured chordae or, in extreme circumstances, a ruptured papillary muscle. Frequently, the degree of regurgitation is variable on an hour-by-hour basis as changes in ischemia effect papillary muscle function. Because vasodilator therapy is such a specific mode of therapy for mitral regurgitation (4), it is important to make this diagnosis so that this therapy can be applied. The hallmark of acute mitral regurgitation is a large V wave in the pulmonary capillary wedge pressure trace (4). Since the left atrium is frequently of normal size in patients with acute mitral regurgitation, the V wave is relatively larger than in patients with chronic mitral regurgitation and a large compliant left atrium.

In some patients with severe hypotension and a very low forward cardiac output, the usual holosystolic murmur of mitral regurgitation may be indistinct or even absent (9). In such a situation, it is important to make this diagnosis in order to avoid vasopressor drugs, which might worsen the regurgitation and even further reduce forward cardiac output.

The catheter may also be used to measure oxygen saturation in mixed venous (pulmonary artery) blood. This measurement helps in determining directional changes in cardiac output and also in assessing the relative balance between oxygen supply to the body and overall oxygen consumption. Recalling the Fick principle, if overall body oxygen consumption and arterial oxygen remain relatively constant, then changes in mixed venous oxygen content will reflect changes in cardiac output. Thus, an increase in mixed venous oxygen content indicates a rise in cardiac output, while a reduction indicates a reduction in cardiac output.

A ruptured interventricular septum can also be diagnosed with the pulmonary artery catheter. This syndrome usually produces abrupt and catastrophic hemodynamic consequences in the patient with acute myocardial infarction. It is generally accompanied by an abrupt deterioration of ventricular function and the sudden appearance of a loud holosystolic murmur along the lower left sternal border (which may or may not be accompanied by a thrill). In some instances, it is difficult to distinguish a ruptured septum from acute mitral regurgitation. The balloon-tip catheter can help greatly in this regard. First, one can identify the characteristic regurgitant V waves of severe mitral regurgitation. More importantly, one can detect the oxygen step-up in blood that occurs because of the left to right shunt at the ventricular level. With a triple-lumen balloon-tip catheter in place, a right atrial blood sample and a pulmonary artery sample may be sufficient to document the step-up in oxygen content of the blood. Serial withdrawal of blood samples as the catheter is withdrawn through the right side of the circulation will also be satisfactory in making this diagnosis.

With the triple-lumen balloon-tip catheter, venous or right atrial pressure is monitored through the proximal lumen. Right atrial pressure represents the filling pressure of the right ventricle, and therefore is a measure of right ventricular function. The relation between right and left ventricular filling pressure is discussed below. Newer versions of the ballon-tip catheter provide further capabilities. Some catheters have electrodes for right ventricular pacing, which may be helpful in patients with advanced atrioventricular block. In addition, one version of the balloon-tip catheter has two sets of electrodes, which sit in the right ventricle near the septum and in the right atrium. By recording from these electrodes, one can often sort out the mechanisms involved in serious arrhythmias. For example, in patients with a wide QRS tachycardia, it is not always easy to distinguish between ventricular tachycardia or supraventricular tachycardia with aberrant conduction. Recordings from the right atrial electrodes will clearly identify the P wave of atrial depolarization, while recordings from the right ventricle will identify ventricular depolarization. A comparison of these two spikes therefore allows one to sort out the mechanism of individual arrhythmias.

In addition, this catheter can be used for atrial or ventricular pacing. Pacing from the right ventricle is more reliable and easier to measure than pacing from the right atrium. Nevertheless, where the atrial contribution to ventricular contraction is desired, atrial or sequential atrioventricular pacing can be implemented with this catheter in many patients.

HEMODYNAMIC DESCRIPTORS OF ACUTE MYOCARDIAL INFARCTION

Of the various measurements that have been proposed to describe the hemodynamic status of patients with acute infarction, one of the most useful is the ventricular function curve, which is illustrated in Fig. 3. In this representation of cardiac performance some measure of ventricular function such as stroke volume or stroke work is plotted as a function of some measure of preload such as pulmonary capillary wedge pressure. The curve has an ascending limb, which flattens out at approximately 15–20 mmHg.

Since the right and left ventricle each has its own ventricular function curve, the relation between the two is of some importance. First, right atrial pressure and

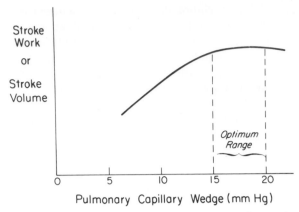

FIGURE 3 Representative ventricular function curve with stroke work or stroke volume plotted as a function of pulmonary capillary wedge pressure. The optimum pulmonary capillary wedge pressure is approximately 15–20 mmHg.

pulmonary capillary wedge pressure, respectively, represent the filling pressures of the right and left ventricles of the heart, as conceptually illustrated in Fig. 4. In Fig. 4, stroke volume from each ventricle is plotted as a function of the respective atrial pressure. The normal right ventricular function curve is situated to the left of the normal left ventricular function curve, since the right ventricle operates at a lower filling pressure. Thus, in this patient, the right ventricle normally might be at point A with a stroke volume of 80 cc and a right atrial pressure of about 3 mmHg. The left ventricle would be at point B with the same stroke volume and a left atrial pressure of 10 mmHg. For practical purposes, the stroke volume from the two sides of the heart is the same, so that the two ventricles operate on the same horizontal line. If this patient had an acute myocardial infarction that predominantly affected left ventricular function, stroke volume might be reduced to 50 cc. Since right ventricular function is initially intact, the right ventricle is now operating at point C with a filling pressure of about 2 mmHg. The left ventricular function curve has shifted down and to the right to point D because of the infarction and now has a filling pressure of 15 mmHg. Because this patient was hypotensive with a low cardiac output and yet had a normal central venous pressure, it might be tempting to consider a volume challenge. If this were done, as illustrated in Fig. 4, an increase in intravascular and ventricular volumes might shift the stroke volume up to 60 cc. Note that the right atrial pressure is now about 3 mmHg and the right ventricle is operating at point E. Because of the very flat left ventricular function curve, however, the left ventricle now operates at point F with a left atrial pressure of 30 mmHg, and the patient might go into pulmonary edema.

In the example above, it is apparent that the central venous pressure cannot be used as a reliable measure of the filling pressure of the left ventricle. The central venous or right atrial pressure is primarily an indicator of right ventricular function, whereas pulmonary capillary wedge pressure is the better indicator of left ventricular function. This is further illustrated in Fig. 5, in which simultaneous central venous and pulmonary capillary wedge pressures were plotted in a group of patients with acute myocardial infarction. Note that there is no overall relation. Furthermore, one cannot use central venous pressure in an individual patient to predict with confidence what the pulmonary capillary wedge pressure would be. Since the left ventricle is primarily responsible for maintaining cardiac output and systemic pressure, one must concentrate on optimizing its function in patients with power failure.

Studies with volume loading and diuresis in patients with acute infarction have suggested that the optimal left ventricular filling pressure is approximately 15-20 mmHg (6). Thus, in a patient who is either hypotensive or has a low cardiac output or power failure, it is important to optimize this filling pressure. In such hypovolemic patients with a filling pressure lower than 15 mmHg, administration of volume (100 cc every 3-5 min) to bring the filling pressure up to 15-20 mmHg may be all that is required to improve hemodynamic performance. In patients with a higher filling pressure, the use of diuretics can reduce filling pressure to 15-20 mmHg and relieve the symptoms and signs of pulmonary congestion.

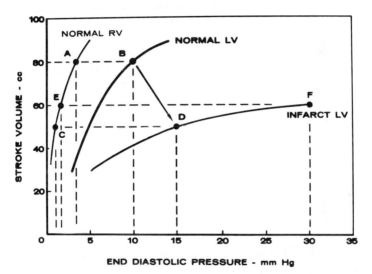

FIGURE 4 Schematic right ventricular (RV) and left ventricular (LV) function curves before and after left ventricular infarction. The normal RV function curve is to the left of the normal LV function curve, since RV end-diastolic pressure is less than LV end-diastolic pressure. Since the two ventricles have approximately the same stroke volume over any reasonable period of time, however, they operate on the same horizontal line. Under normal circumstances, the right ventricle would be at point A and the left ventricle at point B, both with a stroke volume of 80 cc. Following infarction, which predominantly affects the left ventricle, the LV curve is shifted down and to the right, although the RV curve may not be initially affected. Stroke volume decreases to 50 cc and the right ventricle is at point C with the left ventricle at point D. A volume load at this point might increase stroke volume to 60 cc and the right ventricle would go to point E, whereas the left ventricle would move to point F. At this high filling pressure, the patient might well go into pulmonary edema. This diagram illustrates the important fact that central venous pressure reflects only right ventricular function and pulmonary capillary wedge pressure reflects left ventricular function.

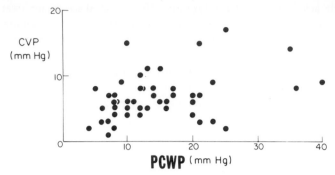

FIGURE 5 Lack of correlation between central venous pressure (CVP) and pulmonary capillary wedge pressure (PCWP) in acute myocardial infarction. The relation between CVP and PCWP is illustrated for a group of patients with acute myocardial infarction who had hemodynamic monitoring. Note that there is no relation that would allow one to use CVP as a predictor of PCWP. For example, at a CVP of approximately 8 mmHg, PCWP ranged from 5 to 40 mmHg.

The measurements of filling pressure and stroke work that characterize the left ventricular function curve are also important in defining the status and prognosis of individual patients. This is illustrated by data from a large group of patients with acute myocardial infarction shown in Fig. 6. Left ventricular stroke work index is plotted as a function of pulmonary capillary wedge pressure (left ventricular filling

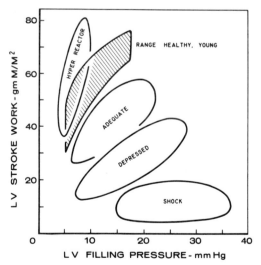

FIGURE 6 Hemodynamic consequences of myocardial infarction. The hatched area represents the range of left ventricular (LV) function in healthy young individuals. Following acute myocardial infarction, there is tremendous variability in the hemodynamic response. Some patients with small infarcts and increased sympathetic tone may be in the normal or hypernormal range. As the size of the infarct increases, however, function is progressively shifted down and to the right, so that all patients with cardiogenic shock fall in the lower right-hand group. From Sodeman and Sodeman (21).

pressure). The hatched area represents the range for healthy young people who had undergone cardiac catheterization. The four elliptical areas in general define some of the responses of patients to acute myocardial infarction. Some patients with small infarcts and a large adrenergic response may be in the normal or hypernormal range. These patients have a very good prognosis and little therapy other than the usual observation is needed. One proposed therapy for these patients has been propranolol, which might be beneficial in reducing the deleterious effects of increased sympathetic tone on both ischemic myocardium and arrhythmias (13).

As the size of the infarct increases, function is shifted down and to the right, so that patients with severe power failure invariably have a filling pressure greater than 15 mmHg and a left ventricular stroke work index less than 20 g · m/m^2. The prognostic value of these measurements is quite important. In patients who have an initial left ventricular filling pressure that is less than 15 mmHg (before any vasodilator or diuretic therapy), mortality is close to zero. In patients with a stroke work index less than 20 g · m/m^2 and a filling pressure greater than 15 mmHg, the mortality approaches 85% with conventional therapy, although vasodilator drugs may improve that mortality somewhat. Many patients in this group have classical cardiogenic shock, although in some patients the clinical picture does not indicate the tremendous hemodynamic deficit that is present. Patients with a filling pressure greater than 15 mmHg and a stroke work index greater than 20 g · m/m^2 have approximately 10-20% mortality, which is generally related to the magnitude of their stroke work index (3). Thus, hemodynamic measurement can provide important base line information on the status of patients and their overall course.

More importantly, such information can be helpful in evaluating the response of patients to specific therapeutic measures. Since patients vary considerably in their response to particular therapeutic interventions, hemodynamic monitoring helps in selecting an intervention and carefully following the response to it. It is of use in optimizing therapy or in discontinuing therapy to which the patient does not respond. This principle has been one of the most important aspects of individual hemodynamic monitoring in critically ill patients.

The data of Fig. 6 make it clear that acute myocardial infarction cannot be considered as a single entity. It appears more appropriate to divide patients into specific subsets, which can then be considered for therapy separately. Several subset classifications might be applied to these patients (8), and one is listed in Table 1. These subsets will be briefly described, although it should be understood at the outset that these are only general guidelines and are not to be considered as absolute divisions. The three measurements that are used in this subset classification are systolic arterial pressure, left ventricular filling pressure, and cardiac index.

Subset 1 represents patients who have low left ventricular filling pressure and, as a consequence, low arterial pressure and cardiac index. As previously discussed, they benefit mostly from volume administration to raise their left ventricular filling pressure to the optimal level of 15-20 mmHg. In such circumstances, it is usual for the hypotension to disappear and the cardiac index to increase appropriately. These patients represent at most 10% of patients with acute infarction. They are often patients who have previously been on diuretic therapy or who may have had inadequate fluid intake (e.g., elderly people in hot climates). Subset 2 is a more

TABLE 1 Therapeutic classification of subsets in acute myocardial infarction[a]

Subset	Description	Systolic arterial pressure (mmHg)	Left ventricular filling pressure (mmHg)	Cardiac index (liter/min · m²)	Therapy
1	Hypovolemic	< 100	< 10	< 2.5	Volume
2	Pulmonary congestion	100–150	> 20	> 2.5	Diuretics
3	Peripheral vasodilation	< 100	10–20	> 2.5	Nothing or vasoactive drugs
4	Power failure and/or mitral regurgitation	< 100	> 20	< 2.5	Vasodilators
5	Severe shock	< 90	> 20	< 2.0	Circulatory assist
6	Right ventricular infarct	< 100	< 15 (RVFP > 10)	< 2.5	Avoid diuretics; volume for low LVFP

[a]The numerical values given in this table are representative ones and are intended to provide general guidelines. They should not be considered as absolute cutoff points. The arterial pressures apply to patients who were previously normotensive and should be adjusted upward for patients who were previously hypertensive.

common group of patients with acute infarction who have a reasonable arterial pressure and cardiac index, but a high left ventricular filling pressure and the symptom of dyspnea. Since the predominant hemodynamic abnormality is a high filling pressure, diuretics represent the therapy of choice. When the left ventricular filling pressure is reduced, this symptom will often disappear. Diuretics reduce filling pressure by increasing systemic venous compliance and then promoting diuresis through the kidneys (7). It should be noted that once one has given diuretics to a patient, one cannot follow basilar rales as a guide to the left ventricular filling pressure. There may be an abrupt reduction in the left ventricular filling pressure, but it may take a day or two for rales to clear. Therefore, it is important not to continue administering diuretics merely because basilar rales are present, because one might lower the filling pressure to hypovolemic levels. An evaluation of left ventricular filling pressure can often be made from the upright chest X-ray. Redistribution of blood flow to the upper lobes is fairly closely correlated with a left ventricular filling pressure greater than 15 mmHg (13).

Subset 3 represents an unusual group of patients who have a low systolic arterial pressure, but relatively normal cardiac index. The usual response to the insult of an acute myocardial infarction is peripheral vasoconstriction in an attempt to maintain arterial pressure. In some patients this does not occur, and they have a good cardiac output despite severe hypotension. The left ventricular filling pressure may be relatively normal or slightly elevated. It may not be necessary to administer any therapy, although with extremely low blood pressure a vasoactive drug such as dopamine should be considered.

Subset 4 represents a common group of patients with moderate to severe power failure. They have a low arterial pressure and cardiac index and a filling pressure greater than 20 mmHg. Vasodilator therapy can be extremely beneficial to patients in this group by reducing filling pressure and increasing cardiac output. Similarly, in patients with severe mitral regurgitation, vasodilator therapy has its most prominent effect in increasing forward cardiac output and reducing regurgitant volume (4). In patients with a ruptured interventricular septum, vasodilator therapy might also be of benefit until definitive surgery can be considered. This is because a reduction of forward systemic vascular resistance may increase forward cardiac output and decrease the left to right shunt across the interventricular septum.

Subset 5 represents patients with cardiogenic shock who are markedly hypotensive with a very low cardiac index and a high left ventricular filling pressure. In addition to many of the other therapies listed, these patients should probably be put on circulatory assist devices such as the intra-aortic balloon. This device may help somewhat in their short-term management, although the long-term prognosis is still poor (17).

The last subset in Table 1 includes patients with an inferior myocardial infarction that predominantly affects the right ventricle. Infarction of the right ventricle causes it to fail and the right ventricular filling pressure to rise. This may be accompanied by some hypotension and a reduced cardiac output. It is important to recognize this syndrome to avoid diuretics, even though the right ventricular filling pressure is markedly elevated. Left ventricular filling pressure may be normal or reduced, and in fact it may be necessary to administer volume to raise it up to an optimal level of 15-20 mmHg, which will usually maintain arterial pressure and cardiac index. Diagnosis has recently been facilitated by use of technetium pyrophosphate scanning, which can specifically document infarction of the right ventricle (19).

One aspect of the hemodynamic approach to the therapy of power failure that should be mentioned is the consideration that must be given to the preservation of ischemic myocardium. Since a variety of therapeutic and hemodynamic interventions may alter the balance between myocardial oxygen supply and demand, it is important to consider these effects conceptually when selecting a therapeutic intervention. The four primary determinants of myocardial oxygen demand are heart rate, arterial pressure, heart size, and myocardial contractility. A number of experimental and clinical reports have shown that techniques that reduce myocardial oxygen demand are effective in preserving ischemic myocardium (11).

In general, it is not practical to consider routinely reducing sinus heart rate in patients with acute infarction. Prevention or control of tachyarrhythmias, however, can be extremely beneficial in controlling myocardial oxygen consumption. In some hypertensive patients (systolic pressure greater than 160 mmHg) a cautious reduction of arterial pressure may be beneficial in reducing infarct size (20). In patients with heart failure who are hypertensive, reduction of blood pressure is also effective in reducing pulmonary capillary wedge pressure and the symptoms and signs of pulmonary congestion. Heart size can be reduced by a number of techniques. Diuretic agents are effective in lowering pulmonary capillary wedge pressure, by both increasing systemic venous compliance and reducing intravascular volume. Various vasodilator drugs are also effective in reducing heart size. Drugs such as sodium nitroprusside and nitroglycerin both pool blood peripherally and reduce pulmonary capillary wedge pressure (2). In patients with acute pulmonary edema, tourniquets, phlebotomy, or positive pressure breathing might also be employed to reduce pulmonary congestion.

Reduction of myocardial contractility is usually not a desirable goal in patients with borderline or overt congestive heart failure. It may be important, however, to avoid certain markedly positive inotropic agents (e.g., isoproterenol) in patients who have considerable amounts of ischemic myocardium. This increased stimulation increases the need for oxygen and may actually increase the size of the infarct.

A number of other techniques have been proposed to reduce ischemic myocardium [e.g., propranolol (14), hyaluronidase, mannitol, steroids, glucose-insulin-potassium]. These have been discussed elsewhere (11). It is sufficient to note that in applying the principles of hemodynamic monitoring to patients with acute myocardial infarction, it is mandatory to consider the potential effect of these interventions on the balance between myocardial oxygen supply and demand.

SUMMARY

Several currently available techniques are extremely helpful in the evaluation and management of patients with acute myocardial infarction and ischemic disease. Balloon-tip catheters have been particularly useful for measurements of pulmonary artery and pulmonary capillary wedge pressures and cardiac output. Such measurements have made it possible to select therapy on the basis of hemodynamic abnormalities and to evaluate the response of each patient to such therapy. The most useful approach has been to quantitate a left ventricular function curve by plotting stroke work index against filling pressure. Initial values have considerable prognostic importance, while changes help to define a beneficial or deleterious response to therapeutic interventions. This approach has greatly simplified patient management and has provided a better understanding of the overall pathophysiology of acute myocardial infarction.

REFERENCES

1. Berman, D. S., Salel, A. F., DeNardo, G. L., Bogren, H. G., and Mason, D. T. Clinical assessment of left ventricular regional contraction patterns and ejection fraction by high-resolution gated scintigraphy. J Nucl Med 16:865–874, 1975.
2. Chatterjee, K. and Parmley, W. W. The role of vasodilator therapy in heart failure. Progr Cardiovasc Dis 19:301–325, 1977.
3. Chatterjee, K., Parmley, W. W., Ganz, W., Forrester, J. S., Walinsky, P., Crexells, C., and Swan, H. J. C. Hemodynamic and metabolic responses to vasodilator therapy in acute myocardial infarction. Circulation 48:1183–1193, 1973.
4. Chatterjee, K., Parmley, W. W., Swan, H. J. C., Berman, G., Forrester, J., and Marcus, H. S. Beneficial effects of vasodilator agents in severe mitral regurgitation due to dysfunction of subvalvar apparatus. Circulation 48:684–690, 1973.
5. Cohn, J. N. and Daddario, R. C. Mechanism of disappearance of Korotkoff sounds in clinical shock. Circulation 32(II):II-69, 1965.

6. Crexells, C., Chatterjee, K., Forrester, J. S., Dikshit, K., and Swan, H. J. C. Optimal left heart filling pressures in acute myocardial infarction. N Engl J Med 289:1263–1266, 1973.
7. Dikshit, K., Vyden, J. K., Forrester, J. S., Chatterjee, K., Prakash, R., and Swan, H. J. C. Renal and extrarenal hemodynamic effects of furosemide in congestive failure after acute myocardial infarction. N Engl J Med 288:1087–1090, 1973.
8. Forrester, J. S., Chatterjee, K., and Swan, H. J. C. Medical therapy of acute myocardial infarction by application of hemodynamic subsets. N Engl J Med 295:1356–1362, 1404–1413, 1976.
9. Forrester, J. S., Diamond, G., Freedman, S., Allen, H. N., Parmley, W. W., and Matloff, J. M. Silent mitral insufficiency in acute myocardial infarction. Circulation 44:877–883, 1971.
10. Ganz, W., Donoso, R., Marcus, H. S., Forrester, J. S., and Swan, H. J. C. A new technique for measurement of cardiac output by thermodilution in man. Am J Cardiol 27:392–396, 1971.
11. Hillis, L. D. and Braunwald, E. Myocardial ischemia. N Engl J Med 296:971–977, 1034–1041, 1093–1096, 1977.
12. Julian D. G. Coronary care. In: Acute Myocardial Infarction, D. G. Julian and M. F. Oliver, eds. Edinburgh: Livingstone, 1968, pp. 34–36.
13. McHugh, J. J., Forrester, J. S., Adler, L., Zion, D., and Swan, H. J. C. Pulmonary vascular congestion in acute myocardial infarction: Hemodynamic and radiologic correlations. Ann Intern Med 76:29–33, 1972.
14. Mueller, H. S., Ayres, S. M., Religa, A., and Evans, R. G. Propranolol in the treatment of acute myocardial infarction: Effect on myocardial oxygenation and hemodynamics. Circulation 49:1078–1087, 1974.
15. Page, D. L., Caulfield, J. B., Kastor, J. A., DeSanctis, R. W., and Sanders, C. A. Myocardial changes associated with cardiogenic shock. N Engl J Med 285:133–137, 1971.
16. Parmley, W. W., Chuck, L., Kivowitz, C., Matloff, J. M., and Swan, H. J. C. In vitro length-tension relations of human ventricular aneurysms: The relationship of stiffness to mechanical disadvantage. Am J Cardiol 32:887–894, 1973.
17. Sanders, C. A., Buckley, M. J., Leinbach, R. C., Mundth, E. D., and Austen, W. G. Mechanical circulatory assistance: Current status and experience with combining circulatory assistance, emergency coronary angiography and acute myocardial revascularization. Circulation 45:1292–1313, 1972.
18. Schiller, N. B., Drew, D., Acquatella, H., Boswell, R., Botvinick, E., Greenberg, B., and Carlsson, E. Non-invasive, biplane quantitation of left ventricular volume and ejection fraction with a real-time two-dimensional echocardiography system. Circulation 54(II):II-234, 1976.
19. Sharpe, N., Botvinick, E., Shames, D., Chatterjee, K., Massie, B., Schiller, N., and Parmley, W. W. Noninvasive diagnosis of right ventricular infarction: A common clinical entity. Circulation 53 and 54:II-76, 1976.
20. Shell, W. E. and Sobel, B. E. Protection of jeopardized ischemic myocardium by reduction of ventricular afterload. N Engl J Med 291:481–486, 1974.
21. Sodeman, W. A. and Sodeman, W. A., Jr., eds. Pathologic Physiology: Mechanisms of Disease. Philadelphia, Pa.: Saunders, 1974, p. 287.
22. Swan, H. J. C., Ganz, W., Forrester, J., Marcus, H., Diamond, G., and

Chonnette, D. Catheterization of the heart in man with use of a flow-directed balloon-tip catheter. N Engl J Med 283:447–451, 1970.

23. Theroux, P., Franklin, D., Ross, J., Jr., and Kamper, W. S. Regional myocardial function during acute coronary occlusion and its modification by pharmacologic agents in the dog. Circ Res 35:896–908, 1974.

CHAPTER 9

INSTANTANEOUS FORCE–VELOCITY–LENGTH RELATIONS OF THE LEFT VENTRICLE: METHODS, LIMITATIONS, AND APPLICATIONS IN HUMANS

KIRK L. PETERSON

Over the past decade there has been a sustained interest in improved characterization of the failing, intact heart as it is encountered in both the animal laboratory and the clinical setting. The impetus for such efforts has arisen primarily from the recognized limitations of the classical ventricular function curve in providing a comprehensive description of the major elements that control or influence myocardial shortening. In our clinical hemodynamic laboratory we have worked on developing methods that allow computation of ventricular afterload, as defined by various equations for wall stress; myocardial fiber stretch, as defined by the ventricular volume or the length of the minor axis circumference; and velocity of myocardial shortening, as defined by the rate of change of a minor axis chord measured at either the endocardium or the mid-wall of the ventricular musculature. Such measurements are analogous to traditional and well-accepted modes of analysis of myocardial function with isolated papillary muscle. Moreover, they provide a more direct and selective analysis of the known determinants of left ventricular performance: for example, peak or mean velocity of minor axis shortening of the ventricle is often depressed even though stroke volume or stroke work remains normal; end-diastolic diameter and volume are frequently increased even though end-diastolic pressure is normal, or conversely, end-diastolic pressure is elevated at times although ventricular size is normal because of enhanced ventricular stiffness; or wall stress, a measure of the force that resists shortening, may be augmented but may not be appropriately accounted for in the computation of stroke work or power.

In the application of force-velocity-length analysis to the intact heart during ejection, assumptions about separate contractile, series elastic, and parallel elastic elements have been avoided, and only the calculated velocity of myocardial shortening has been utilized to assess muscle displacement. Isotonic contractions in the intact left ventricle of the dog demonstrate an inverse relation between the initial velocity of circumferential shortening and wall stress, analogous to that between contractile element velocity and tension in the isolated papillary muscle (1). Also, earlier studies with variably afterloaded auxotonic contractions demonstrated that the inverse relation between velocity of wall motion and wall tension was sensitive to interventions that altered inotropic state (11). Thus, when analyzing the ejection phase, there would appear to be justification for using velocity of wall motion, although the behavior of the myocardium during diastole and isovolumetric systole cannot be adequately explained without some consideration of elastic components of muscle.

In most of the clinical studies in which instantaneous force-velocity-length relations have been used to assess left ventricular performance, only the circumferential or equatorial component of ventricular shortening has been measured and radial and meridional components have been variably ignored (8). The exclusion of the meridional component has been justified by animal and human studies demonstrating that the shortening of the longitudinal axis is approximately 13% or less in the normal and the diseased ventricle, and thus accounts for only a small proportion of the global change in left ventricular cavity size during systole (9). We have included or excluded radial shortening (i.e., that due to wall thickening) depending on the definitions used for the calculation of ventricular afterload. Where a relatively simple, thin-wall definition of chamber wall forces was utilized in the form of wall tension (proportional to the product of intracavitary pressure and minor axis radius), we accounted for both circumferential and radial components of shortening by measuring the extent and speed of shortening of the minor axis at the *endocardium*. However, if more complex thick-wall equations for wall forces were utilized, in particular those that attempt to assess average wall stress at the *mid-wall*, we calculated a comparable mid-wall circumferential velocity of shortening and ignored the radial contribution to change in cavity size. Moreover, our intention has been to model a vectorial component of left ventricular shortening in order to describe its behavior in terms of constructs found useful in isolated papillary muscles. These assumptions are supported by work of Gould et al. (6) demonstrating that changes in wall forces and velocity of shortening for all three directional components (equatorial, radial, and meridional) occur concordantly in various types of human heart disease.

Up to the present, three methods have been developed for the assessment of instantaneous force-velocity-length relations in the human left ventricle. The first technique was used initially by Glick et al. (5) and involved implantation of radiopaque epicardial markers at the time of cardiac surgery. Although it was a valuable first step, the method had the limitations that a thoracotomy was necessary and the velocity of shortening could be measured only at the outer wall of the ventricle. Also, the epicardial markers were not useful for making interpatient comparisons of myocardial function. Other investigators extended this technique by global implantation of the markers either on the epicardium or in the mid-wall at the time of cardiac surgery. High-speed cineangiography of the markers then provided a noninvasive means of assessing velocity-length relations, and in combination with cardiac catheterization provided the essential measurements for ventricular mid-wall force-velocity-length relations.

The next method, chronologically, was the use of high-speed left ventricular cineangiography simultaneously with the recording of a left ventricular pressure pulse (4). Gault et al. (4) reported that the peak as well as the mean velocity of circumferential shortening (V_{CF}), measured as a minor axis radial chord at the midpoint of the long axis and normalized per unit length, was significantly depressed in patients with congestive heart failure. Moreover, the profile of the force-velocity relation for the ventricular mid-wall was clearly different; normal subjects demonstrated generation of peak wall stress early in systole and before the time of peak velocity of shortening, giving rise to a counterclockwise loop, while subjects with myocardial failure manifested significant delay in the development of peak stress, which also tended to come after the development of peak velocity of shortening, giving rise to a closed loop (Fig. 1). The velocity of circumferential fiber shortening at peak calculated wall stress [where, if a two-element Hill model is assumed, the velocity of series elastic extension (V_{SE}) equals zero, and thus the velocity of the contractile element (V_{CE}) should equal V_{CF}] was also shown to identify patients with depressed myocardial contractile function. Although this

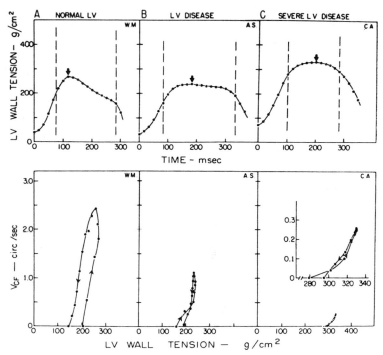

FIGURE 1 Profile of the force-velocity relation for the ventricular mid-wall. (Top) Left ventricular (LV) wall tension versus time (A) in a patient with normal LV function, (B) in a patient with myocardial failure, and (C) in a patient with severe myocardial failure. Arrows indicate the point of maximum tension. Vertical dashed lines represent the beginning and end of ejection. (Bottom) Instantaneous relation between velocity of circumferential fiber shortening (V_{CF}) at mid-wall of minor axis and wall tension throughout ejection. Arrows denote the direction of the tension-velocity loop. From Gault et al. (4), by permission of the American Heart Association, Inc.

cineangiographic method is useful for quantitating depressed myocardial function, it is tedious to execute frame by frame and is often dependent on a subjective determination of the cavity-endocardial interface, particularly during the middle and latter portions of ejection, when significant trabecular infolding is known to occur.

Subsequently, an ascending aortic catheter with an enclosed electromagnetic velocity probe was utilized to calculate instantaneous changes in left ventricular volume when left ventricular end-diastolic volume had been determined angiographically (10). The velocity of circumferential fiber shortening was computed at the mid-wall as $(dV/dt)/2r^2$ where dV/dt is the instantaneous rate of change of volume and r is a radius calculated from the instantaneous volume when the ventricle is assumed to be the shape of a sphere. Wall tension was also derived, by using the product of intracavitary pressure and radius. Then, in order to simultaneously demonstrate the velocity of shortening, operating length, wall force, and time, we developed a time-labeled three-dimensional perspective plot that permitted simultaneous graphic display of four variables. As shown in Fig. 2, each adjacent vertical line represents the computer printout for a 5-msec interval. The base of the three-dimensional plot represents the length (circumference)-tension relation during systole. The projection to the left provides the length (circumference)-velocity plot and indicates the extent of circumferential shortening as well, while the projection to the right represents the tension-velocity relation. In patients with normal ventricular function, represented by the loop toward the near corner of the three-dimensional plot, velocity of shortening rose sharply and continued to rise even as tension fell, and wall tension was lower during the second than during the first portion of ejection. In patients with impaired function (far corner), velocity of shortening rose sharply but was not sustained as systole progressed and as wall tension continued to increase. In contrast to normal patients,

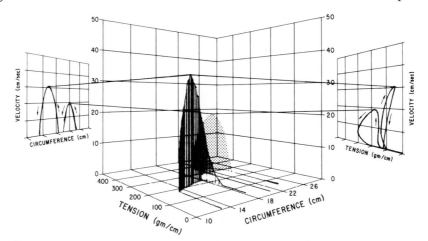

FIGURE 2 Three-dimensional perspective plot of left ventricular velocity, tension, and circumference. Velocity is plotted on the Y axis, circumference on the Z axis, and tension on the X axis. The loop for a patient with normal ventricular function is in the background, toward the far corner. Each adjacent vertical line in the loop indicates a 5-msec interval. From Peterson et al. (10), by permission of the American Heart Association, Inc.

those with depressed function showed considerably higher wall tension during the second than during the first half of ejection. In patients with impaired ventricular function, the peak velocity of circumferential fiber shortening occurred at a greater circumference and tended .to occur at a higher tension than in patients with normal function. Consequently, the peaks of the abnormal patients' three-dimensional loops clustered toward the far corner, where velocity is low and tension and circumference are high. This approach to the analysis of ventricular function appears to characterize the failing myocardium by its manifestations of depressed peak velocity of shortening, delayed dissipation of wall stress or tension, and operation at greater end-diastolic fiber lengths. Moreover, the asynchronous development of peak velocity and peak wall force in the failing heart was again identified by the directional change in the force-velocity loop.

Although the use of a velocity probe during cardiac catheterization represents a relatively novel means of assessing instantaneous changes in ventricular shortening, the shortcomings of the method should also be emphasized. First, this technique does not provide a direct measurement of myocardial shortening and is dependent on an arbitrary geometric model for the left ventricle and on left ventriculography for the determination of the beginning or end-diastolic volume and circumferential length. Second, blood flow velocity is directly proportional to flow only if the cross-sectional area of the ascending aorta is constant and the profile of flow is relatively flat. Previous studies by Greenfield and Patel (7), performed at the time of thoractomy, indicated that the average deviation in the cross-sectional area of the ascending aorta was 11% of the diastolic value with a range of 5.4–16.5%. Thus, the mean error in calculating flow from a velocity signal would be affected by a deviation of ±5.5% around the average value for cross-sectional area between end-diastolic and peak systolic pressures. The profile of flow as it emerges through the aortic valve may not be totally flat; however, this source of error can be minimized by placing the sensing electrodes just above the sinuses of Valsalva near the inlet of flow, where a nonflat velocity profile might not yet have had the opportunity to develop. A further problem in the derivation of ventricular shortening rates from a velocity probe signal is that the method depends on all ejected flow being sensed by the velocity probe signal. The method is thus not applicable to disease states in which all ejected flow does not exit through the aorta, such as mitral valve regurgitation or a ventricular septal defect.

Another method of analyzing the instantaneous force-velocity-length relations of the left ventricle in humans that has been developed in our laboratory consists of recording a high-fidelity micromanometer left ventricular pressure pulse simultaneously with an M mode echocardiogram across the minor axis of the left ventricle (Fig. 3). The long axis of the left ventricle can be determined approximately by simultaneously measuring stroke volume by an indicator dilution technique, or it can be assumed that the ratio of major to minor axes is approximately 2:1 throughout the cardiac cycle. All the necessary data are then available to calculate ventricular minor axis or circumferential shortening, at either the endocardium or the mid-wall, and mid-wall hoop stress, based on standard equations. For data processing, echocardiographic tracings of the endocardium and epicardium as well as the left ventricular pressure pulse are digitized every 10 msec

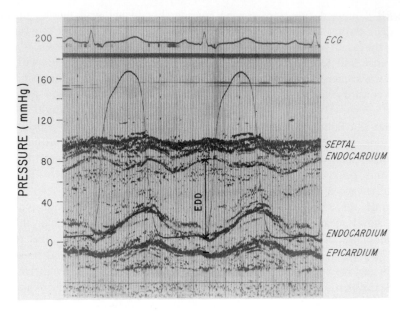

FIGURE 3 Strip-chart recording of M mode echocardiogram obtained simultaneously with recording of high-fidelity left ventricular pressure and electrocardiogram in patients undergoing cardiac catheterization. EDD indicates end-diastolic diameter. The calibration for left ventricular pressure is given on the left.

on an electromagnetic tablet; thereafter a least-squares best fit of a polynomial equation of fifth or lower order is utilized to "smooth" and allow differentiation of the raw data. Stress-velocity, stress-radius, and velocity-radius curves can then be plotted in an instantaneous fashion through systole. This technique has the notable advantage of allowing assessment of force-velocity-length relations of the ventricle both before and after a physiological or pharmacological intervention. It is limited, however, by assumptions about the geometry of the ventricular cavity, the difficulty of obtaining adequate echocardiographic resolution and visualization of the ventricular dimensions and posterior wall thickness in some individuals, and uncertainty about the constancy of the minor axis chord that is measured throughout the course of systole. Nevertheless, in patients in whom we have applied this technique, there has been a satisfactory correlation with similar data derived by measuring ventricular dimensions by cineangiography and pressure by a micro-manometer-angiographic catheter.

USE OF FORCE–VELOCITY–LENGTH RELATIONS IN VALVULAR HEART DISEASE

A commonly cited application of instantaneous force-velocity-length relations in humans is that of Gault et al. (3) in patients with free aortic regurgitation. In this study left ventricular contractile function was analyzed before and after aortic valve replacement for free aortic regurgitation, using data derived from cineventriculo-graphic measurements of chamber dimensions and wall thickness with simultaneous registration of left ventricular pressure. Although all the patients demonstrated an improved cardiac index, increased diastolic aortic pressure, and decreased end-diastolic pressure, four of the five manifested no improvement in instantaneous velocity of circumferential fiber shortening (V_{CF}) at maximum wall stress, and four of the five had abnormal values for peak V_{CF} preoperatively with no significant improvement in this parameter of myocardial contractile state postoperatively (Fig. 4). These data are perhaps most illustrative of the relative inadequacy of constructs that relate end-diastolic pressure to either cardiac output or stroke action as a sensitive and specific measure of myocardial function, and the relative superiority of direct assessment of wall forces, operating length, and velocity of shortening for characterizing the important factors that control myocardial shortening.

A further application of force-velocity-length analysis in clinical heart disease is the study reported by Eckberg et al. (2) in patients with chronic severe mitral regurgitation. Previous studies in experimental animals demonstrated that acute mitral regurgitation caused reduced impedance to left ventricular ejection associated with a marked reduction in intramyocardial wall tension, enhanced ventricular emptying, and increased myocardial fiber shortening. However, human subjects with chronic, severe mitral regurgitation showed a reduced velocity of shortening during ejection at maximum wall stress and reduced values for peak as well as mean velocity of circumferential fiber shortening. These depressed velocity indices were present despite increased resting fiber lengths and relatively normal levels of wall stress. In no case was a supernormal velocity of circumferential fiber shortening

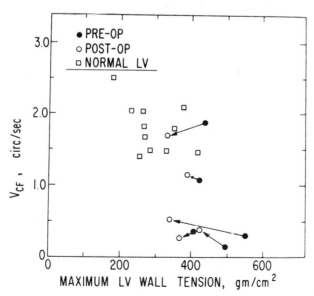

FIGURE 4 Velocity of circumferential fiber shortening at maximum wall tension plotted as a function of maximum wall tension before (●) and after (○) aortic valve replacement in five patients with free aortic regurgitation. The directional change in each case is indicated by the arrow. (□) Tension-velocity measurements in 11 normal subjects. From Gault et al. (3), by permission of the American Heart Association, Inc.

noted, which might be expected from the behavior of the left ventricle in the setting of acute experimental mitral regurgitation. Inspection of representative instantaneous force-velocity profiles throughout ejection for the patients with mitral regurgitation and for normal subjects demonstrates that in the former, ejection begins from an elevated end-diastolic tension, immediately after the onset of systole, and peak tension and peak velocity of circumferential fiber shortening occur nearly simultaneously, giving rise to a clockwise force-velocity loop (Fig. 5). Interestingly, the extent of shortening of the left ventricle in the 11 subjects remained normal, as evidenced by normal ejection fractions and a normal percentage of shortening across the chamber minor axis. It was again concluded from these studies that force-length-velocity analyses in mitral regurgitation uncovered depression of myocardial contractile state, which would not have been apparent from an analysis of left ventricular hemodynamic performance alone.

As a further example of the usefulness of instantaneous measurements of force, velocity, and length of the left ventricle, we recently studied 19 subjects with valvular aortic stenosis and compared the findings with those for 11 patients who were catheterized for atypical chest pain but found to have no evidence of left ventricular dysfunction or coronary artery disease. The questions addressed in this study were: 1) Can instantaneous force-velocity-length relations characterize more fully the status of myocardial function in the presence of concentric hypertrophy? 2) More specifically, when reduced myocardial shortening is encountered in the presence of valvular aortic stenosis, does this imply depression of myocardial contractility, or can abnormal loading conditions (i.e., brought about by inadequate hypertrophy) give rise to a state of excess wall stress and associated reduction of ventricular shortening? 3) Is there a process of reapportionment of

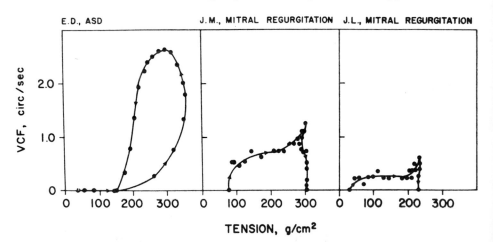

FIGURE 5 Representative plots of velocity of circumferential fiber shortening against wall stress on tension in a control subject and two patients with mitral regurgitation. In the control subject, contraction begins at a low end-diastolic tension and shortening begins after significant tension development. With mitral regurgitation, end-diastolic tension is increased and shortening begins immediately after the onset of contraction. Note also that peak V_{CF} is depressed and the loop is clockwise in the patients with mitral regurgitation. From Eckberg et al. (2), by permission of the American Heart Association, Inc.

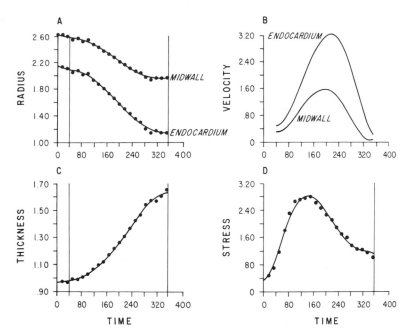

FIGURE 6 Analysis of instantaneous force-velocity-length relations in valvular aortic stenosis. Plotted as a function of time (milliseconds) are (A) radius (centimeters), (B) velocity of endocardial and mid-wall circumferential shortening (circumferences per second), (C) wall thickness (centimeters), and (D) wall stress (grams per square centimeter divided by 10). Data were obtained from normal subjects by simultaneous cine left ventriculography and micromanometer measurement of left ventricular pressure. All raw data were fit to a fifth-order polynomial function, using the least-squares technique.

mid-wall forces and shortening vectors, and what are the correlations between mid-wall measurements of equatorial shortening velocities and endocardial measurements of minor axis shortening, where both equatorial and radial (wall thickening) components of shortening are accounted for?

To obtain this information in patients with valvular aortic stenosis, the left ventricle was catheterized either with a Millar micromanometer-angiographic catheter or by placing two catheters into the left ventricle, one by the transseptal approach (for angiographic injection) and the other by the retrograde route (for micromanometer pressure recording). Wall stress at the mid-wall was calculated by using an equation for thick-walled structures; end-diastolic mass was determined by assuming uniform wall thickness of the reference ellipsoid of revolution and then, assuming a constant mass throughout systole, calculating the wall thickness appropriate to this mass and the instantaneous volume measurements. Endocardial radial shortening was computed from frame-by-frame measurements of ventricular volume, using the area-length method. Mid-wall radius change was obtained from the summation of the instantaneous endocardial radius determinations and half the computed wall thickness. Values for stress, wall thickness, endocardial radius, and mid-wall radius were then individually plotted against time through ejection, and the respective curves were fitted to a polynomial function by a least-squares iterative routine (Fig. 6).

In addition, mean wall stress and mean V_{CF} were obtained by integration of the stress-time and velocity-time curves, respectively. Peak isovolumic dP/dt was derived by digital differentiation of the pressure-time curve in order to obtain an independent index of myocardial contractile state that would be relatively free of the abnormal loading conditions imposed by aortic valve obstruction.

Several interesting observations emerged from this analysis of the instantaneous force-velocity-length relations for patients with valvular aortic stenosis. First, both peak and mean wall stress were generally elevated over the group of 11 normal subjects, suggesting that concentric hypertrophy was not a "perfect" adaptation and did not completely normalize left ventricular wall stress (Table 1). Analysis of the stress-time plots in aortic stenosis showed that not only was peak stress higher in the patients but also the dissipation of stress was delayed, and both served to elevate mean stress value throughout systole. Second, comparison of measurements of mid-wall and endocardial V_{CF} revealed a proportionately greater role of radial than of circumferential shortening in patients with aortic stenosis compared with normal subjects; thus, as shown in Fig. 7, a particular mean V_{CF} at the endocardium was correlated with a significantly lower mid-wall measurement, indicating that muscle thickening plays an important role in aortic stenosis in maintaining the extent of cavity shortening (ejection fraction) within the normal range. The data also suggest that in the equatorial direction at the mid-wall (where presumably there is an "average" myofibril) the rate and extent of myocardial shortening are depressed because of excessive circumferential wall stress. However, as shown by Gould et al. (6), the mid-wall equatorial power, defined as the product of stress and velocity of shortening, is not significantly changed, nor is the mean circumferential work obtained by integrating the equatorial power-time curve.

We also noted in our subjects with valvular aortic stenosis that those with clearly depressed values for the mean velocity of circumferential fiber shortening, measured at the mid-wall or the endocardium, also had values of peak dP/dt below 1483 mmHg/sec, while most patients with normal *endocardial* but abnormal *mid-wall* mean V_{CF} values had peak dP/dt above 1483 mmHg/sec (Fig. 8). Thus, the independent use of a simple isovolumetric phase contractile index that is not dependent on a particular muscle model helped to distinguish between depressed myocardial contractile state and changes in mid-wall mean V_{CF} values that are attributable to enhancement of equatorial stress.

TABLE 1 Comparison of endocardial and mid-wall velocity of circumferential fiber shortening, mid-wall stress, and myocardial mass in normal subjects and patients with aortic stenosis

	Normal ($n = 11$)	Aortic stenosis ($n = 19$)
Endocardial mean V_{CF} (circ/sec)[a]	1.75 ± 0.11	1.22 ± 0.12
Mid-wall mean V_{CF} (circ/sec)[a]	1.00 ± 0.05	0.63 ± 0.05
Mid-wall mean stress (g/cm²)	197 ± 15	282 ± 12
Mid-wall peak stress (g/cm²)	259 ± 18	371 ± 12
Left ventricular mass (g/m²)	64 ± 4	149 ± 16

[a]Given in circumferences per second.

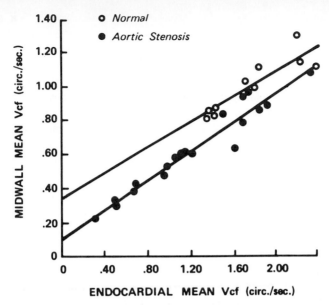

FIGURE 7 Plot of mid-wall and endocardial mean velocities of circumferential fiber shortening in normal subjects (○) and patients with valvular aortic stenosis and left ventricular hypertrophy (●). A straight line was fitted to the data points for each group by the least-squares method. Note that for any particular endocardial value for V_{CF}, the corresponding mid-wall value is less in patients with valvular aortic stenosis.

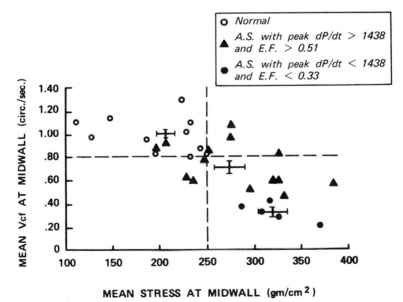

FIGURE 8 Mean V_{CF} at mid-wall plotted as a function of mean stress at mid-wall in normal subjects, patients with aortic stenosis who have an ejection fraction greater than 0.51 and peak dP/dt greater than 1438 mmHg/sec, and patients with aortic stenosis who have an ejection fraction less than 0.33 and peak dP/dt less than 1438 mmHg/sec. The mean ± SE is shown also for each group of patients. Analysis suggests that both myocardial failure (●) and excess equatorial stress (▲) are operative in depression of mid-wall circumferential velocity of shortening.

131

Thus, in the analysis of valvular aortic stenosis, instantaneous force-velocity-length relations served to characterize this pathophysiological state as one in which operating fiber lengths remain relatively normal, but equatorial and radial wall stress are both elevated and inadequately compensated for by myocardial hypertrophy. In addition, radial wall thickening plays a relatively more important role in maintaining overall chamber shortening within normal limits, since mid-wall or equatorial shortening is often depressed in the face of elevated mid-wall circumferential stress. Moreover, correlation of the mid-wall circumferential shortening rates with iso-volumetric dP/dt measurements serves to distinguish between patients who have depressed mid-wall shortening velocities because of elevated circumferential stress and/or myofibril realignment, and those who have a decrease in shortening velocity because of depression of myocardial contractile state.

REFERENCES

1. Covell, J. W., Fuhrer, J. S., Boerth, R. C., and Ross, J., Jr. Production of isotonic contractions in the intact canine left ventricle. J Appl Physiol 27:577–581, 1969.
2. Eckberg, D. L., Gault, J. H., Bouchard, R. L., Karliner, J. S., and Ross, J., Jr. Mechanics of left ventricular contraction in chronic severe mitral regurgitation. Circulation 47:1252–1259, 1973.
3. Gault, J. H., Covell, J. W., Braunwald, E., and Ross, J., Jr. Left ventricular performance following correction of free aortic regurgitation. Circulation 42:773–780, 1970.
4. Gault, J. H., Ross, J., Jr., and Braunwald, E. Contractile state of the left ventricle in man: Instantaneous tension-velocity-length relations in patients with and without disease of the left ventricular myocardium. Circ Res 22:451–463, 1968.
5. Glick, G., Sonnenblick, E. H., and Braunwald, E. Myocardial force-velocity relations studied in intact unanesthetized man. J Clin Invest 44:978–988, 1965.
6. Gould, L. K., Kennedy, J. W., Frimer, M., Pollack, G. H., and Dodge, H. T. Analysis of wall dynamics and directional components of left ventricular contraction in man. Am J Cardiol 38:322–331, 1976.
7. Greenfield, J. C. and Patel, D. J. Relation between pressure and diameter in the ascending aorta of man. Circ Res 10:778–781, 1962.
8. Hawthorne, E. W. Dynamic geometry of the left ventricle. Am J Cardiol 18:566–573, 1966.
9. Lewis, R. P. and Sandler, H. Relationship between changes in left ventricular dimensions and the ejection fraction in man. Circulation 44:548–557, 1971.
10. Peterson, K. L., Uther, J. B., Shabetai, R., and Braunwald, E. Assessment of left ventricular performance in man: Instantaneous tension-velocity-length relations obtained with the aid of an electromagnetic velocity catheter in the ascending aorta. Circulation 47:924–935, 1973.
11. Ross, J., Jr., Covell, J. W., Sonnenblick, E. H., and Braunwald, E. Contractile state of the heart characterized by force-velocity-length relations in variably afterloaded and isovolumic beats. Circ Res 18:149–163, 1966.

CHAPTER 10

POSTOPERATIVE EVALUATION
OF CARDIAC FUNCTION

NICHOLAS T. KOUCHOUKOS
LOUIS C. SHEPPARD

As new knowledge about the pathophysiological changes occurring in patients after cardiac surgical procedures has accumulated, particularly with regard to the cardiovascular subsystem, optimal management of such patients has become a complex and often a multidisciplinary endeavor. The abnormalities of cardiac function that occur postoperatively are related primarily to 1) the degree of cardiac dysfunction present preoperatively, 2) the duration and adequacy of extracorporeal circulatory support, 3) the extent of intraoperative myocardial injury, and 4) the completeness of repair of the specific cardiac or vascular abnormalities. Effective management of the patient in the postoperative period requires knowledge of these factors and of the usual effects of extracorporeal circulatory support on other organ systems, and aggressive management of abnormalities that are life-threatening or result in significant morbidity.

SIGNIFICANCE OF IMPAIRED CARDIAC
FUNCTION POSTOPERATIVELY

Mean values for cardiac output after intracardiac operations vary with the type of cardiac malformation, the operative procedure, and the age of the patient. Impaired cardiac performance following open intracardiac operations, manifested chiefly by low cardiac output, is associated with substantial mortality and morbidity in the early postoperative period (3, 5, 19). The consequences of low cardiac output in the presence of increased sympathetic activity have been documented by Dietzman et al. (5). In a series of 25 adult patients with cardiac indices less than 3.0 liter/min · m^2 in the early postoperative period, they noted a significant difference in survival between patients with cardiac indices between 2.0 and 3.0 liter/min · m^2 who had normal peripheral vascular resistance and adequate tissue perfusion, and those with indices less than 2.0 liter/min · m^2 who had evidence of increased sympathetic activity (increased peripheral vascular resistance, reduced tissue perfusion, and increased serum catecholamine levels). Even though cardiac output was slightly below normal in the former group of patients, it was adequate to meet the metabolic requirements of the various organ systems. In other studies, deaths from acute cardiac failure early postoperatively have occurred most commonly in patients with low cardiac output (3, 19). In adult patients after mitral valve replacement, a mean postoperative cardiac index of 1.5 liter/min · m^2 was associated with a 10% probability of hospital death (Fig. 1b) (3). In infants and small children, after a variety of cardiac operations, a mean postoperative cardiac index of less than 2.0 liter/min · m^2 was associated with a 10% probability of death

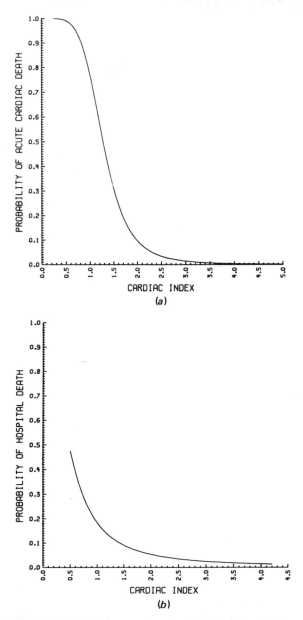

FIGURE 1　Probability of death from acute cardiac failure from the average cardiac index (liter/min · m^2). (a) Probability for 139 infants and children in the early postoperative period. From Parr et al. (19). (b) Probability for 125 patients following mitral valve replacement. From Appelbaum et al. (3).

from acute cardiac failure (Fig. 1*a*) (19). The probability of death rose steeply in both groups at indices below these levels.

In patients with low cardiac output and impaired left ventricular function, as evidenced by abnormally elevated mean left atrial and left ventricular end-diastolic pressures, the mortality and morbidity rates early postoperatively are also appreciably increased. Of 16 adult patients with cardiac indices less than 2.2 liter/min · m^2 and left atrial pressures greater than 15 mmHg, whom we evaluated at a time when low cardiac output was not systematically treated, 3 died within 24 hr of operation of irreversible ventricular fibrillation and another 2 died within 2 wk of operation of ventricular arrhythmias. Both of the latter patients had persistently low cardiac outputs. Two additional patients had episodes of ventricular fibrillation but survived. Among 14 patients evaluated simultaneously, who had mean left atrial pressures below 15 mmHg and higher cardiac outputs, there was only 1 postoperative death (11). Thus, impaired cardiac performance remains a major cause of mortality and moribidity after cardiac surgery and must be actively sought and aggressively treated if results of operation are to be optimal. In general, this implies direct measurement.

ROUTINE POSTOPERATIVE MEASUREMENTS

Certain parameters assessing the function of the cardiovascular system are measured routinely in the early postoperative period. Arterial pressure is obtained with an indwelling cannula, usually placed percutaneously in the radial artery. Heart rate and rhythm are determined from standard electrocardiographic leads. Left atrial and right atrial (central venous) pressures are determined from fine polyvinyl catheters placed at the time of operation. Alternatively, a flow-directed catheter may be passed into the pulmonary artery from a peripheral vein to measure central venous, pulmonary arterial, and capillary wedge pressures, and to estimate left ventricular filling pressure. Measurements of arterial and atrial pressures (in mmHg) are obtained at 5–15-min intervals in the first 24–28 hr after operation. In our experience, the use of indwelling arterial and cardiac catheters for this period of time has been associated with an extremely low incidence of complications, and they are used in all patients undergoing surgical procedures involving extracorporeal circulatory support.

The volume of drainage from pericardial, mediastinal, and pleural tubes, the amount of blood infused, and the output of urine from a urethral catheter are recorded at hourly intervals. Arterial blood-gas analyses are obtained as often as necessary to ensure optimal gas exchange and acid-base balance.

Cardiac output is usually determined by the indicator dilution technique, injecting indocyanine green dye into the left atrial catheter and sampling from the arterial catheter, or alternatively, injecting dye into the right atrial catheter and sampling from a catheter placed in the pulmonary artery at the time of operation. The latter system is preferred when the left-sided cardiac chambers are large or the cardiac output is low, in order to minimize distortion of the dilution curves and errors in the calculated value for cardiac output. In infants and small children, dye is injected into the right atrium and blood is withdrawn from the radial or brachial artery to allow adequate time for stabilization of the absorption spectrum. With the use of appropriate densitometers and portable or large computers, cardiac output and index are calculated. When the thermal dilution technique is employed, cold saline (4°C) is used as the indicator and is injected into the right atrium. The change in temperature of the blood in the pulmonary artery is measured with a thermistor-tipped catheter. This method has the advantage of allowing repeated determinations of cardiac output without the need for withdrawal of blood. Determination of stroke volume and cardiac output from the arterial pressure pulse contour, a method explored 20 yr ago by Starr (23), has not proved reliable enough in the postoperative period to supplant the techniques outlined above (16).

All the measurements discussed above can be automatically made and the data can be analyzed and displayed by using a digital computer, as shown in Table 1. Use of such an automated system has, in our experience, greatly facilitated the management of patients after cardiac surgical procedures (14). It provides data that can be retrieved more rapidly and are more accurate than those obtained by conventional manual techniques.

Arterial pressure has generally been thought to be a reliable indicator of cardiac function postoperatively. If arterial hypotension is present (systolic arterial pressure less than 70-80 mmHg) cardiac function is generally suboptimal. If the arterial pressure is normal or above normal, however, the cardiac output may be high, normal, or low (11). Central venous (right atrial) pressure is not consistently related to blood volume deficit, left ventricular filling pressure, cardiac output, or the response to blood replacement in the postoperative period. In our experience, a measurement (or estimate) of cardiac output, combined with a measurement of arterial pressure and mean left atrial pressure (which, in the absence of either stenosis or incompetence of the mitral valve, approximates left ventricular end-diastolic pressure), allows the most accurate assessment of cardiac function and the response to various therapeutic interventions.

TABLE 1 Oscilloscopic display of hemodynamic data from a three-second interval for two patients connected to an automated monitoring system[a]

Data	Patient 1	Patient 2
Time	1636	
Systolic pressure, mmHg	196	101
Diastolic pressure, mmHg	137	43
Heart rate, beats/min	95	136
Temperature, °C	34.9	37.1
Right atrial pressure, mmHg	9	14
Left atrial pressure, mmHg	12	12
Blood volume, ml	40	60
Chest drainage, ml[b]	193	96
Chest drainage, ml/hr[b]	134	0
Urine output, ml[b]	1051	0
Urine output, ml/hr[b]	920	0

[a]From Kouchoukos et al. (14).

[b]Chest drainage and urine output are expressed as total milliliters and milliliters for the previous clock hour.

ETIOLOGY, DIAGNOSIS, AND MANAGEMENT OF IMPAIRED CARDIAC FUNCTION IN THE POSTOPERATIVE PERIOD

Hypovolemia

Inadequate blood volume is a frequent cause of impaired cardiac performance early after operation. The magnitude of the blood volume deficit during this period depends on several factors, the most important being 1) the adequacy of volume replacement at the termination of the operative procedure, 2) the degree of vasoconstriction present, particularly in the venous capacitance vessels, and 3) the volume of blood lost as mediastinal drainage relative to the volume of blood replaced. In general, blood is infused from the pump-oxygenator at the termination of the perfusion to achieve a mean left atrial pressure of 14-18 mmHg in adults and 10-14 mmHg in infants and children. These levels of left atrial pressure result in optimal stretching of the sarcomeres (preload) and thus maximal stroke volume, but do not produce pulmonary congestion or edema. The left and right atrial pressures generally decrease to more normal levels later in the postoperative period. The ultimate values for right and left atrial pressures are determined primarily by the volume of blood in the systemic and pulmonary venous beds, the venous tone of these two systems, and the pressure-volume characteristics of the left- and right-sided cardiac chambers.

As noted previously, central venous (or right atrial) pressure is not consistently related to blood volume deficit or the response to blood replacement after operation. A measurement of mean left atrial pressure (or pulmonary wedge or diastolic pressure) is the most reliable guide to the adequacy of volume replacement during this period. Among adult patients with acquired heart disease, the effects of volume infusion on cardiac output early postoperatively are a function of the base line value for left ventricular filling pressure. Among 9 patients with normal (< 12 mmHg) mean left atrial pressures early postoperatively, we observed that infusion of blood to increase left atrial pressure by an average of 3.4 mmHg produced a statistically significant increase in cardiac index (2.52 to 2.93 liter/min $\cdot$ m^2) while heart rate remained constant. In 9 patients with mean left atrial pressures before blood infusion of greater than 12 mmHg (mean, 15.6 mmHg), comparable increases (mean, 4.1 mmHg) in left atrial pressure were produced, but cardiac index did not increase and the mean value actually decreased (2.58 to 2.41 liter/min $\cdot$ m^2) (13). Thus, if cardiac output is low and left atrial pressure is low or normal (< 12-14 mmHg), infusion of blood will generally increase cardiac output early post-operatively. If left atrial pressure is already elevated above this level, further augmentation of blood volume and filling pressure does not usually increase cardiac output. A study of left ventricular pressure-volume relations in patients with mitral valvular disease has shown that at filling pressures above 14 mmHg, minimal increases ($< 3\%$) in calculated left ventricular fiber length (preload) are produced, while at the same time marked increases in left ventricular wall tension result, particularly in dilated ventricles (20). With the automated system currently in use in our intensive care unit, blood or albumin can be automatically infused in 20-ml portions every 2 min to achieve a desired level for left atrial pressure, which is entered into the computer (14).

Cardiac Tamponade

Persistent bleeding into the pericardial cavity and mediastinum resulting in cardiac tamponade is a relatively uncommon but serious cause of impaired cardiac performance after operation. Bleeding of sufficient quantity to require reoperation occurs in approximately 2-3% of patients undergoing cardiac operations. Cardiac tamponade generally becomes apparent in the early postoperative period, but can be delayed in its presentation for up to several weeks after operation, particularly when anticoagulants are being administered.

The diagnosis of cardiac tamponade may at times be difficult to make with certainty. Significant drainage from the mediastinal tubes, combined with a trend toward equalization and gradual increase of the right and left atrial pressures, strongly suggests its presence. Subsequently, arterial hypotension and clinical evidence of low cardiac output may develop. A chest roentgenogram often demonstrates an increase in the mediastinal silhouette. Treatment consists of urgent operation to evacuate clot and identify and control the point or points of bleeding. If the bleeding is generalized, deficiencies of various clotting factors (platelets, factors V and VIII, and fibrinogen) must be sought by appropriate tests. Administration of fresh frozen plasma, fresh whole blood, and platelet and plasma concentrates is indicated when deficiencies of these substances are demonstrated.

Myocardial Dysfunction

Total cardiac performance can be significantly affected in the postoperative period by several mechanisms that impair myocardial function.

Preoperative Cardiac Dysfunction

Abnormalities of myocardial function may be present preoperatively in patients with both acquired and congenital heart disease, and these may persist or actually become more severe after operation. In our experience with patients after mitral, double, or triple valve replacement, the severity of the preoperative cardiac disability, as reflected by the functional class, clearly affects the hospital mortality rate (Table 2) (1, 25, 26).

Impairment of myocardial contractility has been demonstrated preoperatively in patients with aortic and mitral valvular disease (7, 8) and in patients with coronary atherosclerotic heart disease, particularly those with predominant symptoms of congestive failure (10). Higher operative and late mortality rates have been observed in the latter group of patients after myocardial revascularization than in patients with more normal ventricular function (10, 12).

Intraoperative Myocardial Injury

Myocardial injury can occur during cardiopulmonary bypass and, if severe, or if imposed on myocardium that is already abnormal (i.e., left ventricular hypertrophy, left ventricular fibrosis, coronary arterial occlusive disease), can be an important cause of imparied cardiac performance in the postoperative period. Ischemia,

TABLE 2 Hospital mortality after valve replacement according to preoperative functional class

Valve(s) replaced	Preoperative functional class[a]	No. of patients	Hospital deaths	
			No.	%
Mitral (1)	III	109	3	3
	IV	24	4	17
Aortic and mitral (26)	III	180	17	9
	IV	52	15	29
Aortic, mitral, and tricuspid (25)	III	28	5	18
	IV	10	4	40

[a]New York Heart Association classification.

hemorrhage, and necrosis of the myocardium, particularly of the inner layers of the left ventricular wall, have been observed in patients dying after cardiopulmonary bypass, many of whom had low cardiac output postoperatively. Studies of myocardial metabolism and measurements of specific enzymes to detect myocardial necrosis indicate that myocardial damage of varying severity occurs in many patients during or after operations in which cardiopulmonary bypass is employed (21).

The presence of markedly hypertrophic left ventricular myocardium may predispose to severe ischemic myocardial injury following cardiopulmonary bypass. A small, contracted left ventricle that does not eject effectively has been observed in patients of this type and has been termed the "stone heart" (4). This type of myocardial injury has been observed when normothermic cardioplegia or hypothermic coronary perfusion has been used as a method for myocardial preservation. The incidence of this complication has apparently been reduced after the use of hypothermic cardioplegia (31), suggesting that the adequacy of protection of the myocardium during cardiac surgical procedures plays an important role in the etiology of this complication.

Embolization of air to the coronary arteries can occur during operations in which the ascending aorta or left-sided heart chambers are opened, and can impair myocardial contractility. Embolization of aggregates of blood elements into the myocardial vasculature may also affect myocardial function. Injury to the coronary arteries during the operative procedure (i.e., by direct cannulation or by inadvertent injury to normally located or aberrant coronary arteries during repair of various congenital and acquired cardiac lesions) can produce myocardial infarction and severely impair cardiac performance.

Residual Cardiovascular Disease

The presence of residual cardiovascular abnormalities may also contribute to impaired myocardial function after operation. Examples include the presence of significant tricuspid valvular incompetence after mitral and aortic valve replacement, aortic valvular incompetence after mitral valve replacement, coronary arterial occlusive disease after valve replacement, and the persistence of significant pulmonary arterial hypertension after correction of left to right shunts. The inadequate repair of congenital or acquired lesions (i.e., incomplete relief of right ventricular outflow obstruction in tetralogy of Fallot, incomplete closure of ventricular septal defects, incomplete correction of valvular stenosis or incompetence, and perivalvular leaks) may also impair myocardial function postoperatively. Careful preoperative and intraoperative evaluation should allow detection and treatment of most myocardial and valvular lesions. When there is evidence for significant impairment of cardiac performance postoperatively, prompt reoperation should be considered in any patient in whom correctable residual lesions are present.

Impaired Myocardial Contractility

If evidence for impaired myocardial contractility is present after operation, the use of pharmacologic agents that have positive inotropic effects is indicated. Isoproterenol is an effective agent since it exerts a chronotropic as well as an inotropic action on the myocardium, and cardiac output can be augmented by both these mechanisms. In addition, it can produce peripheral vasodilation, which may be beneficial if there is significant vasoconstriction. Tachycardia and ventricular arrhythmias often occur with infusion of this drug, however, and not infrequently limit its use. Although isoproterenol can produce an increase in cardiac output postoperatively, myocardial oxygen demand is also increased and anaerobic myocardial metabolism may result (17).

Epinephrine is also a useful agent, particularly when arterial hypotension is present. If infused in sufficient amounts, it will increase myocardial contractility and peripheral vascular resistance, and thus increase cardiac output and arterial pressure. In smaller doses, it may actually result in a fall in peripheral vascular resistance because of the beta adrenergic effect on blood vessels (6). Dopamine, a naturally occurring catecholamine with inotropic and chronotropic effects on myocardium, has been shown to be effective in the management of some patients after cardiac operations (9, 24). It has a smaller chronotropic effect than isoproterenol in postoperative patients and may be preferable because of this. Use of *l*-norepinephrine or metaraminol is indicated only when marked arterial hypotension is present. The latter drugs produce marked vasoconstriction and may significantly impair organ system function.

Digitalis preparations may be used postoperatively to improve myocardial contractility and treat specific arrhythmias (see below). Rapidly acting preparations (digoxin, deslanoside, ouabain) should be administered postoperatively when there is evidence of impaired myocardial function and there are no contraindications to their use. These agents are often used in conjunction with catecholamine infusions. As a therapeutic level of digitalis is obtained, the catecholamine drugs may be tapered off and discontinued. Digitalis preparations should be administered cautiously, taking into account the status of digitalization preoperatively, as well as the presence of hypokalemia and alkalosis, which may increase the sensitivity of the patient to usual maintenance doses. We routinely discontinue digitalis preparations 24–48 hr before operation to minimize the occurrence of intraoperative and postoperative arrhythmias.

Although the use of propranolol preoperatively in patients with coronary arterial occlusive disease has been reported to result in severe impairment of cardiac function postoperatively (28), withdrawal of the drug, particularly in patients receiving large doses, can result in acute myocardial infarction (18). Since the effects of propranolol can be counteracted by isoproterenol, calcium, and digitalis, we prefer not to discontinue the drug before operation in patients with severe angina pectoris and continue to give up to 120-160 mg/d until the evening before operation.

Impedance to Left Ventricular Ejection

Increased impedance to left ventricular ejection that results in an increase in systolic wall tension (afterload) has been shown to reduce stroke volume and left ventricular stroke work in patients with diseased myocardium. In postoperative adult patients with elevated mean arterial pressure, high peripheral vascular resistance, and low cardiac output, improvement in cardiac output has been achieved by the reduction of arterial and left atrial pressure. In a group of 8 patients with mean arterial pressure greater than 100 mmHg and evidence of impaired cardiac performance (cardiac index less than 2.1 liter/min $\cdot$ m^2) and mean left atrial pressure greater than 15 mmHg, infusion of Arfonad (trimethaphan camsylate), a ganglionic blocking and vasodilating agent, produced significant increases in stroke index and cardiac output, which averaged 18 and 15%, respectively. A comparable reduction of arterial pressure in patients with higher cardiac indices and lower left atrial pressures, suggesting more normal left ventricular function, resulted in a decrease in stroke volume, presumably as the result of a decrease in left ventricular filling pressure (preload) (15). We and others (27) observed similar hemodynamic changes when sodium nitroprusside, a potent vasodilator, was used in adult patients with impaired cardiac function. More recently, we evaluated sodium nitroprusside in infants with low cardiac output and relative hypertension after intracardiac surgery. When the mean arterial pressure was reduced to normal levels by infusion of the drug, a significant increase in cardiac output and a reduction in the markedly elevated peripheral vascular resistance were observed in all the patients studied (2). Although other pharmacological agents such as phentolamine and phenoxybenzamine produce similar hemodynamic effects, we prefer trimethapan or sodium nitroprusside because of the rapid onset and short duration of their action and because of the minimal side effects produced. The infusion rates of these agents can be adjusted relatively easily to achieve the desired reduction in arterial pressure. We are currently evaluating a computer-controlled system for regulation of mean arterial pressure by automatic infusion of these drugs (22), and have employed it in more than 500 patients in the early postoperative period.

Use of vasodilating agents to reduce arterial pressure and impedance to left ventricular ejection should be considered in all postoperative patients with low cardiac index and with elevated left atrial pressure, mean aortic pressure, and peripheral vascular resistance. Reduction of arterial pressure under these circumstances allows more effective emptying of the left ventricle and may, with a reduction of left ventricular end-diastolic pressure, reduce left ventricular wall stress and allow more efficient perfusion of the subendocardial region of the left ventricle. Reducing left ventricular systolic pressure will also reduce myocardial oxygen consumption. If the cardiac output remains low and the filling pressure high after the administration of these vasodilating agents, the addition of an inotropic agent, such as epinephrine, dopamine, or isoproterenol, may be effective in increasing cardiac output.

Intra-Aortic Balloon Counterpulsation

Assistance of the failing circulation with the intra-aortic balloon counterpulsation device has been employed in patients in whom cardiopulmonary bypass cannot be discontinued without hemodynamic deterioration or in patients who deteriorate later in the postoperative period. Intra-aortic balloon counterpulsation reduces left ventricular work and oxygen consumption and may improve myocardial perfusion. The device has been used primarily in patients with severe coronary artery disease and evidence for severely impaired left ventricular function. It has also been applied in a smaller number of patients after other cardiac surgical procedures such as single or multiple valve replacement. The indications for its use are not completely defined, but in general it is employed when there is evidence of deterioration of the hemodynamic state (mean aortic pressure less than 80–90 mmHg, mean left atrial or left ventricular end-diastolic pressure greater than 25 mmHg, and low cardiac output). The patients have usually received maximal pharmacologic support. In patients of this type, hospital mortality has been approximately 50%, and 40% of patients are long-term survivors. While these results are not optimal, it must be recognized that the majority of these patients would have died without the period of circulatory support. The encouraging results being accumulated at several centers may result in expanded use of the device postoperatively, possibly as a substitute for catecholamine support, which may have detrimental effects, particularly in patients with ischemic myocardium.

Acid-Base and Electrolyte Abnormalities

Metabolic acidosis occurs infrequently after extracorporeal circulatory support with the currently used pump-oxygenator systems and priming techniques. When metabolic acidosis is present postoperatively, it may reflect inadequate perfusion during bypass, particularly if the period of bypass was prolonged. More commonly, it results from low cardiac output and poor tissue perfusion. Since metabolic acidosis may adversely affect myocardial function it should be treated vigorously, and improvement in cardiac output is obviously an important aspect of therapy. Arterial hypoxemia, if present, should also be corrected to ensure adequate oxygen delivery to the tissues.

Alkalosis is present postoperatively more often than acidosis. Metabolic alkalosis may result from the citrate ion present in ACD blood and is often compounded by the respiratory alkalosis that occurs in patients who are receiving assisted ventilation. Patients who require ventilatory support should have careful control of the ventilator to avoid severe respiratory alkalosis (arterial PCO_2 less than 30 mmHg and arterial pH above 7.60). Alkalosis above this level may impair myocardial contractility.

Low serum potassium concentrations are frequently present after procedures in which cardiopulmonary bypass is used, and they may result in arrhythmias that can significantly impair cardiac performance. Preoperative diuretic therapy may deplete total body potassium, and potassium ion should be administered preoperatively in patients who have been on long-term diuretic therapy, if the serum potassium concentration is low. The diuresis that occurs after cardiopulmonary bypass, particularly when hemodilution has been employed, promotes the urinary excretion of potassium. Respiratory alkalosis resulting from mechanical ventilation reduces the serum potassium concentration, which may be reduced further by the increase in urinary potassium excretion. To minimize these potassium losses, diuretic therapy should be discontinued several days before operation, if possible. In addition, potassium chloride should be administered postoperatively when potassium levels are below 3.5 meq/liter, to minimize the occurrence of arrhythmias.

Calcium ion may exert a positive inotropic effect on myocardium. If serum calcium levels are low in the presence of a low cardiac output, calcium should be administered. This is of particular importance when large amounts of citrated blood are infused, since serum calcium may be inactivated by the citrate.

Abnormalities of Rate and Rhythm

Arrhythmias occur commonly after cardiac surgical procedures and, although generally transient and well tolerated, may occasionally impair cardiac performance. This is particularly true if other mechanisms are also contributing to impaired cardiac function. Factors that predispose to the development of arrhythmias after cardiac procedures include electrolyte imbalance (particularly low serum potassium), metabolic acidosis, hypoxemia, digitalis excess, surgical trauma, and preexisting cardiac disease. If any or all of these abnormalities are present early postoperatively, they should be corrected promptly when possible.

Placement of epicardial wires at the time of operation allows for accurate diagnosis of arrhythmias after operation and for therapy by pacing. These wires should be placed on the right atrium and the left or right ventricle, preferably in pairs 0.5-1.0 cm apart so that accurate recordings can be made from them and low-current stimulation can be used if necessary (30).

Arrhythmias affect cardiac performance chiefly by their effect on heart rate. Arrhythmias associated with bradycardia often result in a decrease in cardiac output even though there may be an initial compensatory increase in stroke volume. Ventricular extrasystoles may also occur at slow ventricular rates and further impair cardiac function. Arrhythmias resulting in tachycardia (more than 120-140 beats per minute) decrease cardiac output by impairing diastolic filling, which results in a reduction in stroke volume. This may be an important factor after valve replacement, since the function of some prosthetic valves is adversely affected at rapid heart rates. Perfusion of the myocardium, particularly the subendocardial layers, may also be impaired by tachycardia because of the reduction of coronary blood flow during diastole.

Supraventricular Arrhythmias

Sinus Tachycardia

This arrhythmia occurs frequently after cardiac surgical procedures and is generally transient. If myocardial function is normal and the rate is not excessive, it is usually well tolerated. Occasionally, the rate may be excessively rapid (more than 150–160 beats per minute), and under these circumstances therapy may be required to improve cardiac function. Obvious causes for tachycardia (hypovolemia, fever, pericardial tamponade) must be sought and appropriately treated. Neostigmine (Prostigmin) in small doses (0.5–1.0 mg) may be successful in slowing the rate. Digitalis is also effective, particularly if the tachycardia originates from an ectopic focus, since it should slow the rate of the ectopic pacemaker and prolong atrioventricular conduction, thus slowing the ventricular rate.

Paroxysmal Atrial Tachycardia

This can often be interrupted by maneuvers that increase vagal tone (carotid massage, infusion of neostigmine, or elevation of systolic blood pressure with vasopressor agents). Atrial pacing that is faster than the spontaneous rate of paroxysmal atrial tachycardia can capture the atria and interrupt the arrhythmia.

Atrial Flutter and Fibrillation

Atrial flutter generally results in an atrial rate of 280–320 beats per minute, and the ventricular response is most often a fixed ratio of the atrial rate (i.e., 2:1 or 4:1). Pacing the atrium at a faster rate is occasionally successful in interrupting this arrhythmia and restoring sinus rhythm. More often, the flutter can be converted to atrial fibrillation by overdrive pacing (29). If the resulting ventricular rate is high, it can be lowered with digitalis. If the ventricular rate with atrial fibrillation is low, it can best be controlled by ventricular pacing, particularly in the presence of ventricular extrasystoles. In addition to suppressing the ectopic beats, pacing under these conditions may improve cardiac output.

Junctional Arrhythmias

If a junctional tachycardia is present, digitalis is contraindicated since it may further enhance the automaticity of the junctional pacemaker. Intravenous lidocaine is the drug of choice under these circumstances, since it suppresses the automaticity of the junctional pacemaker without significantly affecting myocardial contractility or atrioventricular conduction. If the tachycardia is significantly impairing cardiac function with resulting hypotension, paired ventricular pacing to halve the rate may occasionally be effective. Junctional arrhythmias resulting in bradycardia can usually be managed by atrial or ventricular pacing, which often increases cardiac output.

Ventricular Arrhythmias

Ventricular extrasystoles may be treated by pacing the ventricles at a slightly higher rate than the intrinsic ventricular rate, either atrially or ventricularly, to suppress the ectopic foci. When this is not successful or the ventricular rate is already high, use of lidocaine or procainamide is generally effective.

Ventricular tachycardia can occasionally be treated by pacing, but generally cardioversion combined with appropriate drug therapy (lidocaine or procainamide) is necessary. If hypokalemia is present, it should be treated with intravenous potassium chloride.

Atrioventricular Dissociation

Spontaneous or surgically induced atrioventricular dissociation is often transient, but it should be treated by ventricular pacing if the ventricular rate is low. A normally conducted rhythm usually ensues, although occasionally permanent pacing is required. If serious atrioventricular conduction abnormalities are present preoperatively or occur intraoperatively, we place permanent as well as temporary epicardial electrodes on the right or left ventricles at the time of operation. The permanent electrodes are implanted in the subcutaneous layer of the anterior abdominal wall. If conduction disturbances persist in these patients early postoperatively, they are managed by the temporary wires. If the use of a permanent pacer becomes necessary, a pulse generator can be connected to the implanted electrodes as a secondary procedure.

SYSTEMATIC DETECTION AND TREATMENT OF IMPAIRED CARDIAC PERFORMANCE

On the basis of the information summarized above, we employ in our cardiac surgical intensive-care unit a systematic approach to the detection and treatment of impaired cardiac performance. As noted previously, appropriate selection of patients for operation and precise and proper conduct of the operative procedure are the most important factors in preventing or minimizing the occurrence of impaired cardiac function postoperatively.

Clinical evidence for low cardiac output may be present in some patients. If the usual clinical signs are not present, however, one may have a high index of suspicion that cardiac output is low if arterial hypotension, high left atrial pressure, poor peripheral perfusion, and metabolic acidosis are present. If low cardiac output is present preoperatively, the likelihood that it will be present postoperatively is high. Provisions should be made to measure cardiac output postoperatively in all these types of patients. Correctable factors contributing to low cardiac output, such as residual cardiac defects, excessive bleeding with cardiac tamponade, and acid-base and electrolyte abnormalities, should be systematically sought and treated. If the heart rate is less than 80-90 beats per minute, cardiac output may be augmented by increasing the rate to 90-110 per minute with appropriate atrial or ventricular pacing. If the heart rate is rapid (more than 130-140 beats per minute), the type of tachycardia should be accurately identified and treated.

Once these abnormalities have been identified and the appropriate measures taken to correct them, cardiac output is remeasured; if it is still low, interventions to improve myocardial performance directly are indicated (Table 3). As noted above, cardiac output, mean aortic pressure, and left atrial pressure are the most useful parameters for assessing cardiac function during this period.

TABLE 3   Logic for analysis and treatment of impaired cardiac function early after operation

Mean left atrial pressure (mmHg)	Mean arterial pressure (mmHg)	Cardiac index (liter/min · m²)		
		< 2.0	2.0–3.0	> 3.0
≤ 7		Blood[a]	Blood[a]	Blood[a]
7–14		Blood[a]	Blood[a]	–
15–18	< 100	Epinephrine	–	–
	> 100	Epinephrine, dopamine[b], or Isuprel[b]	Trimethaphan or nitroprusside[c]	–
> 18	< 100	Epinephrine, dopamine[b], or Isuprel[b]	–	–
	> 100	Epinephrine, dopamine[b], or Isuprel[b] plus trimethaphan or nitroprusside	Trimethaphan or nitroprusside[c]	–

[a]Use albumin if the hemoglobin concentration is > 16 g%.

[b]If frequent premature contractions are present or heart rate is above 120 beats per minute, use epinephrine.

[c]Optional in this category.

Cardiac Index Less Than 2.0 Liters per Minute per Square Meter

As noted previously, a cardiac index of less than 2.0 liter/min · m² early postoperatively is associated with high morbidity and mortality. If the cardiac index is below this level and the mean left atrial pressure is 14 mmHg or less, fluid should be infused to augment left ventricular filling pressure and volume and to increase cardiac output. If the hemoglobin level is greater than 12 g per 100 ml, we employ albumin rather than whole blood. Volume is administered under these circumstances regardless of the level of mean arterial pressure. Occasionally, if the arterial pressure is high with evidence of significant peripheral vasoconstriction, trimethaphan or sodium nitroprusside may be administered concomitantly to reduce arterial pressure, particularly if bleeding is excessive. This may depress cardiac output further, however, and additional volume infusion may be required.

If the mean left atrial pressure is between 15 and 18 mmHg and the mean arterial pressure is less than 100 mmHg, epinephrine is administered. If the mean arterial pressure is greater than 100 mmHg, dopamine or isoproterenol may be used unless the heart rate is greater than 120 beats per minute or if there is ventricular irritability, in which case epinephrine is used. If the mean left atrial pressure is greater than 18 mmHg and the arterial pressure is less than 100 mmHg, epinephrine, dopamine, or isoproterenol should be infused. If the mean arterial pressure is greater than 100 mmHg, trimethaphan or nitroprusside is infused to reduce arterial pressure and left ventricular afterload. Epinephrine, dopamine, or isoproterenol is infused concomitantly to improve myocardial contractility. Cardiac index should be measured at intervals while these interventions are employed to assess the response to therapy. An example of the use of this logic is shown in Fig. 2. If cardiac performance does not improve or further deteriorates after this treatment program, intra-aortic balloon pumping should be considered.

Cardiac Index Between 2.0 and 3.0 Liters per Minute per Square Meter

If the mean left atrial pressure is less than 14 mmHg, blood or albumin should be infused to achieve an optimal ventricular filling pressure (12–14 mmHg). Other interventions are generally not necessary unless the mean arterial pressure is above 100 mmHg and the left atrial pressure above 15 mmHg. Under these conditions, trimethaphan or nitroprusside may be infused to reduce arterial pressure and ventricular afterload.

Cardiac Index Over 3.0 Liters per Minute per Square Meter

Under these conditions, no therapy is indicated except that blood can be infused if left atrial pressure is less than 7 mmHg. This again ensures optimal left ventricular filling pressure.

Although it has not always been successful, the logic described above has resulted in a more precise analysis of impaired cardiac performance after cardiac

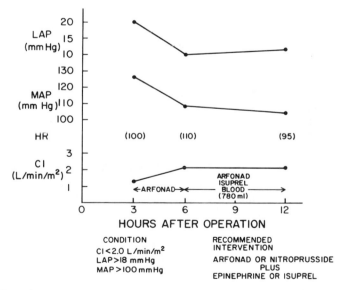

FIGURE 2 Hemodynamic data in a patient following coronary artery bypass grafting. Initial cardiac index (CI) was 1.3 liter/min · m²; mean left atrial pressure (LAP), 22 mmHg; and mean arterial pressure (MAP), 128 mmHg. Recommended interventions are infusion of an impedance-reducing agent and an inotropic agent. After the infusion of Arfonad, LAP decreased to 10 mmHg, MAP decreased to 108 mmHg, and CI increased to 2.3 liter/min · m². With the addition of Isuprel and infusion of blood (LAP fell below the limit of 14 mmHg), LAP rose slightly, MAP remained below 110 mmHg and CI remained above 2.2 liter/min · m².

surgical procedures than previous methods, and has provided a systematic plan of treatment that alters left ventricular filling pressure (preload), impedance to ejection (afterload), and contractility. This logic is based primarily on data accumulated in adult patients, although information on cardiac performance in infants and children has recently become available (2, 19). By using the automated system for infusion of volume, and when techniques for automatic infusion of vasodilating and inotropic agents and for the detection and treatment of arrhythmias are perfected, it should be possible to set and automatically maintain appropriate levels of left atrial pressure (preload), mean arterial pressure (afterload), heart rate, and contractility, thereby achieving optimal cardiac performance.

REFERENCES

1. Allen, W. B., Karp, R. B., and Kouchoukos, N. T. Mitral valve replacement: Starr-Edwards cloth-covered composite-seat prosthesis. Arch Surg 109:642–647, 1974.

2. Appelbaum, A., Blackstone, E., Kouchoukos, N. T., and Kirklin, J. W. Afterload reduction and cardiac output in infants early after intracardiac surgery. Am J Cardiol 39:445–451, 1977.

3. Appelbaum, A., Kouchoukos, N. T., Blackstone, E. H., and Kirklin, J. W. Early risks of open heart surgery for mitral valve disease. Am J Cardiol 37:201–209, 1976.

4. Cooley, D. A., Reul, G. J., and Wukasch, D. C. Ischemic contraction of the heart: "Stone heart." Am J Cardiol 29:575–577, 1972.

5. Dietzman, R. H., Ersek, R. A., Lillehei, C. W., Castaneda, A. R., and Lillehei, R. A. Low output syndrome: Recognition and treatment. J Thorac Cardiovasc Surg 57:138–150, 1969.

6. Fordham, R. M. M. and Resnekov, L. Comparison of hemodynamic effects of intravenous isoprenaline and adrenaline after aortic valvular homograft replacement. Br Heart J 32:393–398, 1970.

7. Gault, J. H., Covell, J. W., Braunwald, E., and Ross, J., Jr. Left ventricular performance following correction of free aortic regurgitation. Circulation 42:773–780, 1970.

8. Hildner, F. J., Javier, R. P., Cohen, L. A., Samet, P., Nathan, M. J., Yahr, W. Z., and Greenberg, J. J. Myocardial dysfunction associated with valvular heart disease. Am J Cardiol 30:319–326, 1972.

9. Holloway, E. L., Stinson, E. B., Derby, G. C., and Harrison, D. C. Action of drugs in patients early after cardiac surgery. I. Comparison of isoproterenol and dopamine. Am J Cardiol 35:656–659, 1975.

10. Kouchoukos, N. T., Doty, D. B., Buettner, L. E., and Kirklin, J. W. Treatment of postinfarction cardiac failure by myocardial excision and revascularization. Circulation 45:72–78, 1972.

11. Kouchoukos, N. T. and Karp, R. B. Management of the postoperative cardiovascular surgical patient. Am Heart J 92:513–531, 1976.

12. Kouchoukos, N. T., Kirklin, J. W., and Oberman, A. An appraisal of coronary bypass grafting. Sixth Annual George C. Griffith Lecture. Circulation 50:11–16, 1974.

13. Kouchoukos, N. T., Kirklin, J. W., Sheppard, L. C., and Roe, P. Effect of elevation of left atrial pressure by blood infusion on stroke volume early after cardiac operations. Surg Forum 22:126–127, 1971.

14. Kouchoukos, N. T., Sheppard, L. C., and Kirklin, J. W. Automated patient care following cardiac surgery. In: Cardiovascular Clinics, A.N. Brest ed. Philadelphia: Davis, 1971, vol. 3, no. 3, pp. 109–120.

15. Kouchoukos, N. T., Sheppard, L. C., and Kirklin, J. W. Effect of alterations in arterial pressure on cardiac performance early after open intracardiac operations. J Thorac Cardiovasc Surg 64:563–572, 1972.

16. Kouchoukos, N. T., Sheppard, L. C., McDonald, D. A., and Kirklin, J. W. Estimation of stroke volume from the central arterial pressure contour in postoperative patients. Surg Forum 20:180–182, 1969.

17. Mueller, H., Gianelli, S., Jr., Ayres, S. M., Conklin, E. F., and Gregory, J. J. Effect of isoproterenol on ventricular work and myocardial metabolism in the postoperative heart. Circulation 37:146–153, 1968.

18. Olson, H. G., Miller, R. R., Amsterdam, E. A., Wood, M., Brocchini, R., and Mason, D. T. The propranolol withdrawal rebound phenomenon: Acute and catastrophic exacerbation of symptoms and death following the abrupt cessation of large doses of propranolol in coronary artery disease. Am J Cardiol 35:162, 1975.

19. Parr, G. V. S., Blackstone, E. H., and Kirklin, J. W. Cardiac performance and mortality early after intracardiac surgery in infants and young children. Circulation 51:867–874, 1975.

20. Riley, S. M., Jr., Blackstone, E. H., and Kouchoukos, N. T. Left ventricular diastolic pressure-volume relations in patients with mitral valvular disease. Surg Forum 26:220–222, 1975.

21. Sapsford, R. N., Blackstone, E. H., Kirklin, J. W., Karp, R. B. Kouchoukos, N. T., Pacifico, A. D., Roe, C. R., and Bradley, E. L. Coronary perfusion versus cold ischemic arrest during aortic valve surgery. Circulation 49:1190–1199, 1974.

22. Sheppard, L. C., Kouchoukos, N. T., Shotts, J. F., and Wallace, F. D. Regulation of mean arterial pressure by computer control of vasoactive agents in postoperative patients. In: Computers in Cardiology, IEEE 75 CH 1018-1C, Rotterdam, October 1975, pp. 91–94.

23. Starr, I. and Schild, A. Studies made by stimulating systole at necropsy. IX. A test of the aortic compression chamber hypothesis and of two stroke volume methods based upon it. J Appl Physiol 11:169–180, 1957.

24. Stephenson, L. W., Blackstone, E. H., and Kouchoukos, N. T. Dopamine vs. epinephrine in patients following cardiac surgery: Randomized study. Surg Forum 27:272–275, 1976.

25. Stephenson, L. W., Kouchoukos, N. T., and Kirklin, J. W. Triple-valve replacement: An analysis of eight years' experience. Ann Thorac Surg 23:327–332, 1977.

26. Stephenson, L. W., Kouchoukos, N. T., Kirklin, J. W., Karp, R. B., and Pacifico, A. D. Combined aortic and mitral valve replacement: Results in 251 patients. Circulation 51:II-31, 1975.

27. Stinson, E. B., Holloway, E. L., Derby, G., Oyer, P. E., Hollingsworth, J., Griepp, R. B., and Harrison, D. C. Comparative hemodynamic responses to chlorpromazine, nitroprusside, nitroglycerin and trimethaphan immediately after open heart operations. Circulation 52:26–33, 1975.

28. Viljoen, J. F., Estafanous, F. G., and Kellner, G. A. Propranolol and cardiac surgery. J Thorac Cardiovasc Surg 64:826–830, 1972.

29. Waldo, A. L., MacLean, W. A. H., Karp, R. B., Kouchoukos, N. T., and James,

T. N. Sustained rapid atrial pacing to control supraventricular tachycardias following open-heart surgery. Circulation 51:II-13, 1975.

30. Waldo, A. L., Ross, S. M., and Kaiser, G. A. The epicardial electrogram in the diagnosis of cardiac arrhythmias following cardiac surgery. Geriatrics 26:108-112, 1971.

31. Wukasch, D. C., Reul, G. L., Milam, J. D., Hallman, G. L., and Colley, D. A. The "stone heart" syndrome. Surgery 72:1071-1080, 1972.

PART III

INDIRECT (NONINVASIVE) ASSESSMENT OF CARDIAC PERFORMANCE

CHAPTER 11

BALLISTOCARDIOGRAPHY

ISAAC STARR

If one keeps one's sense of humor no harm is likely to come from a symposium such as this one, and some good may. Thus, the occasion gives me an opportunity to thank all those who have helped me during a lifetime of experimental research; they are far too numerous to mention by name. I must also thank the University of Pennsylvania for permitting me to continue working for an unconscionably long time after attaining the statutory age of retirement, and perhaps I can add something to quiet the criticism of such an unorthodox proceeding by passing around a folder that contains reprints of the 42 papers I have published after reaching retirement age. President Carter has now come out on the side of the elderly, so let me support his endeavors by giving you a brief account of my scientific stewardship.

HISTORY

My interest in the physiological way of looking at things had been initiated by a teacher at Princeton, Dr. E. Newton Harvey, and I encountered the physiological viewpoint again at Woods Hole, where I spent the three summers of my medical school years. Also, stimulated by the bumbling and ineffectual efforts of the good kind family doctor in handling ill health in my family, I developed an interest in therapeutics that was later stimulated by Dr. A. N. Richards, who put me to work assessing the effect of drugs on the hearts of my patients by measuring cardiac output.

I worked in this field for about 8 yr, investigating the action of the commonly used drugs on the cardiac outputs of my patients. To interpret such data I needed a method of testing for the significance of differences and found it in Fisher's book (2); so I was one of the first, if not the first, to apply modern statistical techniques to clinical problems (9). The drugs worked just about as one would have expected from animal experiments, and no exciting information was gained. So I began to think of my cardiac output studies as very laborious and not very rewarding.

While in this state of mind, I was invited to take part in a cardiac output symposium organized by the circulation section of the American Physiological Society, of which I was a founding member; others on the program were Dr. Arthur Grollman and Professor Yandell Henderson of Yale; the latter talked of experiments he had done 20 yr before. Henderson had noticed that when he stood on a spring scale to weigh himself, the pointer moved in time to his heart; he made records of that movement with a kimograph and smoked drum. After exercise the record became larger, so he believed its amplitude to be related to cardiac output (11).

Apparently Henderson died without the knowledge that he had not been the first in the field. Twenty-eight years before Henderson's study, a young Scot named J. W. Gordon, at that time about 24 yr old, had also stood on a spring scale, and he had also seen the pointer move in time to his heartbeats (11). He made records and described his results before an English scientific society. The presentation was discussed by Couts-Trotter of Trinity college, a name that meant nothing to me until, reading the curriculum vitae of the late Sir Henry Dale, I found that Dale had once held the Couts-Trotter Fellowship at Cambridge; Couts-Trotter must have been a considerable person to have had a fellowship named after him. When discussing Gordon's paper, about 100 yr ago, he remarked that the explanation of the phenomenon should be sought in the movement of the body's center of gravity, and he was 100% right (11).

As I listened to Henderson over 50 yr later I realized at once that by using a light beam and a photokimograph, methods developed since Henderson's experiments had been performed, apparatuses could now be built that would give a much more accurate account of the body's movement. So my first ballistocardiograph was conceived.

MODELS

Seeking to test such methods, I made models of the simple physical aspects of the circulation with a pump, valves, elastic tubing, and resistances arranged to mimic the anatomy and physiology of the human circulation (11). Such models give records of the pulse and ballistocardiogram (BCG) that closely resemble those secured in normal men and women. Many students of the subject have set up models of this type, but doubt of my ability to mimic the physiological effects of arteriosclerosis in such a model led me to work on fresh cadavers, where "real" arteriosclerosis was to be found.

In charge of a medical ward for many months each year, I was in an ideal position to get autopsy permission soon after death and to begin experimenting soon afterward. After I had received such permission, the pulmonary artery and aorta were cannulated and attached to syringes (11), and the movement of their pistons was recorded.

After filling the syringes and arteries with blood, blood was perfused into the femoral artery until the desired diastolic pressure was reached; inflow was then stopped and aortic pressure declined, as it does in diastole during life. During this decline, systole was simulated by releasing the mallet, which struck a blow of known energy, or by pushing in the syringe pistons by hand. The cardiac output was recorded at each instant of ejection, as far as I know for the first time; therefore one could readily differentiate the record to get velocity at each instant and calculate work instant by instant, the way Newton would have us do. Besides the record of flow, we recorded central and peripheral blood pressures at each instant and also the force BCG. The relations of these records to one another were compared in statistical studies (11).

I had started with the expectation that all I had to do to simulate normal cardiac action was to push a normal amount of blood into the aorta and pulmonary artery in a normal ejection time. When I simulated systole by a push from my arm this requirement was easily met, but the left ventricular ejection velocity curve looked like the dashed line of Fig. 1 and both BCG and pulse wave contours were abnormal. To make such records normal in form I needed to increase the initial acceleration of the injected blood, and to accomplish this came close to requiring more strength than my arm possessed. Evidently, to accelerate the blood normally, a strong cardiac contraction is required.

With a series of results like these before me I could now ask, If our vision is limited to the observations that can be easily made in patients during life, how can one distinguish the strong from the weak contraction? One cannot distinguish this by the cardiac output, for this, represented by the area under the two velocity curves, is the same in strong and weak systoles, nor by maximum ejection velocity, for the altitudes of the two velocity curves are the same in both. It is the differences in initial slopes of the velocity curves that distinguish the strong from the weak systoles; in other words, differences in the forces. One must conclude that cardiac output will be worthless for the detection of early cardiac weakness, and I lost my interest in it.

NEWTONIAN CONSIDERATIONS

When I went to talk about these unexpected results with my friends who were physicists or engineers, they laughed at me. Why, they said, what you think you have discovered, Newton could have told you 300 yr ago. So I became a Newtonian, and this has had a profound effect on my work.

In order to describe motion Newton had to invent a new kind of mathematics,

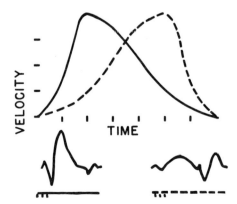

FIGURE 1 Velocity of ejection in strong hearts (solid line) and weak hearts (dashed line). (Lower left) Force BCG of a strong heart; (lower right) force BCG of a weak heart. Note that the cardiac output (the area under the curves) is the same for the strong and for the weak heart, and that the maximum velocity (the height of the curves) is also the same. These measurements, therefore, will not distinguish strong from weak hearts. Strong and weak systoles are easily distinguished by differences in the slopes of the wave fronts.

the calculus, and so the distinction between normal and abnormal cardiac function is a problem in the calculus. The complete description of a movement is given by the differential equation in Table 1, which is one of the basic equations of physics. It says that the force applied to move an object can be accounted for by the sum of a series of terms: the displacement times a constant, the velocity times a constant, the acceleration times a constant, and so on as far as one needs to go.

The displacement aspect of cardiac ejection is related to the stroke volume, the area under the pulse, and the displacement BCG, which records the second integral of my present record. Related to the velocity aspects are the items in the middle column of Table 1; related to acceleration are the slope of the pulse wave front and the force BCG, the records I use routinely.

HIGH-FREQUENCY INFORMATION

Therefore, I have interested myself in aspects of the circulation different from those studied by my predecessors. Mathematically, they are derivatives of the familiar functions and so of higher frequency. The reason for studying these derivatives is Newtonian, but everyone is familiar with it from experience with a car. When the motor is slightly weakened, the displacement aspects of its performance remain normal—the car will get you home; the velocity aspects may remain normal—the car will still do 50 mph on the expressway; but the acceleration aspects are abnormal—the car will not accelerate properly when the light changes to green. So I readied myself to study the cardiac forces of my patients and had collected considerable clinical experience when help arrived from an unexpected source.

DUTCH EXPERIENCE

As part of their training program for recruits, the Dutch army used forced marches and long bicycle rides. During such unaccustomed exertion one of the

TABLE 1 Relation of the items in the force (or energy) equation to various aspects of the movement of your car and of blood ejected from the heart

	Total force or energy =		
	AX +	BX' +	$CX'' + \cdots$
Measurement	Displacement	Velocity	Acceleration
For your car	Mileage meter	Speedometer	Accelerometer
For the heart			
Cardiac output	Stroke volume	Stroke volume/ejection duration	
Pressure pulse	Area under pulse	Amplitude of pulse	Slope of pulse wave front
Center of gravity ⎰	Displacement	Velocity	Force BCG
Movement ⎱	ULF BCG	ULF BCG	
ECG ⎱			
Venous pressure ⎰	No information		
Apex beat ⎱			

recruits suddenly collapsed and died; he had had the usual physical examination, the electrocardiogram (ECG) had been found normal, the autopsy was negative, and there was no explanation. Such things are well known to happen occasionally, but when a second recruit suffered the same fate the authorities were aroused. Eventually the problem was put in the hands of H. C. Burger, the professor of biophysics at Utrecht, a mathematician and physicist, best known in the United States for his work with the ECG. The ECG had not helped in this instance and, casting about for a lead, Burger learned about Yandell Henderson's work. As a class demonstration, he suspended a ladder from the ceiling of his laboratory and, with a student lying on it, took records. The records fascinated him, as they have everyone with a mathematical inclination, for the movement of the body in space must have a quantitative mathematical relation to the movements of blood in the body, through Newton's laws of motion. But before any publication could be made, the Germans invaded Holland, the university closed, and Burger, his wife, and his three small children nearly starved.

MATHEMATICAL STUDIES

Concerned chiefly with survival during the occupation, Burger could do no experiments, but the mathematical problems presented by the BCG kept returning to his mind and when, the war over at last, one of his Ph.D. candidates, Noordergraaf, asked for permission to tackle them, he was glad to agree. To do so Noordergraaf needed a computer, and there was none in war-ravaged Utrecht.

Peace returned eventually, and current American scientific journals began to arrive in Holland once more, so Burger learned of my work, which, in contrast to his own, had been stimulated by the war. He soon came to the United States to see me and my apparatus. There was a digital computer—the first electrical one—at the University of Pennsylvania. The U.S. Public Health Service provided the money to bring Noordergraaf over. Even with much help from the computer it took him 2 yr to complete the calculation.

The array of differential equations that constitutes Noordergraaf's general theory of the circulation is to be found in our book (11). Suffice it to say that the normal BCG is quantitatively explained as originating from the movements of the body's center of gravity during the cardiac cycle, as Couts-Trotter predicted 100 yr ago.

With the calculation accomplished, Noordergraaf was able to proceed further. With today's techniques, almost every mathematical statement can also be expressed electrically, so the mathematical relations appearing in the theory were used by him and Verdouw to create an electric model of the circulation on which all sorts of interesting experiments could be readily performed. It was soon evident that the results of my own experimentation and the calculations of the Dutch mathematicians permitted similar conclusions regarding the interpretation of the BCG records, which I will present in Fig. 2.

ORIGIN OF BALLISTOCARDIOGRAM FORCES

The large initial deflections, the I and J waves, are results of the initial cardiac forces; the heart's energy accelerates the blood headward initially, and the body, when free to move in accord with Newton's law, goes footward.

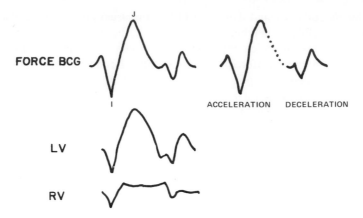

FIGURE 2 Components of the normal force BCG. (Upper left) Typical normal record of one systole. The first footward wave is called I, the large headward wave J. The vertical distance between the I and J wave tips, adjusted for the calibration, is the standard method of measuring force BCG amplitude and the usual index of cardiac strength. (Upper right) The first part of this record, represented by the *first solid line*, records the resultant of the forces generated by blood acceleration, and so it is directly related to cardiac strength. The part to the right, represented by the *second solid line*, is caused by the forces of blood deceleration, and so it is *not* related to cardiac strength. In the part represented by the *dotted line*, forces of both acceleration and deceleration are acting. (LV) Force BCG of the left ventricle alone; (RV) force BCG of the right ventricle alone.

Later in systole the outrushing blood reaches the arch of the aorta and the curve of the pulmonary artery, where the headward movement of most of it is arrested and a large part is then accelerated footward, both movements creating headward forces that first bring the I wave to an end and then push the body headward, causing the J wave.

Normally, about half of the forces recorded in the initial footward deflection, the I wave, come from the left ventricle, which is also responsible for almost all of the J wave. The right ventricle causes the remaining half of the I wave. The smaller forces seen late in systole (Fig. 2) result from the deceleration of the blood as ejection draws to a close, and so they are unrelated to cardiac strength or weakness and have been little studied.

In the cadaver experiments the I-J amplitude, the measurement chiefly used to define the size of a force BCG, is strongly correlated with the integral of the left ventricular forces (11). In the electric model I wave depth is almost perfectly correlated with blood acceleration in simulated systole (15). In dogs (18) and baboons (6) given isoproterenol, ultralow-frequency (ULF) BCG amplitude is correlated with blood acceleration in the ascending aorta. These experiments are not perfect because they compare the force BCG, which is generated chiefly but not exclusively by the left ventricle, with aortic flow, generated solely by the left ventricle; but the relations are so good that one does not hesitate to use the BCG I-J amplitude as a measure of cardiac strength.

While the BCG has a small component from the right ventricle, the pulse is generated by the left ventricle alone, so knowledge of abnormalities in the relative contributions of right and left hearts of any case can be much improved by taking the pulse derivative and BCG simultaneously. These two records always have a certain resemblance and sometimes look very much alike (11). This is because their forms have a common origin in the time course of the heart's energy.

CLINICAL INTERPRETATION MADE
BY AN ELECTRIC MODEL

Obviously we were soon in a position to use our electric model to improve the clinical interpretation of our records, and with the help of Dr. Verdouw we started a type of clinical study that had not been attempted before (15). I took interesting records secured in the clinic and challenged Verdouw to reproduce my findings by altering the simulated physiological properties of his model. Thus I sent him a record secured from a case of pulmonary stenosis with an abnormality in the BCG I wave, as shown in Fig. 3, and Verdouw duplicated this abnormality in the model by simulating a contraction in which the forces of ejection from one ventricle preceded those of the other.

The doubled waves of the pulse derivative (PD) and BCG found in one of my uremic patients were reproduced in the model by simulating an ejection velocity curve that has a double peak, so that the forces of one part of the left heart of my patient manifested themselves later than the rest.

The extremely distorted BCG found in conjunction with a normal PD in a case with hypercholesterolemia was reproduced by Verdouw by simulating normal forces from the right heart, while those coming from the left side were greatly diminished, the ejection being opposed by increased systemic impedance.

Therefore it seems evident that we are in a position to interpret in quantitative physiological terms any pair of simultaneous records, BCGs and PDs, that we may secure in the clinic. The fascinating prospect of such a detailed physiological analysis of heart disease makes me wish I were young again. But I would not have you think that we are ready to make such an analysis routinely on our patients at this time. We are not. Verdouw has returned to Holland, and he was the one who, under Noordergraaf's direction, both constructed and operated the electric model, and his replacement will be hard to find. It is always hard to find people with the combination of clinical, physiological, mathematical, and engineering interest that work such as mine requires. Perhaps such work should be attempted only in universities where, as in this one, medical and engineering facilities are located close to one another.

THE NONINVASIVE TEST USED
IN THE CLINIC

There are, however, simpler means of getting ahead with an analysis of the physiological problems of heart disease, and for the rest of this lecture let me ask you to accept two propositions strongly supported by the behavior of our models: 1) the I-J amplitude of the force BCG is a measure of the initial cardiac forces and

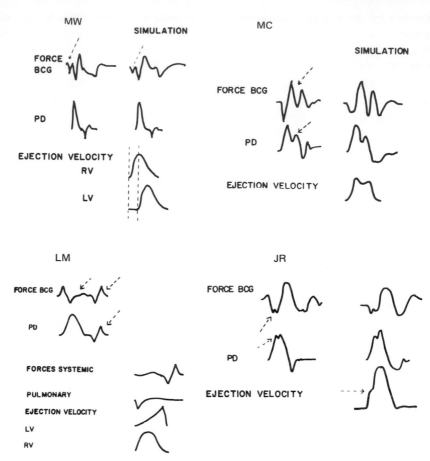

FIGURE 3 Force BCGs and carotid PDs in four patients. Verdouw adjusted the electric model until it duplicated these records. The physiological abnormalities present in the patients are disclosed by the adjustments of the model needed to mimic the clinical records. (Upper left) Patient MW, pulmonic stenosis, age 18, after operation. (Upper right) Patient MC, uremia, age 31, blood pressure 178/120. (Lower left) Patient LM, hypercholesteremia, age 42, blood pressure 132/75. (Lower right) Patient JR, angina, age 48, blood pressure 132/90. From Starr et al. (15).

so of cardiac strength, and 2) the consistent distortions of contour indicate irregularities in the cardiac ejection curve caused by incoordination of the cardiac contraction—or, if one has a compulsion to speak Greek rather than English, this can be called akinesis or dyskinesis. One notes that we have a numerical measure of cardiac strength, but not of cardiac coordination, although we are ready to judge the severity of the incoordination from the relative amount of distortion in the records, as has been described (11).

Before I review the clinical results, let me remind you of the main features of the simple tests of cardiac function we have been using. 1) We make these tests while the patients are resting comfortably under standard conditions. 2) We take records of 50-100 consecutive systoles at each test, and so we have an array of duplicates in every test. I believe this to be much more important than most doctors realize. 3) We use methods that neither frighten nor hurt the subject, so we believe that errors caused by the emotion generated by any clinical test have been held to a minimum in our data. 4) We measure the two main aspects of cardiac ejection simultaneously—pressure (by the pulse) and flow (by the BCG). 5) We are interested in the components of the pressure and flow curves that have frequencies higher than those studied by our predecessors. So we are using new ways of detecting cardiac disabilities, in the expectation that our findings will contain important clinical information that has been missed by conventional cardiac studies. 6) Our test is so completely innocuous that the investigator does not hesitate to order as many tests as the study needs.

In doing this work we have had to face certain difficulties, which we have learned to minimize but not to abolish. 1) As everyone who has worked with the pulse knows, the proper application of the transducer to the artery is essential, and it is sometimes difficult to attain and to be sure that you have attained it in any particular case. 2) Forces other than those arising from the heart and circulation appear in our BCG. These artifacts come chiefly from movements of the patient and vibrations in the building. Attention to the comfort of the subject minimizes the subject's movements; despite progress in eliminating them, building vibrations remain a continuing problem. We rely on a simple rule to distinguish abnormal physiological forces from the artifacts present in all our recrods; the artifacts are random, forces of interest are regularly repeated. The engineers tell us that forces are so ubiquitous that all force records are "noisy" records; ours certainly are.

With such tests we have had a most extensive clinical experience, about 200 patients a year for 40 yr. Let me start by reviewing briefly the most interesting of the newer findings.

INCOORDINATION OF THE CARDIAC CONTRACTION: METHODS OF DETECTING IT

That one part of the heart might contract differently from the other parts has long been known. Over 50 yr ago fluoroscopy showed that, in some cases of cardiac aneurism, part of the cardiac silhouette moved quite differently from the more normal remainder. In a classic pharmacological demonstration witnessed by thousands of medical students, an overdose of digitalis causes the ventricle of an animal preparation to lose the normal coordination of its contraction in what we call ventricular fibrillation. In an animal experiment repeated by many, Tennant and Wiggers (17) ligated a coronary branch in an exposed dog heart in 1935 and observed that the ischemic area bulged with each systole. In an experiment in 1936 I damaged part of a dog's ventricle by a cautery, and as the damaged area bulged with systole, an extra wave appeared on the BCG (11). In the cadaver experiments mentioned, a jerky cardiac ejection caused a distorted pulse and BCG (11).

Evidently when the contractility of one part of the cardiac muscle differs from that of another, abnormalities can be expected to appear in the BCG, as they do in our models. But a puzzling difficulty caused me to postpone publication for several years. If one part of the left ventricle is contracting differently from the other, as my theory supposes, why does not an abnormality of contour appear in the conventional pulse wave? Why is it that studies on the pulse wave of patients with cardiac infarction give no hint of the disorganization of the cardiac contraction that is so very commonly demonstrated by the force BCG in such cases? It was several years before I saw my way through the difficulty. My first study on this subject was not finally published until 1962, with Ogawa collaborating (12). By that time I was confident that the explanation of the discrepancy lay in the deficiencies of the older methods of recording the pulse and in the damping present in the arteries; for both reasons the high-frequency (HF) abnormalities in the pulse wave were not recorded by the older techniques.

If this idea was correct, we could easily take several steps that would provide us with a better record of the HF components of the pulse in noninvasive clinical work: 1) we would take the record as close to the heart as possible; i.e., from the carotid, 2) we would differentiate the record to bring out its HF components, and 3) we would use modern electric apparatuses capable of recording HF phenomena. We have been taking pulses this way for the last 20 yr.

Figure 4 will acquaint you with the evidence we now secure on all our patients.

N.K.

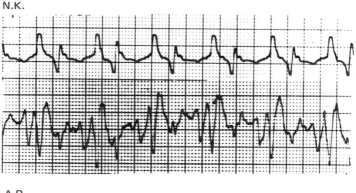

A.R.

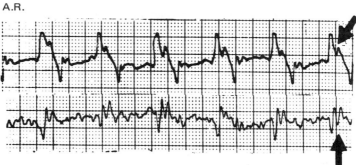

FIGURE 4   Carotid PD and force BCG of two patients. (Upper pair) Age 45, blood pressure 130/85, postbypass operation for angina. The ventriculogram was normal. Angiography revealed open bypass; coronary arteries filled well. The heart is beating with normal strength and coordination. (Lower pair) Age 46, blood pressure 126/74, angina. The ventriculogram showed an incoordinate cardiac contraction. Slight coronary artery disease on angiogram. The PD shows an abnormal notch (arrow); the force BCG J wave also shows an abnormal notch (arrow). From Starr and Shelburne (14). Reprinted by permission of S. Karger AG, Basel.

TABLE 2 Consistency of diagnosis of cardiac incoordination or its absence in 112 cardiacs studied by three tests

Agreement	% of time
All three tests agree	37
BCG and ventriculogram agree	55
BCG and PD agree	65
PD and ventriculogram agree	52

The upper pair of records, PD above BCG, are both normal; in the lower pair the PD is distorted by an HF abnormality, indicated by an arrow, and there is a corresponding abnormal wave in the BCG. So the two tests agree that the subject whose records are shown below has cardiac incoordination and that the other has not.

More recently we have been using a third test for cardiac incoordination, the ventriculogram (3), which has been performed by Shelburne in most of the cases subjected to cardiac catheterization (14). In the subject whose records are shown at the top in Fig. 4, the ventriculogram was normal; in the subject shown below, irregular wall movement was interpreted as indicating cardiac incoordination. In more than 100 subjects all 3 tests have been made, and it is of great interest to compare the results, shown in Table 2, which do not always agree as nicely as Fig. 4 suggests.

I believe that such discrepancies can be explained by the different deficiencies of the three tests, for none of them is perfect. In taking a ventriculogram (Fig. 5),

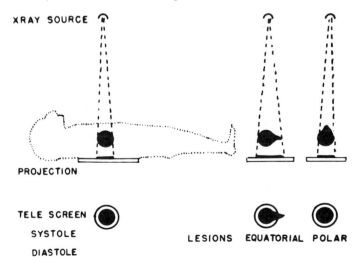

FIGURE 5 Two sources of error in the ventriculogram. The cine records not the ventricular silhouette, but a projection of it, and the angle of projection is not known. Movement of the silhouette at a right angle to the X-ray beam is well recorded, but movement in the line of the beam is not recorded, so abnormalities of movement in this direction would be missed.

the X-ray source is above the patient, the screen below. So the movies show, not the movement of the ventricular wall, but its projection, and since the angle of projection is unknown, the measurement may have a large error. The position of the lesion must also affect the result. Think of the heart as a sphere with its pole toward the X-ray source: if the abnormality were equatorial the abnormal movement would be seen, but if the abnormality were polar it would not. Such a setup is sure to miss many cases of abnormal wall movement. It is not surprising that the BCG often detects cardiac incoordination when the ventriculogram does not (14).

The damping to which the PD is subject also tends to diminish the number of cases of cardiac incoordination detected by that method. Indeed, the pulse behaves as if it were the least sensitive of the three methods of detecting incoordination; it often fails to show abnormalities judged to be present by the other two methods.

The artifacts to which the BCG is subject would lead to errors in the other direction, for one might interpret artifacts as evidence of incoordination. Obviously it is of great interest to compare the evidence of cardiac incoordination secured by these three methods in a series of cases.

With the help of Dr. Shelburne, I made a blind study (14) and Table 2 shows the results obtained. In more than one-third of our cases all three tests agreed that incoordination was present, or that it was absent. This is not as good agreement as one would like, but studies of this kind have just begun, and when all three tests do agree we seem to have strong evidence of the presence or absence of cardiac incoordination.

CLINICAL CHARACTERISTICS OF CARDIAC INCOORDINATION

Both invasive and noninvasive tests agree on certain characteristics. 1) Cardiac incoordination is very common in elderly cardiacs (7). 2) It can be induced by exercise or by driving the heart. 3) The anginal attack is accompanied by the appearance of cardiac incoordination or its increase (11). 4) Nitrites improve cardiac coordination when they relieve the pain of angina (11); they may also improve or abolish cardiac incoordination when no pain is present (13). 5) Cardiac incoordination is usually found in association with coronary heart disease.

Evidence secured by the two noninvasive tests shows the following in addition. 1) Incoordination shows a strong respiratory variation in many cases. During inspiration, when the heart is better filled, cardiac coordination improves (Starling's law). 2) In arrhythmias ventricular incoordination may be present in some beats and not in others. 3) Cigarette smoking may cause temporary cardiac incoordination in older people and not in young ones (11). 4) Coronary bypass usually improves cardiac incoordination when it improves angina, but it seldom restores the cardiac contraction to normal (10). The maximum effect of the operation is temporary, but in many patients prolonged improvement has been demonstrated (10). 5) Cardiac incoordination is never seen in healthy young adults, although hundreds have been tested.

RELATIONS OF CARDIAC INCOORDINATION TO CORONARY HEART DISEASE

In most of our cases Dr. Shelburne rated the amount of coronary sclerosis by means of angiograms, so we could study the relation between his findings and the results of our three tests (Table 3). In the 23 cases in which the BCG was normal the average coronary arteriosclerosis rating was 4.1. In the 44 cases in which the BCG indicated cardiac incoordination the coronary rating averaged 6.5, 55% higher. The two means are significantly different. This is also true when data secured by the ventriculogram and pulse derivative are studied (14).

When one takes the cases in which all three tests were normal and compares them with those in which all three tests indicated cardiac incoordination, the difference in the amount of arteriosclerosis in the normal and abnormal group is even more impressive; the mean for the latter is almost 200% higher, and this is, of course, highly significant (14). So one must conclude that the presence of cardiac incoordination is associated with increased coronary arteriosclerosis.

These new physiological conceptions of coronary heart disease reconcile the anatomic and physiological findings. We can now think that the parts of the cardiac muscle with diminished blood supply contract less vigorously than the rest of the heart. The difference in performance between the normal and abnormal areas of cardiac muscle, the degree of incoordination, is not fixed but labile; apparently situations of stress are not as well met by the ischemic as by the normal parts, and during stress the incoordination increases.

Missed altogether by the cardiology of the past, cardiac incoordination is now identified as the characteristic physiological manifestation of coronary heart disease, present in all severe cases.

CARDIAC STRENGTH AND FACTORS THAT ALTER IT

Medical interest in cardiac incoordination is of recent date, but interest in cardiac weakness goes back centuries. In planning this lecture I proposed to consider

TABLE 3 Is ventricular incoordination related to arteriosclerosis? Comparison of three tests for ventricular incoordination and arteriosclerosis ratings made from coronary angiograms

Test	Result of test	No. of cases	Average rating[a]
BCG	Normal	23	4.5
	Abnormal	44	6.5
Ventriculogram	Normal	28	2.7
	Abnormal	29	8.0
PD	Normal	31	6.0
	Abnormal	28	7.3
All three tests	Normal	13	3.0
	Abnormal	12	8.7

[a]In the range 0–15.

next the new information secured about it, but I found my data too extensive to present in the time allotted, and must content myself with mentioning a few examples.

The few studies I shall describe in detail should be interpreted against a background of information gained over the years by studying healthy medical students in the pharmacology course. In such subjects the records secured were all normal in form and amplitude, and epinephrine never failed to increase the initial cardiac forces, which testifies to our ability to detect differences in cardiac strength by the methods used.

The favorable effects of nitroglycerin on cardiac strength and coordination in cases of coronary heart disease have been clearly demonstrated (13). By taking records before, soon after, and years after operative procedures, we have tested their effectiveness; the coronary bypass operation, in contrast to its largely ineffective predecessors, was often followed by improved cardiac strength and coordination (10). The effect of maintenance doses of digitoxin in old people in normal sinus rhythm was investigated by a blind experiment of several years' duration made with Dr. Luchi; the results were negative. In a report still in press (9a), data secured by noninvasive testing were found more closely correlated with coronary sclerosis than were data secured at catheterization.

EFFECT OF AGE ON CARDIAC STRENGTH

Most bodily functions decline as age advances, and every worker in the field has found that the average force BCG of older people is smaller than that of healthy young adults. The first question is, Is this finding a result of the unwitting inclusion of asymptomatic cases of coronary heart disease in the healthy group? A long-term follow-up permits one to identify those who developed symptoms of coronary heart disease later, and so may well have had it at the time of the original test. If these cases of incipient disease are withdrawn from our series of healthy people, the average force BCG of the remainder, who continued healthy for the next 17 yr, still declines at the average rate of 1.5% a year. There is, therefore, a slow weakening of the heart as age advances that is not due to coronary disease, and I think this is the best evidence of it that has been presented (11).

In my subjects, as in other data, the blood pressure goes up as age advances, leading some to think that the heart might grow stronger with age; but this is not true of the pulse derivative, for PD_{max} declines as age advances at a rate close to that of the force BCG, averaging 1.1% a year.

The aging of a few subjects has been followed very carefully. In one subject we have made over 250 tests during a span of 40 yr. As he grew older his blood pressure slowly rose and his force BCG became smaller, reaching a minimum when he was 71 yr old, at which time he was still asymptomatic and in good health. But shortly after this minimum a left bundle branch block was detected for the first time. In later years the BCG improved, and at age 82 it is remarkably good for so old a man, but the left bundle branch block has persisted. Evidently he had asymptomatic cardiac damage from which he recovered, except for the electric abnormality. My bet is that the necropsy will show a healed lesion, but I am not the one to complete this study.

Another healthy person followed for 40 yr has also developed clear BCG evidence of asymptomatic cardiac damage, from which he recovered completely. Today he is in tolerably good health at the age of 86.

LONG AFTER-HISTORIES

Before discussing the results secured in the much larger group not followed so intensively, we must pause to pay tribute to Sir James Mackenzie, who, at the height of his career and at what must have been a great financial sacrifice, left London and moved to a small town where he would be better able to keep track of his patients. Soon overtaken by ill health, Mackenzie did not succeed in his endeavor, but I and many others have found his example inspiring and have adopted his method.

In 1936, as soon as my first ballistocardiograph was completed and clinical studies became possible, I secured records of all the healthy subjects I could get my hands on, chiefly medical students, faculty, friends, and family. Interesting patients drawn from the medical wards were also tested. Arrangements were made to follow as many of these subjects as possible, and between 10 and 20 yr later they were examined by Dr. Francis Wood, who had been kept in ignorance of the BCG findings (11). When their after-histories were compared with the contour and amplitude of their original records the results were very striking; those with small BCGs developed heart disease and died of it far more frequently than those with normal records, and this could not be explained by differences in age (11).

There were not enough subjects with BCGs abnormal in form in the group who were originally healthy to make possible a study of the clinical consequences of this abnormality. But when the data from the patients were added, the relation between contour abnormalities and after-histories was striking. Those whose BCG form abnormalities were judged to be small did not differ in duration of life from those with normal records. But when the contour abnormalities were greater, the effect on average life duration was very striking (11). Abnormalities of contour had far more prognostic significance than did abnormalities of amplitude.

This strong evidence for the prognostic value of the BCG soon attracted others into the field. Baker et al. (1) studied their subjects on an HF table like the one I had used. Four hundred controls and 300 patients with ischemic heart disease were studied. They were followed for 9 yr, coronary events such as the development of angina, of infarction, and sudden death being recorded. Record amplitude was not studied, and BCG form was classified by the method I had used (11). Figure 6 shows a very informative arrangement of Baker's data, made by B. M. Wright of England. Baker et al. concluded:

After correction for age, healthy controls with abnormal BCGs developed ischemic heart disease three times as frequently as did those whose BCGs were normal .... Patients with clinical evidence of IHD who also had abnormal BCGs, developed twice as many recurrences as did those having IHD and normal records.

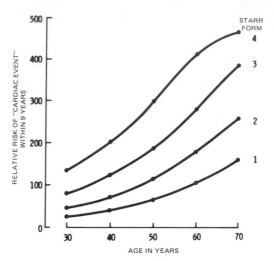

FIGURE 6 Relation between age in years and force BCG form with the risk of a cardiac event within 9 yr. The subjects were apparently normal males. The form of the force BCG was classified in four groups, group 1 being normal and group 4 extremely abnormal, as has been described (11). This is an arrangement of the data of Baker et al. (1) made by B. M. Wright.

Another important study has recently been reported from Wolf's clinic (5). These authors used a modern ULF table and took repeated records in each patient, four times a year. Great care was taken to make the study blind; the predictions were made and locked up years before the results were in.

Lynn and Wolf concluded that "predictions of subsequent myocardial infarction or sudden death based on qualitative assessment of BCG pattern were highly accurate at the 0.0001 level of confidence." Wolf and his collaborators have also found that their data support a very interesting new conception: the bad heart can be distinguished from the good one by the inconsistency of its performance.

Dr. Kiessling of the Prudential insurance company studied more than 2000 male employees by Dock's shin-bar method (4). He divided them by the form of their records into three groups: normal, questionable, and abnormal. Among those whose records were judged to be normal, the deaths during the period of observation were only about half those expected from the life table; among those whose records were judged abnormal, the deaths exceeded those expected by 27%.

Taylor et al. (16) followed 261 businessmen aged 48-57 yr, using Nickerson's ballistocardiograph (11). In 14 yr of follow-up, coronary events occurred in those with abnormal BCGs 3 times more frequently than in those with normal records. The authors concluded that the BCG has prognostic power independent of other risk factors.

A FORTY-YEAR FOLLOW-UP

In view of these completely consistent conclusions, all of which confirm and extend my work of 20 yr ago, you may well wonder why I was attracted back into the field, and indeed I have wondered about it myself. My best reason I talk about with my tongue in my cheek; I never heard of a clinical series that was followed for 40 yr, so why not break the record when it seemed so easy to do? For, largely because of the generosity of my colleagues and of the University, I have been able to continue my work long after the ordinary age of retirement.

By taking the data nearest at hand and combining the two series started in 1936, I soon located data from 115 people who had been first tested 40 yr ago and had been followed until death (74%), or were known to be alive 40 yr after the first test.

Figure 7 shows the dot diagram; obviously, the coefficient of correlation between the initial cardiac forces and life duration is very strong, 0.71. The possibility that this might be due to chance is so remote that the probability is quite off the table in Fisher's book (2).

Figure 8 shows that BCG form is also significantly related to life duration, both when the abnormality is severe and when it is slight, and this latter finding deserves comment. In the study of Baker et al. (1) and in my own first study (11) subjects with BCGs markedly or extremely abnormal in form developed heart disease and died much more frequently than did those with normal records. In the data of Baker et al. this was also true of those whose BCGs were slightly abnormal, but in my first study this difference was not significant. In my present study, this difference is highly significant, so Baker et al. are upheld. Both slight and severe deviations of BCG contour from the normal must be regarded as having adverse prognostic significance.

SIGNIFICANCE OF COMMON CLINICAL DATA

I do not think it can be disputed that an abnormal BCG is a bad thing for one to have, and that chance will not explain our findings. But a final question must be

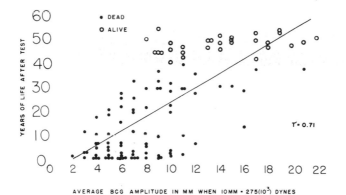

FIGURE 7 Relation of BCG amplitude measured 40 yr ago with life duration after the initial test. (●) Those who died during the period of observation; (○) those who survived. The latter can be handled in three ways: 1) by omitting them, 2) by using the known duration of their life after the first test (40 yr), and 3) by adding to this known duration the expected duration of life from the life table. The third method has been used here. The correlation is highly significant for all three methods.

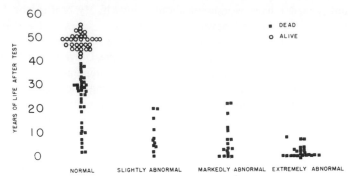

FIGURE 8 Life duration after the initial test compared with abnormalities of BCG contour rated according to a method described (11). (■) Those who had died and (○) those who were alive 40 yr after the original test. Life duration of the survivors was calculated by adding life expectancy from the life table to the 40 yr of the study. The average differences in life duration between those with force BCGs normal in form and those with BCGs slightly, markedly, and extremely abnormal are very striking and highly significant.

raised that is not easy to answer; granted that the BCG is of value in predicting longevity and defining cardiac incoordination and weakness, is it really any better than the simple symptoms and signs long used by the medical profession to assess the severity of cardiac disease? With much hesitation I attacked this difficult problem and culled the medical records for the signs and symptoms of a group of 221 patients whom I had also tested by my methods (8). Table 4 shows that five items of the clinical study were significantly related to life duration and that BCG form abnormalities had the largest chi-square. The mathematical difficulties inherent in comparing one chi-square with another deter me from claiming that BCG form is better or more useful than the other items because its chi-square is larger; but I, and other statisticians, would have no hesitation in pointing out that BCG form is not inferior to the more usual items of the clinical study when used for this purpose. The exact evaluation of common clinical data is a field that needs much more exploration, and I have only made a start.

TABLE 4 Comparison of ballistocardiogram form and clinical items for relation to life duration

Item	Chi-square
Significantly related to life duration	
Abnormal force BCG form	69
Reduced exercise tolerance	38
Increased cardiac silhouette	26
Diagnosis of cardiac abnormality	24
ECG evidence of infarction	13
Not related to life duration	
BCG amplitude, atrial fibrillation, conduction defects, blood pressure, heart rate, age, weight	

CONCLUSION

Finally, taken together, what do my studies show? When the heart is viewed as a pump and when one is interested in the HF aspects of its performance, information new to clinicians appears. Physiologically, this information is related to the strength or weakness of the heart and to the coordination of its contraction. Clinically, it can be properly used to determine the nature and severity of the heart's physiological abnormalities, the likelihood of complications, the need for therapeutic measures, and their effectiveness.

REFERENCES

1. Baker, B. M., Jr., Davis, F. W., Jr., Mason, R. E., Scarborough, W. R., and Singewald, M. L. Ballistocardiography and ischemic heart disease. Predictive considerations and statistical evaluation. Proc R Soc Med 60:6–12, 1967.
2. Fisher, R. A. Statistical Methods for Research Workers. Edinburgh: Oliver & Boyd, 1930.
3. Grossman, W. Cardiac Catheterization and Angiography. Philadelphia: Lea & Febiger, 1976.
4. Kiessling, C. E. A preliminary appraisal of the prognostic value of ballisto-cardiography. Bibl Cardiol 26:292–295, 1970.
5. Lynn, T. N. and Wolf, S. The prognostic significance of the ballistocardiogram in ischemic heart disease. Am Heart J 88:277–280, 1974.
6. Smith, N. T., van Citters, R. L., and Verdouw, P. D. The relation between the ultralow frequency ballistocardiogram and ascending aortic flow acceleration in the baboon. Bibl Cardiol 26:198–205, 1970.
7. Starr, I. Cardiac weakness and incoordination in a large population of ambulatory patients. Bibl Cardiol 32:37–41, 1973.
8. Starr, I., Askowitz, S. I., and Mandelbaum, E. M. Items of prognostic value in the clinical study. J Am Med Assoc 192:83–87, 1965.
9. Starr, I., Jr., Collins, L. H., Jr., and Wood, F. C. Studies of the basal work and output of the heart in clinical conditions. J Clin Invest 12:13–43, 1933.
9a. Starr, I., Karreman, G., Bering, T., and Shelburne, J. C. Blind study on the relations between the extent of coronary arteriosclerosis and the strength of the myocardial contraction as measured by invasive and non-invasive tests. Am Heart J, in press.
10. Starr, I. and MacVaugh, H. Early and late effects of the coronary bypass operation on cardiac contractility and coordination. Am Heart J 90:179–189, 1975.
11. Starr, I. and Noordergraaf, A. Ballistocardiography in Cardiovascular Research. Amsterdam: North-Holland, and Philadelphia: Lippincott, 1967.
12. Starr, I. and Ogawa, S. Incoordination of the cardiac contraction in clinical conditions. Am J Med Sci 244:663–679, 1962.
13. Starr, I., Pedersen, E., and Corbascio, A. Effect of nitroglycerine on the ballistocardiogram of persons with and without clinical evidence of coronary heart disease. Circulation 12:588–603, 1955.
14. Starr, I. and Shelburne, J. C. A comparison of 3 methods of detecting ventricular incoordination in man and their relation to the amount of coronary arteriosclerosis. Bibl Cardiol 35:109–114, 1976.

15. Starr, I., Verdouw, P. D., and Noordergraaf, A. Clinical evidence of cardiac weakness and incoordination secured by simultaneous records of the force BCG and carotid pulse derivative and interpreted by an electrical analogue. Am Heart J 85:341–348, 1973.
16. Taylor, H. L., Blackburn, H., Parlin, R. W., and Keys, A. Coronary heart disease risk and the Nickerson ballistocardiograms. Circulation 38(suppl 6):24, 1968.
17. Tennant, R. and Wiggers, C. J. Effect of coronary occlusion on myocardial contraction. Am J Physiol 112:351–356, 1935.
18. Winter, P. J., Deuchar, D. C., Noble, M. I. M., Trenchard, D., and Guz, A. A relation between the ballistocardiogram and the movement of blood from the left ventricle of the dog. Cardiovasc Res 1:194–200, 1967.

CHAPTER 12

ECHOCARDIOGRAPHY

NICHOLAS J. FORTUIN

Although Edler and co-workers (2) in their pioneering investigations recognized 25 yr ago that pulsed reflected ultrasound could provide images from the moving walls of the left ventricle, application of this important finding to the evaluation of cardiac function has occurred only in recent years. Ultrasonic imaging of the left ventricle provides direct information about ventricular performance similar to that obtained from angiographic study. The development of this technique has permitted bedside application of many of the principles for the evaluation of ventricular function that were established previously by catheterization studies in humans and animals. Echocardiography has the advantages that it is safe, relatively low in cost, repeatable, and does not require the injection of contrast medium.

TECHNIQUE AND PRINCIPLES

This technique employs repeated microsecond pulses of ultrasonic energy (2–5 MHz), which are passed through the heart. When sonic waves encounter interfaces of differing acoustic density, such as blood and ventricular endocardium, they are reflected backward or "echoed." The same transducer that transmits the sonic impulses functions as a receiver of the returning or echoed waves, which are displayed on an oscilloscope or permanently recorded on photographic paper. Since the speed of sound in tissue is known, distances of structures from the transducer or distances between intracardiac structures can be calculated.

Figure 1 illustrates a normal left ventricular echocardiogram. It is obtained by placing the ultrasonic transducer in standard recording position in the third and fourth intercostal space adjacent to the sternum and angulating the beam so that it transects the left ventricle in an area just below the mitral valve leaflets. Using the mitral leaflets as a reference point makes it possible to compare studies in the same or different subjects. The ultrasonic beam is like an ice pick that passes through successive cardiac structures including the anterior right ventricular wall, the cavity of the right ventricle, the interventricular septum in its upper anterior position, the left ventricular cavity, and the posterolateral free wall of the left ventricle (Fig. 1). This view of the left heart is analogous to what is seen in a steep left anterior oblique ventriculogram, although a much smaller area of myocardium is actually visualized.

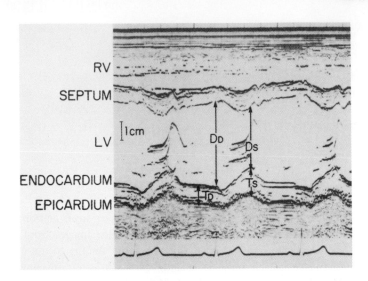

FIGURE 1 Left ventricular (LV) echocardiogram from normal subject illustrating measurement of minor axis dimension at end-diastole (D_D) and end-systole (D_S). The measurement is made from the endocardial surface of the posterior wall to the endocardial surface of the left side of the septum. Wall thickness in systole (T_S) and diastole (T_D) is measured from the epicardial to the endocardial surface of the posterior wall (RV, right ventricle).

EVALUATION OF SYSTOLIC FUNCTION

It is necessary to understand the left ventricular geometry of the normal heart to appreciate how this small ultrasonic view of the left heart can provide information about overall ventricular function. The left ventricle is a complex geometric form that can be most simply reduced to a prolate ellipsoid (Fig. 2). This ellipsoidal model has a long axis (L) and perpendicular and equal minor axes (D_1 and D_2). When the ventricle contracts, the major work of ejection is accomplished by a change in the minor axis, which shortens by 35%, whereas the long axis changes by only 10–12%. Angiographic studies have established two facts about the minor axis that have an important bearing on the study of left ventricular function by echocardiography (11). First, there is a linear correlation between the percentage change in the minor axis during systole ($\%\Delta D$) and the percentage change in ventricular volume, which is the left ventricular ejection fraction (EF). Second, there is an equally close linear correlation between the minor axis dimension and the overall volume or size of the left ventricular chamber in both systole and diastole. Thus, the minor axis dimension and its change during the cardiac cycle are direct correlates of overall ventricular chamber size and ejection fraction. Most of the information about left ventricular performance derived from echocardiographic studies utilizes the minor ventricular axis in a single plane. As noted, this is the area of the left ventricle sampled by the ultrasound technique. Using present single-dimension systems it is not possible to measure the ventricular long axis.

An important question in early investigations in which this technique was applied was how closely the minor axis of the ventricle determined by echocardiography compared with the minor axis measured in angiographic studies. Several studies confirmed the fact that the two minor axis measurements were remarkably similar in ventricular chambers of varying sizes (4). Further, the echocardiographic minor axis is readily reproducible. There is a close and linear correlation between the minor axis determined by echocardiography and the overall chamber volume measured from angiocardiograms in both systole and diastole (4). This relation forms the basis for extrapolating the minor axis determination to ventricular volume. Ventricular volume can be calculated most simply by cubing the minor axis, $V = D^3$ (9), or by employing regression equations derived from the linear relation between minor axis dimension and chamber volume (4); that is,

$$\text{End-diastolic volume (EDV)} = 59D_D - 153$$

$$\text{End-systolic volume (ESV)} = 47D_S - 120$$

where D_D and D_S are the minor axis dimensions at end-diastole and end-systole. The cube method overestimates volume in large chambers, but both methods yield good statistical correlations when echocardiographic and angiographic measurements are compared. Unfortunately, with either method the standard error of the estimate is high, so that individual determinations may be inaccurate. Because of this inaccuracy and because it is difficult to conceive that a complex function such as chamber volume can be derived from a single measurement of chamber dimension, I do not advocate converting echocardiographic data to volume. Minor axis dimensions are best employed as correlates of chamber volume by themselves. The same can be said for the artificial extrapolation to ejection fraction, which requires conversion of dimension to volume. The $\%\Delta D$ is the basic measurement that can be utilized as a correlate of ejection fraction. Normal values are more than 25%.

The $\%\Delta D$ or EF provides information about overall pump function of the ventricle. Minor axis measurement by echocardiography also allows determination of velocity indices of chamber shortening, which may reflect muscle function more directly (3). Since the ventricle is circular at its minor axis, the endocardial circumference is equal to πD. The mean velocity of circumferential shortening (mean V_{CF}) is then the change in circumference between end-diastole and

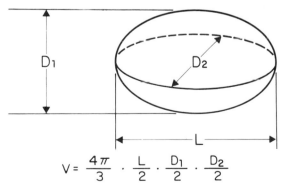

$$V = \frac{4\pi}{3} \cdot \frac{L}{2} \cdot \frac{D_1}{2} \cdot \frac{D_2}{2}$$

FIGURE 2 Geometric representation of a normal left ventricle as a prolate ellipsoid with the volume (V) formula shown. Abbreviations: D_1 and D_2, minor axes in perpendicular plane; L, long axis. An echocardiographic study of the left ventricle measures only D in a single plane.

end-systole divided by the duration of circumference shortening (dt) and normalized for end-diastolic circumference:

$$\text{Mean } V_{CF} = \frac{D_D - D_S}{dt\, D_D}$$

where dt is the ejection time, which is most conveniently determined from an externally recorded carotid pulse tracing or less accurately measured directly from the echocardiogram. The echocardiographic V_{CF} has been closely correlated with the V_{CF} measured by cineangiography.

Mean V_{CF}, like %ΔD, is influenced by acute changes in the loading conditions of the ventricle, particularly afterload (10). This is not a serious restriction in chronic heart disease, where compensatory hypertrophy serves to normalize abnormal systolic wall stress. In spite of the theoretical advantages of the velocity indices of systolic function over those reflecting pump function, studies in patients with chronic valvular heart disease have not shown that V_{CF} is superior to %ΔD.

Measurement of ventricular wall thickness during the cardiac cycle provides a potentially important application of echocardiography in describing regional systolic function. Several studies have documented that this technique provides accurate measurements of the thickness of both the interventricular septum and the left ventricular posterolateral wall (12). The percentage change in thickness during systole or the mean velocity of wall thickening is easily calculated from high-quality echocardiograms. Ischemic injury resulting in regional dysfunction in areas visualized by the ultrasound beam results in early change in these indices so that hypokinesis, akinesis, or dyskinesis can be quantitated.

Combining an instantaneous measurement of ventricular dimension with a measurement of intraventricular pressure in the catheterization laboratory allows construction of pressure-dimension loops that are well correlated with the pressure-volume loops determined from angiographic studies. Combined pressure, dimension, and wall thickness measurements can be employed to calculate left ventricular work, cycle efficiency, power, and wall stress during diastole and systole (5).

EVALUATION OF DIASTOLIC FUNCTION

Certain disease states, particularly those in which hypertrophy or ischemia plays a role, may produce an alteration in the diastolic properties of the left ventricle even in the absence of systolic abnormalities. Digitization of the instantaneous dimensions of the minor axis throughout the cardiac cycle by a simple computer program allows a graphic display of dimension versus time (6). The diastolic portion of this curve describes the lengthening rate of the minor axis, which is related to both ventricular relaxation and ventricular filling. The peak lengthening rate is reduced in patients with mitral stenosis or idiopathic hypertrophic subaortic stenosis (IHSS) and increased in patients with mitral regurgitation. In IHSS the filling rate declines progressively with increasing stages of hypertrophy, even though systolic function remains normal or supernormal. Recently, Gibson and co-workers (13) described a kind of discoordinate relaxation in patients with ischemic heart disease. They used computerized data to relate mitral valve motion to diastolic events in the left ventricular wall. In normal subjects the mitral valve begins its opening movement shortly after the ventricular dimension begins to lengthen and achieves its maximal opening velocity at the time when the lengthening rate of the ventricle is maximal. In patients with ischemic heart disease, who show regional injury, the mitral valve opening is delayed considerably, so that the ventricle expands before valve opening allows a change in diastolic volume. Thus, the shape change precedes ventricular filling and results in abnormal diastolic performance. This abnormality was noted even when the ultrasound beam did not sample injured myocardium. Thus, an important advantage of the ultrasound technique is that it allows quantitative characterization of rapidly changing events during the cardiac cycle. It is likely that analysis of regional wall motion in diastole, such as the rate of diastolic thinning, may also provide important information about regional ischemic injury, since studies in isolated heart muscle have demonstrated that relaxation abnormalities precede contraction abnormalities in acutely ischemic myocardium.

CLINICAL APPLICATIONS

Practical application of this technique for the evaluation of ventricular performance in patients with heart disease has followed the validation of much of the material discussed above. Heretofore, invasive studies have been required to evaluate left ventricular function in patients with valvular heart disease. In these patients it is important to know the extent to which clinical symptoms and signs may be ascribed to altered valvular function or to altered ventricular function. It is equally important to know what effect the altered valve function is having on ventricular function with the passage of time. An echocardiographic study of the left ventricle provides answers to these questions in most instances. In states of chronic volume overload, such as mitral or aortic regurgitation, the overall increase in ventricular dimension is a good guide to the magnitude of the valvular leak. Because of the low-impedance systolic runoff in mitral regurgitation, $\%\Delta D$ or EF is increased until the ventricle begins to fail. Normal or low values for $\%\Delta D$ are indicative of left ventricular dysfunction, which, if it is declining progressively, may be an indication for surgical intervention. Patients with aortic regurgitation pose a particularly difficult clinical problem because the symptoms do not occur until late in the natural history of the disease and usually reflect altered ventricular performance. These patients may be managed more intelligently than in the past by using serial echocardiographic assessment or left ventricular size and function. Progressive dilation or deterioration in systolic functional indices may allow earlier selection for surgical therapy, before the development of symptoms and before irreversible changes in the ventricle occur. In patients with aortic stenosis, the severity of the lesion will be mirrored by the severity of left ventricular hypertrophy or wall thickness increase. Because of the high impedance to emptying in this condition, ejection phase indices of systolic function may be lower than normal. These indices, along with the extent of left ventricular dilatation, will provide important information about the adequacy of function.

The left ventricle may be affected by numerous disease states and by many drugs or other environmental agents. In the past, recognition of cardiac effects has required extensive involvement, since only a greatly advanced alteration in performance could be detected by the available clinical techniques. With the use of echocardiography it is possible to describe more subtle effects. For instance, reproducible depression of V_{CF} has been found in normal subjects given small amounts of alcohol (1). Cardiac toxicity from antineoplastic agents such as adriamycin can be recognized long before clinical signs appear. Figure 3 shows an example of the deterioration of left ventricular function in a patient treated with adriamycin. The ejection fraction declined before there was clinical evidence of heart failure. In connective tissue disorders such as systemic lupus erythematosus, scleroderma, or polymyositis we have seen evidence of depression of myocardial functional indices in the absence of clinical findings. Primary cardiac muscle disease or cardiomyopathy is diagnosed readily at the bedside when the patient presents with congestive heart failure. Echocardiography in this setting confirms the presence of severe left ventricular dysfunction and obviates the need for catheterization. The challenge to the clinician is to recognize myocardial disease in its early form, when

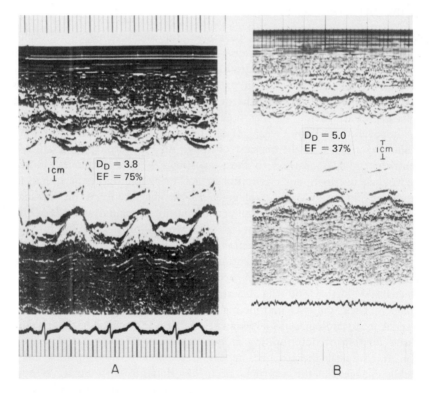

FIGURE 3   Adriamycin cardiotoxicity detected before clinical evidence of cardiac involvement. (A) Control echocardiogram of the left ventricle before institution of adriamycir therapy of breast carcinoma. (B) After several weekly treatments, the left ventricular diastolic dimension (D_D) has increased and the ejection fraction (EF) has declined. Movement of both septum and free wall has decreased.

presenting symptoms may be vague or nonspecific (e.g., arrhythmias, chest pain, or fatigue) and before obvious signs of heart failure are present. We have used echocardiography for early recognition as well as to obtain important information regarding improvement or deterioration of function in follow-up.

The ability to measure left ventricular wall thickness makes this a potentially useful technique for the evaluation and subsequent follow-up of patients with hypertension or other conditions that produce left ventricular hypertrophy. As noted above, the effects of hypertrophy are best studied by analyzing the diastolic properties of the wall and minor axis, since changes here precede changes in systolic functional indices.

CORONARY ARTERY DISEASE AND LIMITATIONS OF THE TECHNIQUE

In coronary artery disease the applications of single-dimension echocardiography are limited, largely because of technical factors. When damaged myocardium can be imaged, it is possible to recognize alterations in systolic and diastolic function both qualitatively and quantitatively. The major problem is that it is not possible to image the majority of left ventricular myocardium from the standard transducer position. This is illustrated in Fig. 4, which shows that the standard echocardiographic view area involves the upper anterior septum and the proximal portion of the posterolateral wall beneath the mitral annulus. Angulating the transducer toward the apex and moving it laterally or to other interspaces will provide images from other areas of the myocardium, but much of the ventricle will still not be seen. Determining what area of the ventricle one is looking at is difficult when the mitral valve is not available as a reference point.

Overall indices of systolic function such as V_{CF} or $\%\Delta D$ are inaccurate in patients with regional ventricular disease. One of the basic tenets in the use of the echocardiogram in assessing cardiac function is that the ultrasound beam is sampling a representative portion of the remaining unsampled myocardium. This assumption is valid in conditions that affect the entire ventricle, but it is particularly invalid in coronary artery disease, where regional involvement and compensatory hyperfunction in other regions are the rule.

The other major limitation to this technique is that the left ventricle cannot be adequately imaged in a significant proportion of patients. The proportion will vary with the patient groups studied, being higher in older adults and in patients who are acutely ill or have chronic lung disease, obesity, or recent chest surgery. Improvements in the technique should reduce the magnitude of this problem.

TWO-DIMENSIONAL ECHOCARDIOGRAPHY

Recent technological advances have resulted in the development of several types of ultrasound equipment capable of providing two-dimensional images of the heart in real time. The earliest instrument of this type, which employed multiple miniature transducers emitting and receiving parallel beams, has been replaced in this country by two newer devices. One utilizes a single transducer, mechanically

180   N. J. FORTUIN

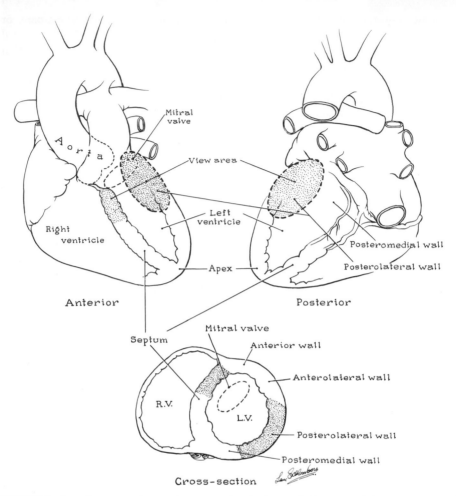

FIGURE 4 Anterior, posterior, and cross-sectional views of the normal heart to show the relationship of the ultrasound beam to intracardiac structures. The shaded areas represent portions of myocardium imaged from the standard transducer position. Note that the apex; the posteromedial, anterolateral, and anterior walls; and the posterior portion of the septum are difficult to visualize with this technique.

oscillated through an arc, which produces a pie-shaped 30° view of intracardiac structures (7). The other device, which is more expensive, utilizes multiple transducers in a single probe; electronic beam steering angulates the direction of ultrasound transmission from each transducer, thus avoiding the problem of parallel direction and enhancing resolution (8). A wide sector angle of 90° can be achieved. Early studies have established that these units provide images from many areas of the left ventricle (apex, lateral wall, posterior and inferior septum) that cannot be imaged easily with single-dimension systems. Both longitudinal and cross-sectional views of several areas of the left ventricle can be obtained. This technique holds great promise for future investigations of left ventricular function, particularly in patients with coronary artery disease.

REFERENCES

1. Delgrado, C. E., Fortuin, N. J., and Ross, R. J. Acute effects of low doses of alcohol on left ventricular function by echocardiography. Circulation 51:535–540, 1975.
2. Edler, I. Diagnostic use of ultrasound in heart disease. Acta Med Scand [Suppl] 308:32–36, 1955.
3. Fortuin, N. J., Hood, W. P., Jr., and Craige, E. Evaluation of left ventricular function by echocardiography. Circulation 46:26–35, 1972.
4. Fortuin, N. J., Hood, W. P., Jr., Sherman, M. E., and Craige, E. Determination of left ventricular volumes by ultrasound. Circulation 44:575–584, 1971.
5. Gibson, D. G. and Brown, D. J. Assessment of left ventricular systolic function in man from simultaneous echocardiographic and pressure measurements. Br Heart J 38:8–17, 1976.
6. Gibson, D. G. and Brown, D. J. Measurement of instantaneous left ventricular dimension and filling rate in man, using echocardiography. Br Heart J 37:677–683, 1975.
7. Griffith, J. M. and Henry, W. L. A sector scanner for real time two-dimensional echocardiography. Circulation 49:1147–1152, 1974.
8. Kisslo, J., vonRamm, O. J., and Thurstone, F. L. Cardiac imaging using a phased array ultrasound system. II. Clinical technique and application. Circulation 53:262–267, 1976.
9. Popp. R. L. and Harrison, D. C. Ultrasonic cardiac echography for determining stroke volume and valvular regurgitation. Circulation 41:495–502, 1970.
10. Quinones, M. A., Gaasch, W. H., Cole, J. S., and Alexander, J. K. Echocardiographic determination of left ventricular stress-velocity relations in man: With reference to the effects of loading and contractility. Circulation 51:689–700, 1975.
11. Sandler, H. and Ghista, D. N. Mechanical and dynamic implications of dimensional measurements of the left ventricle. Fed Proc 28:1344–1349, 1969.
12. Troy, B. L., Pombo, J., and Rackley, C. E. Measurements of left ventricular wall thickness and mass by echocardiography. Circulation 45:602–611, 1972.
13. Upton, M. T., Gibson, D. G., and Brown, D. J. Echocardiographic assessment of abnormal left ventricular function by echocardiography. Br Heart J 38:1001–1009, 1976.

CHAPTER 13

EXERCISE STRESS TESTING

ROBERT A. BRUCE
L. JOHN CLARKE

Exercise stress testing reveals variations in cardiovascular and electrocardiographic responses to the augmented aerobic requirements of muscular work. If the intensity of work performed is allowed to progress to symptom-limited capacity, the functional limits of the cardiovascular system are defined and many of the pathophysiological mechanisms contributing to dysfunction or failure of the heart may be identified. It provides a means for earlier detection, as well as functional evaluation, of the severity of chronic ischemic heart disease, whatever its etiology. It also provides an excellent noninvasive means of assessing the efficacy of treatment of ambulatory cardiac patients; indeed, with a low-level protocol it aids in determining the optimal time and safety of discharging patients from the hospital to unsupervised self-care at home after acute myocardial infarction or after aorto-coronary bypass surgery.

HISTORICAL DEVELOPMENTS

There are many more physiologists, physicians, cardiologists, electrocardiographers, and others who have contributed to our knowledge of exercise testing than can be cited in this brief overview. Yet it should be noted that in 1889 Maximowitsch and Rieder (30) noted the increase in both heart rate and blood pressure with exercise, and in 1895 Frank (20) recognized that the resistance component of cardiac work per minute was represented by the product of pressure-volume work per beat times the heart rate. In 1908 Einthoven (18) recorded electrocardiographic responses to exercise that showed increases in the amplitude of P and T waves as well as in heart rate, and in 1918 Bousfield (5) observed abnormal variations in these responses in patients with angina pectoris. In 1928 Feil and Siegel (19) recorded ST-T changes with spontaneous attacks of angina pectoris and their resolution when nitroglycerin relieved pain and lowered blood pressure.

Dr. Starr's contemporaries Wood et al. (37) reported in 1931, in 30 patients with angina pectoris, the association of symptoms induced by various types of exertion with electrocardiographic findings. Half exhibited temporary changes in the ventricular complexes during pain; the others showed no specific changes. Interestingly, on the basis of the frequent absence of electrocardiogram (ECG) changes in their studies of temporary coronary artery occlusion in animals, they stated that the absence of changes during attacks of angina in patients did not rule out the possibility of temporary myocardial ischemia. They also postulated that the majority of anginal attacks are "associated with a localized circulatory disturbance in the heart." Although no untoward complication occurred, they were not prepared to recommend this ECG procedure as a diagnostic test. In 1932, however, Goldhammer and Scherf (21) employed a variety of exercises to observe ECG responses, and other studies were reported by L. N. Katz, V. Puddu, and M. Missal.

Another of Dr. Starr's contemporaries, A. M. Master, introduced the two-step exercise test in 1929 (28). He focused on the amount of work done with "every day muscular activity" and designed a step test simple enough for clinical application in hospital or office practice. He reported differences in foot-pounds of work performed in relation to sex, age, and body weight in 115 normal subjects when they exercised for $1\frac{1}{2}$ min at a rate that would allow recovery in 2 min of heart rate and blood pressure to within 10 points of the resting values (Fig. 1). His data on 444 normal subjects show considerable variation in the work achieved in relation to age and sex, yet the trends resemble those observed years later by others with respect to functional aerobic capacity or maximal oxygen uptake of normal subjects (2). Master emphasized that men have a greater tolerance for exercise than women and that children show the greatest efficiency. He suggested that this test could aid diagnosis and evaluation of cardiovascular disease and help decide how much activity should be permitted. In 1935 Master (26) reported the ratio of the observed number of climbs in the two-step test to the expected number to derive a "percentage of efficiency." This indicated whether "an adult or child is fit to

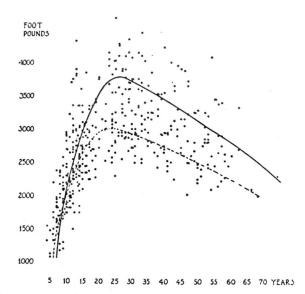

FIGURE 1 Variations in foot-pounds of work performed with the single two-step test in 1.5 min in healthy males (solid curve) and females (dashed curve). Note the lower values in children, peak responses at about 25 yr of age, higher values in men than in women, and progressive decline with age. From Master (26), with permission from the American Heart Journal.

perform the average physical work for his sex, age, and weight, but one can learn also what is actual physical capacity, be he an invalid or athlete." Of three case examples Master cited, the first was a woman with an enlarged heart, mitral valve disease, and 77% efficiency. The second was a patient who had recovered from "an acute coronary artery occlusion" and had negative physical and chest X-ray findings, minor abnormalities in "R-T" in lead I, and only 67% efficiency on testing; this patient had a recurrent event the following year. The third patient, whose history was similar, markedly reduced his weight, and serial exercise testing over 9 mo showed an improvement in efficiency from 86%, which was interpreted as a "good prognosis," to normal exercise tolerance 2 yr later. It was not until 1941 that focus was placed on the electrocardiographic responses to the test when Master and Jaffee (27) reported a single case in which ST changes were induced by exercise.

The duration of the test was later extended from $1\frac{1}{2}$ to 3 min and it was called the double two-step test. Clinical attention shifted from the cardiovascular responses to graded amounts of work to the ECG changes, which, by selection of a middle-aged American population, often reflected the ischemic myocardial consequences of coronary vascular disease. This noninvasive technique was extensively adopted by physicians as an aid to diagnosis of angina pectoris, coronary insufficiency, or ischemic heart disease; it became the standard diagnostic test in the United States for the next two to three decades.

The concept that ST depression reflects the balance between the metabolic demands of the myocardium and the adequacy of coronary circulation in angina patients was stated by Lloyd-Thomas (25). Evidence that a reduced exogenous supply of oxygen as well as the increased circulatory demands induced by exercise reproduce the ECG sign of myocardial ischemia in healthy young men was shown by Yu et al. (38). The prognostic value of ST depression induced by the Master step test was reported by Mattingly (29) and Robb and Marks (33). With the advent of invasive coronary arteriography within the last decade, numerous cardiologists defined the moderately high sensitivity and specificity of this functional sign for significant evidence of coronary vascular disease. Redwood and Epstein (32), however, seriously questioned its diagnostic value. Although Master recognized that the amount of ST depression increases with the severity of exercise, he believed that stresses or the number of ascents in his step test should be weight-adjusted for each sex.

By use of the treadmill, which makes the work load proportional to body weight (15), the aerobic requirements of exercise can be expressed in terms of oxygen uptake per unit of weight. Doan et al. (17) compared the prevalence of a 0.5-mm ST depression in the 12-lead ECG after the double two-step test with the prevalence of a 1-mm or greater depression in a single precordial ECG lead after a multistage treadmill test of symptom-limited exercise capacity in almost equal numbers of habitually active and sedentary healthy subjects. A greater prevalence of ST depression with maximal exercise on the treadmill suggested a stronger potential for early detection of latent coronary heart disease. Several investigators reported variations in sensitivity with different lead placements (3), marked intra- and interobserver variations in the interpretation of responses, as well as variations in subjects and patients, technical limitations of the frequency response, damping characteristics, millivolt calibration of the electrocardiograph, and use of vector-cardiography and polarcardiography (8, 14) for QRS, ST, and T changes with exercise. Different types of testing procedures, single versus multistage or ramp functions, continuous or discontinuous testing, various types of ergometers, differences in posture, and the use of arms and/or legs have also been explored for the past 75 yr.

CLINICAL EXPERIENCE, RISKS OF COMPLICATIONS, AND SALIENT DEVELOPMENTS

A 1970 survey of experience with 170,000 exercise tests performed in 73 clinical centers indicated the need for preliminary clinical examination of patients and their resting ECG before exercise testing (34). The needs for professional supervision of testing and facilities for emergency treatment when needed (on rare occasions) were recognized; furthermore, safety was not compromised when more stressful tests were used. The mortality risk was 1 in 10,000 tests and the morbidity risk was 2.4 in 10,000 tests. The importance of exertional hypotension, defined by an inadequate rise in systolic pressure of less than 10 mmHg, as a precursor to postexertional cardiac arrest from ventricular fibrillation in 2.2% of men with coronary heart disease has been reported; with prompt defibrillation, all survived without the complication of evolving myocardial infarction.

Comparison of a symptom-limited multistage treadmill test with the clinically accepted double two-step test indicated a greater prevalence of ST depression and greater sensitivity and predictive risk ratio for detection of asymptomatic middle-aged men who were at risk for later clinical manifestations of coronary disease events with the treadmill test (1, 17). This applied to a lesser extent in Chinese men, who experience coronary disease less frequently (24). These findings led to further measurements to define the normal standards for maximal oxygen uptake in middle-aged men and women (12) and the amount of restriction imposed by heart disease. This permitted statistical prediction of normal limits of the functional aerobic capacity and estimation of an individual's capacity from regression on duration of exercise with a standardized multistage protocol (12). Then the amount of functional aerobic impairment (FAI) could be determined for each individual (12) (Table 1). With a nomogram this could be readily estimated from elapsed time, which, under these conditions, represented the integrated limits of the entire cardiovascular system (12). The individual's functional aerobic capacity, expressed as a percentage of the average normal maximal oxygen uptake, then equaled 100% minus FAI%.

PROSPECTIVE COMMUNITY STUDY OF SYMPTOM–LIMITED MAXIMAL EXERCISE

These developments prompted the initiation in 1971 of a prospective community project, which became known as the Seattle Heart Watch (10), to test three hypotheses: 1) that physicians in routine clinical practice could perform multistage, symptom-limited tests and use the observed responses as an aid to evaluating the severity of cardiovascular disease; 2) that significant differences in

TABLE 1 Regression equations for estimation of functional aerobic impairment from duration of symptom-limited maximal exercise, sex, age, and activity status[a]

Age-predicted normal values of $\dot{V}O_2$ max in milliliter per kilogram of body weight per minute

$= 57.8 - 0.445$ (age in years) for sedentary men

$= 41.2 - 0.343$ (age in years) for sedentary women

$= 69.7 - 0.612$ (age in years) for active men

$= 44.4 - 0.343$ (age in years) for active women

Estimated $\dot{V}O_2$ max in milliliter per kilogram of body weight per minute

$= 3.88 - 0.056$ (duration in seconds) for men

$= 1.06 - 0.056$ (duration in seconds) for women

$= 10.5 + 0.035$ (duration in seconds) for cardiac men

$$\text{FAI\%} = \frac{\text{Age-predicted } \dot{V}O_2 \text{ max} - \text{estimated } \dot{V}O_2 \text{ max}}{\text{Age-predicted } \dot{V}O_2 \text{ max}} \times 100$$

Percentage of average normal $\dot{V}O_2$ max $= 100\% - \text{FAI\%}$

[a]See Bruce et al. (12).

responses, representing mechanisms of cardiac impairment, could be obtained in cardiac patients and would permit noninvasive assessment of left ventricular function; and 3) that useful prognostic information could be identified by retrospective analysis of morbidity and mortality through appropriate follow-up surveillance. It is interesting to report that more than 50 physicians, including cardiologists, internists, and general practitioners in both clinical and industrial facilities, cooperated. In 6 yr after July 1971 more than 9000 persons were tested, and in the past 2–3 yr at least another 3000 persons and more than 9000 tests were added by means of peripheral terminals linked by dial telephone to a central computer. During part of this time, when research funds for dataphone rentals were available, continuous ECG signals from single precordial leads in nearly 4000 persons were also transmitted by telephone for on-line computer averaging and analysis of QRS and ST responses before, during, and 5 min after such exercise tests. This objective evaluation supplemented the clinical interpretations by the physicians. This method increased the signal-to-noise ratio nearly tenfold when approximately 100 beats were averaged for each period of observation. Data were sampled at 400 Hz, and a statistical study of 5 measurements of ST forces indicated a greater differentiation of responses of cardiac patients from those of healthy subjects during the fixed interval of 50–69 msec after the nadir of the S wave (which was designated ST_B), especially at 1 min into recovery from symptom-limited maximal exercise (R. A. Bruce, unpublished observations). Initial classifications of risk factors, physical activity status, cardiovascular disease, and types of treatment of individuals were made by the physician before exercise testing. Subsequent follow-up surveillance for possible morbidity or mortality was achieved by mailing questionnaires to patients every 6 mo, and to healthy subjects originally enrolled in the Seattle Heart Watch every year. What have we learned from the first 6 yr of this study, which is still in progress?

Feasibility, Safety, and Pathophysiological Significance

First, the feasibility of multistage treadmill testing of symptom-limited capacity in various clinical environments has been demonstrated. In the latest tabulation of the community experience during the past 6 yr, more than 17,000 tests were performed, of which 11,390 (66%) were on cardiovascular patients and 5756 (34%) were on asymptomatic healthy persons (Fig. 2). Although 6 instances of exertional hypotension and postexertional cardiac arrest from ventricular fibrillation occurred, with an incidence of 0.04%, all were successfully defibrillated, and there have been no deaths. Even fewer examples of acute myocardial infarction with (11) or without arrest and no deaths have been reported. It is of interest to note that the range of exercise duration is very broad in both groups, with modal values of stage III in the cardiac patients and stage IV in the healthy persons. The weight-adjusted maximal oxygen uptake is highly correlated with the duration of exercise with this testing protocol (12), and the estimated values for this variable at the modal durations of exercise are 34.1 and 24.0 ml/kg · min, respectively. The average functional aerobic capacity in the cardiac patients, over all ages and both sexes, is only 70% of that in the healthy persons. Thus, it is apparently feasible for physicians to exercise cardiac patients with safety, even to their symptom-limited capacity, and to derive reasonable quantitative estimates of the limits of functional cardiovascular performance. Since the relation of cardiac output to oxygen uptake is nearly the same in patients with coronary heart disease as in normal persons (13) and may be roughly estimated by regression on oxygen uptake, the peak cardiac output responses of these two groups are approximately 18.7 and 13.5 liter/min,

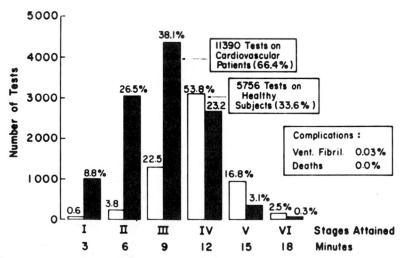

FIGURE 2 Distribution of work loads obtained in 5756 multistage treadmill tests in healthy men and 11,390 tests in patients with cardiovascular disease in Seattle experience, 1971–1977.

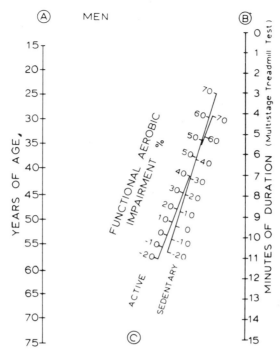

FIGURE 3   Nomogram to derive functional aerobic impairment from age, duration of exercise, and activity classification of men who are tested by the multistage treadmill test of symptom-limited exercise. From Bruce et al. (12), with permission from the American Heart Journal.

respectively. Indeed, on the basis of these modal values, where peak cardiac output in cardiac patients averages only 73% of that of normal subjects, functional impairment in the absence of clinical manifestations of congestion at rest is a common finding.

Evaluation of Functional Impairment

Three types of functional impairment of cardiac patients may be evaluated quantitatively from noninvasive measurements at symptom-limited maximal exercise.

The first is FAI, or the percentage deviation of an individual's weight-adjusted maximal oxygen uptake, estimated by regression from the total duration in seconds of this particular multistage treadmill test, from the weight-adjusted average for normal subjects of the same sex, age, and activity classification.

Fortunately, with a nomogram (Fig. 3), FAI may be derived from a single measurement of the duration of exercise when sex, age, and activity classification are known (12). When FAI% is subtracted from 100%, the individual's aerobic capacity is derived as a percentage of that of average normal subjects similar in sex, age, and activity classification. This evaluates the aerobic capacity of the entire body since, according to the Fick equation, $\dot{V}O_2$ is the product of cardiac output and the difference between the arterial and the mixed venous oxygen content (31). Because there is a high correlation between oxygen uptake and cardiac output, even in patients with symptomatic coronary heart disease (13), this is a first approximation to cardiac capacity, and the FAI estimates the severity of cardiac dysfunction or heart failure at symptom-limited exercise. The nomogram may also be used to estimate how much longer the impaired patient needs to continue the exercise test to show normal function. Conversely, and this is of greater interest to the patient, one can ascertain the equivalent age at which the observed performance would coincide with the expected average normal response.

The cumulative percentage distributions of FAI derived by nomogram for 2404 normal men; 1244 men who were hypertensive or had atypical chest pain, specifically not angina pectoris, and showed no clinical evidence of heart disease; 1751 unoperated men with coronary heart disease; and 343 men who were tested before aortocoronary bypass surgery are shown in Fig. 4. The normal range extends from −23 to +23%. Of men in these four groups, 95, 84, 48, and 20%, respectively, had aerobic capacities within the normal range. Stated differently, 5% of the normal men were equally divided between those with negative values of FAI, which represent greater than normal maximal oxygen uptakes, and those with positive values, which represent subnormal uptakes. Likewise, 16, 52, and 80% of men in the 3 patient groups had aerobic impairment or subnormal limits of maximal oxygen uptake. Hypertension and atypical chest pain syndromes are included together because the functional aerobic impairment is only mild or borderline, in contrast to the definite impairment exhibited by the majority of coronary heart disease (CHD) patients. Variations in percentile values for these four groups of men are easily derived from this chart.

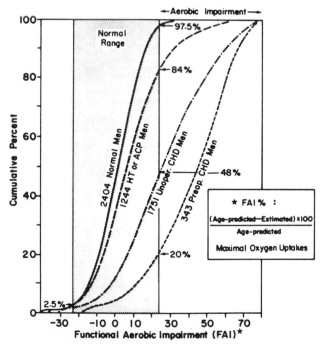

FIGURE 4 Cumulative distribution curves of functional aerobic impairment in four groups of healthy men and cardiovascular patients.

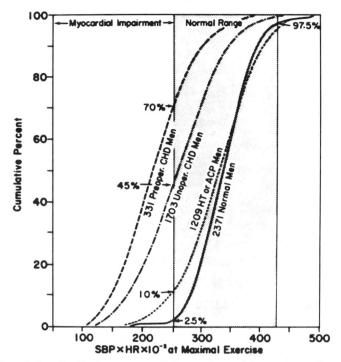

FIGURE 5 Cumulative distribution curves of the product of heart rate and systolic pressure times 10^{-2} at maximal exercise in the four groups of men represented in Fig. 4.

The second type of functional impairment that may be evaluated refers to myocardial capacity, more specifically to the amount of functional left ventricular impairment. It is the product of heart rate and systolic pressure at maximal exercise, times 10^{-2}, called the pressure rate or double product. The cumulative percentage distribution of this variable, which in humans is highly correlated with myocardial requirement for oxygen during exercise (23), is shown in Fig. 5 for 2371 normal men, 1209 hypertensive men or men with atypical chest pain specifically not angina pectoris, 1703 unoperated men with CHD, and 331 men with CHD who were tested before aortocoronary bypass surgery. The normal range, representing the 2.5 and 97.5 percentiles, extends from 250 to 430. Of men in the 3 groups of patients, 10, 45, and 70%, respectively, exhibited subnormal values. From this chart it is possible to ascertain the percentile relationship of an individual patient to the group of his peers. It should be noted that the effects of antihypertensive therapy, or treatment with beta blockers in about 7% of the coronary patients, are disregarded in this analysis. Likewise, these values do not apply to women, who characteristically show smaller increments in systolic pressure with exercise. Since the decline in heart rate with aging is almost exactly balanced by the increased systolic pressure responses observed by sphygmomanometry, there is little necessity to adjust the pressure rate product for differences in age within the range 30-60 yr.

The magnitude of functional left ventricular impairment can also be evaluated by the percentage difference between age-predicted and observed values of the pressure rate product at maximal exercise (9). For normal men, the predicted value is $364 - 0.58$ (years of age).

The third type of functional cardiac impairment refers to the heart rate response defined as the percentage deviation from age-predicted maximal heart rate for normal men; this represents the chronotropic impairment (9). The predicted normal maximal rate is $210 - 0.662$ (years of age). The cumulative distribution curves for normal men and the same three groups of cardiovascular patients are shown in Fig. 6. The normal range, defined by the 2.5 and 97.5 percentiles, is from -10 to $+10\%$. Since this is a derived variable representing differences from age-adjusted normal averages, abnormal values are shown when the curves are shifted to the right. In this instance, 80% of the hypertensive or atypical chest pain syndrome cases, 44% of the men with unoperated CHD, and 22% of the men with CHD and subsequent bypass surgical treatment have heart rate responses that are within the normal range. The others show subnormal capacity or chronotropic impairment. Again, the effect of propranolol in a small fraction of these patients is disregarded; actually, this increases the amount of chronotropic impairment.

Mechanisms of Cardiac Dysfunction

Many of the cardiac mechanisms of functional aerobic impairment can also be identified by simple, noninvasive observations. One or more precordial ECG leads also reveal the occurrence of premature beats or other arrhythmias and, occa-

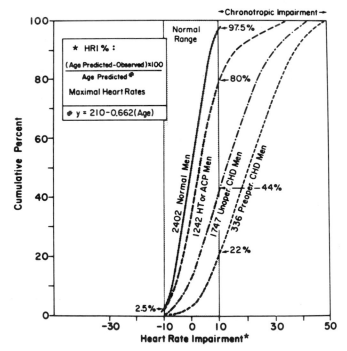

FIGURE 6 Cumulative distribution curves of chronotropic capacity and impairment in the four groups of men represented in Figs. 4 and 5.

sionally, changes in intraventricular conduction. The appearance of three or more consecutive ventricular premature beats is an indication to stop the test. Invasive studies in selected patients have documented acute reductions in cardiac output when these disorders occur. The subjective awareness of chest discomfort or pain initiated by the testing usually indicates angina pectoris. Often, but not always, objective evidence of subendocardial ischemia may be demonstrated by horizontal or downsloping ST depression. The earlier this becomes apparent during exercise, the greater the amount of depression, and the longer it persists after exercise, the greater the severity of subendocardial ischemia. Yet the absence of this response in patients with transmural ischemia, prior myocardial infarction, and scarring with occurrence of dyskinesis of that portion of the ventricular wall with exercise is a commonly observed false negative ST response. A statistical analysis of computer measurements indicates that the criterion for an abnormal response is a depression of 1.5 mm or -0.15 mV or more in a left precordial CB_5 lead, particularly at 1 min after maximal exercise (R. A. Bruce, unpublished observations).

The significance of ST depression, which has been the primary focus of clinical interest in exercise testing since Master and Jaffe (27), Mattingly (29), Robb and Marks (33), and others emphasized its clinical value, should be discussed briefly from the viewpoint of pathophysiology, prevalence, and diagnostic and prognostic implications in relation to CHD. Even marked ST depression, appearing early and lasting for a few minutes after exertion, is not necessarily a diagnostic sign of coronary vascular disease, since, as Mattingly (29) observed, anemia may cause myocardial ischemia. Therefore it is only a nonspecific functional sign of imbalance, primarily at the subendocardial cell membrane, between the myocardial oxygen demand, defined by left ventricular volume, wall tension, pressure, contractility, and heart rate, and the supply of oxygenated arterial blood provided by the coronary circulation. It may be accentuated by positive inotropic agents, such as digitalis (4, 22), or by hypokalemia. When the ST segment depression is a result of ischemia, whatever the cause, it is associated with an intracellular shift toward anaerobic glycolysis and with release of potassium and lactate (16). ST depression also occurs at least mildly with tachycardia (Sjöstrand effect) (36)—especially with greater than average increases in heart rate and systolic pressure as well as prolonged exertion, and usually as a modest upsloping depression—in healthy persons, especially women, and more frequently with advancing age.

ST change is quantitatively variable in amount, even under tightly controlled conditions of retesting 1 wk later, and observers may agree on responses only 70% of the time, although computer analysis of ST depression shows reproducible changes more than 80% of the time (R. E. Traylor, personal communication).

The prevalence of ST depression varies with designated criteria, with age, and with the presence of heart disease, especially coronary disease with associated infarction and scarring of the myocardium. The diagnostic value of ST changes in relation to coronary arteriographic criteria is controversial and disappointingly low. In the Seattle Heart Watch, using the criterion of 1 mm or more of horizontal or downsloping ischemic depression, the sensitivity is only 47% while the specificity is 81% for detecting at least 70% stenosis of one or more coronary arteries (7). Indeed, the poorest performance for detection of coronary disease through exercise-induced ST changes is in patients with ventricular dyskinesis, usually associated with severe coronary disease, both with and without clinical infarction (10). These patients frequently exhibit false negative responses with minor ST depression at rest, which disappears with exercise or is even replaced by elevation. This change is hypothesized to be a consequence of transmural ischemia or dyskinesis of the ventricular wall adjacent to the lead electrode induced by the increase in systolic pressure during exercise. Accordingly, about half, or even a majority, of postmyocardial infarction coronary patients do not exhibit the expected true positive response. However, the prognostic value, confirming the earlier observations of Mattingly (29) and Robb and Marks (33), who used the double two-step test, is somewhat greater.

Comparative Incidence of Primary and Secondary Coronary Heart Disease Events

After approximately 3 yr of follow-up surveillance, enough morbidity and mortality events have occurred in the Seattle Heart Watch to indicate important changes in the natural history of CHD. The frequency is much lower for primary events in previously healthy asymptomatic men than for secondary events in patients with clinically manifested CHD (Fig. 7). In order of importance, the morbidity in primary events from myocardial infarction and angina pectoris greatly exceeds the mortality from cardiac deaths. In contrast, the secondary events in patients with previously recognized CHD occur about 18 times as often. Again in order, very sudden cardiac death (within 1 hr) is exceeded only by angina pectoris, partly because the contemporary clinical trend is to treat patients with angina pectoris by aortocoronary bypass surgery. Myocardial infarction is a less frequent event than cardiac death. Thus, not only is the incidence of secondary events much greater, but the more frequent type of event is quite different. How many of these changes reflect progressive cardiac dysfunction?

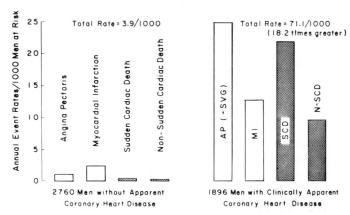

FIGURE 7 Incidence of primary and secondary CHD events within 3 ± 1 yr of follow-up surveillance after maximal exercise testing in Seattle experience. Note that myocardial infarction is the most frequent primary event, sudden cardiac death is the most frequent spontaneous secondary event, and secondary events occur 18 times as often, in part because of the frequent use of surgical treatment of angina.

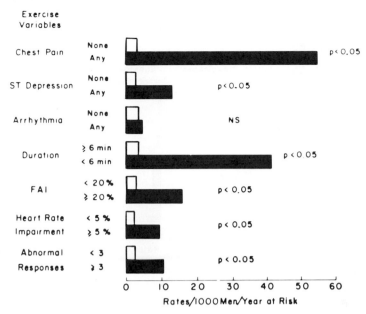

FIGURE 8 Comparison of the predictive value of exercise variables in 2760 men clinically free of CHD at the initial examination and testing.

Clinical and Exercise Predictors of Coronary Heart Disease Events

The available data for an industrial and clinical cohort of 2760 healthy men with 3 ± 1 yr of follow-up surveillance reveal no cardiac events in 98.6% (6). Of the 1.4% who developed CHD events, univariate analyses of the event rates per 1000 men at risk per year indicate the predictive value of any one or more of the commonly identified risk factors, including a positive family history of cardio-vascular disease and particularly smoking and systolic pressure over 140 mmHg at rest. Of the exercise responses, chest pain on exercise testing, duration of symptom-limited exercise of less than 6 min (corresponding to the first two stages of the multistage test), and ischemic ST depression are much stronger predictors (Fig. 8). In this population sample, the prognostic importance of ischemic ST depression was limited to one-third of the sample who had one or more conventional risk factors (Fig. 9).

Univariate analyses of secondary CHD events in patients with clinical manifestations of CHD indicate that two parameters of maximal left ventricular function, along with an enlarged heart or cardiomegaly, are major predictors (Fig. 10). The two exercise parameters are duration of less than 3 min, which represents a maximum $\dot{V}O_2$ of less than 17 ml/kg · min or about 4–4.5 multiples of the resting oxygen requirement (mets), and a systolic pressure at symptom-limited maximal exercise of less than 130 mmHg. For the absence of all 3 predictors and the presence of any 1, and 2, or all 3, respectively, the annual CHD mortality risks are 20, 96, 252, and 884 per 1000 men at risk. Of the patients with none of these predictors, 78% have

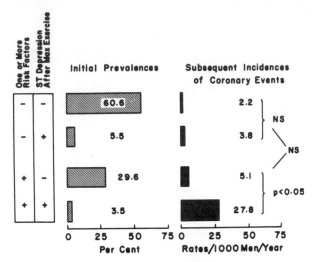

FIGURE 9 Comparison of the predictive value of conventional risk factors and of ST depression after maximal exercise in men initially free of CHD.

the lowest risk and less than 1% have the highest risk. With multivariate analysis, five predictors are identified (7): the total number, rather than the type, of abnormalities in the resting ECG, followed by cardiomegaly, maximal systolic pressure, exercise duration, and the exertional arrhythmia severity score. Of CHD patients with the lowest mortality risk who remain unoperated, 85% have a 3-yr survival rate of nearly

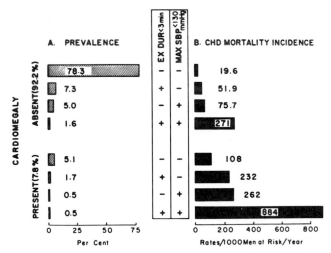

FIGURE 10 Variations in prevalence of three parameters of left ventricular function and subsequent incidence of CHD mortality in men with clinically manifest CHD on initial examination and exercise tests. Note that 78% without any of these risk variables had the lowest annual risk of cardiac death (20 per 1000 men at risk), and the range of the risk gradient varied markedly as the number of these variables increased. The overall annual rate of cardiac deaths is 29 per 1000 men at risk.

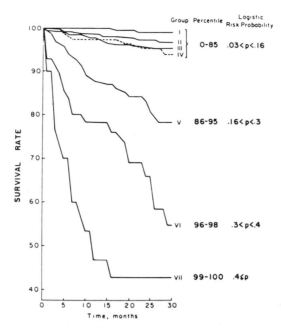

FIGURE 11   Variations in prevalence of ischemic parameters in the CHD patients represented in
Fig. 10. Note the narrow range of the risk gradient.

95%. Although parameters of myocardial ischemia have some predictive value, the
differentiation of mortality risk is meager (Fig. 11).

LOW-LEVEL TESTING FOR SAFETY
OF AMBULATORY SELF-CARE AT HOME

As medical and surgical care improves and the duration of hospitalization
diminishes, an entirely new application of exercise stress testing is now emerging.
Accordingly, we have developed a low-level multistage test for patients with acute
myocardial infarction or aortocoronary bypass surgery (35). This protocol begins at
1.2 mph and 0% gradient for 3 min and increases to 3 and 6% gradients. The test is
given when the responsible physician or surgeon is ready to discharge the patient
from the hospital. In the uncomplicated infarct patient this occurs at about 11 d,
and in the surgical patient it may be as early as 6 or 7 d. There are three major
differences between this symptom-threshold testing protocol and symptom-limited
testing for determination of capacity. First, even the highest work load does not
exceed 3–3.5 mets, which is less than the first stage of the established multistage test
of capacity. Second, the purpose is to test the wisdom and safety of the clinical
decision to discharge the patient at that time. Actually, about 80% of uncomplicated
patients continue this low-level test for 9 min without distress. When the exceptional
patient who manifests a threshold symptom or sign in a shorter time is allowed a
longer period of convalescence in hospital, he usually completes the test two or more
days later without difficulty. Third, unlike symptom-limited capacity testing, the

purpose of the low-level test is to define the threshold for any symptom (usually chest pain) or sign such as excessive tachycardia, fall in blood pressure, premature beats, or ST displacement (whether depression or elevation). It seems more prudent to test patients under professional supervision than to discharge them prematurely on the basis of no adverse symptoms or signs at rest and then to have a clinical relapse occur unnecessarily and unexpectedly even with the very modest energy requirements of self-care at home. Furthermore, when this low-level testing is performed pre-operatively, it provides an opportunity for very early evaluation of the effects of surgical treatment. Much more experience is needed to express the merits of this application in statistical terms.

Exercise testing is most useful for assessing the severity of myocardial ischemia, the amount of ventricular dysfunction or failure, and the risk of arrhythmias that may be induced by even mild exercise, when there is no evidence available at rest, particularly in patients with CHD who are recovering from acute myocardial infarction or from aortocoronary bypass surgery.

COMMENTS

Now, nearly 50 yr later, we seem to have come full circle to recognize, as Master originally did, how important these measurements of heart rate and systolic blood pressure are. There is, of course, a major difference in study design, since he originally attempted to define work loads that were only moderate for normal persons and would permit heart rate and systolic pressure to return to within 10 points of resting levels within 2 min. Although he did not intend to evaluate responses to symptom-limited maximal exertion in cardiac patients, the fact that some could not achieve the prescribed number of ascents revealed symptom-limited capacity, which he originally appraised in terms of percentage "efficiency." In my experience, single-stage testing was used for several years before it was recognized that if exercise testing were safely withstood by the more impaired patients who could not complete even a moderate stress test because of symptomatic limitations, then it should be equally possible for all ambulatory persons to be tested to symptom-limited exertion. It is essential in any testing situation that proper guidelines be followed, specifically that a preliminary clinical and ECG examination be made to exclude any persons who should not be tested. Professional supervision and monitoring, use of the multistage principle with continuous increments in work load (even if it requires lower work loads initially for the most limited patients), and mandatory rules for stopping exertion, even in the absence of symptoms, are important constraints to ensure safety. With these clinical guidelines and precautions, the safety of symptom-limited exercise testing exceeds that of the previously reported general experience, which was based primarily on submaximal stress testing, and far exceeds that of the commonly used invasive examinations by coronary arteriography and left ventriculography.

CONCLUSIONS

Low-level and symptom-limited exercise testing provides the physician with a noninvasive means of examining the patient that will aid not only in evaluating and managing but also in assessing the prognosis of the patient. The predominent limitation during exercise is set by the functional limits of the cardiac patient's heart. Hence, exercise is a tool for detecting ventricular dysfunction before it progresses to overt congestive heart failure at rest.

The primary risk faced by patients with clinical manifestations of coronary heart disease is sudden death. Noncongestive left ventricular dysfunction and heart failure are the major predictors of sudden cardiac death. Exercise testing may be used to define the severity of the cardiac dysfunction and has the advantage that it can be performed either at the time of initial work-up of the patient in the office or at the last examination before discharge from the hospital.

Finally, Dr. Starr's contemporaries who pioneered clinical investigation of angina patients and who conducted experimental animal studies recognized the limitations of electrocardiographic procedures and wisely refrained from recommending them for diagnosis. Taking cognizance of cardiomegaly in their patients and the blood pressure responses during the anginal pain, they stated, "The clinical observations are more likely to be significant from a diagnostic standpoint than the electrocardiographic phenomena" (37). The latter statement has greater validity if "clinical observations" are extended to include responses to symptom-limited exercise.

REFERENCES

1. Aronow, W. S., Cassidy, J., and Yueyama, R. R. Resting and postexercise apexcardiogram correlated with maximum treadmill stress tests in normal subjects. Circulation 44:397–402, 1971.
2. Åstrand, P. O. Physical performance as a function of age. J Am Med Assoc 205:729–733, 1968.
3. Blackburn, H., Taylor, H. L., Okamoto, N., Rautaharju, P., Mitchell, P. L., and Kerkhof, A. C. Standardization of the exercise electrocardiogram. A systematic comparison of chest lead configurations employed for monitoring during exercise. In: Physical Activity and the Heart, M. J. Karvonen and A. J. Barry, eds. Springfield, Ill.: Thomas, 1967, pp. 101–133.
4. Blackmon, J. R., Hellerstein, H. K., Gillespie, L., and Berne, R. M. Effect of digitalis glycosides on the myocardial sodium and potassium balance. Circ Res 8:1003–1012, 1960.
5. Bousfield, G. Angina pectoris: Changes in electrocardiograms during paroxysm. Lancet 2:457–458, 1918.
6. Bruce, R. A., DeRouen, T. A., and Blake, B. Maximal exercise testing: A preliminary report of the Seattle Heart Watch. In: Royal College of Physicians Symposium, L. McDonald, ed. London, in press.
7. Bruce, R. A., DeRouen, T. A., Peterson, D. R., Irving, J. R., Chinn, N., Blake, B., and Hofer, V. Non-invasive predictors of sudden cardiac death in men with coronary heart disease. Am J Cardiol 39:833–840, 1977.
8. Bruce, R. A., Detry, J. M., Early, K., and Early, R. Polarcardiographic responses to maximal exercise in healthy young adults. Am Heart J 83:207–218, 1972.
9. Bruce, R. A., Fisher, L. D., Cooper, M. N., and Gey, G. O. Separation of effects of cardiovascular disease and age on ventricular function with maximal exercise. Am J Cardiol 34:757–763, 1974.
10. Bruce, R. A., Gey, G. O., Cooper, M. N., Fisher, L. D., and Peterson, D. R.

Seattle Heart Watch: Initial clinical, circulatory and electrocardiographic responses to maximal exercise. Am J Cardiol 33:459–469, 1974.

11. Bruce, R. A., Hornsten, T., and Blackmon, J. R. Myocardial infarction after normal responses to maximal exercise. Circulation 38:552–558, 1968.

12. Bruce, R. A., Kusumi, F., and Hosmer, D. Maximal oxygen intake and nomographic assessment of functional aerobic impairment in cardiovascular disease. Am Heart J 85:546–562, 1973.

13. Bruce, R. A., Kusumi, F., Niederberger, M., and Peterson, J. L. Cardiovascular mechanisms of functional aerobic impairment in patients with coronary heart disease. Circulation 49:696–702, 1974.

14. Bruce, R. A., Li, Y. B., Dower, G. E., and Nilson, K. Polarcardiographic responses to maximal exercise and to changes in posture in healthy middle-aged men. J Electrocardiol 6:91–96, 1973.

15. Buskirk, E. and Taylor, H. L. Maximal oxygen intake and its relation to body composition with special reference to chronic physical activity and obesity. J Appl Physiol 11:72–78, 1957.

16. Case, R. B., Roselle, H. A., and Cramptom, R. S. Relation of ST depression to metabolic and hemodynamic events. Cardiologia 48:32–41, 1966.

17. Doan, A. E., Peterson, D. R., Blackmon, J. R., and Bruce, R. A. Myocardial ischemia after maximal exercise in healthy men: A method for detecting potential coronary artery disease? Am Heart J 69:11–21, 1965.

18. Einthoven, W. Weiteres über das Elektrokardiogram. Arch Gesamte Physiol Menschen Tiere 122:517–584, 1908.

19. Feil, H. and Siegel, M. L. Electrocardiographic changes during attacks of angina. Am J Med Sci 175:255–260, 1928.

20. Frank, O. Zur Dynamik des Herzmuskels. Z Biol 14:370–437, 1895.

21. Goldhammer, S. and Scherf, D. Elektrokardiographische Untersuchungen bei Kranken mit Angina Pectoris ("Ambulatorischer Typus"). Z Klin Med 122:134–151, 1932.

22. Hirsch, E. Z. The effects of digoxin on the electrocardiogram after strenous exercise in normal men. Am Heart J 70:196–203, 1965.

23. Kitamura, K., Jorgensen, C. R., Gobel, F. L., Taylor, H. L., and Wang, Y. Hemodynamic correlates of myocardial oxygen consumption during upright exercise. J Appl Physiol 32:516–522, 1972.

24. Li, Y. B., Ting, N., Chiang, B. N., Alexander, E. R., Bruce, R. A., and Grayston, J. T. Electrocardiographic response to maximal exercise: Treadmill and double master exercise tests in middle-aged Chinese men. Am J Cardiol 20:541–548, 1967.

25. Lloyd-Thomas, H. G. The exercise electrocardiogram in patients with cardiac pain. Br Heart J 23:561–577, 1961.

26. Master, A. M. The two-step test of myocardial function. Am Heart J 10:495–510, 1935.

27. Master, A. M. and Jaffe, H. L. Electrocardiographic changes after exercise in angina pectoris. J Mt Sinai Hosp 7:629–632, 1941.

28. Master, A. M. and Oppenheimer, E. T. A simple exercise tolerance test for circulatory efficiency with standard tables for normal individuals. Am J Med Sci 177:223–243, 1929.

29. Mattingly, T. W. The postexercise electrocardiogram. Its value in the diagnosis and prognosis of coronary arterial disease. Am J Cardiol 9:395–409, 1962.

30. Maximowitsch, V. Untersuchungen über die durch Muskelarbeit und Flussigkeits-

aufnahme bedingten Blutdruchsschwankungen. Dtsch Arch Klin Med 46:329–368, 1889–1890.

31. Mitchell, J. H., Sproule, B. J., and Chapman, C. V. The physiological meaning of the maximal oxygen intake tests. J Clin Invest 37:538–547, 1958.

32. Redwood, D. R. and Epstein, S. E. Uses and limitations of stress testing in the evaluation of ischemic heart disease. Circulation 46:1115–1131, 1972.

33. Robb, G. P. and Marks, H. H. Postexercise electrocardiogram in arteriosclerotic heart disease. J Am Med Assoc 200:918–926, 1967.

34. Rochmis, P. and Blackburn, H. Exercise tests: A survey of procedures, safety and litigation experience in approximately 170,000 tests. J Am Med Assoc 217:1061–1066, 1971.

35. Sivarajan, E., Snydsman, A., Smith, B., Irving, J. B., Mansfield, L. W., and Bruce, R. A. Low-level treadmill testing of 41 patients with acute myocardial infarction prior to discharge from hospital. Heart Lung 6:975–980, 1977.

36. Sjöstrand, T. The relationship between the heart frequency and the ST level of the electrocardiogram. Acta Med Scand 138:191–200, 1950.

37. Wood, F. C., Wolferth, C. C., and Livezey, M. M. Angina pectoris: The clinical and electrocardiographic phenomena of attack and their comparison with effects of experimental temporary occlusion. Arch Intern Med 47:339–365, 1931.

38. Yu, P. N. G., Bruce, R. A., Lovejoy, F. W., and McDowell, M. E. Variations in electrocardiographic responses during exercise. Studies of normal subjects under unusual stresses and of patients with cardiopulmonary diseases. Circulation 3:368–376, 1951.

CHAPTER 14

SYSTOLIC TIME INTERVALS

ARNOLD M. WEISSLER
RICHARD S. STACK
YOUNG H. SOHN
DAVID SCHAFFER

Early studies of systolic time intervals (STI) were focused on their validation in the overall assessment of left ventricular performance and, in particular, in designating group differences among normal subjects and patients with various forms of left ventricular disease. Their acceptance as useful quantitative measures of left ventricular performance in individual patients has evolved slowly. In part, this reflects the different nature of the STI, which denote the timing of the events of the cardiac cycle rather than the more customary dimensions of pressure, flow, and volume. In addition, the fact that the STI are subject to transient circulatory influences, such as changes in end-diastolic wall stress and resistance to systolic emptying (as are virtually all other physiological measures of contractile function) has deterred some from accepting these measures as valid physiological expressions of cardiac performance. With the recent understanding that, despite the potential influence of sudden changes in ventricular loading, temporal events of the cardiac cycle can be delineated accurately and can reflect sustained alterations in left ventricular function, the STI have gained more widespread application.

Probably the greatest value of the STI is in following the course of left ventricular performance in patients with chronic cardiovascular disease, particularly coronary artery disease. In our laboratory, we have applied STI to two of the most challenging questions facing noninvasive technology: Do the methods afford information that current clinical approaches cannot provide, and are the noninvasive methods as accurate as the invasive techniques in defining the status of left ventricular performance?

PRINCIPLES OF SYSTOLIC TIME INTERVALS

The STI, which constitute the sequential phases of left ventricular systole, are determined from simultaneous high-speed recordings of the electrocardiogram, the phonocardiogram, and the carotid arterial pulse tracings (9, 10). In clinical practice, three primary measurements of the phases of systole are determined. Total electromechanical systole (QS_2) is the interval that spans the entire period of systole from the onset of the QRS complex on the electrocardiogram to the closure of the aortic valve as reflected in the second heart sound. The left ventricular ejection time (LVET) is the phase of systole during which the left ventricle ejects into the arterial system. The preejection period (PEP), the interval from the onset of ventricular depolarization to the beginning of ejection, is derived by subtracting the LVET from the QS_2 interval. Calculation of the PEP in this manner discounts the error resulting from the delay in transmission of the arterial pulse from the proximal aorta to the point of its detection over the carotid artery (usually a 20-msec delay). Alternatively, the PEP can be derived by measuring the interval from the onset of ventricular depolarization to the beginning of the upstroke of the carotid arterial pulse, from which the arterial pulse transmission time (the A_2 incisural interval) is subtracted.

By using recordings of the first heart sound and the apex cardiogram, some investigators have attempted to subdivide the PEP into its component intervals, the electromechanical delay and the isovolumetric contraction time. In our experience, the difficulty in delineating the onset of the mitral component of the first heart sound on the phonocardiogram and the beginning of mechanical systole on the apex cardiogram makes the measurement of these subintervals of the PEP so variable that it limits their general application. Furthermore, the time of registration of the first heart sound is not a valid indicator of the onset of isovolumetric systole.

To make these measurements, one should apply the same meticulous methodological approach that one would use in the cardiac catheterization laboratory. In practice, an electrocardiographic lead demonstrating a clear onset of ventricular depolarization is selected. The phonocardiogram should be recorded over the upper precordium in the frequency range 100–500 Hz. The carotid or subclavian arterial pulse must be recorded with high-fidelity instrumentation, preferably a strain gauge transducer that permits flat frequency and phase response between 0.1 and 30.0 Hz and at least a 2.0-sec time constant. For best definition of the STI, one must be certain that the recordings delineate a sharp inscription of the initial high-frequency vibrations of the aortic component of the second heart sound on the phonocardiogram, and a clearly discernible upstroke and incisural notch on the carotid arterial pulse tracing. Photographic recordings are preferred, and a minimum paper speed of 100 mm/sec is deemed necessary for accurate determination of the STI. Calculations of the STI are derived from the mean of at least 10 consecutive beats obtained while the patient is supine during quiet respiration. A critical review of these technical factors has recently been presented by Lewis et al. (6).

In simplest terms, the STI delineate the durations of the two major components of the systolic cycle of the heart, namely the preejection and ejection phases. The durations of these two sequential phases comprise total electromechanical systole. Their application in clinical practice is based on the fact that, like heart rate, cardiac output, and arterial pressure, the STI are well regulated under normal circumstances, so that QS_2, PEP, and LVET corrected for sex and heart rate fall within narrow physiological limits. The narrow distribution of the STI relative to heart rate readily allows detection of deviations from normal.

CLINICAL APPLICATION OF SYSTOLIC TIME INTERVALS

Of greatest importance in the clinical application of the STI is the finding that as left ventricular performance diminishes in patients with cardiac disease, a distinct pattern of change in the STI evolves: PEP lengthens and LVET shortens, while QS_2 remains unchanged (9, 10). The alterations in PEP and LVET have been found to be closely correlated with the reduced stroke volume, cardiac output, and ejection fraction, as well as with indices of left ventricular performance based on measurement of the first derivative of isovolumetric left ventricular pressure, in patients with coronary artery, primary myocardial, and hypertensive disease (1, 2, 4, 5). These data provide evidence that the changes in STI are related to the diminished contractile performance of the left ventricle in these states. It has been demonstrated that abnormal intervals are frequently in evidence in these states despite the absence of other abnormal clinical findings and when symptoms are minimal or absent.

The physiological alterations in the decompensated myocardium that are responsible for the changes in systolic intervals described above have been discussed earlier in this book. They include decreases in the rate of contraction and tension development relative to systolic load, which result in a diminished rate of pressure development during isovolumetric systole and a decreased extent and rate of contraction during ejection. The latter alterations in turn result in a diminished stroke volume and ejection fraction during an abbreviated ejection period. It is notable that just as the duration of mechanical systole (active state) remains unchanged in experimental left ventricular failure, the QS_2 remains remarkably normal in the decompensated left ventricle in humans (when inotropic drugs are withheld).

Application of STI measurements has shown that a simplified expression of alterations in the intervals is provided by the ratio PEP/LVET. This ratio requires no correction for sex or heart rate in the range 50–110 beats per minute. Since PEP lengthens while LVET shortens, the presence of left ventricular dysfunction is shown by an increase in PEP/LVET. In the normal population the range of PEP/LVET follows a normal distribution with a mean of 0.34 and a standard deviation of 0.04. When interpreting changes in individual patients, one should recognize that in addition to intrinsic left ventricular dysfunction, other clinically pertinent factors may influence the STI. Among these are digitalis therapy, beta receptor stimulation of the heart, beta receptor blocking agents, vasopressors, and transient alterations in ventricular volume (5). The influence of these factors on PEP/LVET is summarized in Table 1.

Digitalis administration improves left ventricular performance, as reflected in a

TABLE 1 Factors influencing preejection period/left ventricular ejection time

Factor	Effect
Left ventricular decompensation	Increase
Digitalis	Decrease
Beta receptor stimulation	Decrease
Beta receptor blockade	Increase
Vasopressors	Increase
Decreased ventricular volume	Increase
Left bundle branch block	Increase

diminution in PEP/LVET from levels that were previously high. However, in patients with moderate to marked left ventricular dysfunction, administration of digitalis rarely reduces the ratio to normal. Beta receptor stimulation with such agents as isoproterenol and epinephrine markedly diminishes PEP/LVET and may reduce it to normal from previously abnormal levels. A hallmark of the effects of positive inotropic agents, including digitalis and beta receptor stimulants, is an abbreviation of total electromechanical systole (QS_2). This finding helps one ascertain when left ventricular performance is influenced by positive inotropic agents, and it lends insight into the analysis of factors influencing left ventricular compensation.

The diminution in left ventricular performance induced by beta receptor blockade in standard clinical doses is usually of a mild degree. For this reason the finding of a moderate or severe abnormality in PEP/LVET (> 0.50) in patients receiving these agents probably reflects diminished intrinsic performance of the heart. Administration of vasopressor agents rarely interferes with the interpretation of STI since the clinician is aware of their administration. An acute reduction in left ventricular volume, such as occurs when a normal person assumes an upright posture or after a brisk diuresis, may induce or accentuate an abnormal PEP/LVET. In clinical states in which diuretic agents have been administered, the findings on STI may seem paradoxical, in that the patient experiences a diminution in symptoms of dyspnea while left ventricular performance appears to be diminished. In fact, the "unloading" of the ventricle under these circumstances does induce diminished left ventricular systolic performance, which is accompanied by lowered left atrial and pulmonary capillary pressures, the latter accounting for the improvement in dyspnea. It is to be noted that in all these circumstances the STI offer a measure of overall left ventricular systolic performance, reflecting the combined influences of intrinsic disease, compensating mechanisms, and the effects of administered agents.

In applying measurements of STI it should be recognized that alterations in ventricular conduction may themselves induce changes in left ventricular performance. Characteristically, the presence of left bundle branch block tends to prolong the PEP selectively, predominantly by lengthening the electromechanical interval. Patients with isolated left-axis deviation or with combined bundle branch block may demonstrate a similar disproportionate lengthening of the PEP. In contrast, in right bundle branch block, in the absence of left ventricular dysfunction, there is no abnormality in the left ventricular STI. It is our impression that the changes in PEP that accompany intraventricular conduction disturbances of the left ventricle reflect a combination of factors, including a delay in onset of mechanical activity, dyssynergic contractile patterns induced by the disturbances in ventricular depolarization, and alterations in intrinsic contractile function induced by the associated disease process.

The STI are useful in the analysis of valvular heart disease as well. Patients with compensated aortic stenosis or aortic insufficiency (or both) exhibit an abbreviation of the PEP and a lengthening of the LVET, with a consequent decrease in PEP/LVET. The QS_2 is often lengthened. With the development of left ventricular decompensation in the presence of aortic valvular disease, the PEP lengthens while the LVET shortens, and PEP/LVET increases from previously diminished levels. Thus, the development of left ventricular failure in aortic valve disease is attended by a return of the STI toward normal. In patients with severe mitral regurgitation PEP/LVET may be increased to a level of 0.50 even when the left ventricle remains well compensated. However, an increase in PEP/LVET beyond 0.50 in the presence of mitral regurgitation is consistently associated with a diminution in left ventricular performance. In patients with isolated mitral stenosis PEP/LVET is a reliable index of left ventricular chamber performance.

THE UNIQUE VALUE OF SYSTOLIC TIME INTERVALS

Do the STI afford information that current clinical approaches cannot provide? As an approach to this question, we sought to ascertain the relative frequency of residual symptoms and signs of abnormal STI in 37 patients who had convalesced from a documented injury to the left ventricular myocardium (7). The patients had recovered from an acute transmural myocardial infarction occurring 3–60 mo before the studies. They ranged in age from 35 to 75 yr. Documentation of acute myocardial infarction included a typical history of precordial chest discomfort, characteristic serum enzyme changes, and sequential electrocardiographic alterations with persistence of pathological Q waves. The location of previous myocardial infarction was anteroseptal or anterolateral in 14 patients, diaphragmatic in 16, and combined anterior and diaphragmatic in 7. Each patient was categorized according to the New York Heart Association classification. The cardiothoracic ratio was calculated for each patient on the basis of a standard posterior-anterior chest radiograph. The presence of S_3 and S_4 sounds was documented phonocardiographically.

Compared to the values for a group of 25 normal subjects studied concurrently, the preejection period index (PEPI) was prolonged, the left ventricular ejection time index (LVETI) was shortened, and PEP/LVET was increased. For each of these indices, the differences between the controls and the patients were statistically significant ($p < 0.001$). Of the three, PEP/LVET allowed best discrimination between normal and abnormal groups (7, 11). Of special relevance to the question that was framed above are the observations on the patients who were asymptomatic—that is, who had neither dyspnea nor fatigability nor angina pectoris. Among these asymptomatic patients (Fig. 1), all of whom had convalesced from a previously documented myocardial infarction, the majority exhibited abnormal left ventricular performance as defined by the PEP/LVET measurement.

Having defined this high incidence of abnormality in left ventricular performance among asymptomatic patients, we asked whether the presence of such an abnormality could have been detected by other common clinical indicators, namely the presence of an S_3 or S_4 gallop or of cardiomegaly on chest X-ray. Figure 2 shows the range of left ventricular performance measured by PEP/LVET among the 20 patients who were asymptomatic for dyspnea and fatigability. The distribution of abnormal diastolic sounds among these patients is also shown. It is apparent from this distribution that the presence of S_3 or S_4 could not reliably detect the patients with abnormal left ventricular performance. It should be noted that the

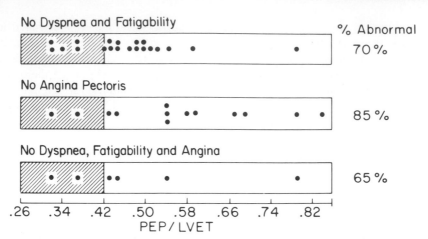

FIGURE 1 Distribution of PEP/LVET among patients with previous myocardial infarction grouped according to absence of symptoms of dyspnea and fatigability and angina pectoris. Hatched areas represent the normal data range. From Stack et al. (7).

presence of S_4 was frequent among individuals in whom ventricular performance remained within normal limits.

It is appropriate to indicate at this point that in contrast to the measurements of the STI, which reflect systolic events in the left ventricle, the presence of S_3 and S_4 denotes alterations in the diastolic filling characteristics of the ventricle. It is therefore not unexpected that these auscultatory indicators of left ventricular dysfunction are not closely correlated with the presence of abnormal systolic performance. Equally unreliable in detecting abnormality of the left ventricle was the presence of an abnormal cardiothoracic ratio (> 0.5), a finding that was apparent in only 4 of the 14 patients who demonstrated abnormal PEP/LVET.

Among patients who have convalesced from a previous insult to the myocardium, the STI reveal the presence of residual abnormality when clinical and radiological evidence for such cardiac abnormality is absent. While it was not surprising to learn that the common clinical indicators are somewhat insensitive, the degree to which the clinical findings underestimate the prevalence of residual abnormality was unexpected. Indeed, the observations raised the question of whether the STI truly reflect ventricular dysfunction. The second question challenging the noninvasive method is whether the STI are as accurate as invasive

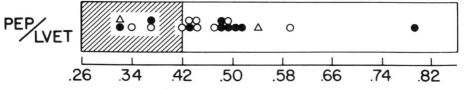

FIGURE 2 Distribution of PEP/LVET among patients who were asymptomatic for dyspnea and fatigability. The presence or absence of phonocardiographically documented S_3 and S_4 is shown: (○) neither S_3 nor S_4, (●) S_4, and (△) S_3 and S_4.

measures in defining the status of left ventricular performance. This has been reinvestigated in studies designed to test the relationship of the STI to the left ventricular ejection fraction (EF). The EF was measured from a single-plane right anterior oblique view, employing injections of 76% methylglucamine diatrizoate (Renografin). The study was based on 29 patients with angina pectoris who had not experienced a myocardial infarction and 54 patients with angina pectoris who had survived a documented acute myocardial infarction. All of the patients had coronary artery disease that had been demonstrated by angiography ($> 50\%$ narrowing of the diameter of at least one major coronary artery). A third group of 41 patients was studied because of atypical chest pain. Each of the latter had a normal coronary arteriogram and a normal EF and showed no local contraction abnormalities on contrast ventriculography. The average data for STI and EF among the three groups of patients are compared in Table 2.

Among the patients with a normal coronary arteriogram and a normal left ventricular EF, the EF was 0.68 ± 0.08 (mean $\pm$ SD). Among the same patients PEP/LVET was 0.34 ± 0.04 (mean $\pm$ SD). These values correspond almost precisely to norms previously established for these measures (3, 9, 10). It is evident that highly significant deviations in EF, PEPI, LVETI, and PEP/LVET occurred among the patients with coronary artery disease who had had a previous myocardial infarction compared with the group with normal angiograms and normal left ventricular performance. The third group, the patients with documented coronary artery disease but without a record of a previous myocardial infarction, did not differ significantly in these measures from normal. The STI and the EF thus demonstrated concordant changes on group analysis.

The correlation of the three STI measures with EF for the entire series of observations is summarized in Table 3. In confirmation of previous studies, among the STI the PEP/LVET was most closely correlated with the left ventricular EF ($r = 0.89$ for the entire series).

TABLE 2 Ejection fraction and systolic time intervals: Mean data[a]

Measure	Normal patients[b] ($n = 41$)	CAD without MI[c] ($n = 29$)	CAD with MI[c] ($n = 54$)
Ejection fraction, %	68 ± 1.3	70 ± 1.6	44 ± 2.1^d
PEPI, msec[c]	129 ± 1.9	131 ± 2.2	151 ± 2.4^d
LVETI, msec[c]	410 ± 2.3	409 ± 2.0	390 ± 2.5^d
PEP/LVET[c]	0.34 ± 0.005	0.35 ± 0.007	0.46 ± 0.012^d

[a]Mean $\pm$ SE.

[b]Those found to have normal coronary arteriograms and left ventricular performance on contrast angiography and ventriculography.

[c]Abbreviations: CAD, coronary artery disease; MI, myocardial infarction; PEPI, preejection period index; LVETI, left ventricular ejection time index; PEP/LVET, ratio of left ventricular preejection period to ejection time.

[d]$p < 0.001$ for difference from normal.

TABLE 3 Correlation of systolic time intervals with ejection fraction[a]

	r	
Measure[b]	Patients with CAD ($n = 83$)	All patients[c] ($n = 124$)
PEP/LVET	−0.89	−0.87
PEPI	−0.81	−0.77
LVETI	0.65	0.61

[a]Values are significant at $p < 0.01$ for all data.
[b]For abbreviations see Table 2.
[c]Includes normal patients plus those with CAD.

PREEJECTION PERIOD/LEFT VENTRICULAR EJECTION TIME

As a test of the accuracy of PEP/LVET in defining the presence of abnormal left ventricular performance in the individual patient, the distribution of PEP/LVET among the patients with coronary artery disease was related to the EF (Fig. 3). Abnormal left ventricular chamber performance was defined by an EF less than 0.52 (2 SD below the normal mean). A PEP/LVET greater than 0.42 (2 SD above the normal mean) was also considered to be abnormal. It is evident that the patients with a normal EF clustered in the range of PEP/LVET below 0.42, whereas those with an abnormal EF fell in the range above 0.42. Only two individuals with a normal PEP/LVET had an abnormal EF; only three individuals with an abnormal PEP/LVET had a normal EF.

An additional test of the accuracy of PEP/LVET is afforded by the calculation of the specificity and sensitivity of the PEP/LVET with respect to the EF determination. The specificity of PEP/LVET was defined as the percentage of all patients with a normal EF who are detected by a normal PEP/LVET. For the

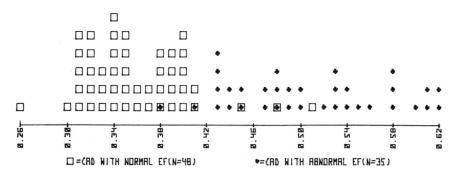

FIGURE 3 Distribution of PEP/LVET among the 83 patients with coronary artery disease: (□) patients with a normal EF (> 0.52), and (+) patients with abnormal EF (< 0.52).

calculations all patients, with and without coronary artery disease, were included. As above, a PEP/LVET of 0.42 was considered the upper limit of normal and an EF of 0.52 was considered the lower limit of normal. At these limits, the specificity of PEP/LVET (calculated as detected norms/detected norms + missed norms) was 97%. The sensitivity of PEP/LVET (calculated as detected abnormals/detected abnormals + missed abnormals) was 94%.

A more comprehensive analysis is provided by the calculated specificity and sensitivity throughout the range of PEP/LVET observed in this series. For this analysis all individuals—those with normal left ventricular performance in the absence of coronary artery disease and all patients with coronary artery disease— were included. The data illustrated in Fig. 4 again demonstrate the high degree of specificity and sensitivity of the PEP/LVET measurement at the 2 SD limit of 0.42. For limits above and below 0.42 there is an increasing disparity between the sensitivity and the specificity of PEP/LVET in detecting normal and abnormal EF. Thus, 0.42 is the limit of optimum combined sensitivity and specificity and hence the most useful limit for clinical application of PEP/LVET.

The analysis shown in Fig. 4 includes another element that pertains to the clinical application of PEP/LVET. At the PEP/LVET limit of 0.51, the point of 100% specificity is reached. All individuals above this limit demonstrated abnormal left ventricular performance (EF < 0.52). At a PEP/LVET of 0.37, 100% sensitivity is reached. All individuals below this limit demonstrated normal left ventricular EF.

On the basis of these observations, it seemed reasonable to suppose that the results obtained by using PEP/LVET to determine abnormal left ventricular function in patients with coronary artery disease would correspond closely with those obtained by determining the EF. This hypothesis was tested in several clinical

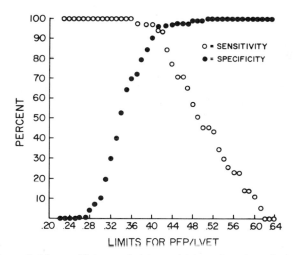

FIGURE 4 Display of (●) specificity and (○) sensitivity of various limits of PEP/LVET in defining abnormal left ventricular performance, using an EF determination of 0.52 as the lower limit of normal performance. The point of optimal combined specificity and sensitivity is at a limit of PEP/LVET = 0.42. A specificity and sensitivity of 100% occurs at limits of 0.37 and 0.51, respectively.

subsets of patients with coronary artery disease (Table 4). The data indicate that the prevalence of abnormal left ventricular performance in the four groups in Table 4 determined by PEP/LVET was virtually identical to that determined by EF. Agreement between PEP/LVET and EF estimates of the prevalence of abnormal function exceeded 90% in each subset.

It is evident that PEP/LVET is a noninvasive measure of left ventricular performance that is superior to current clinical approaches in detecting abnormal left ventricular performance. Indeed, PEP/LVET appears equivalent to the measurement of left ventricular EF in defining the presence of normal or abnormal ventricular performance in patients with coronary artery disease. If the STI are truly useful measures, their clinical application should give as much insight into the pathogenesis of coronary artery disease as do invasive measurements. A most important observation related to factors determining the course of coronary artery disease is that longevity in patients with coronary artery disease is markedly influenced by the presence of abnormal left ventricular function. This relationship was cited by Gorlin earlier in this book (Chapter 7). In view of these observations, we have initiated studies of the potential application of PEP/LVET as a prognostic index in patients with coronary artery disease. All of the patients had survived a previous myocardial infarction by at least 3 mo when the STI measurement was made. Although the data are preliminary, we offer them here since the first observations linking ventricular dysfunction and longevity were reported by Dr. Starr in his classic studies employing the ballistocardiogram. Among 42 patients followed to date, 23 had abnormal left ventricular performance and 19 normal performance according to the initial PEP/LVET. The survival data for a complete 18-mo follow-up period are plotted in Fig. 5. It is clear from these limited observations that patients with an abnormal PEP/LVET have reduced longevity. The STI thus appear to be useful in prognosticating longevity in patients with coronary

TABLE 4 Comparison of preejection period/left ventricular ejection time with ejection fraction in detecting prevalence of abnormal left ventricular performance

		n	EF < 0.52 (%)	PEP/LVET > 0.42 (%)	Agreement[a] (%)
Number of	1	18	28	22	94
vessels involved	2	23	30	30	100
(< 50%)	3	42	55	60	90
Extent of	None	26	0	0	100
contraction	Local	44	55	52	91
abnormality	General	13	92	100	92
End-diastolic	⩽ 14	53	30	32	91
pressure (mmHg)	> 14	30	63	63	100
Old myocardial	Present	54	65	67	91
infarction	Absent	29	0	0	100
All patients with CAD		83	42	43	94

[a]Number of patients with concordant PEP/LVET and EF × 100/total patients.

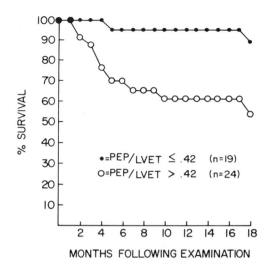

FIGURE 5 Cumulative longevity among two groups of patients with previous myocardial infarction during 18 mo after initial determination of STI: (●) those with initial normal PEP/LVET, and (○) those with initial abnormal PEP/LVET.

artery disease. These observations indicate that the STI will be useful in future investigations of factors that influence both ventricular function and overall mortality in patients with coronary artery disease.

We will bring our discussion to a close by citing a paragraph from one of Dr. Starr's papers (8):

> *The message with which I wish to close this presentation is a brief one. To me the evidence shows clearly that when the Newtonian conceptions of motion are applied to heart disease a new window is opened. When one looks through this window one sees abnormalities in cardiac performance not recognized by conventional techniques; these abnormalities are important, for they are related to the later development of disease and to diminishing longevity. Looking through this window one sees new facts about familiar diseases. One sees the effects of cardiac therapy demonstrated in striking fashion; so one becomes better able to adapt therapy to the needs of the patient. And let us not forget that this new knowledge can be gained without disturbing the patient in any way, without subjecting him to either discomfort or danger and, after the apparatus is set up, with little trouble and expense.*

Dr. Starr's astute observations of a decade ago related to the diagnostic use of the ballistocardiogram are applicable today to the measurement of the time intervals of the cardiac cycle.

REFERENCES

1. Ahmed, S. S., Levinson, G. E., and Schwartz, C. J. Systolic time intervals as measures of the contractile state of the myocardium in man. Circulation 46:559–571, 1972.

2. Garrard, C. L., Jr., Weissler, A. M., and Dodge, H. T. The relationship of alterations in systolic time intervals to ejection fraction in patients with cardiac disease. Circulation 42:455–462, 1970.

3. Kennedy, J. W., Baxley, W. A., Figley, M. M., Dodge, H. T., and Blackman, J. R. Quantitative angiography. 1. The normal left ventricle in man. Circulation 34:272–277, 1966.

4. Lewis, R. P., Boudoulas, H., Welch, T. G., and Forester, W. F. Usefulness of systolic time intervals in coronary artery disease. Am J Cardiol 37:787–796, 1976.

5. Lewis, R. P., Leighton, R. F., Forester, W. F., and Weissler, A. M. Systolic Time Intervals in Noninvasive Cardiology. New York: Grune & Stratton, 1974, pp. 301–368.

6. Lewis, R. P., Rittgers, S. E., Forester, W. F., and Boudoulas, H. A critical review of the systolic time intervals. Circulation 56:146–158, 1977.

7. Stack, R. S., Lee, C. C., Reddy, B. P., Taylor, M. L., and Weissler, A. M. Left ventricular performance in coronary artery disease by systolic time intervals and echocardiography. Am J Cardiol 37:331, 1976.

8. Starr, I. The place of the ballistocardiogram in a Newtonian cardiology, and the new light it sheds on certain old clinical problems. Proc R Soc Med 60:1297–1306, 1967.

9. Weissler, A. M., Harris, W. S., and Schoenfield, C. D. Bedside technics for the evaluation of ventricular function in man. Am J Cardiol 23:577–583, 1969.

10. Weissler, A. M., Harris, W. S., and Schoenfield, C. D. Systolic time intervals in heart failure in man. Circulation 37:149–159, 1968.

11. Weissler, A. M., Stack, R. S., Lee, C. C., Reddy, B. P., and Taylor, M. L. Left ventricular performance in coronary artery disease by systolic time intervals and echocardiography. Trans Am Clin Climatol Assoc 87:36–47, 1976.

CHAPTER 15

MYOCARDIAL IMAGING WITH RADIOACTIVE TRACERS IN CONGESTIVE HEART FAILURE

BERTRAM PITT

Radioactive tracer techniques are playing an increasing role in the evaluation of patients with congestive heart failure (1, 7, 9, 10). Myocardial perfusion imaging following intravenous injection of ^{201}Tl (15) and evaluation of ventricular function following injection of ^{99m}Tc human serum albumin (16) have proved particularly useful and show promise of becoming routine diagnostic procedures in both diagnosis and evaluation of therapy.

THALLIUM-201

Thallium-201 is used primarily in the evaluation of patients who are suspected of having either ischemic heart disease or myocardial infarction (10). It is taken up by normal myocardium in proportion to myocardial blood flow, myocardial mass, and the intracellular cation pool (15). Areas of myocardial ischemia or infarction can be detected by a focal decrease in tracer uptake (Fig. 1). However, a decrease in activity at the apex of the left ventricle is a normal variant since the left ventricular myocardium is thinnest at this point (5) (Fig. 2). Myocardial ischemia can be detected within minutes of experimental coronary artery occlusion, and areas of myocardial infarction can be detected several years after the initial event. Acute ischemia can be differentiated from old infarction by serial myocardial imaging (11).

The relative thickness of the ventricular myocardium and the size of the ventricular cavity can also be estimated. In normal patients, the left anterior oblique image after administration of ^{201}Tl reveals uptake in the intraventricular septum, apex, and lateral walls of the left ventricle; the left ventricular cavity can be faintly discerned. Activity within the right ventricular myocardial free wall is not usually detected. Although tracer is taken up by the right ventricular free wall, it is not normally visualized with current imaging techniques, since the blood flow per gram of the right ventricular free wall is considerably less than that of the left ventricular free wall. In patients with chronic right ventricular hypertrophy caused by pressure and/or volume overloading, the right ventricular free wall is easily visualized and the right ventricular cavity is often found to be dilated (4) (Fig. 3). Detection of right ventricular hypertrophy by ^{201}Tl myocardial imaging appears to be more sensitive

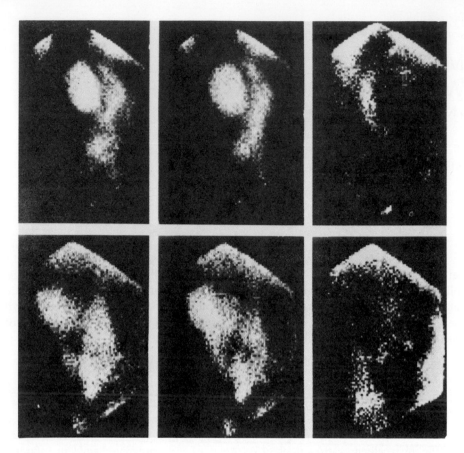

FIGURE 1 Previously asymptomatic patient with electrocardiographic evidence of an acute
anteroseptal myocardial infarction. (Top row, left to right) Anterior [201]Tl
myocardial perfusion image; anterior end-diastolic gated cardiac blood pool image
and anterior end-systolic gated cardiac blood pool image. (Bottom row) Left
anterior oblique images in same sequence as on the top. Note a perfusion defect in
the anterior atypical (anterior view) and apical septal (left anterior oblique) regions
of the myocardium in the ^{201}Tl image. The gated cardiac blood pool image reveals
decreased left ventricular function and akinesis of the anterior apical and septal
areas of myocardium corresponding to the perfusion defect seen in the ^{201}Tl image.
From Pitt and Strauss (10).

than detection by standard electrocardiography, especially in the presence of
concomitant left ventricular hypertrophy (4). Left ventricular hypertrophy can also
be detected by the ^{201}Tl myocardial image by assessing the relative thickness of the
left ventricular free wall and septum. Although only relative measurements are
possible from the ungated ^{201}Tl image because of myocardial wall motion, more
precise measurements can be made by gating the image and making measurements
from the end-diastolic and systolic images. In patients with concentric left
ventricular hypertrophy resulting from hypertension and/or valvular heart disease,
the thickness of the left ventricular free wall and that of the septum are increased

approximately equally. Idiopathic hypertrophic aortic stenosis (IHSS) can be detected by the finding of a thickening of the apex and intraventricular septum that is out of proportion to the thickening of the left ventricular free wall (asymmetric septal hypertrophy, ASH) (2). Although the diagnosis of IHSS is most frequently made by echocardiography, we have found several instances in which M mode echocardiography suggested ASH and IHSS but the left anterior oblique ^{201}Tl myocardial image revealed a thickened interventricular septum that was equal in size to the left ventricular free wall; the latter observation was confirmed in at least one instance by postmortem examination. In other instances in which the finding of ASH on the echocardiogram has led to the diagnosis of IHSS, the left anterior oblique ^{201}Tl myocardial image has shown the ASH, but also increased right ventricular activity and right ventricular dilation, suggesting that the cause of

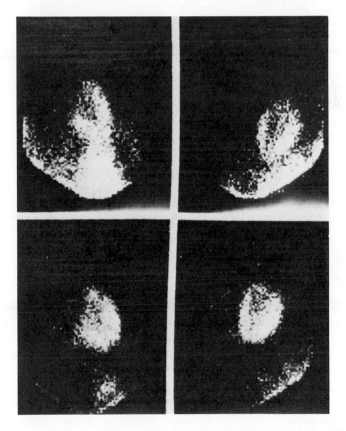

FIGURE 2   Thallium scan in a subject without coronary artery disease obtained in the anterior position (left panels) and left anterior oblique (right panels) with injection at rest (upper panels) and during stress (lower panels). The zone visualized is the left ventricular myocardium with associated left ventricular cavity. A hint of right ventricular myocardial activity is seen on the stress scan in the left anterior oblique view. A zone of decreased tracer concentration at the apex is a normal variant. The tracer concentration of splanchnic activity is greatly decreased during stress compared with rest. From Strauss and Pitt (14).

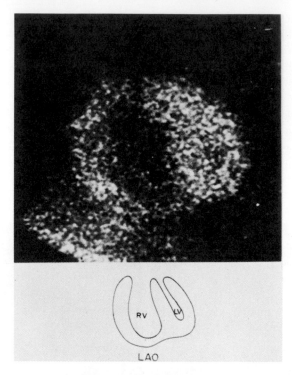

FIGURE 3 Patient with long-standing cor pulmonale. (Top) Left anterior oblique (LAO) [201]Tl
myocardial perfusion image. (Bottom) Schematic drawing: LV, left ventricular
cavity; RV, right ventricular cavity. Note the markedly dilated right ventricular
cavity and the appearance of a relatively thickened right ventricular myocardium.
From Pitt and Strauss (10).

the disproportionate septal hypertrophy was right ventricular hypertrophy
rather than IHSS.

The ^{201}Tl myocardial image has been useful in evaluating patients with
congestive heart failure of uncertain etiology and in distinguishing patients with
idiopathic congestive cardiomyopathy from those with ischemic cardiomyopathy
(1). Although the clinical history usually suffices for this distinction, in occasional
patients it is not sufficient. Thus, patients with autopsy-proved myocardial
infarction sometimes failed to experience an episode of precordial chest pain, or a
bout of chest pain was occasionally misinterpreted as being of gastrointestinal or
pulmonary origin. The electrocardiogram sometimes fails to show the diagnostic
changes of infarction; conversely, Q waves suggestive of myocardial infarction are
occasionally found in patients with idiopathic congestive cardiomyopathy and
normal coronary arteries. Patients with idiopathic congestive cardiomyopathy also
have episodes of atypical precordial chest pain that are often interpreted as
myocardial infarction in the context of other cardiovascular signs and symptoms
such as congestive failure and/or recurrent ventricular arrhythmias.

In the patient with congestive heart failure due to idiopathic congestive
cardiomyopathy, ^{201}Tl myocardial imaging reveals a dilated left ventricular cavity

with relatively uniform ^{201}Tl uptake with no, or only small, focal defects that involve less than 20% of the left ventricular circumference. In patients with congestive heart failure resulting from previous myocardial infarction and in those with ischemic cardiomyopathy, ^{201}Tl myocardial imaging reveals a dilated left ventricular cavity and a relatively large focal defect in tracer uptake, usually greater than 20% of the left ventricular circumference (1).

Although the most frequent explanation for the finding of a focal defect in ^{201}Tl uptake is myocardial infarction, other infiltrative diseases of the myocardium must be considered, including tumors and granulomas such as sarcoidosis (3). Thallium-201 myocardial imaging has been particularly useful in the evaluation of cardiac involvement in patients with pulmonary sarcoidosis. In patients with chronic pulmonary hypertension, the right ventricular myocardium undergoes dilation and hypertrophy. Focal tracer defects indicative of sarcoidosis of the left ventricular myocardium are sometimes seen. In some of those in whom myocardial sarcoidosis was demonstrated at postmortem examination it was unsuspected clinically, whereas in others intraventricular conduction disturbances and dysrhythmias had suggested possible myocardial involvement. The finding of myocardial involvement in a patient with pulmonary sarcoidosis is an indication for steroid therapy, whether or not the patient is symptomatic.

THALLIUM-201 IN CONJUNCTION WITH OTHER TECHNIQUES

Although ^{201}Tl myocardial imaging is of value in the assessment of patients with congestive heart failure, it is of even greater value when combined with isotope angiography and/or gated cardiac blood pool imaging. Left ventricular function can be monitored noninvasively following the injection of ^{99m}Tc intravenously. Circulation time, mean pulmonary transit time, right and left ventricular volumes, and ejection fraction can be determined by monitoring the initial passage of tracer through the circulation and observing beat-to-beat changes in activity over the right and left ventricles. This technique is simple, noninvasive, and can be repeated by subsequent imaging of the same dose of tracer or by injecting tracers, such as ^{113m}In, which have a different activity. Another approach is to allow the tracer to reach equilibrium in the circulatory system and to trigger the scintillation camera by using a physiological marker such as the R wave of the electrocardiogram (16). Using this technique, it is possible to select specific phases of the cardiac cycle, such as end-diastole or end-systole, for imaging, or to divide the cardiac cycle into any number of segments, each 20–40 msec in duration. Using systems that are currently available commercially, the cardiac cycle can be divided into 28–56 frames, each frame a composite of several beats so as to achieve sufficient activity for statistical reliability. The 56-frame multiple-gated acquisition cardiac blood pool image (MUGA) can then be shown in a cine format similar to standard contrast angiography. Using semiautomatic edge detection programs, left ventricular ejection fraction and rates of ventricular filling and emptying can be automatically calculated from the left ventricular time-activity curve and displayed at the bedside (8). Left ventricular ejection fraction can be measured serially from the initial injection of tracer for approximately 3–6 hr. The correlation between left ventricular ejection fraction and rates of ventricular emptying and filling determined by standard contrast angiography and those determined by MUGA has been excellent in our own and other laboratories. In addition to overall ventricular function, regional myocardial wall motion can be assessed and calculated automatically by measuring the changes in activity and area around the center of gravity of the left ventricle. Although first-pass and MUGA imaging appear to be similar in their ability to measure overall left ventricular and right ventricular function, the latter technique is superior for measuring regional myocardial wall motion because of the greater number of counts that it provides, and hence the enhanced statistical reliability of each individual frame.

APPLICATION TO CONGESTIVE HEART FAILURE

The ability to determine noninvasively the left ventricular ejection fraction and regional motions of the myocardial wall, both at rest and during exercise, has opened a new era for evaluating patients with congestive heart failure. Objective assessment of ventricular function should be very helpful in the initial evaluation of a patient complaining of dyspnea on exertion or fatigue. Although most patients with congestive heart failure are treated with digitalis and diuretics until symptomatic improvement occurs, it is likely that a further improvement in left ventricular function could be obtained by adjusting therapy on the basis of objective indices of ventricular function. The potential for this technique in the evaluation and therapy of congestive heart failure can be seen from our initial experience with gated cardiac blood pool imaging in the coronary care unit. Left ventricular ejection fraction appears to be a more sensitive index of left ventricular dysfunction in patients with acute myocardial infarction than are standard measures of left ventricular filling pressure and cardiac output. A group of patients with acute myocardial infarction studied within the first 24 hr of the onset of symptoms were divided into those with normal left ventricular filling pressure, those in mild to moderate left ventricular failure with an abnormal left ventricular filling pressure and/or cardiac output, and those with manifest cardiogenic shock (12) (Fig. 4). Left ventricular ejection fraction was subnormal even in those with normal left ventricular filling pressures and cardiac outputs. In those with mild to moderate cardiac failure and those in cardiogenic shock there was a progressive decrease in ejection fraction. Left ventricular ejection fraction also proved to be an objective index of clinical improvement. In those with obvious clinical improvement, left ventricular ejection fraction increased over the initial 10–14 d of hospitalization. In contrast, in those who failed to show clinical improvement the ejection fraction either did not increase from the initial measurement or showed a decrease.

Left ventricular ejection fraction determined by gated cardiac blood pool imaging has also proved to be a good indicator of prognosis after hospital discharge in acute myocardial infarction. Patients who died after hospital discharge had a significantly lower left ventricular ejection fraction than those who survived. Multiple-gated cardiac blood pool imaging is proving useful in the evaluation of therapeutic interventions both during and after hospitalization. In our experience,

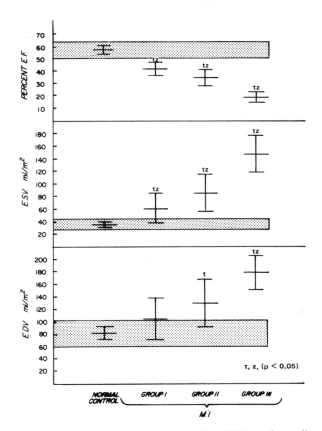

FIGURE 4 Distribution of left ventricular ejection fraction (E.F.), end-systolic volume (E.S.V.), and end-diastolic volume (E.D.V.) in normal control subjects and patients with myocardial infarction (M.I.). Group I patients had normal left ventricular filling pressures and cardiac output, group II had an elevated left ventricular filling pressure, and group III had cardiogenic shock. The shaded areas represent the normal range ± 2 SD. The mean values are plotted with 1 SD. Note the significant reduction in E.F. and increase in E.S.V. in group I, those with M.I., and normal left ventricular filling pressures and cardiac outputs. From Rigo et al. (12) by permission of the American Heart Association, Inc.

gated cardiac blood pool imaging has been useful in assessing the effects of intravenous nitroglycerin on left ventricular function.

Gated cardiac blood pool imaging is of special value in patients with severe left ventricular failure and/or cardiogenic shock following acute myocardial infarction. In the usual patient with cardiogenic shock, the ^{201}Tl myocardial image reveals a large defect in tracer uptake by the left ventricle; the gated cardiac blood pool image shows a dilated left ventricle, a low left ventricular ejection fraction, and extensive abnormalities in the motion of regions of the myocardial wall. Occasionally, however, patients with cardiogenic shock are found to have relatively trivial or no defects on their ^{201}Tl myocardial image and a small left ventricle that contracts well on the gated cardiac blood pool image. The right ventricle in these patients is dilated, and the right ventricular ejection fraction is reduced (13) (Fig. 5). These patients with massive right ventricular infarction as the cause of their cardiogenic shock require prompt recognition and institution of plasma volume expansion. If they are properly recognized and treated, the long-term prognosis in these patients is relatively good, whereas in those with massive left ventricular failure the prognosis is poor.

Myocardial imaging is also of value for the patient with severe congestive heart failury and the sudden appearance of a loud systolic murmur, suggesting either rupture of a papillary muscle or a ventricular septal defect. Although these two conditions can often be distinguished clinically, or by demonstrating evidence of the defect by serial determination of blood oxygenation in consecutive chambers of the right side of the heart using a balloon flotation catheter, confirmation of the diagnosis is often necessary. It can be provided at the bedside by injecting ^{99m}Tc human serum albumin through the lumen of the balloon flotation catheter in the pulmonary artery while the patient is in the left anterior oblique projection. The simultaneous appearance of tracer in both right and left ventricles suggests the diagnosis of a ventricular septal defect, whereas delayed filling of the right ventricle occurs in papillary muscle rupture or dysfunction. Measurements of left ventricular ejection fraction and assessment of regional myocardial wall motion by the multiple-gated cardiac blood pool image in this type of patient are of even greater value in timing therapy and in assessing prognosis. In those whose left ventricle is relatively small and contracts well, surgical correction of the septal defect or papillary muscle rupture has a good prognosis. Conversely, in those whose left ventricle is large and contracts poorly, the extent rather than the site of infarction is of importance; surgical correction of the defect is associated with high mortality and poor long-term prognosis even if the initial surgery is successful.

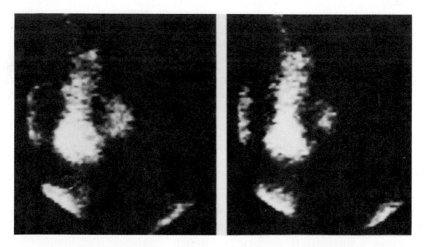

FIGURE 5 Patient with electrocardiographic evidence of an acute inferior myocardial infarction and cardiogenic shock. Left end-diastolic and right end-systolic left anterior oblique gated cardiac blood pool images. Note the small left ventricle with only moderately reduced contraction and large, dilated, poorly contracting right ventricle. From Pitt and Strauss (10).

The ability to assess prognosis and to judge the effectiveness of therapy in patients with ischemic heart disease should be even further improved by the clinical introduction of gamma tomography (6). Using this technique, it is possible to measure the extent of infarction and of the remaining viable myocardium. Clearly, a new era in the evaluation of patients with congestive heart failure is approaching. The clinician will have the ability to assess ventricular function objectively and to determine the effectiveness of therapeutic intervention at the bedside. Decisions concerning the choice of therapeutic agent and the duration of therapy will be based on these objective data and will provide more effective therapy and reliable prognostic indices.

REFERENCES

1. Bulkley, B. H., Hutchins, G. M., Bailey, I., Strauss, H. W., and Pitt, B. Thallium-201 imaging and gated cardiac blood pool scans in patients with ischemic and idiopathic cardiomyopathy: A clinical and pathologic study. Circulation 55:753–760, 1977.
2. Bulkley, B. H., Rouleau, J. R., Strauss, H. W., and Pitt, B. Idiopathic hypertrophic subaortic stenosis: Detection by thallium-201 myocardial perfusion imaging. N Engl J Med 293:1113–1116, 1975.
3. Bulkley, B. H., Rouleau, J., Strauss, H. W., and Pitt, B. Sarcoid heart disease: Diagnosis by thallium-201 myocardial perfusion imaging. Am J Cardiol 37:125, 1976.
4. Cohen, H. A., Baird, M. G., Rouleau, J. R., Fuhrmann, C. F., Bailey, I. K., Summer, W. R., Strauss, H. W., and Pitt, B. Thallium-201 myocardial imaging in patients with pulmonary hypertension. Circulation 54:790–796, 1975.
5. Cook, D. J., Bailey, I., Strauss, H. W., Rouleau, J., Wagner, H. N., and Pitt, B. Thallium-201 for myocardial imaging: Appearance of the normal heart. J Nucl Med 17:583–589, 1976.
6. Keyes, J. W., Jr. Emission computed tomography of the myocardium. In Cardiovascular Nuclear Medicine, ed. 2, H. W. Strauss and B. Pitt, eds. St. Louis: Mosby, in press.
7. Pitt, B. and Strauss, H. W. Combined use of thallium-201 myocardial perfusion imaging and gated cardiac blood pool imaging. Herz 2:212–214, 1977.
8. Pitt, B. and Strauss, H. W. Current concepts: Evaluation of ventricular function by radioisotopic technics. N Engl J Med 296:1097–1099, 1977.
9. Pitt, B. and Strauss, H. W. Myocardial imaging in the non-invasive evaluation of patients with suspected ischemic heart disease. Am J Cardiol 37:797–806, 1976.
10. Pitt, B. and Strauss, H. W. Myocardial perfusion imaging and gated cardiac blood pool scanning: Clinical application. Am J Cardiol 38:739–746, 1976.
11. Pond, M., Rehn, T., Burow, R., and Pitt, B. Early detection of myocardial infarction by serial thallium-201 imaging. Circulation 56:893, 1977.
12. Rigo, P., Murray, M., Taylor, D. R., Kelly, D. T., Weisfeldt, M. L., Strauss, H. W., and Pitt, B. Left ventricular function in acute myocardial infarction evaluated by gated scintiphotography. Circulation 50:678–684, 1974.
13. Rigo, P., Murray, M., Taylor, D. R., Weisfeldt, M. L., Kelly, D. T., Strauss, H. W., and Pitt, B. Right ventricular dysfunction detected by gated scintiphotography in patients with acute inferior myocardial infarction. Circulation 52:268–274, 1975.

14. Strauss, H. W. and Pitt, B. Common procedures for the non-invasive determination of regional myocardial perfusion, evaluation of regional wall motion and detection of acute infarction. Am J Cardiol 38:731–738, 1976.
15. Strauss, H. W. and Pitt, B. Thallium-201 as a myocardial imaging agent. Semin Nucl Med 7:49–58, 1977.
16. Strauss, H. W., Zaret, B. L., Hurley, P., Natarajan, T. K., and Pitt, B. A scintiphotographic method for measuring left ventricular ejection fraction in man without cardiac catheterization. Am J Cardiol 28:575–580, 1971.

PART IV

CONSEQUENCES
OF HEART FAILURE

CHAPTER 16

HEMODYNAMIC PULMONARY EDEMA

ALFRED P. FISHMAN
GIUSEPPE G. PIETRA

Water has a separate circulation within the lungs. Its circulation is closely related to the supporting structures of this organ and is open at both ends: water enters the interstitial spaces in the vicinity of minute vessels and leaves the lungs by way of pulmonary lymphatics. Although the minute vessels are *predominantly* anatomic capillaries, arterioles and venules also allow water to traverse their walls. For the sake of simplicity, in this chapter we will designate the fluid-exchanging vessels of the pulmonary circulation as capillaries. One important caveat to this approach is that the bronchial microcirculation and particularly the bronchial venules are also capable of water exchange. Since their major contribution appears to be leakage resulting from increased permeability (10) rather than hemodynamic upset, the bronchial venules will not be considered further here.

Pulmonary edema is said to exist when abnormal quantities of water (and protein) accumulate in the lungs. The *entry* of large quantities into the interstitial spaces is not synonymous with pulmonary edema, nor is a high rate of *exit* via the lymphatics. The sine qua non is the demonstration that abnormally large quantities of water have been *retained*. For the clinician to detect excess water by using rales and an abnormal chest radiograph as criteria, the normal water content of the lungs has to increase from four- to sixfold (3). For this reason, interest is high in detecting smaller quantities, such as occur in the interstitial edema that follows acute myocardial infarction.

In this chapter, hemodynamic pulmonary edema will be considered with respect to its pathogenesis, the "stretched pore" phenomenon, and recent approaches to early detection.

PATHOGENESIS OF HEMODYNAMIC PULMONARY EDEMA

There are two prerequisites for understanding the pathogenesis of hemodynamic pulmonary edema: an appreciation of the functional anatomy of the fluid transport system, and an awareness of the way in which Starling's law of capillary exchange applies to the lungs.

Functional Anatomy

The notion was long ago dispelled that the minute pulmonary vessels are simply biologic tubes, lined by sheets of inert membranes across which the exchange of water occurs. As shown in Fig. 1, specialized cells line both the capillary and the alveolar surfaces; irregular cell-cell junctions are seen where the tips of the cells meet. That these cells also engage in biologic transport processes, particularly pinocytosis, is well known (4, 12).

Exceedingly important for gas exchange is the unique way in which the minute vessels are incorporated into the lung. At the capillary level, one side of the minute vessel abuts on the interstitial space that lies between the alveolar and endothelial basement membranes. At the opposite side, the alveolar interstitial space is lacking because of the fusion of the epithelial and endothelial basement membranes (Fig. 1). When excess fluid is to be stored in the lung, it accumulates in the interstitial space on the thick side (2). Greater impermeability of the epithelium than of the endothelium helps to confine water to the interstitial space, thereby preventing alveoli from flooding (Fig. 2) (12). Gradients of subatmospheric pressure favor the subsequent movement of interstitial fluid to the peribronchial-perivascular interstitium, away from the gas-exchanging regions of the lung. At the corners of

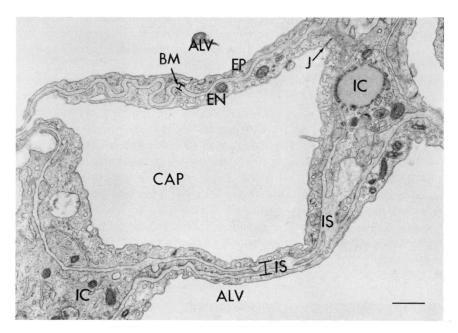

FIGURE 1 Electron micrograph of an alveolar septum of a rat lung. The capillary (CAP) is lined by thin endothelial cells (EN) connected to each other by junctions (J). In this picture, the alveolar surfaces (ALV) are lined by flat epithelial cells (EP). On one aspect of the alveolar septum, epithelium and endothelium are separated only by a thin basement membrane (BM) (thin side). On the opposite side the interstitial space (IS) contains cells (IC) and connective tissue (thick side). Scale bar, 0.85 μm.

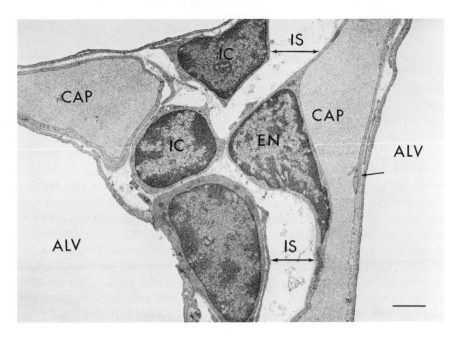

FIGURE 2 Interstitial edema causing swelling and electron lucency of the thick side of the interstitium at the confluence of three alveolar septa. The thin side is indicated by the single-headed arrow. Scale bar, 8.0 μm.

the alveoli in the primary septa located at the base of the alveoli are not only capillaries but also venules (5). Anatomic considerations indicate that during spontaneous breathing blood flows from the arterioles preferentially through the capillary located in the primary septa into these venules, whereas capillaries located in the secondary septa between alveoli are perfused only when favorable vascular and alveolar pressure conditions prevail (5). When intrathoracic pressures are high, as during some applications of positive pressure breathing, the venules also seem to have the potential for serving as sources of leakage of fluid into the interstitium (15).

Quite misleading with respect to the origin of interstitial fluid can be the histological demonstration of excess water (and protein) near airways (14). Although water and protein do localize there, they generally do not originate there. Instead, the bulk of evidence favors the idea that during spontaneous breathing, water and protein enter the interstitial spaces almost exclusively at the level of the capillaries and are transported toward lymphatics along the supporting structures of the lungs by favorable hydrostatic pressure gradients in the interstitium. The process of moving excess water from the thick portions of the alveolar-capillary barriers results in accumulation around bronchioles. This depot function of the peribronchiolar interstitial space favors premature closure of terminal airways, a promising prospect for the early detection of interstitial pulmonary edema.

It is important to recognize that the interstitial space is a complicated structure specialized for mechanical function and for coping with excess water.

Interspersed in this interstitial space are pools of hydrophilic proteoglycans (ground substance), which act as local sumps. Of great interest is the notion that specialized receptors, "juxtacapillary" or J receptors, in the connective tissue are deformed when swelling of ground substance occurs, and respond by stimulating the ventilation, a response that promotes lymphatic drainage (7). The resulting increase in respiratory frequency, which is characteristic of interstitial edema, thereby emerges as a mechanism for promoting the drainage of excess water by the lungs as well as a valuable clinical sign that the lungs contain excess water.

Starling Equation

Although physiologists have been refining the Starling equation (Fig. 3) to take into account the transcapillary exchange of proteins, clinicians have been turning measurements of only the intravascular pressures to practical advantage. For example, it has been repeatedly shown that acute interstitial edema of the lungs is associated with an increase in vascular pressure and is abetted by a concomitant decrease in intravascular colloid osmotic pressure. Although these empirical observations are useful clinically, they should not obscure the fact that pressures in the interstitial space are not uniform, that they derive from complicated interactions ranging from pleural pressures to the "antiedema" effects of surfactant, and that the ability to predict the occurrence of pulmonary edema by using vascular hydrostatic and oncotic pressures only implies automatic adjustments of corresponding pressures in the interstitial space that are currently beyond comprehension.

STRETCHED PORE PHENOMENON

Sporadic observations of the systemic circulation have suggested that under some circumstances, "pores" open in the microcirculation, resulting in increased permeability to macromolecules (13). This stretched pore phenomenon has now been demonstrated directly in the pulmonary circulation by use of electron microscopy and suitable tracers (Figs. 4 and 5). Thus, as hydrostatic pressures

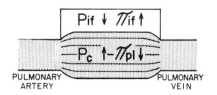

$$Q = k\,[(P_c - P_{if}) - \sigma(\pi_{pl} - \pi_{if})]$$

where Q = net flow of fluid across the vessel wall
  k = filtration coefficient
  P_c = capillary hydrostatic pressure
  P_{if} = interstitial fluid hydrostatic pressure
  σ = reflection coefficient
  π_{pl} = osmotic pressure of plasma proteins
  π_{if} = osmotic pressure of interstitial fluid proteins

FIGURE 3 Starling's equation.

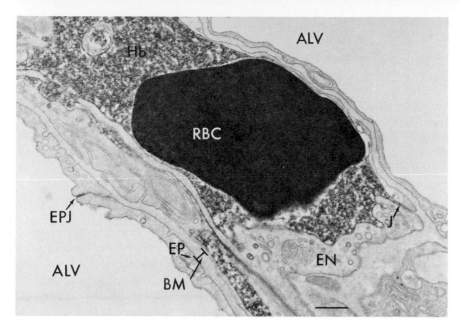

FIGURE 4 Normal perfusing pressures. The tracer (hemoglobin, Hb) is confined to the capillary lumen and appears in the electron micrograph as osmiophilic granular material after incubation of the tissue in 2,2′-diaminobenzidine and H_2O_2. RBC, red blood cell; EPJ, epithelial cell junction. Scale bar, 0.65 μm.

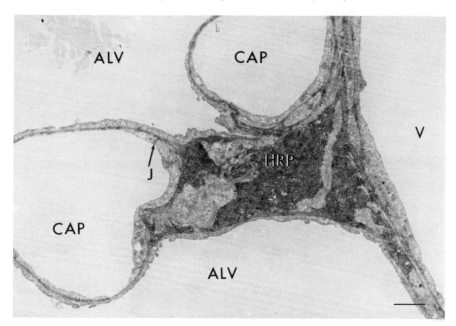

FIGURE 5 Interstitial edema. The tracer (horseradish peroxidase, HRP) has accumulated in the collagenous portions of the interstitium and appears as a granular osmiophilic material after incubation of the tissue as described for Fig. 4. The capillaries are empty since the lung was fixed by intravascular perfusion. The arrow indicates an endothelial junction through which the tracer has escaped into the interstitium. Scale bar, 6.0 μm.

increase in the small pulmonary vessels, the interendothelial junctions appear to dilate sufficiently to increase the access of circulating proteins to the interstitial space—that is, the vessels become more "permeable" to water and proteins (9).

Alveolar junctions appear to be less stretchable than endothelial junctions. There is good correlation between the functional difference in permeability to proteins of the endothelium and epithelium and the structure of their junctions as seen in freeze-fracture preparations (6, 8, 11). Endothelial junctions of alveolar capillaries are composed of one or two rows of particles located in shallow grooves on the external half (E) of the fractured cell membrane (Fig. 6). Epithelial junctions are instead composed of several anastomosing ridges located over the internal half (P) of the epithelial cell membrane (Fig. 7). Although much must still be learned about the functional significance of images seen on freeze-fracture preparations, the permeability of cell junctions to ions appears to be related to the number and appearance of junctional strands (1). The simpler the structure of the junctions, the greater are its porosity to ions and the susceptibility of the junctions to mechanical stresses. It is clear that the differential stretchability of endothelial and epithelial junctions favors the formation of interstitial rather than alveolar edema.

The concept of stretchable junctions has several practical implications. The first is the localization of early pulmonary edema. In the normal lung, hydrostatic

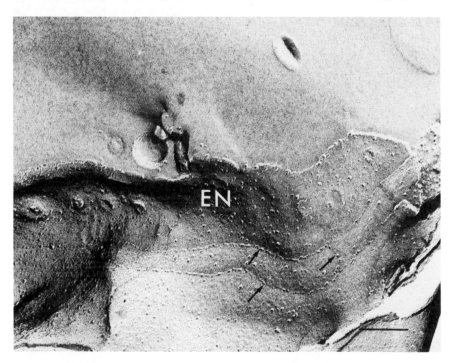

FIGURE 6 Endothelial junction. Micrograph of a freeze-fracture replica of an alveolar capillary of the rabbit lung showing double rows of particles (arrows) over the E face (exoplasmic) of the endothelial cell at the level of the junction. This appearance of the junction has been associated with high permeability to ions (1). Scale bar, 0.3 μm.

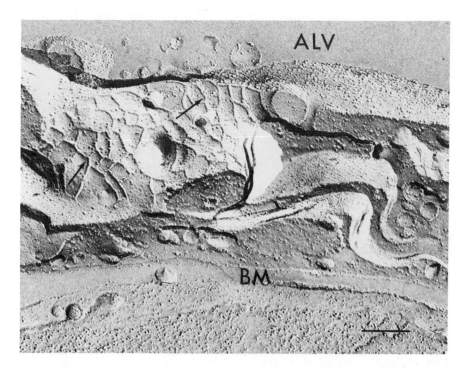

FIGURE 7 Epithelial junction. Micrograph of a freeze-fracture replica of a type I pneumocyte of a rabbit lung. The junction is composed of anastomosing solid ridges (arrows) over the P face (protoplasmic) of the pneumocyte. This appearance has been associated with impermeability of the junction. Scale bar, 0.3 μm.

pressures are maximal at the bases. Should pulmonary capillary pressure increase for any reason, such as acute myocardial infarction and decreased compliance of the ventricular wall or left ventricular failure, stretched pores at the bases promote local edema. Another implication concerns the composition of vascular and interstitial fluid. If the increase in capillary pressure is modest, molecular sieving will be manifested: the fluid transversing the interendothelial junctions into the interstitium will be hypo-oncotic, leaving hyperoncotic pressure behind because of the greater loss of water than of proteins into the interstitial space of the lungs. Should hydrostatic pressures rise sufficiently to stretch pores widely, fluid iso-oncotic with plasma will be lost into the interstitial spaces (Fig. 8). The implications of these changes in pore size for the protein and water content of blood and of pulmonary interstitial fluid have just begun to be explored.

EARLY DETECTION OF PULMONARY EDEMA

The first consequences of left ventricular failure are manifested in the lungs. Heavy reliance has traditionally been placed on the detection of rales. Unfortunately, this stage represents rather severe pulmonary edema, since by the time rales appear excess water is not only present in the interstitial spaces but has also risen

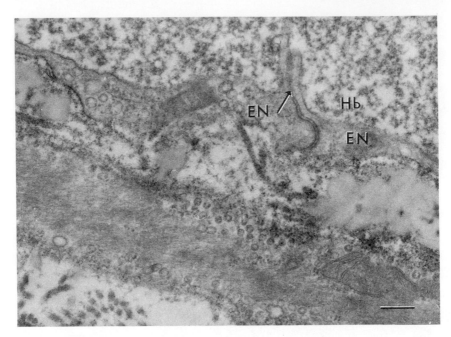

FIGURE 8   Electron micrograph of a "leaky" pulmonary venule from a rat injected with hemoglobin and high doses of epinephrine. Under these extreme hemodynamic conditions, small vessels other than capillaries became leaky to proteins. The animal was killed 5 min after injection. The arrow points to an endothelial cleft filled with the osmiophilic reaction product of hemoglobin and diaminobenzidine. The reaction product is seen both in the vascular lumen and between the endothelium and the medial muscle, but the direction of flow cannot be established in a static picture. Scale bar, 0.5 μm.

above alveoli to the bronchiolar level. The chest radiograph is most helpful when the heart is enlarged and alterations in the vascular pattern in favor of the apices accompany evidences of interstitial and alveolar edema. However, these manifestations are least equivocal when the pulmonary changes are quite striking and large quantities of water have accumulated in the interstitial spaces, alveoli, and bronchioles.

An earlier manifestation than either of the above, and one that has attracted too little clinical attention, is the increase in respiratory frequency that accompanies stiffening of the lungs by excess fluid. As indicated above, this manifestation presumably originates in a reflex pathway that begins with stimulation by the excess fluid of J receptors that are adjacent to collagen bundles in alveolar-capillary septa.

Pulmonary function tests have been more useful for making serial observations of the course of pulmonary edema than for quantifying its degree. Most valuable in this regard has been consecutive determination of the vital capacity. This approach has the advantage of simplicity and reproducibility, but it is limited with respect to detecting interstitial edema by the large spread of normal values.

Because of these limitations in conventional pulmonary function tests, interest turned naturally to the "closing volume" test, which has proved valuable for the early detection of interstitial disease that affects the peribronchial and peri-bronchiolar areas of the lungs—that is, the areas in which water tends to pool during interstitial edema. The principle of the test is shown schematically in Fig. 8.

CONCLUDING REMARKS

In this chapter only a few aspects of the pathogenesis and early detection of pulmonary edema have been considered. Emphasis has been placed on the anatomic and physiological bases of clinical manifestations. A major conclusion is that the clinical evidences of pulmonary edema are late manifestations and that approaches appear to be on hand for earlier detection. Another conclusion is that in advanced edema, when intercellular junctions are widely stretched by high intravascular pressures, distinctions between permeability and hemodynamic edema tend to blur because in both instances leakage of proteins into the interstitial spaces is facilitated, albeit by different mechanisms.

Finally, preoccupation with the intercellular junctions should not obscure other aspects of water and protein transport across alveolar-capillary barriers in the lungs. For example, water is presumably transported not only by bulk flow through intercellular clefts but also by flow across cell surfaces. Indeed, the trans-cellular flow probably predominates. Moreover, pinocytosis is involved in the transcellular movement of proteins. How both of these processes are affected by the raised vascular pressures that accompany hemodynamic pulmonary edema remains to be clarified.

REFERENCES

1. Claude, P. and Goodenough, D. A. Fracture faces of zonulae occludentes from "tight" and "leaky" epithelium. J Cell Biol 58:390–400, 1973.
2. Cottrel, T. S., Levine, O. R., and Senior, R. M. Electron microscopic alterations at the alveolar level in pulmonary edema. Circ Res 21:783–797, 1967.
3. Fishman, A. P. Pulmonary edema. The water-exchanging function of the lung. Circulation 46:390–408, 1972.
4. Fishman, A. P. and Pietra, G. G. Handling of bioactive materials by the lung. N Engl J Med 291:884–890, 953–959, 1974.
5. Gil, J. Morphologic aspects of alveolar microcirculation. In: Symposium on the Pulmonary Circulation. Fed Proc, in press.
6. Inoue, S., Michel, R. P., and Hogg, J. C. Zonulae occludentes in alveolar epithelium and capillary endothelium of dog lungs studied with the freeze-fracture technique. J Ultrastruct Res 56:215–225, 1976.
7. Paintal, A. S. Fluid pump of type J receptors of the cat. J Physiol (Lond) 238:53–54, 1974.
8. Pietra, G. G. The basis of pulmonary edema with emphasis on ultrastructure. In: The Lung—Structure, Function and Disease, W. M. Thurlbeck, ed. Baltimore: Williams & Wilkins, 1978, pp. 391–421.
9. Pietra, G. G., Szidon, J. P., Leventhal, M. M., and Fishman, A. P. Hemoglobin as a tracer in hemodynamic pulmonary edema. Science 166:1643–1646, 1969.
10. Pietra, G. G., Szidon, J. P., Leventhal, M. M., and Fishman, A. P. Histamine and pulmonary edema in the dog. Circ Res 29:323–337, 1971.

11. Schneeberger, E. E. and Karnovsky, M. J. Substructure of intercellular junctions in freeze-fractured alveolar capillary membrane of mouse lungs. Circ Res 38:404–411, 1976.
12. Schneeberger, E. E. and Karnovsky, M. J. The influence of intravascular fluid volume on the permeability of newborn and adult mouse lungs to ultrastructural protein tracers. J Cell Biol 49:319–334, 1971.
13. Shirley, H. H., Wolfram, C. G., Wasserman, K., and Mayerson, H. S. Capillary permeability in macromolecular stretched pore phenomenon. Am J Physiol 190:189–193, 1957.
14. Staub, N. C. Pulmonary edema. Physiol Rev 54:678–811, 1974.
15. Toung, T., Sahavia, P., Permutt, S., Zuidema, G. D., and Cameron, J. L. Aspiration pneumonia: Beneficial and harmful effects of positive end-expiratory pressure. Surgery 82:279–283, 1977.

CHAPTER 17

AUTONOMIC ADJUSTMENTS TO CONGESTIVE HEART FAILURE AND THEIR CONSEQUENCES

ROBERT ZELIS
STEPHEN F. FLAIM
STEPHEN NELLIS
JOHN LONGHURST
RALPH MOSKOWITZ

In Chapter 5 of this book, Dr. Braunwald proposed the following definition of congestive heart failure: "Heart failure is the pathophysiologic state in which an abnormality of *cardiac* function is responsible for the failure of the heart to pump blood at a rate commensurate with the requirements of the metabolizing tissues." It is the latter half of that definition that we wish to consider here. When the delivery of blood is insufficient, the peripheral circulations must adjust the distribution of the cardiac output to ensure survival of the individual.

Clearly, there are various degrees of congestive heart failure and, as might be expected, the quality and magnitude of peripheral circulatory adjustments depend on the severity of myocardial dysfunction. When heart failure has progressed to the point where cardiac output is depressed in subjects at rest, there is a characteristic redistribution of regional blood flow to ensure adequate perfusion of the heart and brain at the expense of the skin, kidneys, and gut (8, 12, 31) (Fig. 1). It is not fortuitous that the circulations to which flow is most restricted are those that respond most vigorously to enhanced sympathetic tone, the factor that appears to be a primary mechanism for this redistribution of regional blood flow (5). Although an excessive sympathoadrenal response plays an important role in this redistribution of flow to the circulations, especially when blood flow is measured in the awake state and the subject is uncomfortable at rest, other factors may contribute to this phenomenon. Such circulatory adjustments in heart failure are multiple and include altered levels of vasoactive hormones, altered vasomotion reflexes, and so on. These will be covered in more detail in Chapter 18.

In this chapter we will concentrate on skeletal muscle, the tissue that has major fluctuations in metabolic rate. It is this tissue that most often unmasks circulatory decompensation in heart failure when the needs of actively metabolizing exercising

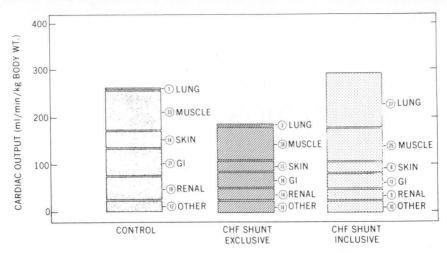

FIGURE 1 Distribution of the cardiac output in normal rats and rats with congestive heart failure produced by aortocaval fistula in the awake resting state. Regional blood flows were determined from the distribution of radionuclide-tagged microspheres in the peripheral organs after left ventricular injection. The magnitude of the left to right shunt is shown by the large lung blood flow portrayed in the panel on the far right. It should be noted that the circulations that are most compromised when systemic cardiac output is reduced by heart failure are those with the highest capacity to respond to alpha adrenergic receptor stimulation (renal, splanchnic, and cutaneous).

skeletal muscle cannot be met because of an inability of the heart to deliver sufficient blood. When this occurs during exercise, there is clearly an enhanced sympathoadrenal response. The consequences of this response and its causes are addressed here. This can be accomplished best by considering how blood flow to skeletal muscle is regulated in heart failure.

METABOLIC VASODILATION

It has been known for some time that in congestive heart failure the resistance vessels fail to dilate normally to a maximal metabolic stimulus (30). Whereas normal subjects might achieve a limb blood flow of 40 ml/min · 100 ml following restoration of circulation to an ischemic limb (reactive hyperemia response), patients with heart failure achieve a blood flow of only 25 ml/min · 100 ml. This inability to dilate normally has also been noted when blood flow has been measured after exercise, during static exercise, or during regional or systemic dynamic exercise in both humans and animals in heart failure (14, 28, 30). Since this response returns toward normal after diuresis, it was suggested that augmented sodium retention might be responsible for this vascular stiffness. A series of studies in animals and humans has presented considerable evidence that this limited arteriolar vasodilator response is probably secondary to increased vascular sodium and water content and, in certain conditions, increased tissue pressure (10, 25, 26, 29).

Since blood flow may be inadequate to certain skeletal muscle beds during exercise in heart failure, what are the metabolic consequences that ensue? A common feature noted in patients with congestive heart failure is a widened arteriovenous oxygen difference. One would therefore predict that a low cardiac output would lead to enhanced oxygen extraction in the peripheral circulations. At rest, this is accomplished by enhanced sympathetic nervous system tone, which effects a regional redistribution of flow away from organs of low metabolic requirements to those more metabolically active (8, 12, 31).

Is this true for the limb circulations as well? If sympathetic tone were entirely responsible for the reduced forearm blood flow of heart failure, then skin blood flow should be restricted more than skeletal muscle flow. However, blood flow is reduced equally to both skin and muscle in heart failure, which suggests that increased vascular stiffness must also be important in restricting blood flow to skeletal muscle during the resting state (31). But is nutritional flow altered? In patients with heart failure with a low forearm blood flow, the oxygen extraction across the nonexercising forearm is enhanced and normal oxygen consumption is maintained (14, 28) (Fig. 2). However, with forearm dynamic exercise of graded

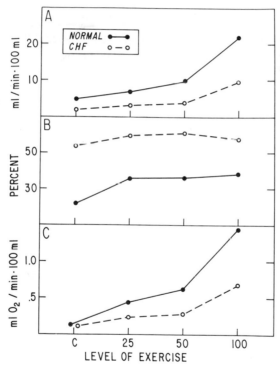

FIGURE 2 Comparison of nutritional blood flow in (●) a normal subject and (○) a patient with congestive heart failure. (A) Forearm blood flow; (B) forearm oxygen extraction; and (C) forearm oxygen consumption. Data were taken at rest (point *C*) and during rhythmic grip exercise of progressively increasing severity, induced by squeezing a hand dynamometer to 25, 50, or 100 mmHg for 5 sec 4 times per min for 5 min. Although forearm blood flow is reduced at rest in the patient with heart failure, the increased oxygen extraction is sufficient to maintain a normal basal forearm oxygen consumption. The higher level of oxygen extraction is not adequate to keep pace with muscle metabolic requirements during exercise and results in a greater shift to anaerobic metabolism, which is reflected in a reduced forearm oxygen consumption. From Zelis et al. (27).

intensity, forearm blood flow fails to rise normally; forearm oxygen extraction increases, but it is not sufficient to keep up with oxygen requirements (28). In other words, for any level of blood flow during exercise, oxygen extraction fails to increase proportionally (Fig. 3). Oxygen consumption of the exercising forearm is therefore reduced below normal for any particular level of external work. Thus, during exercise, it appears that nutritional blood flow suffers significantly.

Is it the increased vascular stiffness or the exaggerated sympathoadrenal response that is more important in limiting metabolic vasodilation, leading to the observed failure of oxygen consumption to rise normally? Generally, when metabolic vasodilator stimuli compete with the vasoconstrictor effects of alpha adrenergic receptor stimulation, it is the metabolic influences that predominantly control local blood flow (3, 13, 19, 22, 23). However, this overriding of sympathetic constrictor vascular tone by local metabolites (functional sympatholysis) is a relative phenomenon, and a true competition exists when there is a submaximal metabolic stimulus.

INTERACTION BETWEEN METABOLIC VASODILATION AND ADRENERGIC VASOCONSTRICTION

To test the hypothesis that alpha adrenergic receptor stimulation might influence skeletal muscle oxygen consumption during exercise, a canine gracilis muscle preparation was utilized (1) (Fig. 4). With this preparation, gracilis muscle tension could be recorded continuously and, through a feedback mechanism, could

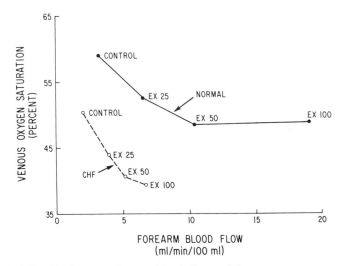

FIGURE 3 Relationship between forearm blood flow and forearm venous oxygen saturation at rest (control) and during three levels of forearm grip exercise (see Fig. 2) for (●) normal subjects and (○) patients with congestive heart failure (CHF). For any level of forearm blood flow, CHF patients have a much greater reduction in venous oxygen saturation, indicating that blood flow is not able to keep pace with the metabolic needs of the exercising muscle; a compensating enhancement of oxygen extraction by the tissues is observed.

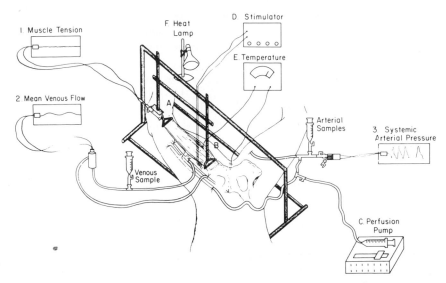

FIGURE 4 Canine gracilis muscle preparation utilized to evaluate the effects of intra-arterial norepinephrine infusion on gracilis muscle blood flow and oxygen extraction during static exercise to a predetermined level of maximal contractile force. In this preparation, mean venous flow was measured with a rotameter; in other studies, gracilis muscle artery blood flow was measured directly by flowmeter.

be used to control motor nerve stimulation voltage to maintain skeletal muscle tension at a constant percentage of maximal contractile force (MCF). The effects of intra-arterial infusion of norepinephrine on gracilis muscle blood flow, oxygen extraction, and oxygen consumption were evaluated during static exercise of variable duration and intensity. Table 1 shows the results of one such study at 10% MCF during serial 2-min exercise periods interrupted by a period of rest. Similar results were seen with 2.5% MCF maintained for 10 min. As the dose of norepinephrine infused intra-arterially was increased, there was a progressive stepwise reduction in gracilis muscle blood flow during exercise. This resulted in enhanced oxygen extraction. The oxygen extraction was sufficient to maintain normal oxygen consumption during the two lower doses of norepinephrine; however, during the highest level of infusion oxygen consumption fell significantly.

In these studies, norepinephrine could have been working at either of two

TABLE 1 Effects of intra-arterial norepinephrine on gracilis muscle blood, oxygen extraction, and oxygen consumption during 2 min of static exercise at 10% maximum contractile force

Measurement	Control	Norepinephrine infusion (μg/min)		
		0.11	0.22	0.44
Blood flow, ml/min	20.3	16.0	13.6	6.3
Oxygen extraction, %	54.4	72.8	80.7	83.2
Oxygen consumption, ml/min	2.2	2.3	2.12	0.88

levels, the resistance vessels or the precapillary sphincters. If it exerted its effect primarily at the resistance vessel level, the effect would be comparable to that produced by mechanical occlusion of the feeding artery. For that matter, arterial mechanical occlusion might also be comparable to an increase in resistance vessel stiffness—that is, a limited vasodilator capacity, the phenomenon described above, which is characteristic of severe heart failure. If the norepinephrine effect were working predominately at the precapillary sphincter level, one might expect to see a different effect on skeletal muscle metabolism, since nutritional blood flow appears to be regulated at this level (9, 21, 24). Therefore, the effect of mechanical occlusion of blood flow to the gracilis muscle during exercise was compared with the effect of intra-arterial norepinephrine producing a comparable degree of blood flow restriction.

The results of this study were quite informative (17). It was found that for any particular reduction in blood flow caused by mechanical occlusion of the gracilis artery during gracilis muscle exercise, there was a *greater* reduction in oxygen consumption than could be produced by a comparable reduction in blood flow induced by intra-arterial norepinephrine infusion. This strongly suggests that the inability of oxygen consumption to rise normally in exercising skeletal muscle in heart failure patients is caused predominantly by an effect at the resistance vessel level—that is, the vascular stiffness factor related to increased vascular sodium content.

On the other hand, the exaggerated sympathoadrenal response to exercise in heart failure may in part be compensatory. With a modest stimulation of alpha adrenergic receptors (i.e., low-dose norepinephrine) and constriction of the pre-capillary sphincters, one would expect that there would be an *intramuscular* redistribution of blood flow away from the fibers of low metabolic activity and toward fibers of high metabolic activity. Precapillary sphincters in the region of fibers of high metabolic activity would have the constrictor effects of alpha adrenergic receptor stimulation overriden by the accumulation of local metabolites. Such an effect would not occur in the microcirculation supplying less metabolically active fibers. Alpha adrenergic receptor stimulation of vessels in resting skeletal muscle is quite different. Most observers have suggested that in resting skeletal muscle nutritional blood flow is restricted and regional oxygen consumption falls (2, 18, 20). The selective intramuscular redistribution of flow to the more metabolically active fibers during exercise and maintenance of a normal oxygen consumption must be an important protective physiological mechanism in normal subjects.

When the sympathetic nervous system is turned on more strongly, however, as in heart failure during exercise or during high-dose intra-arterial norepinephrine infusion, one might expect the level of blood flow control to the microcirculation to shift from the precapillary sphincters to the resistance vessels. Thus, the effects of high-dose norepinephrine might severely restrict total flow. This would cause oxygen consumption to fall, because of inability of the precapillary sphincters to have a major effect on nutritional flow in the face of severely limited total flow. The metabolic results of this series of events are predictable. The maintenance of skeletal muscle high-energy phosphate stores would shift from oxidative processes to less efficient anaerobic processes. Systemically, this would lead to the well-known lactic acidosis seen when heart failure patients exercise, the early appearance of fatigue, and the slow recovery from exercise.

CONSEQUENCES OF SKELETAL MUSCLE HYPOXIA

With the limitation of nutritional blood flow, it is likely that exercising skeletal muscles in patients with heart failure become more ischemic and hypoxic than those of normal subjects. To study the systemic consequences of local skeletal muscle hypoxia, a canine preparation was utilized (15). Venous return from both hind limbs was diverted to an oxygenator and the hind limbs were perfused with a roller pump through an abdominal aortic cannula. Vascular isolation was accomplished by ligating all vessels between the hind limbs and the remaining systemic circulation. When the hind limbs were made hypoxic (PO_2, from 290 to 27 mmHg) the response of the systemic circulation was tachycardia and vasoconstriction. Systemic vascular resistance increased 118%; resistance in the brachial arterial bed increased as well (135%). However, with bilateral hind limb hypercapnia (PCO_2, from 43 to 115 mmHg) and acidosis (pH, from 7.39 to 7.05), no changes were observed in the remaining systemic circulation. It would appear, then, that skeletal muscle hypoxia stimulates somatic afferent nerves and leads to reflex tachycardia and peripheral vasoconstriction. This may be one mechanism by which patients with heart failure produce the exaggerated sympathoadrenal response to exercise. A second mechanism (discussed in Chapter 18) might be related to the reduced low- and high-pressure baroreceptor sensitivity noted in heart failure (7, 11). A blunted baroreceptor response might facilitate and augment the pressor response to stimulation of somatic afferent receptors in skeletal muscle during exercise.

SKELETAL MUSCLE–SYMPATHETIC NERVOUS SYSTEM INTERACTION: INITIATION OF A VICIOUS CYCLE

The events that occur in skeletal muscle during exercise in heart failure may proceed in the sequence shown in Table 2. Initially, locally produced metabolites

TABLE 2 Skeletal muscle circulation in heart failure: One possible sequence of events leading to the excessive sympathoadrenal response to exercise

1. Exercise metabolites lead to vasodilation, which is attenuated in heart failure secondary to stiffness of resistance vessels.
2. Oxygen consumption fails to rise normally, leading to excessive reduction in tissue PO_2, which leads to exaggerated stimulation of somatic afferent nerves.
3. An excessive sympathoadrenal response results and is facilitated by depressed baroreceptor reflexes.
4. Sympathetic alpha adrenergic stimulation in skeletal muscle leads to two responses, depending on whether it is mild to moderate (early effect) or excessive (late effect).
   a. The early effect is a favorable vasoconstriction of precapillary sphincters, leading to a redistribution of flow from less active to more active skeletal muscle fibers and maintenance of normal skeletal muscle oxygen consumption.
   b. The late effect is an unfavorable constriction of the resistance vessels, leading to depressed metabolic blood flow and reduced skeletal muscle oxygen consumption.

lead to vasodilation. This is an attenuated vasodilation because of the stiffness of the resistance vessels secondary to an increased vascular sodium content and perhaps also secondary to an increased tissue pressure. The limited vasodilation leads to failure of oxygen consumption to rise normally in skeletal muscle. This results in an excessive reduction of tissue PO_2. The reduction of PO_2 stimulates somatic afferent nerves, leading to an excessive efferent sympathoadrenal response, which would not be attenuated by a normal feedback mechanism since the baroreceptor response is depressed in heart failure. If the sympathoadrenal response is not grossly exaggerated, an early effect would be constriction of precapillary sphincters, leading to an intramuscular redistribution of blood flow from fibers of low metabolic activity to fibers of high metabolic activity. This enhanced nutritional blood flow would lead to maintenance of normal skeletal muscle oxygen consumption, a favorable response. In fact, in some preliminary studies we have observed that oxygen consumption may even be slightly increased by low doses of norepinephrine (17). The increase in nutritional flow may be a short-lived response in patients with heart failure. A later effect, when neurohumoral vasoconstrictor tone becomes excessive, is a predominant resistance vessel vasoconstriction. The result would be reduced nutritional blood flow, accompanied by a further failure of skeletal muscle oxygen consumption to rise appropriately. This would lead to further stimulation of somatic afferent receptors, and the excessive sympathoadrenal response would therefore be propagated.

IMPLICATIONS FOR VASODILATOR THERAPY

A third form of therapy has been added to the armamentarium of digitalis and diuretics in the treatment of heart failure—vasodilator therapy. This is considered in more detail in Chapter 22. Vasodilators are conveniently classified according to whether they act predominantly on the resistance vessels (hydralazine, phentolamine) or the capacitance vessels (nitrates), or have a balanced effect on arteries and veins (nitroprusside, prazosin) (4, 6, 16). It is clear that these agents reduce left ventricular filling pressure, thereby relieving pulmonary congestive symptoms, and can increase cardiac output, leading to more favorable organ perfusion. However, few studies have been done to evaluate their effects on the regional circulatory responses to exercise. Since the distribution of the cardiac output to skeletal muscle can easily triple with exercise, the effects of these agents on the circulation to skeletal muscle are extremely important. Again, this is a promising field for future study.

CONCLUSIONS

The autonomic adjustments to congestive heart failure appear to be an exaggeration of the sympathoadrenal response to exercise. This may be related to inability of the resistance vessels in skeletal muscle to dilate normally in response to a metabolic stress and a greater stimulation of somatic afferent receptors. The facilitated afferent nerve traffic in skeletal muscle is further facilitated by diminished baroreceptor reflexes, and the efferent response is a greater outpouring of adrenal epinephrine and sympathetic neurogenic vasomotor tone. In skeletal muscle, minimal increases in norepinephrine reaching the vasculature result in a facilitated nutritional blood flow; however, excessive alpha adrenergic receptor stimulation reverses this process and nutritional flow is reduced. The ensuing skeletal muscle ischemia and its attendant hypoxia reinforce the somatic afferent-sympathetic efferent arc and induce an unfavorable cycle. Vasodilator therapy, if it enhances skeletal muscle nutritional flow, could be an effective means of interrupting this cycle and enhancing skeletal muscle metabolism. Thus, even if patients cannot exercise longer with vasodilator therapy, they might have a circulatory response more compatible with long-term well-being, despite a limited improvement in exercise-induced symptoms.

REFERENCES

1. Beech, A., Geiger, J., Crede, W., Mason, D. T., and Zelis, R. Effects of low and high dose norepinephrine on oxygen consumption during low intensity gracilis muscle static exercise. Circulation 50:III-161, 1974.
2. Bolme, P. and Gagnon, D. J. The effects of vasodilating drugs and vasoconstrictor nerve stimulation on oxygen uptake in skeletal muscle. Eur J Pharmacol 29:300–307, 1972.
3. Burcher, E. and Garlick, D. Antagonism of vasoconstrictor responses by exercise in the gracilis muscle of the dog. J Pharmacol Exp Ther 187:75–85, 1973.
4. Chatterjee, K., Parmley, W. W., Swan, H. J. C., Berman, G., Forrester, J., and Marcus, H. S. Beneficial effects of vasodilator agents in severe mitral regurgitation due to dysfunction of the subvalvular apparatus. Circulation 48:684–690, 1973.
5. Chidsey, C. A., Braunwald, D., and Morrow, A. G. Catecholamine excretion and cardiac stores of norepinephrine in congestive heart failure. Am J Med 39:442–451, 1965.
6. Cohn, J. N., Mathew, J. K., Franciosa, J. A., and Snow, J. S. Chronic vasodilator therapy in the management of cardiogenic shock and intractable left ventricular failure. Ann Intern Med 81:777–780, 1974.
7. Eckberg, D. L., Drabinsky, M., and Braunwald, E. Defective cardiac parasympathetic control in patients with heart disease. N Engl J Med 285:877, 1971.
8. Flaim, S. F., Minteer, W. J., and Zelis, R. The effects of volume overload heart failure on the cardiovascular responses to treadmill exercise in the rat. Circulation 56:III-204, 1977.
9. Granger, H. J., Goodman, A. H., and Granger, D. N. Role of resistance and exchange vessels in local microvascular control of skeletal muscle oxygenation in the dog. Circ Res 38:379–385, 1976.
10. Hayduk, K. B., Vladutic, A., Simard, S., Rojo-Ortega, J. M., Belleau, L., Boucher, R., and Genest, J. Renin activity and norepinephrine, cation and water contents of cardiovascular tissue of dogs with congestive heart failure and ascites. Can J Physiol Pharmacol 45:463–468, 1970.
11. Higgins, C. B., Vatner, S. F., Eckberg, D. L., and Braunwald, E. Alterations in the baroreceptor reflex in conscious dogs with heart failure. J Clin Invest 51:715–724, 1972.
12. Higgins, C. B., Vatner, S. F., Franklin, D., and Braunwald, E. Effects of

experimentally produced heart failure on the peripheral vascular response to severe exercise in conscious dogs. Circ Res 31:186–194, 1972.

13. Kjellmer, I. On the competition between metabolic vasodilation and neurogenic vasoconstriction in skeletal muscle. Acta Physiol Scand 63:450–459, 1965.

14. Longhurst, J., Gifford, W., and Zelis, R. Impaired forearm oxygen consumption during static exercise in patients with congestive heart failure. Circulation 54:477–480, 1976.

15. Longhurst, J., Williams, R., Vaughan, M., and Zelis, R. Evidence favoring chemoreceptor activation as the etiology of reflex cardiovascular responses from skeletal muscles. Fed Proc 33:296, 1974.

16. Miller, R. R., Vismara, L. A., Williams, D. O., Amsterdam, E. A., and Mason, D. T. Pharmacological mechanisms for left ventricular unloading in clinical congestive heart failure: Differential effects of nitroprusside, phentolamine, and nitroglycerin on cardiac function and peripheral circulation. Circ Res 39:127–133, 1976.

17. Nellis, S. H., McCauley, K. M., Flaim, S. F., and Zelis, R. Exercise oxygen consumption in skeletal muscle: Norepinephrine- vs mechanically-induced ischemia. Fed Proc 36:585, 1977.

18. Pappenheimer, J. R. Vasoconstrictor nerves and oxygen consumption in the isolated perfused hindlimb muscles of the dog. J Physiol (Lond) 99:182–200, 1941.

19. Remensnyder, J. P., Mitchell, J. H., and Sarnoff, S. J. Functional sympatholysis during muscular activity. Circ Res 11:370–380, 1962.

20. Renkin, E. M. and Rosell, S. The influence of sympathetic adrenergic vasoconstrictor nerves on transport of diffusible solutes from blood to tissues in skeletal muscle. Acta Physiol Scand 54:223–240, 1962.

21. Rosell, S. and Uvnäs, B. Vasomotor nerve activity and oxygen uptake in skeletal muscle of the anesthetized cat. Acta Physiol Scand 54:209–222, 1962.

22. Skinner, N. S. and Costin, J. C. Role of O_2 and K^+ in abolition of sympathetic vasoconstriction in dog skeletal muscle. Am J Physiol 217:438–444, 1969.

23. Strandell, T. and Shepherd, J. T. The effect in humans of increased sympathetic activity on the blood flow to active muscle. Acta Med Scand [Suppl] 472:146–167, 1967.

24. Takeshita, A. A., Mark, L., Abboud, F. M., Schmid, P. G., Heistad, D. D., and Johannsen, U. J. Phentolamine and isoproterenol: Comparison of effects on vascular resistance and oxygen uptake in skeletal muscle during hypotension. J Pharmacol Exp Ther 199:353–359, 1976.

25. Zelis, R., Delea, C. S., Coleman, H. N., and Mason, D. T. Arterial sodium content in experimental congestive heart failure. Circulation 41:213–216, 1970.

26. Zelis, R., Lee, G., and Mason, D. T. Influence of experimental edema of metabolically determined blood flow. Circ Res 34:482–490, 1974.

27. Zelis, R., Longhurst, J., Capone, R. J., and Lee, G. Peripheral circulatory control mechanisms in congestive heart failure. Am J Cardiol 32:481–490, 1973.

28. Zelis, R., Longhurst, J., Capone, R. J., and Mason, D. T. A comparison of regional blood flow and oxygen utilization during dynamic forearm exercise in normal subjects and patients with congestive failure. Circulation 50:137–143, 1974.

29. Zelis, R. and Mason, D. T. Diminished forearm arteriolar dilator capacity produced by mineralocorticoid-induced salt retention in man. Implications

concerning congestive heart failure and vascular stiffness. Circulation 41:589–592, 1970.

30. Zelis, R., Mason, D. T., and Braunwald, E. A comparison of the effects of vasodilator stimuli on peripheral resistance vessels in normal subjects and in patients with congestive heart failure. J Clin Invest 47:960–970, 1968.

31. Zelis, R., Mason, D. T., and Braunwald, E. Partition of blood flow to the cutaneous and muscular beds of the forearm at rest and during leg exercise in normal subjects and in patients with heart failure. Circ Res 24:799–806, 1969.

CHAPTER 18

CIRCULATORY ADJUSTMENTS TO HEART FAILURE

FRANÇOIS M. ABBOUD
PHILLIP G. SCHMID

Circulatory adjustments in heart failure tend to restore cardiac output and tissue perfusion. These include: 1) an increase in blood volume, 2) an increase in peripheral venous tone, 3) an increase in resistance in certain vascular beds, and 4) a change in the capillary surface area-permeability coefficient (12, 21).

MECHANISMS INVOLVED IN THE CIRCULATORY ADJUSTMENTS

The following mechanisms are involved in circulatory adjustments to heart failure: humoral factors such as renin-angiotensin-aldosterone and ADH (antidiuretic hormone), sympathoadrenal control, cardiovascular reflexes, and structural-biochemical changes in heart and blood vessels. Each mechanism has been explored in different preparations of heart failure, and although all may be involved they vary markedly in relative importance, depending on the model of heart failure used (e.g., left versus right failure) or the duration and severity of the disease. The first three mechanisms will be discussed in this chapter.

Humoral Factors

Renin-Angiotensin-Aldosterone

In 1946 Merrill et al. (24) found increased renin levels in renal vein blood of patients with chronic heart failure. DeChamplain et al. (9) demonstrated in 1963 high plasma renin activity as well as high arterial angiotensin levels in similar patients.

Renin-angiotensin-aldosterone activity in heart failure of short duration Morris et al. (26) studied the hormonal and hemodynamic changes in congestive heart failure produced in the rabbit during a period of 2–12 d after aortic constriction. They demonstrated that severe constriction of the suprarenal abdominal aorta and a supplemental daily sodium intake of 10 meq resulted in progressive increases in left ventricular end-diastolic pressure, marked fluid and sodium retention, ascites, and pulmonary congestion. Correspondingly, there were increases in plasma renin activity and angiotensin and aldosterone concentrations. In this preparation, the extra load of salt and water was an important factor in the production of heart failure, and aldosterone levels rose despite the sodium load. The correlation between the renin-angiotensin system and congestive failure in this model was good.

In another study by Watkins et al. (37) the role of the renin-angiotensin-aldosterone system in congestive failure was evaluated in the conscious dog after either pulmonary artery or thoracic inferior vena caval constriction continued for 2 wk. This study emphasized the temporal change in the relationship between the circulatory adjustment and the renin-angiotensin-aldosterone system. *Two phases* were observed. The first phase included increases in plasma renin activity, angiotensin II generation, and plasma aldosterone. In the second phase, the associated retention of sodium and water increased atrial and arterial pressures, which then suppressed the renin-angiotensin-aldosterone system. The animals were edematous, had venous congestion and ascites, and had reached a new steady state of sodium balance. This steady state may not be analogous to human chronic congestive failure, where renin-angiotensin and often aldosterone secretions may be increased despite the presence of hypervolemia.

Angiotensin and sodium retention in heart failure of short duration In the same experiments mentioned above, Watkins et al. (37) administered angiotensin converting enzyme inhibitors (CEI) in the early phases of heart failure and noted persistent hypotension and a reduction in the animal's ability to conserve sodium and water. Angiotensin must be important as a compensatory mechanism in this early phase. CEI were ineffective, however, in the second phase of heart failure after hypervolemia had been established.

The importance of angiotensin in the maintenance of arterial pressure in the low-output states was also demonstrated by Davis et al. (8), who used angiotensin II receptor blocker (saralasin) in sodium-depleted dogs and in dogs with thoracic caval constriction. In these animals, arterial pressure fell, plasma renin levels increased, and aldosterone secretion was markedly reduced after the administration of the receptor blocker. This indicates that 1) angiotensin II acts on specific receptors in vascular smooth muscle, causing constriction; 2) there is a negative feedback control of renin release by angiotensin; and 3) the secretion of aldosterone is determined by activation of specific angiotensin receptors in the adrenal gland and not by sodium concentration.

In addition to the increased rates of excretion and secretion of aldosterone in heart failure, there is a decreased rate of clearance of aldosterone as a result of the fall in hepatic blood flow caused by passive congestion of the liver and decreased rate of extraction and inactivation (5).

Sodium retention may also be related to a reduced glomerular filtration rate (GFR) or rise in renal vein pressure, but a reduced GFR is not essential for sodium retention in heart failure. Barger (1) demonstrated that in dogs with tricuspid insufficiency, marked sodium retention may occur in the absence of changes in glomerular filtration, and Bradley and Blake (3) showed the same effect in patients with congestive heart failure.

Other factors, including the sympathetic tone to the kidney and the release of an "antinatriuretic factor," must also contribute to sodium retention.

The renin-angiotensin-aldosterone system in patients with chronic heart failure Although one is tempted to state simply that a low cardiac output is the trigger for activation of the renin-angiotensin-aldosterone system, there are several unusual features of this system in chronic congestive heart failure in humans. For example, sodium deprivation, which ordinarily causes an increase in angiotensin-aldosterone secretion, has the opposite effect in patients in heart failure. Sodium deprivation and diuresis reduce renin-angiotensin-aldosterone secretion or excretion (10), and conversely, administration of salt to patients in congestive failure leads to a paradoxical increase in aldosterone secretion (20). The type of heart failure, right or left, may also contribute to the magnitude of the aldosterone response to angiotensin. Wolff et al. (38) found normal excretion of aldosterone in most patients with left-sided failure and high values in the majority of patients with right-sided failure. Furthermore, Kloppenborg et al. (18) reported that angiotensin infusions given to patients with congestive failure had little or no effect on aldosterone secretion, either before or after diuretic therapy. This abnormal response may be related to the high circulating levels of this polypeptide.

An explanation for all the responses of the renin-angiotensin-aldosterone system in chronic heart failure is not readily apparent. These effects may involve neural or humoral stimuli that vary with the type, severity, and duration of failure and may be activated by impulses arising in cardiac as well as arterial or pulmonary receptors.

Thirst and the edema of congestive failure   In dogs, constriction of the thoracic region of the inferior vena cava causes an increase in water intake and in intracellular and plasma fluid volume (28). Administration of the angiotensin receptor blocker saralasin to two dogs in congestive failure markedly reduced their water intake (28).

Recent observations suggest that thirst may be induced by a central nervous system action of angiotensin, which may be independently associated with the release of vasopressin. Vasopressin released by angiotensin may account in part for both the central pressor effect of angiotensin (17) and edema. Thus, excessive fluid intake in heart failure could be mediated in part through a central action of the renin-angiotensin system.

Antidiuretic Hormone

Belleau et al. (2) reported a striking increase in plasma ADH activity in six dogs with congestive heart failure and ascites secondary to tricuspid ablation lasting for several weeks. There was no increase of ADH in dogs without ascites. In these experiments, when ADH was elevated 3–17 wk after tricuspid ablation in heart failure, the animals had a markedly positive sodium and water balance, and the changes in plasma aldosterone and norepinephrine activity were not consistent and were not correlated with the symptoms of congestive failure. ADH may thus play a role in the formation of ascites and edema late in congestive heart failure.

Persistence of ADH release in heart failure   It had been demonstrated that, regardless of the state of hydration or plasma osmolality, an increase in left atrial pressure is accompanied by a decrease in plasma ADH. Share (33) showed that inflation of a balloon in the left atrium prevents the increase in ADH plasma levels secondary to occlusion of both common carotid arteries in dogs. It is conceivable that at that stage in heart failure, left atrial receptors have a decreased afferent sensory activity, possibly because of chronic stretch of the left atrium and histological changes in its wall (11, 40). The ADH levels thus fail to be suppressed as the activity of the atrial receptors ceases.

On the other hand, ADH may not be essential for the formation of edema in congestive failure. Hamilton et al. (13) showed that severe sodium retention and ascites persist in dogs with thoracic caval constriction despite injury to the neurohypophysis and production of diabetes insipidus.

Sympathoadrenal Control in Heart Failure

Sympathetic and Parasympathetic Control of the Heart

There is convincing evidence of myocardial depletion of catecholamines and tyrosine hydroxylase in heart failure, particularly in the stressed ventricle (7, 27, 35), but this may be a late development. Soon after pulmonary artery constriction in guinea pigs, we found an increase in the norepinephrine turnover rate, possibly associated with an increase in sympathetic activity selectively directed to the heart (Fig. 1). An increase in sympathetic activity is suggested by measurements of choline acetyltransferase activity in sympathetic ganglia (Fig. 2). Choline acetyltransferase is the enzyme necessary for the synthesis of acetylcholine, which acts as the neurotransmitter in the sympathetic ganglia. Later in heart failure, norepinephrine turnover in the myocardium may be decreased and depletion of norepinephrine becomes more apparent in the right ventricle (32). The increased norepinephrine turnover, suggestive of an increase in sympathetic activity early in

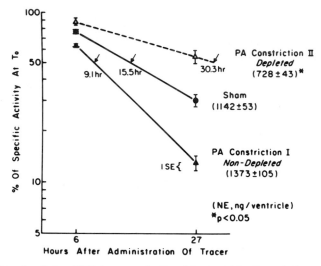

FIGURE 1 Norepinephrine (NE) turnover in the right ventricle. Constriction of the pulmonary artery (PA) resulted in a twofold increase in right ventricular mass, but not all guinea pigs had a depletion of myocardial catecholamines. Maintenance of catecholamines (group I) was associated with a high rate of turnover of neurotransmitter and presumably a high level of sympathetic neural activity to the heart. Depletion of catecholamines (group II) was associated with a decrease in the turnover rate. We speculate that group I represents an early phase and group II represents a later phase of compensation to constriction of the pulmonary artery. (Group I, $n = 5$; group II, $n = 9$; sham group, $n = 11$.)

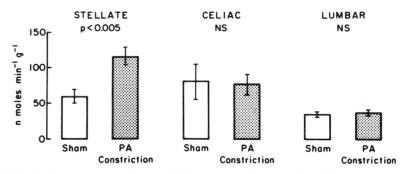

FIGURE 2 Choline acetyltransferase activity in sympathetic ganglia. The neurotransmitter of the preganglionic sympathetic neuron is acetylcholine; synthesis is mediated by choline acetyltransferase (CAT) activity in sympathetic ganglia. An increase in CAT activity in stellate ganglia of guinea pigs with pulmonary artery (PA) constriction suggests a selective increase in sympathetic neural activity to the heart. This corresponds to the early compensatory phase I referred to in the summary and exemplified by group I in Fig. 1. (Sham group, $n = 13$; PA group, $n = 11$; error bars show ± 1 SEM.)

heart failure, is also seen in the cardiomyopathic hamster. Unlike the case of right heart failure in guinea pigs, however, the high norepinephrine turnover in myopathic hamsters persists until death (34).

With respect to parasympathetic activity in the myocardium, as reflected by measurements of choline acetyltransferase in the right and left ventricles, the results in guinea pigs with pulmonary artery constriction indicate that there is no significant reduction in the total activity of that enzyme, in contrast with the marked reduction in tyrosine hydroxylase activity (29). Thus, there appears to be a relative protection of the parasympathetic innervation in the heart compared to the sympathetic innervation.

Altered Adrenergic Tone in Peripheral Vessels

The majority of studies in various models of heart failure indicate that there is no consistent or uniform depletion of catecholamines from the periphery in heart failure (14, 19, 31). Furthermore, there are convincing data indicating overactivity of the peripheral adrenergic system during the stress of exercise.

In our recent studies, the level of adrenergic tone to the peripheral vessels in heart failure produced in guinea pigs varied in the different models (30). In the model of left heart failure (constriction of ascending aorta), there was an increase in resistance caused predominantly by an increase in adrenergic tone, whereas in the model of right heart failure (constriction of the pulmonary artery), the increase in peripheral resistance was related to a humoral factor (Fig. 3). Preliminary studies suggest that the humoral factor in this model may be circulating catecholamines. Furthermore, the responsiveness of the perfused hindquarters of guinea pigs in right and left heart failure to nerve stimulation and to norepinephrine, as well as to angiotensin, is increased (30). Measurements of the catecholamine content of blood vessels in the dog showed that in right-sided failure there are normal vascular levels, despite significant depletion of catecholamines in the heart (31). Others found a

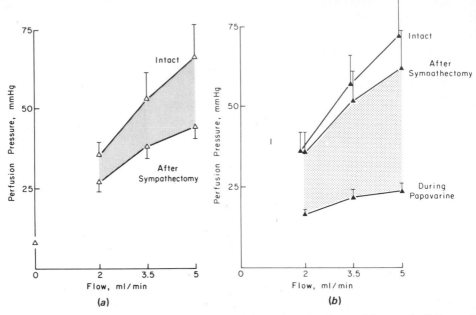

FIGURE 3 Comparison of the models of left and right heart failure. (*a*) Effect of sympathectomy in guinea pigs with tight constriction of the ascending aorta. There was an increased neurogenic contribution to vascular resistance in the hindquarters of the pigs (*n* = 8). (*b*) Nonneurogenic contribution to vascular resistance in guinea pigs with constriction of the pulmonary artery and right heart failure. There was an increased humoral influence (*n* = 7). Error bars show 1 SEM.

slight decrease in the norepinephrine content of the carotid artery and thoracic aorta, but no change in the femoral, saphenous, mesenteric, and renal arteries and an increase in the mesenteric veins (14).

In humans, Kramer et al. (19) suggested that the amount of norepinephrine available for release from the sympathetic nerve endings of resistance vessels in the forearm is augmented in heart failure. This was based on the fact that the responses to tyramine were augmented compared with the responses to norepinephrine. In another study in humans the increase in vascular resistance in heart failure was attributed partly to alpha adrenergic receptor activity (41).

One can summarize the data on the peripheral circulation by concluding that there is no evidence of depletion of catecholamines in peripheral blood vessels and that there may be an increase in sympathetic activity and increased reactivity of vessels. In certain types of heart failure, however, as in the myopathic hamster, the reactivity to nerve stimulation and norepinephrine may be decreased, probably because of changes in smooth muscle reactivity (23).

Perhaps the most dramatic evidence of increased adrenergic activity to the peripheral circulation in heart failure comes from studies in animals and in humans *during exercise*. Chidsey et al. (6) showed that during exercise in heart failure, there is a significant increase in plasma levels of catecholamines. Millard et al. (25) demonstrated that in dogs with experimental failure, there is an intense renal sympathetic vasoconstriction throughout exercise, the major portion of this response being mediated through sympathetic nerves, with an additional contribution from circulating catecholamines. This intense renal vasoconstriction reduces blood flow and causes a redistribution of flow during exercise (25). With respect to changes in venous tone during exercise, Wood (39) demonstrated that there is an increase in sympathoadrenal discharge in humans, causing constriction of the peripheral veins—a response that is blocked by ganglionic blockade. This experiment supports the hypothesis that in congestive failure, excessive venous pressure during exercise occurs in large part as the result of constriction of the veins mediated through adrenergic pathways. It is clear that autonomic control of the peripheral circulation, in addition to humoral factors, plays an important role in the redistribution of blood volume and blood flow during the adjustments in congestive failure.

Reflexes in Heart Failure

Arterial Baroreceptors: Functional Baroreceptor Denervated State

Higgins et al. (16) demonstrated that in conscious dogs with heart failure from tricuspid avulsion and progressive pulmonary stenosis, there is a marked inhibition of the baroreceptor reflex induced by a rise in arterial pressure with phenylephrine (Fig. 4). There is also a marked reduction in the pressor response and in the

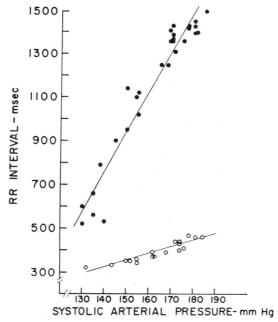

FIGURE 4 Baroreceptor hypertension. Each systolic arterial pressure is plotted against the following RR interval during the transient rise in arterial pressure induced by a bolus intravenous injection of 1-phenylephrine in the same dog in (●) the normal state and (○) heart failure. There is a marked depression in the slope of the regression line in the heart failure state compared with the normal state. (Normal, slope = 173, $r = 0.97$; heart failure, slope = 3.2, $r = 0.92$.) From Higgins et al. (16).

increases in renal and mesenteric resistance during bilateral carotid occlusion. Thus, in heart failure, all measured systemic and regional circulatory adjustments consequent to baroreceptor hypo- or hypertension are attenuated. Because of the integrity of innervation of blood vessels and the integrity of the parasympathetic supply to the heart, one has to postulate that the impairment of the baroreceptor reflex responses must be caused by a defect either at the sensory afferent receptor level or in the central nervous system.

Importance of functional baroreceptor denervation This baroreceptor dener- vated state might explain the exaggerated responses to exercise seen in heart failure. It has been shown that activation of somatic afferents during exercise will cause a rise in arterial pressure, reflex vasoconstriction, and tachycardia. This reflex sympathetic response is exaggerated markedly in the presence of hypotension and decreased carotid perfusion pressure. Activation of somatic afferents during exercise in heart failure causes a marked increase in reflex sympathetic tone; the functional baroreceptor denervation that is prevalent in heart failure may explain this exaggerated response to exercise.

Similarly, the responses to chemoreceptor stimulation are increased when carotid sinuses are perfused at low pressure. When baroreceptor afferent activity is reduced, the chemoreceptor reflex is exaggerated (15). It is possible, therefore, that the chemoreceptor reflex activated during exercise may also be potentiated in heart failure because of the "functional baroreceptor denervation state."

Cardiac Receptors

These are afferent sensory receptors that may be activated by stretch of the ventricles or atria (22). They elicit reflexes that are inhibitory to the sympathetic system and excitatory to the parasympathetic system. Their activation by ventricular stretch, for example, causes vasodilatation and marked brady- cardia.

There are two cardiac conditions in which these cardiac receptors may play a role in circulatory adjustments. Mark et al. (22) proposed that in aortic stenosis, abnormal left ventricular stretch may inhibit the reflex vasoconstrictor response to exercise and cause vasodilation and possibly hypotension. Another cardiac problem that may involve these receptors is acute myocardial ischemia; stretch of the ischemic myocardium could cause withdrawal of sympathetic tone, particularly if the ischemia is localized to the posterior wall of the left ventricle (36). Conversely, a decrease in the stretch of cardiopulmonary receptors caused by hypovolemia in animals or by lower body negative pressure in humans causes an increase in sympathetic tone. The fact is, however, that in heart failure, sympathetic tone may be increased despite left atrial and left ventricular stretch.

Paradoxical increase in sympathetic tone in heart failure Greenberg et al. (11) demonstrated that afferent nerve activity from the heart may be decreased in heart failure. That decrease could account for the increased sympathetic activity, specifically the renal sympathetic tone and sodium retention.

Why is there a decrease in afferent sympathetic activity despite an increase in cardiac size? Could it be that the receptors are sensitive to tension or deformation occurring during atrial or ventricular systole and that the decreased contractility accounts for the decreased activation of these receptors? Could chronic stretch of the atria or ventricles cause histological changes that damage these receptors? Could digitalis, for example, increase their firing and thereby cause vasodilatation, withdrawal of renal sympathetic tone, and diuresis? These are intriguing and potentially very important reflex mechanisms that require further study. Their significance is heightened by two important observations in patients in heart failure:

1. During upright tilt and the consequent decrease in cardiac size, the blood flow to the forearm, which is normally decreased, is increased in heart failure (4).
2. Diuresis, which would tend to increase renin-angiotensin-aldosterone synthesis in normal subjects, tends to decrease the levels of these hormones in heart failure (10).

These paradoxical responses of patients in heart failure to a reduction in cardiac size may reflect restoration of cardiac sensory afferent activity as a more vigorous contraction sets in. The response to the restoration of the cardiac sensory afferent activity is inhibition of sympathetic tone as well as inhibition of the renin-angiotensin-aldosterone system and diuresis.

SUMMARY

One could integrate the experimental results by proposing three phases of circulatory adjustment in heart failure.

Phase I: Low Cardiac Output

Low cardiac output activates the renin-angiotensin-aldosterone system, which causes sodium retention and hypervolemia, increases filling pressure, restores cardiac output, and causes vasoconstriction to maintain arterial pressure. Next, the low output also activates the sympathoadrenal system to cause a redistribution of blood flow to coronary and cerebral vessels, particularly during exercise, and to cause sodium retention and hypervolemia, as well as vasoconstriction to maintain arterial pressure. Finally, increased norepinephrine turnover in the heart may be a manifestation of this phase.

Phase II: Congestion and Hypervolemia

Circulatory congestion causes suppression of the renin-angiotensin-aldosterone system with restoration of sodium balance, but at a new steady state. There may also be a decline in sympathoadrenal tone associated with cardiac distension and manifested by a late decline in norepinephrine turnover.

Phase III: Functional Cardiac and Arterial Baroreceptor Denervation

Late in heart failure there is decreased arterial as well as cardiac baroreceptor sensitivity, with the following hormonal changes: a rise in renin, angiotensin, and possibly aldosterone activity; an increase in ADH; an increase in sympathoadrenal tone, particularly in sympathoadrenal drive to the kidney with increased sodium and water retention; an excessive and sustained sympathoadrenal drive to the heart, which could culminate in depletion of myocardial catecholamines; and an exaggerated pressor response to exercise caused by the baroreceptor denervation state. Restoration of cardiac and possibly arterial baroreceptor activity with reversal of the hormonal responses may result from therapy with digitalis and diuretics.

REFERENCES

1. Barger, A. C. The pathogenesis of sodium retention in congestive heart failure. Metabolism 5:480–489, 1956.
2. Belleau, L., Mion, H., Simard, S., Granger, P. Bertranou, E., Nowaczynski, W., Boucher, R., and Genest, J. Studies on the mechanism of experimental congestive heart failure in dogs. Can J Physiol Pharmacol 48:450–456, 1970.
3. Bradley, S. E. and Blake, W. D. Pathogenesis of renal dysfunction during congestive heart failure. Am J Med 6:470–480, 1949.
4. Brigden, W. and Sharpey-Schafer, E. P. Postural changes in peripheral blood flow in cases with left heart failure. Clin Sci 9:93–100, 1950.
5. Camargo, C. A., Dowdy, A. J., Hancock, E. W., and Luetscher, J. A. Decreased plasma clearance and hepatic extraction of aldosterone in patients with heart failure. J Clin Invest 44:356–365, 1965.
6. Chidsey, C. A., Harrison, D. C., and Braunwald, E. Augmentation of the plasma norepinephrine response to exercise in patients with congestive heart failure. N Engl J Med 267:650–654, 1962.
7. Chidsey, C. A., Kaiser, G. A., Sonnenblick, E. H., Spann, J. F., and Braunwald, E. Cardiac norepinephrine stores in experimental heart failure in the dog. J Clin Invest 43:2386–2393, 1964.
8. Davis, J. O., Freeman, R. H., Johnson, J. A., and Spielman, W. S. Agents which block the action of the renin-angiotensin system. Circ Res 34:279–285, 1974.
9. DeChamplain, J., Boucher, R., and Genest, J. Arterial angiotensin levels in edematous patients. Proc Soc Exp Biol Med 113:932–937, 1963.
10. Genest, J., Granger, P., deChamplain, J., and Boucher, R. Endocrine factors in congestive heart failure. Am J Cardiol 22:35–42, 1968.
11. Greenberg, T. T., Richmond, W. H., Stocking, R. A., Gupta, P. D., Meehan, J. P., and Henry, J. P. Impaired atrial receptor responses in dogs with heart failure due to tricuspid insufficiency and pulmonary artery stenosis. Circ Res 32:424–433, 1973.
12. Habak, P. A., Mark, A. L., Kioschos, J. M. McRaven, D. R., and Abboud, F. M. Effectiveness of congesting cuffs ("rotating tourniquets") in patients with left heart failure. Circulation 50:366–371, 1974.
13. Hamilton, W. F., Ellison, R. G., Pickering, R. W., Hague, E. E., and Rucker, J. T. Hemodynamic and endocrine response to experimental mitral stenosis. Am J Physiol 176:445–451, 1954.
14. Hayduk, K., Brecht, H. M., Vladutiu, A., Simard, S., Rojo-Ortega, J. M., Belleau, L., Boucher, R., and Genest, J. Renin activity and norepinephrine, cation, and water contents of cardiovascular tissue of dogs with congestive heart failure and ascites. Can J Physiol Pharmacol 48:463–468, 1970.
15. Heistad, D. D., Abboud, F. M., Mark, A. L., and Schmid, P. G. Interaction of baroreceptor and chemoreceptor reflexes. J Clin Invest 53:1226–1236, 1974.

16. Higgins, C. B., Vatner, S. F., Eckberg, D. L., and Braunwald, E. Alterations in the baroreceptor reflex in conscious dogs with heart failure. J Clin Invest 51:715–724, 1972.
17. Hoffman, W. E., Ganten, U., Phillips, M. I., Schmid, P. G., et al. Inhibition of drinking in water deprived rats by combined central angiotensin II and cholinergic receptor blockade. Am J Physiol 234:F41–F47, 1978.
18. Kloppenborg, P. W. C., Benraad, T. C., and Majoor, C. L. H. The secretion rate of aldosterone in patients with heart failure. Acta Endocrinol [Suppl] (Kbh) 119:93, 1967.
19. Kramer, R. S., Mason, D. T., and Braunwald, E. Augmented sympathetic neurotransmitter activity in the peripheral vascular bed of patients with congestive heart failure and cardiac norepinephrine depletion. Circulation 38:629–634, 1968.
20. Laragh, J. H. Hormones and the pathogenesis of congestive heart failure: Vasopressin, aldosterone and angiotensin II. Circulation 25:1015–1023, 1962.
21. Laughlin, M. H. and Diana, J. N. Myocardial transcapillary exchange in the hypertrophied heart of the dog. Am J Physiol 229:838–846, 1975.
22. Mark, A. L., Kioschos, J. M., Abboud, F. M., Heistad, D. D., and Schmid, P. G. Abnormal vascular responses to exercise in patients with aortic stenosis. J Clin Invest 52:1138–1146, 1973.
23. Mark, A. L., Mayer, H. E., Schmid, P. G., Heistad, D. D., and Abboud, F. M. Adrenergic control of the peripheral circulation in cardiomyopathic hamsters with heart failure. Circ Res 33:74–81, 1973.
24. Merrill, A. J., Morrison, J. L., and Brannon, E. S. Concentration of renin in renal venous blood in patients with chronic heart failure. Am J Med 1:468–472, 1946.
25. Millard, R. W., Higgins, C. B., Franklin, D., and Vatner, S. F. Regulation of the renal circulation during severe exercise in normal dogs and dogs with experimental heart failure. Circ Res 31:881–888, 1972.
26. Morris, B. J., Davis, J. O., Zatzman, M. L., and Williams, G. M. The renin-angiotensin-aldosterone system in rabbits with congestive heart failure produced by aortic constriction. Circ Res 40:275–282, 1977.
27. Pool, P. E., Covell, J. W., Levitt, M., Gibb, J., and Braunwald, E. Reduction of cardiac tyrosine hydroxylase activity in experimental congestive heart failure: Its role in the depletion of cardiac norepinephrine stores. Circ Res 20:349–353, 1967.
28. Ramsay, D. J., Rolls, B. J., and Wood, R. J. The relationship between elevated water intake and edema associated with congestive cardiac failure in the dog. J Physiol (Lond) 244:303–312, 1975.
29. Roskoski, R., Jr., Schmid, P. G., Mayer, H. E., and Abboud, F. M. In vitro acetylcholine biosynthesis in normal and failing guinea pig hearts. Circ Res 36:547–552, 1975.
30. Schmid, P. G., Mayer, H. E., Mark, A. L., Heistad, D. D., and Abboud, F. M. Differences in the regulation of vascular resistance in guinea pigs with right and left heart failure. Circ Res 41:85–93, 1977.
31. Schmid, P. G., Nelson, L. D., Mayer, H. E., Mark, A. L., Heistad, D. D., and Abboud, F. M. Neurogenic control of vascular tone in heart failure. Clin Res 20:396, 1972.
32. Schmid, P. G. and Roskoski, R., Jr. Regional sympathetic activity in right heart failure (RHF): Choline acetyltransferase activity in ganglia (CATG) and

norepinephrine turnover rate (NETR) in heart and vasculature. Clin Res 24:421A, 1976.

33. Share, L. Effects of carotid occlusion and left atrial distension on plasma vasopressin titer. Am J Physiol 208:219–223, 1965.

34. Sole, M. J., Lo, C. M., Laird, C. W., Sonnenblick, E. H., and Wurtman, R. J. Norepinephrine turnover in the heart and spleen of the cardiomyopathic Syrian hamster. Circ Res 37:855–862, 1975.

35. Spann, J. F., Jr., Chidsey, C. A., Pool, P. E., and Braunwald, E. Mechanisms of norepinephrine depletion in experimental heart failure produced by aortic constriction in the guinea pig. Circ Res 17:312–321, 1965.

36. Walker, J. L., Abboud, F. M., and Mark, A. L. Preferential distribution of inhibitory cardiac receptors in the inferior wall of the left ventricle. Clin Res 25:261A, 1977.

37. Watkins, L., Jr., Burton, J. A., Haber, E., Cant, J. R., Smith, F. W., and Barger, A. C. The renin-angiotensin-aldosterone system in congestive failure in conscious dogs. J Clin Invest 57:1606–1617, 1976.

38. Wolff, H. P., Koczorek, K. R., Buchborn, E., and Rieker, G. Endocrine factors. J Chron Dis 9:554–570, 1959.

39. Wood, J. E. The mechanism of the increased venous pressure with exercise in congestive heart failure. J Clin Invest 41:2020–2024, 1962.

40. Zehr, J. E., Hawe, A., Tsakiris, A. G., Rastelli, G. C., McGoon, D. C., and Segar, W. E. ADH levels following non-hypotensive hemorrhage in dogs with chronic mitral stenosis. Am J Physiol 221:312–317, 1971.

41. Zelis, R., Mason, D. T., and Braunwald, E. Comparison of the effects of vasodilator stimuli on peripheral resistance vessels in normal subjects and in patients with congestive heart failure. J Clin Invest 47:960–970, 1968.

CHAPTER 19

THE KIDNEY IN HEART FAILURE

MARTIN GOLDBERG

Isaac Starr was one of the scientific pioneers who anticipated that the kidney would play the major role in the generation of the expanded circulation and extracellular fluid volume that characterize congestive heart failure. In the 1940s, a lively debate was under way between the proponents of "forward" and those of "backward" heart failure. In 1943, Starr et al. (11) published an article based on observations made in an experimental model of right-sided heart failure in the dog. The article includes the following visionary comments:

The direct experiments on dogs ... and the studies made on man provide evidence against the commonly accepted doctrine of a direct mechanical relation between the heart and what is called congestive heart failure, but this evidence does not deny a relationship of another kind. This evidence ... does not refute the possibility of an indirect relationship ... with time-consuming physiologic steps in between.

A little later in the same paper:

The weakening heart could be thought of as diminishing renal circulation, for there is certainly good evidence of diminished kidney function in cardiac cases; specific renal insufficiency might cause the characteristic retention of fluid and electrolytes; this retained fluid increases blood volume and accumulates in tissues, pressing on the patient's vessels; to accommodate the excess, blood accumulates in the most distensible vessels, the veins, and also in the lungs where it displaces some of the air, and symptoms such as dyspnea result.

Thus, it was clear to Dr. Starr at that time that the congested circulation characterizing congestive heart failure was not merely a mechanical phenomenon, but involved a chain of events that ultimately led to marked expansion of the extracellular fluid volume and that probably involved the kidney.

Today, there is virtually unanimous agreement that, regardless of the initial series of cardiac and systemic hemodynamic events occurring in congestive heart failure, the marked expansion of the extracellular fluid volume and of the circulation requires the participation of the kidney in producing a reduction in sodium excretion and facilitating a positive salt and water balance. But, even today, the controversy of the forward versus the backward failure theory has not been resolved. Still unsettled is the nature of the primary or afferent stimuli from the failing heart that ultimately signal the kidney to retain salt and water. In Chapters 17 and 18, Zelis, Abboud, and co-workers considered the various autonomic and circulatory adjustments that occur in congestive heart failure.

AFFERENT SIGNALS

Some of the factors postulated as being the important afferent signals from the failing heart that eventually reach the kidney are listed below.

1. Reduction in cardiac output
2. Reduction in perfusion pressure
3. Increase in sympathetic activity from baroreceptors
4. Stimulation of "volume" receptors (atria, great vessels)
5. Complex series of hemodynamic alterations in cardiac chambers and great vessels

There are problems with each of these signals. A reduction in cardiac output per se is not closely correlated with renal sodium retention (2, 9). Similarly, renal sodium retention can occur with increases, decreases, or no change in renal perfusion pressure. This may be a very simplistic concept, since it is probable that some combination of changes in perfusion pressure and renal vascular resistance could still be an important signal intrarenally to affect salt and water transport. Increased sympathetic activity from the baroreceptors certainly seems to occur in congestive heart failure and there is evidence that the renal sympathetic nerves as well as the adrenergic hormones affect salt and water transport, but there is also evidence that totally denervated and isolated kidneys can retain salt and water in the presence of congestive failure. Stimulation of volume receptors in the various parts of the circulation, both on the arterial and venous side as well as within the cardiac chambers, has been proposed for many years. Indeed, evidence exists for the presence of pressure and/or volume receptors in both the arterial and the venous circulation. However, the pathway that links these receptors and the kidney is still unknown, and we lack insight into their physiological significance. At present, it can only be said that a complex series of hemodynamic alterations within the various cardiac chambers and the great vessels play on the kidney in some unknown way, to affect its handling of salt and water in congestive heart failure.

CONCEPT OF EFFECTIVE ARTERIAL
PLASMA VOLUME

It has been recognized for several years, and has probably been most effectively expounded by J. P. Peters at Yale, that the kidney is congestive heart failure behaves physiologically very much like the kidney in the hypovolemic state, as occurs with salt depletion or hemmorhage. Peters and others therefore developed the concept of effective arterial plasma volume (EAPV), which to this day has remained an unmeasurable quantity; it is somehow related to some component of the arterial filling pressure or to the relation between the arterial blood volume and the capacity of the vascular tree, but not to the absolute plasma volume per se. The interplay between the component of arterial blood volume and capacity of the tree is generally postulated as a mechanism that ensures perfusion of the vital organs in relation to their homeostatic needs. In this light, it becomes possible to explain why the kidney responds similarly in congestive failure and in acute salt depletion. For example, EAPV may be reduced by external losses of extracellular fluid such as occur by way of the gastrointestinal tract, the skin in burns, or the kidney. This is a state of true sodium depletion. But a similar state can also result from internal fluid rearrangements and shifts of plasma from the vascular tree, as in acute hypo-albuminemic states. The effective arterial plasma volume can also be low not because of a change in absolute volume but because of an increase in the capacity of the vascular bed. Finally, for any particular peripheral resistance, a reduction of effective arterial plasma volume can be brought about by a reduction of left ventricular cardiac output.

RENAL RESPONSE TO REDUCED EFFECTIVE ARTERIAL PLASMA VOLUME

Regardless of the nature of the primary event that leads to decreased EAPV, the physiological consequences to the kidney are the same. First, the kidney shares in the response to the inadequate circulation: as systemic blood pressure falls, or tends to fall, and as heart rate increases, alpha adrenergic outflow increases, both through the nervous system and through the adrenergic hormones. Second, changes in intrarenal hemodynamics are associated with the systemic changes, leading to renal hypoperfusion. Thus, in the presence of established biventricular heart failure, the following hemodynamic phenomena have been frequently observed clinically and experimentally (6): a reduction in renal plasma flow associated with renal vasoconstriction. In this formulation the presence of *bi*ventricular failure is prerequisite, since acute left ventricular failure may evoke a pathophysiologic response that is entirely different (2). The decrease in renal plasma flow is proportionately greater than any change in glomerular filtration rate (GFR), which may be normal early in congestive heart failure. This disproportionate change, therefore, alters the ratio between GFR and renal plasma flow—i.e., the filtration fraction. Changes in filtration fraction alter the protein concentration of the postglomerular capillaries perfusing the proximal renal tubules and may have a large effect on salt and water transport in this nephron segment. Several experimental observations by the inert gas washout technique, in both experimental models and patients with heart failure, have suggested a redistribution of renal blood flow from the outer cortex to the inner cortex, which might affect renal sodium excretion (5).

ENDOCRINE RESPONSE TO DECREASED EFFECTIVE ARTERIAL PLASMA VOLUME

An important series of alterations also occurs in the endocrine systems during congestive heart failure in association with a reduction in EAPV. These include an increased renal secretion of renin, leading to increased production of angiotensin I, which, in the presence of converting enzyme, enhances the elaboration of the vasoconstrictor, angiotensin II; the latter hormone is also a potent stimulus for the adrenal secretion of aldosterone (15). Several laboratories have provided indirect evidence for the presence of a circulating natriuretic factor, the activity of which increases in volume-expanded states and decreases in volume-contracted and edematous states (3). Unfortunately, despite the large number of publications in this field, natriuretic hormone has not yet been characterized or isolated, and its physiological or pathophysiologic importance in relation to other known and unknown natriuretic factors is yet to be clarified. Changes in EAPV may also provide a volume stimulus for the release of antidiuretic hormone. The afferent limb of this effect appears to originate in the left atrial wall and probably also in the arterial baroreceptors (10). With respect to the whole kidney, the net effect of the reduction in EAPV is a decrease in urine output and a marked reduction in sodium excretion: ingestion or parenteral administration of salt and water loads leads to considerable retention in an attempt to repair the effects of hypovolemia.

NEPHRON SITES OF SODIUM AND WATER REABSORPTION

A brief tour through the nephron (Fig. 1) will be helpful in identifying the sites of sodium transport that might be responsive to these various pathophysiologic

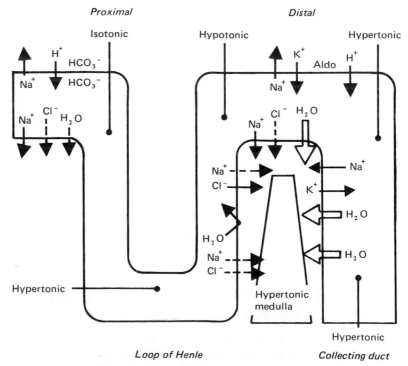

FIGURE 1   Functional anatomy of a single nephron unit.

stimuli in congestive heart failure. First, the classical question must be asked: Can all of the changes in sodium excretion be explained by primary alterations in the rate of glomerular filtration? The answer is, almost certainly not, although reductions in filtration rate, to the extent that they decrease the load of sodium entering the nephron, can limit the access of salt to the various tubular segments.

Several years ago, a series of experiments in which a variety of different maneuvers were used to increase GFR clearly demonstrated in the dog that there was absolutely no relation between even large increments in GFR and alterations in sodium excretion (8). Clearly, therefore, adjustments in tubular sodium transport are the most important mechanisms in the regulation of sodium excretion in health and disease.

To continue through the nephron (assuming, for the moment, nephron homogeneity), in the proximal tubule 60-70% of the filtered load of sodium is reabsorbed into the extracellular space. Most of the sodium is reabsorbed with chloride, which appears to be transported passively, and a minority of the sodium ions are associated with bicarbonate reabsorption, which involves a complex process of hydrogen ion secretion. Water moves passively with sodium, so that the reabsorption is isotonic and no change in sodium concentration occurs by the end of the proximal tubule. Despite this large bulk of salt and water reabsorbed in the proximal tubule, it appears that most of the important regulatory hormones and other factors that influence final urinary sodium excretion do not have an important role in the proximal tubule. In fact, the only hormone that has been clearly demonstrated to affect proximal sodium transport by the micropuncture technique is parathyroid hormone, and this may not be of homeostatic significance with regard to sodium. It is possible that certain adrenergic catecholamines may affect sodium transport in this segment, but this remains to be demonstrated conclusively. More important, this bulk reabsorption of salt and water appears to be quite responsive to a variety of hemodynamic and so-called physical forces, which may be important in reducing the load of sodium delivered out of the proximal tubule and therefore might be contributory to sodium retention, at least in some of the phases of congestive heart failure.

MECHANISM OF PROXIMAL TUBULAR REABSORPTION

As may be seen in a small segment of the proximal tubule shown in Fig. 2, sodium can enter the cell passively from the luminal side since the electrochemical gradient favors downhill movement (7). Once the sodium is within the cell, sodium pumps, which are located along the lateral and basilar surfaces, pump the sodium into the intercellular space. Chloride and water follow sodium passively, so that salt accumulates within these spaces. The "tight junctions" between the proximal tubular cells are not absolutely tight. Therefore, there is always a small backleak of sodium into the lumen, which decreases the efficiency of net sodium reabsorption. The sodium is removed from this region by the peritubular capillaries. Much recent work has been concentrated on the mechanisms whereby sodium enters the capillaries. Although the precise mechanism is unclear, it is somehow related to the factors that primarily affect net fluid uptake, most important of which are the

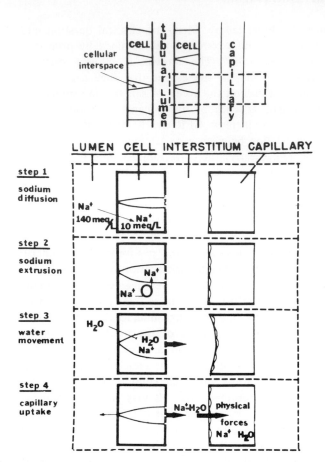

FIGURE 2 Diagrammatic representation of mechanism of fluid and electrolyte reabsorption in the proximal tubule. (Top) Anatomic components of the system. The tubular cell has a luminal and peritubular cell membrane. Adjacent cells are joined luminally by tight junctions. Located between tubule cells is an extracellular interspace. The area bounded by the dotted line is enlarged at the bottom. The reabsorptive process begins with diffusion of sodium down a chemical gradient into the cell (step 1), from which it is actively pumped into the extracellular interspace (step 2), creating an area of local hypertonicity. Water follows along the osmotic gradient, expanding these interspaces. Fluid and sodium movement out of the interspace toward the capillary is accomplished by elevation of the hydrostatic pressure within these compartments (step 3). Finally, fluid and sodium are taken up at the capillary, the result of net balance of hydrostatic and oncotic pressure across the capillary wall (step 4). There is a small backleak of fluid and sodium across the tight junction into the tubule because of the hydrostatic pressure gradient. Reprinted by permission from Agus, Z. S. and Goldberg, M. Renal function in congestive heart failure. In Cardiovascular Physiology, ed. 1, H. J. Levine, ed. New York: Grune & Stratton, 1976.

capillary hydrostatic pressure and the colloid oncotic pressure or protein concentration of plasma in these capillaries. Hence, from the lumen to the intercellular and peritubular space, sodium is the species primarily transported and chloride and water follow passively.

The initial transport step in the interstitial space that is adjacent to the capillaries (Fig. 2) involves the movement of water. The key factor related to this water transport is the difference between the colloid oncotic pressure of capillary plasma and the capillary hydrostatic pressure. Indeed, this difference determines the net uptake of fluid from the interstitium into the capillary. The primary removal of water can then affect sodium transport into the capillary through one or more mechanisms. First, it will transiently increase the sodium concentration in the interstitium and produce a diffusion gradient for sodium into the capillaries. Second, the flow of water creates a bulk flow effect, which can then drag sodium back into the circulation through the mechanism of solvent drag. The more salt and water that move into the capillaries, the less salt and water remain behind in the interstitium and in the intercellular spaces to leak back through the cell and the tight junction into the lumen, and therefore the more effective is the net sodium reabsorption from lumen to capillary. In the volume-expanded state, capillary hydrostatic pressure tends to be higher and plasma proteins are diluted. In this situation, even without a change in the pump transport of sodium, net fluid uptake by the capillary is reduced, leading to retention of the fluid in the intercellular space, distension of this space, and an increase in the backleak of salt and water into the lumen. The net effect of this phenomenon is a decrease in the transport of sodium from the tubular lumen into the capillary. Thus, in the proximal tubule, several pathophysiologic stimuli playing down on the kidney can enhance, at least transiently, the reabsorption of sodium and water; in particular, the increase in filtration fraction, which increases the postglomerular concentration of protein, disturbs the balance between oncotic pressure and hydrostatic pressure so as to enhance fluid uptake from the interstitium into the capillary, thereby promoting the uptake of sodium by the capillary. A similar construct can be made around a reduction in postglomerular capillary hydrostatic pressure, which would also lead to a net enhancement of proximal tubular sodium and water reabsorption through this mechanism.

SODIUM REABSORPTION
IN THE DISTAL NEPHRON

As glomerular filtrate exits from the proximal tubule (Fig. 1), it enters the descending limb of Henle's loop, which enters the deeper recesses of the cortex. In the nephrons that are next to the medulla, the so-called juxtamedullary nephrons, the loop of Henle descends deeply into the renal medulla, often to the level of the papillary tip. Here it makes a hairpin turn to rise in the ascending limb of Henle's loop back to the renal cortex in the region of its own glomerulus. One of the newer and more exciting developments in renal physiology is the recent discovery of a chloride pump in the thick portion of the ascending limb of Henle's loop (4). In this nephron segment, in which the electric potential is positive, chloride is actively reabsorbed and sodium is passively reabsorbed. Furthermore, the epithelium of the ascending limb is quite impermeable to water, which makes this segment an important renal diluting site. Potentially, this salt transport system in the ascending limb is very potent. Under normal physiological conditions it reabsorbs 15-20% of the filtered salt. But it has the capacity to double or even triple its reabsorption rate as loads from the proximal tubule increase. Although this site has the potential for considerable renal sodium retention in pathophysiologic states, even though it is the site of action of the most potent diuretic agents, no hormone that is currently known to exert a major effect on sodium excretion seems to have an important influence on this salt transport system. Micropuncture experiments in the rat and the dog, utilizing models of congestive heart failure, have suggested that the loop of Henle might be an important site of enhanced distal nephron sodium reabsorption (14). However, aldosterone does not have an important action at this segment.

In the distal convoluted tubule within the cortex are sites where sodium is not only reabsorbed with an anion such as chloride, but cations are also secreted concomitantly with sodium reabsorption. These transport processes reflect the role played by the distal tubule and the terminal portions of the nephron as the major sites for the secretion of potassium and hydrogen ions. In the distal convoluted tubule approximately 5-10% of filtered sodium is reabsorbed; part of this reabsorption of sodium is under the influence of aldosterone.

The terminal segment of the nephron consists of the collecting tubule and the collecting duct systems, which account for the reabsorption of approximately 5% of the filtered sodium. This quantity of sodium is large and, should reabsorption cease in this segment, could account for the excretion of more than 500 meq of sodium per day. In fact, a number of recent experimental observations (13) indicate that this terminal nephron segment may be most important in the final regulation of sodium excretion in normal homeostasis. It is also a likely site for enhanced transport in edematous states. Aldosterone probably acts on this segment. But other factors may also influence sodium transport in the collecting system. These factors include not only natriuretic hormones but also other humoral substances that are of potential importance in sodium homeostasis, such as the prostaglandins and the kinen-kallekrein system.

NEPHRON HETEROGENEITY

Up to this point, the regulation of sodium excretion has been considered under the assumption of a homogeneous nephron population. However, this is not so. For example, the population can be viewed as consisting of two groups of nephrons: 1) *cortical nephrons*, which arise in the outer region of the cortex and have short loops of Henle, and 2) *juxtamedullary nephrons*, which originate in the inner recesses of the cortex and have long loops of Henle. Several years ago, the hypothesis was advanced that shifting of the filtrate and the blood flow between the various nephrons might be important in the regulation of sodium excretion (1). The basis for this proposal was the premise that cortical nephrons might be sodium "excretive" whereas juxtamedullary nephrons might be sodium "retentive." Thus, congestive failure might be associated with sodium retention because of the shift of blood flow to the inner nephrons, and diuretics might be natriuretic by virtue of shifting blood flow from the inner to the outer portions of the cortex. This hypothesis was based on observations obtained with the xenon washout technique of estimating renal blood flow. However, serious questions have since been raised about interpretations of regional distribution within the renal cortex based on use of the xenon washout technique (12). Studies of renal blood flow with radioactive microspheres have failed to show a correlation between intracortical shifts and changes in sodium excretion and have indicated the inadequacy of the xenon washout method for showing these changes within the renal cortex. Hence, although the redistribution hypothesis is still a possible explanation for some of the changes in sodium excretion in congestive failure, it is far from established.

When congestive failure is associated with considerable renal sodium retention, more than acute failure of the left ventricle has to be involved. Several years ago, a series of experiments in dogs with left ventricular failure revealed no evidence of enhanced sodium retention. More recently, the GFR and urine volume were found to be high in patients with suspected myocardial infarction and left ventricular failure (2). Finally, a recent series of experiments in conscious dogs, performed at the University of Pennsylvania by Dr. R. A. Grossman in our laboratory and Dr. J. P. Szidon in Dr. A. P. Fishman's laboratory, provided additional evidence that a failing left ventricle may not lead to renal sodium retention. They showed that a reduction in left ventricular cardiac output and in arterial perfusion pressure, following either experimental myocardial infarction or rapid atrial pacing, is not associated with a reduction in renal vascular resistance. A direct relationship was found between increments in left atrial pressure and increases in urine flow, and an inverse relationship was found between increases in left atrial pressure and urine osmolality. These changes occurred even though mean arterial blood pressure decreased. Furthermore, when perfusion pressure was maintained, increased left atrial pressure was associated with an increase in sodium excretion. These observations support the idea that the failing heart, which leads to renal sodium retention and sustained expansion of the extracellular fluid volume, involves more than inadequate function of the left ventricle.

One approach to integration of the current understanding of the renal response in congestive heart failure is to consider it in three phases (Table 1). First, there is an early transient phase in which EAPV is acutely reduced and acute neurohumoral responses are manifested—i.e., increased renin release, increased production of angiotensin, increased aldosterone secretion, increased sympathetic outflow, a rise in filtration fraction, and a tendency toward a fall in renal perfusion pressure. These have been considered above. As also discussed, the redistribution of blood flow has not been proved to be a major factor. The diverse stimuli may affect the hemodynamic and physical forces governing proximal tubular reabsorption and may be associated with enhanced salt and water transport in this segment. The reabsorptive capacity of the more distal portions of the nephron is also increased. However, because the proximal tubule determines the delivery of salt available for reabsorption distally, the proximal tubule may still be the rate-limiting factor in this stage of the process. Enhanced proximal reabsorption will lead to salt and water retention and expansion of the extracellular fluid volume and the circulation until

TABLE 1   Phases of renal response in congestive heart
failure (left and right)

Early transient phase: EAPV sharply reduced
  Neurohumoral response:
    Increased renin, angiotensin, aldosterone
    Increased sympathetic outflow
    Increased filtration fraction
    Decreased perfusion pressure
    Redistribution of blood flow (?)
  Enhanced proximal (and distal) tubular reabsorption until
    new steady state is reached

Moderate sustained CHF
  Increased aldosterone
  Decreased natriuretic hormone(s)
  Other neurohumoral factors (?)
  Enhanced distal nephron reabsorption:
    Loop of Henle
    Collecting duct
  New steady state with expanded extracellular fluid volume

Advanced CHF—pump failure
  Intense neurohumoral and hemodynamic stimuli
  Enhanced proximal and distal reabsorption
    Impaired water excretion—hyponatremia
    Refractoriness to therapy
  Difficult to achieve steady state

---

effective arterial plasma volume is restored and a new steady state is reached. This
state is achieved, however, at the expense of a moderate expansion of the extracellular
fluid volume. During this new steady state, the patient may have the capacity to
excrete salt and water loads normally, as long as the congestive heart failure is mild.

If congestive heart failure is moderate or severe, mechanisms for sodium
retention beyond the proximal tubule may predominate. Therefore, in moderate
sustained congestive failure, increased levels of aldosterone and decreased levels of
natriuretic hormone, as well as other neurohormonal factors that have yet to be
elucidated, enhance reabsorption in the distal nephron. The fraction of filtered salt
and water leaving the proximal tubule in this situation may be normal. But, in the
distal nephron, aldosterone and other agents operate to increase the fraction of the
delivered load of sodium that is reabsorbed. Sodium reabsorption is enhanced and
these patients may again achieve a new steady state, but at the expense of a
considerable expansion in extracellular fluid volume and engorgement of the
circulation. If the cardiac hemodynamic alterations cannot be improved with
digitalis, these patients usually respond quite readily to diuretic therapy and sodium
restriction.

Finally, patients with severe heart disease enter the phase of advanced
congestive heart failure. At this stage, all of the various neurohumoral and
hemodynamic stimuli to sodium reabsorption persist. These patients do not achieve
a steady state; hence, enhanced proximal and distal reabsorption of sodium is

continuous. This state of heart failure is associated with impaired water excretion because of the intense volume stimulus to antidiuretic hormone release as well as the decrease in delivery of salt and water to the distal diluting sites. Hyponatremia and refractoriness to all forms of therapy are common.

REFERENCES

1. Barger, A. C. Renal hemodynamics in congestive heart failure. Ann NY Acad Sci 139:786–797, 1973.
2. Bennett, E. D., Brooks, W. H., Keddie, J., Lin, Y., and Wilson, A. Increased renal function in patients with acute left ventricular failure: A possible hemostatic mechanism. Clin Sci Mol Med 52:43–50, 1977.
3. Bourgoignie, J. J., Hwang, K. H., and Espinel, C. A natriuretic factor in the serum of patients with chronic uremia. J Clin Invest 51:1514–1527, 1972.
4. Burg, M. B. Tubular chloride transport and the mode of action of some diuretics. Kidney Int 9:189–197, 1976.
5. Burger, A. C. Renal hemodynamic factors in congestive heart failure. Ann NY Acad Sci 139:276–284, 1966.
6. Cannon, P. J. The kidney in heart failure. N Engl J Med 296:26–32, 1977.
7. Giebisch, G. Coupled ion and fluid transport in the kidney. N Engl J Med 287:913–919, 1972.
8. Lindheimer, M. P., Lalone, R. C., and Levinsky, N. G. Evidence that an acute increase in glomerular filtration has little effect on sodium excretion in the dog unless extracellular volume is expanded. J Clin Invest 46:256–265, 1967.
9. Migdal, S., Alexander, E. A., and Levinsky, W. G. Evidence that decreased cardiac output is not the stimulus to sodium retention during acute constriction of the vena cava. J Lab Clin Med 89:809–816, 1977.
10. Schrier, R. W. and Berl, T. Nonosmolar factors affecting renal water excretion. N Engl J Med 292:81–88, 1975.
11. Starr, I., Jr., Jeffers, W. A., and Meade, R. H., Jr. The absence of conspicuous increments of venous pressure after severe damage to the right ventricle in the dog, with a discussion of the relation between clinical congestive heart failure and heart disease. Am Heart J 26:291–301, 1943.
12. Stein, J. H., Boinjarern, S., Wilson, C. B., and Ferris, T. F. Alterations in intrarenal blood flow distribution. Circ Res 32-33:61–72, 1973.
13. Stein, J. H. and Reinbeck, H. J. The role of the collecting duct in the regulation of excretion of sodium and other electrolytes (editorial review). Kidney Int 6:1–9, 1974.
14. Stumpe, K. O., Sölle, H., Klein, H., and Krüch, F. Mechanism of sodium and water retention in rats with experimental heart failure. Kidney Int 4:309–317, 1973.
15. Watkins, I., Jr., Burton, J. A., Haber, E., Cant, J. R., Smith, F. W., and Barger, A. C. The renin-angiotensin-aldosterone system in congestive failure in conscious dogs. J Clin Invest 57:1606–1617, 1976.

CHAPTER 20

THE BRAIN IN HEART FAILURE

MARTIN REIVICH

Patients in congestive heart failure not uncommonly have clinical evidence of disturbed cerebral function in the form of irritability, restlessness, apathy, drowsiness, poor attention span, or disorientation (12). Although symptoms of cerebral dysfunction are common in heart failure, they usually do not appear until dyspnea is present at rest. It has been postulated that cardiac output at this stage becomes inadequate to maintain normal perfusion of the brain, resulting in these central nervous system (CNS) symptoms. Circulatory failure produced by myocardial infarction is frequently accompanied by personality change, mild delirium, or depression of mental function. These cerebral symptoms are exaggerated if arterial oxygen saturation is decreased because of concomitant pulmonary edema.

When the decrease in cardiac output is marked, patients in congestive failure often exhibit a shock syndrome characterized by a decreased level of consciousness, restlessness, and stupor, which can go on to coma and death if uncorrected (16).

Cardiac arrhythmia, as well as myocardial failure, can reduce cerebral perfusion to the point of producing cerebral symptoms. In this paper these two concepts will be explored and the information available in support of each will be reviewed.

CEREBRAL PERFUSION AND METABOLISM IN CONGESTIVE HEART FAILURE

In any vascular bed, the perfusion through that organ is directly related to the perfusion pressure across the organ and inversely related to the resistance in the vascular bed. Normally the brain has the capacity to autoregulate, so that changes in perfusion pressure over a wide range do not alter cerebral blood flow (7). As the perfusion pressure declines below normal the cerebral vessels dilate, with a consequent reduction in cerebral vascular resistance (CVR) so as to maintain cerebral blood flow (CBF) constant; conversely, as the perfusion pressure rises the cerebral vessels constrict, CVR increases, and CBF again remains constant.

There is conflicting evidence regarding the effect of congestive heart failure on CBF and metabolism. Scheinberg (12) studied 14 patients who, on clinical grounds, were considered to have chronic congestive heart failure and low cardiac output. At the time of the study all of the patients were alert without evidence of cerebral dysfunction. Mean CBF was significantly reduced, the value being 40 ± 1.9 ml/100 g $\cdot$ min, compared with a normal value of 65 ± 2.1 ml/100 g $\cdot$ min. In addition, the cerebral metabolic rates for oxygen ($CMRO_2$) and glucose (CMR_{gl}) were significantly reduced, the values being 3.29 ± 0.1 ml/100 g $\cdot$ min and 5.14 ± 0.35 mg/100 g $\cdot$ min, respectively, compared with normal values of 3.79 ± 0.09 ml/100 g $\cdot$ min and 6.2 ± 0.26 mg/100 g $\cdot$ min, respectively. CVR was significantly increased to 2.58 ± 0.17 mmHg/ml $\cdot$ 100 g $\cdot$ min, normal being 1.3 ± 0.04 mmHg/ml $\cdot$ 100 g $\cdot$ min.

Cardiac output was not measured in these patients, but in a similar series of patients with congestive failure the cardiac index was 2.1 liter/min $\cdot$ m^2, or a 41% decrease from normal (17). The reduction in CBF (39%) therefore appears to be proportional to the change in cardiac output expected in these patients. Mean arterial blood pressure (MABP) was not reduced below normal, and in fact was significantly elevated—99 compared with 83 mmHg. The normal values with which these changes were compared, however, were obtained in healthy young males 30 yr old or younger, while the average age of the patients was 40 yr. Part of the decline in CBF and metabolism may therefore be related to the older age of the patients, although this would probably not account for the entire change noted.

The observed increase in CVR suggests that there may have been some degree of cerebral atherosclerosis that could contribute to the observed reduction in CBF. Stead et al. suggested that the impairment of cerebral metabolism might result from an inability of the brain to increase its extraction of O_2 from the blood in proportion to the drop in CBF. This, however, is unlikely since the cerebral venous PO_2 was only reduced to 25 ± 1.8 mmHg.

A second study (10) of 15 patients in the early phases of therapy for congestive heart failure has been reported. The mean age of the patients was 60 yr. All were alert, except for one who was disoriented. A "control" group of subjects who had evidence of systemic arteriosclerosis without congestive failure was also included. Their mean age was 62 yr. A group of "normals" under age 40 was also studied. In the first group the CBF was reduced to 40 ± 2.6 ml/100 g $\cdot$ min, but this was not significantly lower than the CBF (48 ± 4.0) of the control group. It was, however, significantly lower than that of the normals (53 ± 5.0).

The $CMRO_2$ was 2.7 ± 0.20 ml/100 g $\cdot$ min, which was not significantly different from the value for the control group (2.9 ± 0.27), but was significantly lower than the normal value (3.4 ± 0.15).

The CMR_{gl} was 4.5 ± 0.91 mg/100 g $\cdot$ min, which was not significantly different from the value for either the control group (6.2 ± 2.5) or the normal group (6.5 ± 1.2).

There was a significant increase in CVR (2.6 ± 0.24 mmHg/ml $\cdot$ 100 g $\cdot$ min) compared with the control group (2.0 ± 0.15) and the normal group (1.8 ± 0.23). In the patients the mean brachial venous pressure (111 mmH$_2$O) was significantly higher than that in the control group (61) and the normal group (70). In addition, the patients' mean jugular venous pressure (120 mmH$_2$O) and cerebrospinal fluid pressure (255 mmH$_2$O) were significantly higher than those of the control group.

The $PaCO_2$ was not significantly different among the 3 groups, being 40 ± 2.1, 45 ± 1.9, and 43 ± 1.5 mmHg for the congestive failure, control, and normal groups, respectively.

CBF and metabolism were not significantly different in the congestive failure group and the control group of patients of the same age with atherosclerosis. There were significant differences from the results for the younger normal subjects. Thus these changes in flow and metabolism cannot be attributed to heart failure but are related to the age of the patients and the presence of atherosclerosis. This probably also explains the changes in flow and metabolism noted in the study of Scheinberg (12). The CVR was significantly higher, but this was probably because of the presence of patients with essential hypertension in the congestive failure group. If these 7 cases are eliminated (i.e., MABP > 115 mmHg) the value for CVR is 2.2 mmHg/ml · 100 g · min, which is not significantly different from the value for the control group.

There was a significant increase in cerebral venous and cerebrospinal fluid pressure, but the degree of elevation probably does not significantly affect CVR. It has been shown that cerebrospinal fluid pressure must exceed 450 mmH$_2$O before CBF is significantly reduced by increased intracranial tension (6).

Thus, in spite of a decrease in cardiac output, the cerebral circulation is maintained. Other studies have shown that the coronary circulation is similarly maintained in congestive failure (2). On the other hand, hepatic blood flow is decreased in proportion to the decrease in cardiac output (8, 9).

In a third report, CBF was measured in 37 men with congestive heart failure (13). In 14 of these subjects, measurements were repeated after cardiac compensation had been achieved. CBF was significantly decreased to 39 ± 2.86 ml/100 g · min in the patients with severe congestive heart failure but was normal—i.e., 51 ± 2.40 ml/100 g · min—in the group with mild to moderate failure. Cerebral oxygen consumption was 3.8 ± 0.14 ml/100 g · min in the patients with mild failure and 3.24 ± 0.19 in the group with severe failure. Although this difference was statistically significant, both values are in the normal range for this age group.

In 10 patients with mild to moderate congestive failure, relief of the cardiac decompensation was associated with a significant decline in CBF to 43 ± 2.9 ml/100 g · min. The MABP also decreased significantly, from 121 ± 6.61 to 100 ± 7.14 mmHg. CVR, on the other hand, remained unchanged, being 2.49 ± 0.19 mmHg/ml · 100 g · min before treatment and 2.44 ± 0.22 after treatment. This suggests that autoregulation was impaired in this group of patients and that the decrease in CBF occurred because of the decline in MABP. Cerebral oxygen consumption decreased slightly, but this change was not significant. Only four patients with severe congestive failure were studied after treatment, and no significant alterations were apparent in this small group.

The earliest and most consistent abnormality in these patients was a significant increase in CVR. CBF was maintained at normal levels in spite of this increased resistance until severe congestive failure supervened. This reduction in flow resulted from a significantly lower mean arterial pressure in severe congestive failure and not a further increase in CVR, again pointing to a loss of autoregulation in these patients. The PaCO$_2$ was normal in these subjects and therefore does not seem to be a cause of the increased CVR. A generalized increase in vascular tone occurs in persons with cardiac decompensation, and it seems that the cerebral vessels participate in this phenomenon, the cause of which is obscure. The degree of impairment of cerebral perfusion in these patients was dependent on the severity of the congestive failure. This decrease in cerebral perfusion with worsening cardiac decompensation is probably linked to the decline in cardiac output that occurs in these patients, particularly if autoregulation is impaired. Although it cannot be excluded on the basis of this study that more severe cerebrovascular disease in the group with the severe failure was the basis of the further reduction of cerebral perfusion, the lack of change in CVR is against this postulate.

All three of these studies were performed in patients who had no CNS symptoms. In a further study, however, a group of 24 patients with severe intractable congestive heart failure and CNS symptoms varying from confusion to somnolence and coma were compared with a group of patients with severe congestive failure without CNS symptoms (5). The mean CBF in the group of patients with CNS symptoms was 26 ml/100 g · min, which was significantly lower than that in the patients without CNS symptoms (39 ml/100 g · min). CVR was significantly higher in the group with CNS symptoms compared with those without (3.61 and 2.66 mmHg/ml · 100 g · min, respectively). There were no significant differences in the metabolic rates for oxygen or glucose between the two groups, the values being 2.71 and 3.24 ml/100 g · min for oxygen and 3.18 and 4.00 mg/100 g · min for glucose, respectively, for the groups with and without CNS symptoms. There were no significant differences in MABP or $PaCO_2$ between these two groups to account for the differences in CBF and CVR.

Six of these subjects were studied during states of mental confusion and at times when they were alert. During periods of mental confusion, CBF decreased significantly and was associated with significant increases in CVR and MABP. There was also a significant decrease in cerebral oxygen consumption during the confused periods. Thus CBF may be profoundly decreased in patients with cerebral symptoms associated with congestive heart failure.

The evidence from these studies seems to indicate that cerebral perfusion and metabolism is reduced in patients with congestive failure, but it is not clear whether this results from the congestive failure itself or concomitant cerebrovascular disease, since all except one study did not control for this important variable, and the one study that did failed to show an effect that could be attributed to congestive failure per se. It does seem that autoregulation is impaired in these patients and that when cerebral perfusion pressure declines CBF is reduced. This underlines the importance of maintaining an adequate MABP in these patients. It also seems that during periods of decreased levels of consciousness, CBF falls significantly.

CARDIAC ARRHYTHMIAS

Now let us turn our attention to the role of cardiac arrhythmias in the production of cerebral symptoms and their effect on cerebral perfusion. It is well documented that extreme bradycardia and cardiac standstill are commonly associated with signs of generalized cerebral ischemia. Several authors have also demonstrated that paroxysmal tachyarrhythmias may also induce dizziness or syncope.

In one study the results of cardiac monitoring for the detection of dysrhythmias in 587 patients were reported (19). In 95 of these cases, unexplained dizziness (55 patients) or syncope (40 patients) was present. In all patients the neurological and cardiac examination was normal and the routine electrocardiogram

(ECG) provided no explanation for the symptoms (Table 1). In 77% of these patients, cardiac abnormalities were detected with cardiac monitoring. Of these abnormalities, 44% were definitely correlated with dizziness or syncope and another 50% were possibly related to the symptoms.

The majority of the abnormalities that were correlated with symptoms were supraventricular tachyarrhythmias (Table 2). The rate of the tachycardia varied from 135 to 218 beats per minute, so that even relatively low rates may have serious hemodynamic effects. Treatment of these abnormalities with antidysrhythmic agents produced complete relief of symptoms in 72% of the patients and partial relief in another 17%.

In another series of 290 patients with cardiac dysrhythmias, 81% had neurological symptoms consisting either of syncope (58%), dizziness (14%), or seizures (9%), while only 1% had focal transient cerebral ischemic attacks, suggesting the rarity of cardiac arrhythmia as a cause of focal neurological manifestations (11).

The role of an arrhythmia in the production of symptoms of cerebral ischemia in a group of 39 patients was evaluated with a continuous 10-hr tape-recorded ECG (20). Twenty-eight of these patients had symptoms of diffuse cerebrovascular insufficiency—i.e., dizziness, giddiness, or syncope—and 11 had classic transient cerebral ischemic attacks. No patient had a prior significant arrhythmia or conduction abnormality diagnosed clinically or by standard ECG. Patients with bradycardia below 40 beats per minute, tachycardia over 150 beats per minute, or high-grade atrioventricular (AV) block, were considered to have arrhythmias capable of producing their symptoms. Ten of the 39 patients had one of these arrhythmias. In seven of these the arrhythmias were correlated with symptoms. Eight of the 10

TABLE 1 Routine electrocardiogram in 95 patients with dizziness or syncope[a]

Observation	No. of patients
Normal electrocardiogram	53
Morphological abnormalities	
Myocardial infarction	6
Left ventricular hypertrophy	1
Abnormal repolarization	2
Dysrhythmias	
Premature atrial contractions	2
Premature ventricular contractions	6
Controlled atrial fibrillation	2
Sinus bradycardia	1
Conduction disturbances	
Left bundle branch block	4
Left anterior hemiblock	1
Bilateral bundle branch block	3
Atrioventricular block, first degree	2
Atrioventricular block, second degree	1
Wolff-Parkinson-White syndrome	1
Normally functioning pacemaker	13

[a]From Van Durme (19).

TABLE 2 Findings with cardiac monitoring in 95 patients with dizziness or syncope[a, b]

Observation	No. of patients
No abnormalities detected	22
Findings definitely correlated with symptoms	46
Paroxysmal atrial fibrillation	6
Paroxysmal atrial flutter	1
Paroxysmal atrial tachycardia	11
Ventricular tachycardia	10
Sinus bradycardia	3
Sinoatrial block or standstill	5
Atrioventricular block, second degree	4
Atrioventricular block, third degree	3
Defective pacemaker	5
Findings possibly related to symptoms	42
Frequent premature atrial contractions	11[c]
Frequent premature ventricular contractions	31[d]
Findings not related to symptoms	17
Sinus tachycardia ($\geq$ 120 beats/min)	8
Sinus bradycardia ($\leq$ 50 beats/min)	1
Intermittent bundle branch block	3
Atrioventricular block, first degree	5

[a]From Van Durme (19).

[b]A patient who presented different types of arrhythmias or conduction defects was always listed under each separate item.

[c]Five patients developed paroxysmal atrial tachycardia; two patients developed atrial fibrillation.

[d]Ten patients developed ventricular tachycardia.

were patients with diffuse cerebrovascular insufficiency. Of these, seven had supraventricular tachycardia and one had sinus bradycardia. Specific antiarrhythmia therapy gave an excellent result in five patients and fair improvement in three.

Thus, about 25% of the patients studied with symptoms of episodic cerebrovascular insufficiency had transient cardiac arrhythmias detected by continuous ECG monitoring. Supraventricular tachycardia was considerably more frequent than bradycardia or AV block. Nine of the 10 "positives" in this series had organic heart disease in addition to cardiac arrhythmia, and most patients were elderly, averaging 68 yr. Both of these factors probably increased their propensity to develop symptoms of cerebrovascular insufficiency from the cardiac arrhythmia.

These studies support the concept that cardiac arrhythmias commonly cause generalized cerebral symptoms but less frequently produce focal neurological manifestations.

Although it has been demonstrated that cardiac arrhythmias have a profound effect on cardiac output and systemic blood pressure (3) only a few studies have examined the effect of cardiac arrhythmias on cerebral perfusion.

Corday and Irving (4) studied the flow through the internal carotid artery in the dog with an electromagnetic flowmeter while various types of cardiac arrhythmias were induced. Frequent premature auricular systoles caused a reduction in internal carotid flow averaging 7%, while frequent premature ventricular systoles caused an average reduction of 12%. Auricular tachycardia caused a reduction in CBF when the rate increased above approximately 200 beats per minute with a reduction in systemic blood pressure and cardiac output, the average decrease in CBF being 14%. Atrial fibrillation caused the most marked reduction in CBF, the average being 23%. The greatest reduction in flow occurred when the ventricular rate exceeded 190 beats per minute.

Similar observations have been made in humans (1). The changes in carotid artery blood flow velocity during pacemaker-induced ventricular tachycardia were examined in a series of 19 patients. The greatest impairment of carotid flow occurred during ventricular tachycardia. The range of reduction in CBF was between 40 and 75%. The average reduction in flow was 50%. Figure 1 illustrates the changes in carotid flow at various pacing rates in one patient.

Right ventricular pacing at rates greater than 120 beats per minute resulted in a decline of carotid artery flow velocity. There was a significant correlation between the pacing rate and the reduction of peak systolic flow velocity. On the other hand, peak diastolic flow velocity was relatively well maintained over a wide range of pacing rates, and declined by only 33% at a rate of 180 beats per minute. These reductions of carotid artery flow velocity are probably based on decreased diastolic cycle length, reduced left ventricular filling, and diminished stroke output. An overshoot of carotid artery flow velocity occurs after bursts of ventricular tachycardia and may be due to reactive hyperemia. At heart rates of less than 120

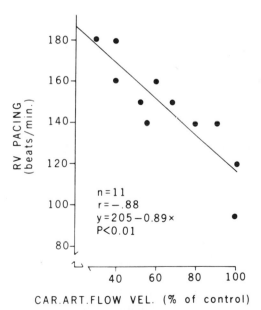

FIGURE 1 Heart rate plotted against percentage of control peak carotid flow velocity in a patient subjected to 11 episodes of rapid right ventricular (RV) pacing at different driving rates. There is a significant ($p < 0.01$) inverse correlation ($r = -0.88$) between heart rate and percentage of control carotid artery flow velocity. From Benchimol et al. (1).

beats per minute no significant differences between peak flow velocity were noted during atrial and ventricular pacing. However, at more rapid rates the atrial contribution to ventricular filling, stroke output, and peak systolic carotid artery flow velocity was more significant, and atrial pacing produced higher peak flow velocity levels. These findings indicate that ventricular tachycardia can significantly reduce CBF and that unexplained episodes of light-headedness and syncope may be based on such arrhythmia-related reductions in flow.

In a few studies in humans the effect of heart block on cerebral hemodynamics has been examined. Sulg et al. (18) studied regional CBF in seven patients with complete AV heart block (five suffering from Adams-Stokes attacks) before and after implantation of a cardiac pacemaker. The mean age of the patients was 69 yr. Preoperatively the heart rate varied between 30 and 48 beats per minute. With the pacemaker, the rate was set to a frequency of about 72 beats per minute in all cases. None of the patients showed any focal neurological signs. However, in all of them there was some reduction in mental capacity but no evidence of pronounced dementia. The initial blood flow measurement revealed a mean value of 40.1 ± 3.9 ml/100 g · min, which represents a significant decrease of approximately 22% from normal (normal was 51.1 ml/100 g · min in that laboratory). Mean hemispheric gray flow was found to be 60.4 ± 5.1 ml/100 g · min, which was also a significant decrease of about 26% (normal being 82.1 ± 5.8). After implantation of the pacemaker, mean flow increased to 43.8 ± 4.5 and gray matter flow increased to 66.0 ± 5.7 ml/100 g · min. Both of these values are significantly higher than the preoperative measurements. There was no significant change in white matter flow,

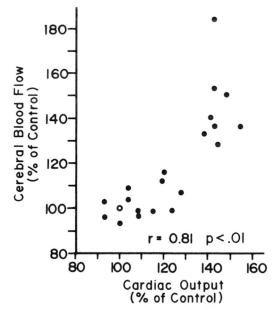

FIGURE 2 Cerebral blood flow plotted against cardiac output, both as percentages of control values (○). The correlation between all simultaneous paced values for cardiac output and CBF (●) is significant ($r = 0.81$, $p < 0.01$). From Shapiro and Chawala (14).

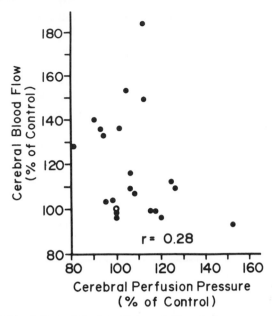

FIGURE 3 Cerebral blood flow plotted against cerebral perfusion pressure, both as percentages of control values (○). There is no correlation between simultaneous values (●) for cerebral perfusion pressure and CBF ($r = 0.28$). From Shapiro and Chawala (14).

which averaged 18.4 ± 3.0 and 19.1 ± 1.6 ml/100 g · min pre- and postoperatively, respectively. The MABP was 121 ± 21 mmHg preoperatively and 112 ± 10 mmHg postoperatively. There was no change in $PaCO_2$ pre- and postoperatively. Clinically, there was a pronounced improvement in one patient, substantial improvement in three, and slight improvement in three. Syncopal-convulsive symptoms disappeared after pacing. Although there was an increase in CBF postoperatively, the values remained subnormal.

In a second study the effects of right ventricular pacing on CBF, cardiac output, MABP, and heart rate were examined in a series of five patients with complete heart block (14). Estimates of CBF were made by calculating the reciprocal of the AV oxygen difference across the brain. Measurements were made in the control state at rates of 30–40 beats per minute and after the heart rate was increased to 60, 70, 90, and 100 beats per minute. No significant changes in blood gases occurred during these measurements. Control cardiac output was reduced—i.e., to 2.8 ± 0.05 liter/min. CBF was also probably below normal during complete heart block. Significant increases in both cardiac output and CBF occurred at the pacing rate of 60 beats per minute. No further changes were recorded at the higher pacing rates. The changes in vascular resistance were not statistically significant, although they declined during pacing at 60 beats per minute. The increases in CBF were well correlated with the increases in cardiac output (Fig. 2) but were unrelated to the observed minor changes in MABP or cerebral perfusion pressure (Fig. 3).

The results of this study appear to show that changes in CBF parallel alterations in cardiac output independent of changes in blood pressure or arterial blood gases and pH. One explanation may be the hypothesis of Shenkin and Novack (15), who suggested that a critical reduction in cardiac output causes the cerebral vessels to constrict in order to participate in the maintenance of an appropriately elevated peripheral resistance, thus leading to a diminution in CBF. This hypothesis requires that the cerebral vessels resist the dilator effects of the local increases in tissue CO_2 tension and decreases in O_2 tension that would be expected when CBF falls. It has been postulated that this reflex vasoconstriction of the cerebral vessels may be mediated by myocardial or pulmonary vascular distension. Whatever the mechanism, it appears that cardiac arrhythmias can significantly alter cerebral perfusion and produce CNS symptoms.

Thus, cerebral hemodynamics and metabolism can be adversely affected by a decrease in cardiac output. In the patient with cardiac failure, the decrease in cardiac output may result either from failure of the heart as a muscular pump or from an arrhythmia. The resulting cerebral hypoperfusion is responsible for cerebral dysfunction.

REFERENCES

1. Benchimol, A., Baldi, J., and Desser, K. B. The effects of ventricular tachycardia on carotid artery blood flow velocity. Stroke 5:60–67, 1974.
2. Bing, R. J., Maraist, F. M., Dammann, J. F., Jr., Draper, A., Jr., Heimbecker, R., Daley, R., Gerard, R., and Calazel, P. Effect of strophanthus on coronary blood flow and cardiac oxygen consumption of normal and failing human hearts. Circulation 2:513–516, 1950.
3. Corday, E., Gold, H., de Vera, L. B., Williams, J. H., and Fields, J. Effect of the cardiac arrhythmias on the coronary circulation. Ann Intern Med 50:535–553, 1959.
4. Corday, E. and Irving, D. W. Effect of cardiac arrhythmias on the cerebral circulation. Am J Cardiol 6:803–808, 1960.
5. Eisenberg, S., Madison, L., and Sensenbach, W. Cerebral hemodynamic and metabolic studies in patients with congestive heart failure. Circulation 21:704–709, 1960.
6. Kety, S. S., Polis, B. D., Nadler, C. S., and Schmidt, C. F. The blood flow and oxygen consumption of the human brain in diabetic acidosis and coma. J Clin Invest 27:500–510, 1948.
7. Lassen, N. A. Cerebral blood flow and oxygen consumption in man. Physiol Rev 39:183–238, 1959.
8. Mokotoff, R., Ross, G., and Leiter, L. Renal plasma flow and sodium reabsorption and excretion in congestive heart failure. J Clin Invest 27:1–9, 1948.
9. Myers, J. D. and Heckam, J. B. An estimation of the hepatic blood flow and splanchnic oxygen consumption in heart failure. J Clin Invest 27:620–627, 1948.
10. Novack, P., Goluboff, B., and Bortin, L. Studies of the cerebral circulation and metabolism in congestive heart failure. Circulation 7:724–731, 1953.
11. Reed, R. L., Siekert, R. G., and Merideth, J. Rarity of transient focal cerebral ischemia in cardiac dysrhythmia. J Am Med Assoc 223:893–895, 1973.
12. Scheinberg, P. Cerebral circulation in heart failure. Am J Med 8:148–152, 1950.

13. Sensenbach, W., Madison, L., and Eisenberg, S. Cerebral hemodynamic and metabolic studies in patients with congestive heart failure. Circulation 21:697–703, 1960.
14. Shapiro, W. and Chawla, N. P. S. Observations on the regulation of cerebral blood flow in complete heart block. Circulation 40:863–870, 1969.
15. Shenkin, H. A. and Novack, P. The control of the cerebral circulation. J Am Med Assoc 178:390–393, 1961.
16. Stead, E. A. Pathologic physiology of heart failure. In: Cecil-Loeb Textbook of Medicine, ed 12, P. B. Beeson and W. McDermott, eds. Philadelphia: Saunders, 1967, pp. 585–587.
17. Stead, E. A., Warren, J. V., and Brannon, E. S. Cardiac output in congestive heart failure. Am Heart J 35:529–541, 1948.
18. Sulg, I. A., Cronqvist, S., Schuller, H., and Ingvar, D. H. The effect of intracardial pacemaker therapy on cerebral blood flow and electroencephalogram in patients with complete atrioventricular block. Circulation 39:487–494, 1969.
19. Van Durme, J. P. Tachyarrhythmias and transient cerebral ischemic attacks. Am Heart J 89:538–540, 1975.
20. Walter, P. F., Reid, S. D., and Wenger, N. K. Transient cerebral ischemia due to arrhythmia. Ann Intern Med 72:471–474, 1970.

PART V

THERAPY OF HEART FAILURE

CHAPTER 21

CURRENT THOUGHTS ON DIGITALIS USE AND INTOXICATION

EDGAR HABER

> *I use it in ascites, anasarca and hydrops pectoris; and so far as the removal of water will contribute to the cure of the patient, so far may be expected from this medicine . . . .*
>
> *Dropsical cases . . . the consequences of scarlet fever and sore throat . . . they were without exception cured by foxglove . . . .*
>
> *In the greater part of what are called asthmatical cases, the real disease is anasarca of the lungs . . . almost always combined with some swelling of the legs . . . .*
>
> *In one case in which it was properly given . . . the urine began to flow freely on the second day. On the third, the swelling began to subside . . . .*
>
> *The foxglove, when given in very large and quickly repeated doses occasions sickness, vomiting, purging, giddiness, confused vision, objects appearing green or yellow . . . slow pulse, even as slow as 35 in a minute . . . .*
>
> *William Withering, 1785*

We have not come a very great deal further than this perceptive observer who understood many of the benefits of digitalis as well as the narrow margin between therapeutic and toxic effects. As these brief quotes from "An Account of the Foxglove" emphasize, he believed the drug to be a diuretic of utility in certain kinds of edema only, the consequence of scarlet fever and sore throat (rheumatic fever?) or pulmonary congestion with peripheral edema (biventricular failure?). Toxic effects were almost completely listed including bradycardia, although, of course, he could not have appreciated other dysrhythmias, given the primitive technology of the day.

EFFECTS OF DIGITALIS ON THE HEART

Regrettably, these insights were much neglected until well into the twentieth century. Clinicians focused on the effect of digitalis on cardiac rate and rhythm and believed it to be effective only in those cases of heart failure associated with atrial fibrillation and a rapid ventricular response. Christian in 1919 (12) and Harrison et al. in 1931 (19) established an improvement in heart failure in patients with sinus rhythm.

Physiological investigations clearly demonstrated that the digitalis glycosides were not primarily diuretics, but produced their beneficial effects by a positive inotropic action on the heart (11, 39). More recently, it has also become clear that there was not a qualitative difference between the effects of the drug on the normal and the failing heart and that both were subject to the same kind of increase in myocardial contractility (7, 17, 24).

In addition to inotropic effects, digitalis acts on the specialized conduction tissue of the heart to increase its refractory period and to diminish conduction velocity. This slows the ventricular response to atrial fibrillation and atrial flutter and prolongs the PR interval in the presence of normal sinus rhythm. In atrial and ventricular myocardium as opposed to specialized conduction tissue, the refractory period is shortened and there is more rapid recovery, reflected in shortening of the QT interval on the electrocardiogram (20).

The digitalis glycosides have potent effects on the autonomic nervous system. It has long been recognized that vagal stimulation is important in slowing sinus node discharge and in decreasing atrioventricular conduction (22). More recently, attention has focused on sympathetic effects that may have a role in the genesis of toxic dysrhythmias (18).

Putting together these pharmacological principles, the beneficial effects of digitalis on dysrhythmias and heart failure are readily comprehended. When cardiac contractility is decreased by excess volume or pressure load or by some intrinsic defect in cardiac muscle, such as may be caused by ischemia or a primary degenerative process, a variety of compensatory mechanisms are brought into play. The end-diastolic pressure rises to increase contractile force by the Frank-Starling mechanism, increased sympathetic tone promotes increased systolic tension and velocity of contraction, and ventricular hypertrophy provides more contractile elements. These compensatory mechanisms operate successfully within a certain range, but when this range is exceeded, an excessive rise in end-diastolic pressure leads to pulmonary or peripheral edema, excess sympathetic tone leads to increased myocardial oxygen consumption, and undesirable tachycardia and ventricular hypertrophy result in decreased cardiac compliance as well as increased oxygen consumption. Finally, these compensatory mechanisms are unable to maintain cardiac output as contractility continues to diminish. Digitalis increases contractility and restores compensatory mechanisms to the ranges in which they are effective. Cardiac output increases and end-diastolic pressure diminishes, relieving pulmonary and peripheral congestion.

In the presence or absence of heart failure, when an atrial dysrhythmia results in a ventricular rate too rapid for complete diastolic filling of the ventricles, cardiac output also diminishes. The effects of digitalis, both *directly* on specialized conduction tissue and *indirectly* via the increase in vagal tone, serve to convert the dysrhythmia to sinus rhythm or diminish the rate of ventricular response, thereby augmenting cardiac output.

Thus the dual action of digitalis, enhancing cardiac contractility and correcting or moderating tachyarrhythmias, results in its very wide application for the treatment of congestive heart failure and four types of supraventricular tachyarrhythmia: paroxysmal supraventricular tachycardia, atrial fibrillation, atrial flutter, and the tachyarrhythmias of the Wolff-Parkinson-White syndrome.

DIGITALIS INTOXICATION

It is regrettable that a drug so broadly useful in the treatment of manifestations of cardiac disease has so narrow a margin between its therapeutic and its toxic dose. As indicated in the quotation at the beginning of this chapter, Withering described many of the toxic manifestations in 1785. Digitalis toxicity persists today as one of the most prevalent adverse drug reactions (21). The incidence in hospitalized patients varies between 8 and 35%, with mortality ranging from 3 to 21% of those experiencing toxicity (33). Digitalis dose, and consequently plasma concentration, is but one of several determinants of toxicity. Whether a patient becomes intoxicated at any particular dose or serum level is dependent on such diverse factors as serum potassium, calcium, and magnesium concentrations; adequacy of tissue oxygenation; acid-base balance; thyroid status; autonomic nervous system tone; concurrently administered drugs; and the nature and severity of the underlying heart disease.

Mechanism

Anorexia, nausea, and vomiting—manifestations referable to the central nervous system and cardiac dysrhythmias—are the principal symptoms of digitalis intoxication. The gastrointestinal effects are probably mediated by chemoreceptors located in the area postrema of the medulla (6) and not by direct effects on the viscera. The mechanism underlying other central nervous system symptoms is poorly understood.

The genesis of cardiac arrhythmias depends on disturbances of impulse formation and conduction as a consequence of alterations in refractory period, impulse transmission, and automaticity of cardiac tissues as well as centrally mediated alterations in vagal and sympathetic tone. At therapeutic levels of digitalis, there is a slowing of sinus rate mediated by vagal effects on the sinoatrial node. At higher doses there may be a depression of sinus node automaticity, leading to marked sinus bradycardia or sinus arrest sometimes seen in intoxication. This predisposes to the emergence of junctional or ventricular escape rhythms. Because digitalis can shorten the refractory period of atrial myocardium, it may lead to an increased atrial rate in patients with atrial flutter.

As with the sinus node, digitalis prolongs the effective refractory period of the atrioventricular node. This is in part related to direct effects and in part to increased vagal tone. The slowing of ventricular response in atrial flutter or fibrillation is accounted for by failure of impulses from the atrium to reach the His-Purkinje system because of decreased conduction in the node. With excessive digitalis administration in patients in sinus rhythm, decreased conduction in the node can lead to second or third degree atrioventricular block.

Digitalis increases the automaticity of the His-Purkinje system, leading to new pacemakers. These are manifest clinically by premature junctional or ventricular beats and later by junctional or ventricular rhythms. Since digitalis has a different effect on ventricular and Purkinje fibers (16), enhanced automaticity, depressed conduction velocity, and local block favor the emergence of arrhythmias of the reentry type. These may lead to ventricular tachycardia and ventricular fibrillation.

Clinical Presentation

Anorexia may be both an early and a persistent manifestation of digitalis intoxication. If allowed to persist, anorexia has been sufficient to cause severe weight loss. Nausea and vomiting are, of course, classically recognized symptoms. Visual manifestations include scotomata, flickering in the peripheral field of vision, changes in color perception, and halos. Toxic effects referable to the nervous system include headache, fatigue, malaise, neurological pain, disorientation, confusion, delirium, and seizures. These are relatively infrequent. Equally rare are allergic skin lesions. Gynecomastia is occasionally seen, particularly in men treated with digitoxin.

Every known rhythm disturbance has been attributed to digitalis intoxication. Most common are atrioventricular junctional escape rhythms, ventricular bigeminy, trigeminy, atrioventricular junctional tachycardia, ectopic ventricular beats, and ventricular tachycardia. Also seen are atrioventricular junctional exit block, paroxysmal atrial tachycardia, atrioventricular block (if second degree, usually Mobitz type I), and sinoatrial block. No electrocardiographic feature distinguishes digitalis toxic rhythms from those due to intrinsic cardiac disease (13).

DETERMINATION OF DIGITALIS PLASMA CONCENTRATION

Na^+,K^+-Adenosine triphosphatase is the probable receptor for the digitalis glycosides. As with all cellular receptors, the degree of occupancy is correlated with the relevant effect and plasma concentration determines receptor occupancy. It is not surprising then that a close correlation has been found between plasma digoxin concentration and electrophysiological effects on the heart (4), but as has been indicated previously, although plasma concentration of digitalis glycosides is not the sole determinant of either therapeutic affect or toxicity, it provides an exceedingly important guide to therapy.

Because of the very low plasma concentrations at which the digitalis glycosides manifest their effects, clinically applicable methods for determining plasma concentration have not been available until quite recently. Practical methods depend on competition between radioactively labeled digitalis glycoside and an unknown concentration of the same compound in plasma for a specific high-affinity binding site. This site may be either a preparation of the enzyme (8) or an antibody (31). The equilibrium between the free and bound species and the labeled and unlabeled digitalis glycoside may be expressed as follows:

$$[Dig^*] + [Dig] + [P] \rightleftharpoons [Dig^*\text{-}P] + [Dig\text{-}P]$$

where $[Dig^*]$ is the concentration of labeled digitalis glycoside, $[Dig]$ that of the unlabeled or unknown digitalis glycoside, and $[P]$ that of the binding protein. It is apparent from this relationship that as [Dig] increases, [Dig*-P] must decrease and [Dig*] increase. In competitive binding assays, the ratio of bound to free radioactive ligand is measured. Thus [Dig*-P]/[Dig*] is proportional to [Dig].

In by far the greatest number of clinical studies specific antibody has been employed as the binding protein in digitalis glycoside assays. This approach is also widely employed in routine clinical laboratories, reagents being readily available from commercial sources. Small volumes of serum or plasma are sufficient for accurate determinations.

Experience in our laboratory has been based on the use of radioimmunoassay with antibodies that bind digoxin (31), digitoxin (30), ouabain (28, 29), and acetylstrophanthidin (27). Antisera may be selected that have exceptional selectivity and affinity, allowing for identification of the particular digitalis glycoside present as well as measurement of subnanogram concentrations. The specificity of antibodies examined has been directed largely at determinants on the C-D ring end of the steroid portion of the molecule. The glycoside part seems to have a smaller role in identification by antibody. Antiserum selected for the digoxin assay (32) bound digoxin with an affinity 50 times greater than that for digitoxin, although the 2 compounds differ only in the presence of a single hydroxyl group at position 12 in the steroid portion of digoxin (31) (Fig. 1). Other steroids that may be encountered in plasma do not interfere when present in physiological ranges.

To carry out the digitalis glycoside radioimmunoassay, it is necessary to have a specific antibody, a reliable standard, a labeled glycoside, and a means of separating antibody-bound from free labeled glycoside. We initially reported a method utilizing tritium-labeled digoxin and dextran-coated charcoal to separate bound from free labeled ligand (31). Digoxin derivatives labeled with ^{125}I are now available from

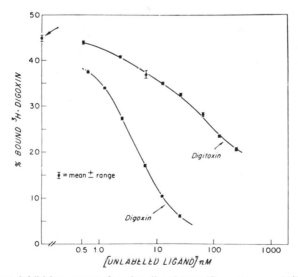

FIGURE 1   Hapten inhibition curves for the digoxin-specific antiserum 46/97, showing on a semilogarithmic scale the extent to which the steroid glycosides digoxin and digitoxin displace tritiated digoxin from the antibody combining site. The control value (no unlabeled ligand added) is indicated by the arrow on the ordinate. Modified from Smith et al. (31).

several commercial sources, increasing the convenience and speed with which the procedure may be carried out as well as obviating some of the problems encountered with liquid scintillation counting of tritium, such as quenching.

All radioimmunoassays are subject to a number of potential errors if attention is not paid to evaluating the affinity and specificity of antisera available, purity of standards, immunological identity of tracers and standards, and interference by other radioactive substances present in the sample. Exogenous radioactivity present in serum after a patient has undergone a radionuclide scanning procedure can produce erroneous results when either beta or gamma counting is utilized. The energy spectrum of these nuclides is invariably different from that of the tritium or ^{125}I utilized in labeling the digitalis glycoside, and they may thus be readily identified on another (higher energy) channel of the counter.

Antisera may lack sufficient affinity or may not be sufficiently specific to differentiate between the digitalis glycoside of interest and other compounds normally present in plasma. Two antisera are compared in Fig. 2 (36). That in Fig. 2A is highly specific whereas that in Fig. 2B reacts significantly with progesterone and testosterone at concentrations likely to be encountered in some patients. Adequate documentation of specificity must be supplied by distributors of antisera before they are accepted in a clinical laboratory.

The dose of a digitalis glycoside administered is generally well correlated with plasma concentration when body size, renal function, and problems in gastrointestinal absorption are taken into account (33). Impairment of renal function particularly affects the plasma concentration of digoxin, since this drug is largely excreted by the kidney, whereas renal function has less effect on digitoxin concentration, the latter drug being largely metabolized in the liver. Digoxin is only partially absorbed from the gastrointestinal tract. The degree of absorption may be profoundly influenced by the compounding of the preparation as well as by gastrointestinal malabsorption syndromes, drugs that decrease gastrointestinal motility, and nonabsorbed substances such as neomycin, cholestyramine, colestipol, and kaolin.

Digitoxin concentration is affected by resins such as cholestyramine that bind the drug and interfere with its enterohepatic cycle. Drugs such as barbiturates that increase hepatic microsomal enzyme activity accelerate the metabolism of digitoxin.

While digitalis toxicity is the result of many factors other than the plasma concentration of the drug, there is a significant correlation between the clinical state and serum or plasma concentration as determined in a great many different centers (36). Whereas mean plasma digoxin or digitoxin concentrations tend to be two to three times higher in patients with toxic dysrhythmias than in patients without signs of toxicity who are receiving conventional doses, the overlap between toxic and nontoxic groups tends to be large. In the individual patient there is no clearly defined therapeutic or toxic dose, toxicity depending on many clinical factors listed previously. For these reasons, plasma concentrations, as measured by radioimmunoassay, should not be used as the only guide to digitalis dosage. Taken in context with other clinical information, they can be of great value in making a therapeutic decision. Indications for ordering a digitalis plasma concentration determination include a questionable history of digitalis ingestion, suspected

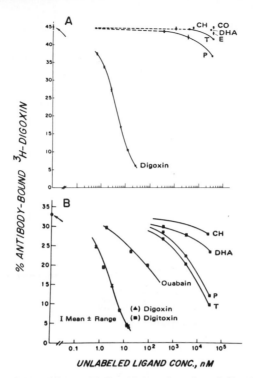

FIGURE 2 Comparison of two antisera. (A) Specificity of a selected digoxin-specific antiserum. Only digoxin competes effectively with [^{3}H]digoxin for antibody binding sites. Cholesterol (CH), cortisol (CO), dehydroepiandrosterone (DHA), 17β-estradiol (E), progesterone (P), and testosterone (T) cause measurable displacement only when present at concentrations more than 1000 times greater than those of digoxin. The arrow on the vertical axis denotes binding in the absence of competing ligand. Horizontal lines indicate ranges of duplicate determinations. Modified from Smith et al. (31). (B) Specificity of another antiserum; progesterone and testosterone interfere at physiological concentrations. Relatively poor specificity is evident, giving the potential for substantial error in the radioimmunoassay. Modified from Smith and Kaplan (36).

manifestations of toxicity, fluctuating renal function, malabsorption, or an unanticipated response, such as the absence of an expected therapeutic effect.

TREATMENT OF DIGITALIS INTOXICATION

Recognition of impending intoxication and withholding of the drug is, of course, the most effective means of dealing with adverse effects. The increased popularity of digoxin as opposed to digitoxin or digitalis leaf is related largely to its far shorter half-life (36 hr versus 4–6 d), which means that toxic manifestations abate much more rapidly on stopping the drug with digoxin than with the other compounds. Rhythm disturbances that impair cardiac output or portend ventricular fibrillation require active intervention. Two-thirds of patients who have ventricular tachycardia consequent to digitalis intoxication do not survive (15).

A number of therapeutic interventions are available. Sinus bradycardia or atrioventricular block resulting in a slow ventricular response may be treated with atropine or electric pacing. Ectopic arrhythmias may be effectively treated with lidocaine or diphenylhydantoin. These drugs do not adversely effect conduction in the atrioventricular node or in the His-Purkinje system. If hypokalemia is present, intravenous administration of potassium is often effective. Propranolol has been used in the treatment of certain toxic arrhythmias, but there is considerable risk of simultaneous depression of pacemakers or atrioventricular conduction, which can result in asystole when the active dysrhythmia is suppressed. Countershock should be used only when all other methods have failed because of the severe arrhythmias that may ensue.

As indicated above, digitoxin undergoes enterohepatic circulation. Orally administered digitoxin-binding resins such as cholestyramine (10) and colestipol (5) may interrupt the enterohepatic circulation and reduce the duration of digitoxin toxicity. The practical efficacy of this maneuver is as yet uncertain.

CARDIAC GLYCOSIDE–SPECIFIC ANTIBODIES IN THE TREATMENT OF DIGITALIS INTOXICATION

Specific antibodies have long been known to inactivate enzymes *in vitro* (1-3) and to neutralize the effects of hormones (23) and toxins *in vivo*. It therefore seemed logical that antibodies might also prove effective in the reversal of drug effects. As indicated earlier, digitalis toxicity is common (34). The diagnosis of toxic dysrhythmias is difficult, and available therapeutic approaches are nonspecific and at times ineffective. A specific antibody that neutralized the effect of the drug would be useful not only in specifically treating life-threatening toxic manifestations, but also in the diagnosis of digitalis intoxication under equivocal circumstances.

Schmidt and Butler (25) demonstrated that rabbits that had been actively immunized with digoxin-protein conjugates and whose sera contained antidigoxin antibodies were protected from the toxic effects of a lethal dose of digoxin. Subsequently, the same authors (26) showed that the administration of digoxin-specific rabbit antiserum would also protect nonimmunized dogs from digoxin intoxication.

The administration of large quantities of crude antiserum could not be readily envisioned as an appropriate intervention in clinical medicine. Consequently, digoxin-specific antibody was purified from antiserum to remove all extraneous protein and thus decrease the risk of sensitization. Affinity chromatography was utilized in which the cross-reacting ligand ouabain was coupled to bovine pancreatic ribonuclease and thence to the solid support bromoacetylcellulose (14). A particularly immunogenic part of the antibody molecule, the F_c fragment, was removed by papain digestion. The remaining univalent F_{ab} fragment had all the binding energy of the original antibody molecule, but could bind only one, rather than two, digoxin molecules. The molecular weight was reduced, however, from 150,000 for the intact molecule to 50,000 for the F_{ab}. Smaller size should permit more rapid diffusion into the interstitial space and also result in more rapid excretion via glomerular filtration with a half-life of about 4–5 hr (37, 38). Immunogenicity studies indicated that the purified F_{ab} fragments of ovine digoxin-specific antibodies were very weakly immunogenic compared with intact gamma globulin in both rabbits and baboons.

When administered to digoxin-treated dogs, antidigoxin F_{ab} fragments produced a marked increase in the total serum concentration of the drug (9). Most of the circulating drug was antibody-bound and thus pharmacologically inactive. Because it is filtered by the glomerulus, F_{ab}-bound digoxin was promptly excreted. In contrast, the administration of intact antibody markedly decreased urinary excretion of digoxin and the biologic half-life of the drug was significantly prolonged (9).

The initial clinical use of purified digoxin-specific F_{ab} fragments to reverse advanced digoxin intoxication in humans has now been reported (35). A 39-yr-old man had ingested approximately ninety 0.25-mg digoxin tablets. On admission, the patient complained of nausea and vomited frequently. The pulse was 40–60 per minute and irregular.

Initial laboratory data included a serum creatinine concentration of 1.3 mg/dl; sodium, 141 meq/liter; potassium, 4.6 meq/liter; chloride, 101 meq/liter; and bicarbonate, 29 meq/liter. An electrocardiogram showed atrial fibrillation with a relatively high degree of atrioventricular block and periods of a regular junctional mechanism at 50 beats per minute as well as occasional runs of atrial tachycardia with high-grade atrioventricular block. The ventricular rate did not respond to a total of 3.0 mg of atropine given intravenously, and a temporary pervenous pacing catheter electrode was placed in the right ventricular apex and pacing was instituted at a rate of 60 beats per minute.

Despite vigorous supportive measures, the spontaneous ventricular rate progressively slowed (Fig. 3) concomitantly with rising serum potassium concentrations (Fig. 4) that were not controlled by frequent intravenous administration of glucose and insulin or of sodium bicarbonate, or by polystyrene sulfonate resin (Kayexalate) given by a retention enema. Twelve hours after ingestion of the digoxin the serum potassium concentration had risen to 8.7 meq/liter (Fig. 4), and the pacing threshold had increased from less than 1 to 2 mA. The interval from last paced beat to an escape beat when pacing was briefly interrupted had risen from 1.8 to 4.6 sec, corresponding to a spontaneous heart rate of 14 beats per minute (Fig. 3). There was marked widening of the QRS complex.

In view of the grave prognosis of advanced digoxin ingestion accompanied by heart block, extreme bradycardia, and intractable hyperkalemia, treatment with F_{ab} fragments of digoxin-specific antibodies was begun. It was estimated that the patient had absorbed approximately 80%, or 18 mg, of the 22.5 mg that he had ingested. Accordingly, an equimolar amount of specific F_{ab} fragments (1100 mg) was administered intravenously in 600 ml of physiological saline over the 2-hr period. There was no evident allergic or toxic manifestations.

One hour after the start of the F_{ab} fragment infusion the escape interval had fallen to 2 sec, and at 90 min atrial fibrillation with a ventricular response of 40–50 beats per minute was observed. Ten minutes after the end of F_{ab} administration and 2 hr after its inception, sinus rhythm at a rate of 75 beats per minute was observed

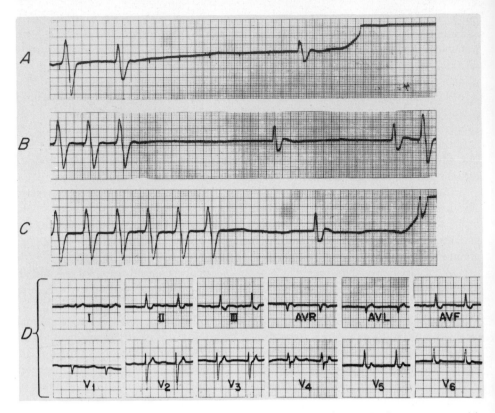

FIGURE 3 Sequential electrocardiograms recorded before, during, and after treatment with digoxin-specific F_{ab} fragments in a patient with severe digoxin toxicity. (A) Tracing recorded immediately before the start of F_{ab} infusion; serum potassium is 8.7 meq/liter; the escape interval when pacer stimulus is reduced below threshold is 4.60 sec. (B) Tracing recorded 15 min after the start of F_{ab} infusion; serum potassium is 8.0 meq/liter; the escape interval is 3.96 sec. (C) Tracing recorded 30 min after the start of F_{ab} infusion; the escape interval is 2.76 sec. (D) Tracing recorded 2 hr after the start of F_{ab} infusion; serum potassium is 7.4 meq/liter; a sinus mechanism is present at a rate of 75 beats per minute, with first degree atrioventricular block (PR interval, 0.24 sec). From Smith et al. (35). Reprinted, by permission, from the New England Journal of Medicine (294:797, 1976).

(Fig. 3). The PR interval was 0.24 sec, and there were ST segment and T wave abnormalities consistent with a marked digitalis effect. The serum potassium concentration had fallen to 7.4 meq/liter and continued to fall steadily, reaching a nadir of 3.4 meq/liter 7 hr after the onset of F_{ab} administration (Fig. 4). Over the subsequent 6 hr, 120 meq of potassium chloride was given by mouth to maintain the serum potassium at about 4 meq/liter.

Serial urinalyses did not demonstrate proteinuria or other evidence of glomerulitis, and creatinine clearance remained stable at 80–100 ml/min.

Figure 4 shows the time course of the total serum digoxin concentration, free serum digoxin concentration, and total serum concentration of sheep F_{ab} fragments. The free digoxin concentration in serum fell precipitously to undetectable levels (less than 1 ng/ml) by the time the first posttreatment serum sample was obtained at 1 hr, and remained below 1 ng/ml through 9 hr.

A sharp rise occurred in the total serum digoxin concentration, from 17.6 ng/ml immediately before infusion to 223 ng/ml 1 hr after the F_{ab} infusion was started. Despite a continuing rise in sheep F_{ab} fragment concentration from 60 μg/ml at 1 hr to 98 μg/ml at 2 hr, total serum digoxin leveled off at 223 and 226 ng/ml, respectively, and remained at about that level until 12 hr after infusion, when an exponential decline with a half-life of 20 hr began and extended through 56 hr.

The peak concentration of sheep F_{ab} fragments in the patient's serum occurred at the completion of the infusion and declined rapidly at first, reflecting distribution through the extracellular space, then more slowly, presumably reflecting both excretion and catabolism. No detectable sheep F_{ab} fragment concentrations were present in serum samples obtained 9 and 21 d after treatment. Antibodies to sheep F_{ab} fragments could not be detected by a sensitive hemagglutination method in samples of the patient's serum obtained 1, 3, and 4 wk after treatment.

Substantial renal digoxin excretion was documented, with urinary total digoxin concentrations as high as 960 ng/ml during the initial 24 hr of observation. Three urine samples collected between the beginning of F_{ab} infusion and 6 hr later

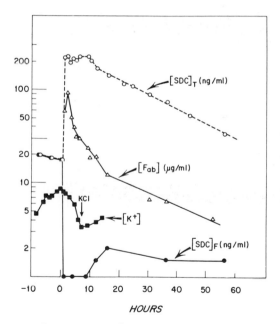

FIGURE 4 Time course of serum potassium concentration [K^+] (meq/liter); total serum digoxin concentration [SDC]$_T$; free serum digoxin concentration [SDC]$_F$; and serum concentration of sheep digoxin-specific F_{ab} fragments, [F_{ab}], in a patient with severe digoxin toxicity. The scale on the vertical axis is logarithmic. On the horizontal axis, administration of digoxin-specific F_{ab} fragments was started at time 0. From Smith et al. (35). Reprinted, by permission, from the New England Journal of Medicine (294:797, 1976).

contained undetectable (less than 1%) amounts to digoxin in the free state, despite total digoxin concentrations ranging from 155 to 660 ng/ml, indicating that digoxin was excreted by the kidney bound to specific F_{ab} fragments during this period. Subsequently, the fraction of total urinary digoxin present in the free state increased gradually to 100% by 30 hr after F_{ab} infusion. These data are consistent with the time course of F_{ab} excretion in urine as measured by radioimmunoassay. Initial urinary F_{ab} concentrations after administration were as high as 42.5 μg/ml, falling to less than 2 μg/ml in a urine sample collected 30–52 hr after F_{ab} infusion.

The rapid fall in free digoxin concentration in serum to near-zero levels after F_{ab} administration was expected from previous observations *in vitro*. Since the interaction of cardiac glycosides with their cellular receptors is a reversible process, this reduction in free digoxin concentration results in progressive removal of the drug from receptor sites as the drug-receptor equilibrium is displaced in the direction of dissociation. The striking rise in total digoxin concentration in serum, previously observed in animal experimental studies (9), occurred as a result of displacement of digoxin from tissue compartments to plasma and other extracellular compartments within which the F_{ab} fragments are distributed. The 50,000-dalton mass of F_{ab} fragments permits glomerular filtration and relatively rapid renal excretion of both F_{ab} fragments (37, 40) and bound digoxin, in contrast to the very slow excretion of digoxin bound to intact gamma globulin before the immune degradation phase.

On the basis of initial clinical experience, one can be optimistic about the potential of purified F_{ab} fragments of digoxin-specific antibodies in the management of advanced, life-threatening toxicity unresponsive to conventional therapeutic measures. This may be but one example of a number of therapeutic opportunities in which the specific inactivation by antibody of an exogenous drug or an endogenous hormone may be undertaken, particularly if nonimmunogenic antibody preparations of desired specificity can be obtained.

REFERENCES

1. Arnon, R. Immunochemical studies on bovine trypsin and trypsinogen derivatives. Immunochemistry 7:241–250, 1970.
2. Arnon, R. and Maron, E. An immunological approach to the structural relationship between hen egg-white lysozyme and bovine α-lactalbumin. J Mol Biol 61:225–235, 1971.
3. Arnon, R. and Shapira, E. Comparison between the antigenic structure of mutually related enzymes. A study with papain and chymopapain. Biochemistry 7:4196–4202, 1968.
4. Barr, I., Smith, T. W., Klein, M. D., Hagemeijer, F., and Lown, B. Correlation of the electrophysiologic action of digoxin with serum digoxin concentration. J Pharmacol Exp Ther 180:710–722, 1972.
5. Bazzano, G. and Bazzano, G. S. Digitalis intoxication: Treatment with a new steroid-binding resin. J Am Med Assoc 220:828–830, 1972.
6. Borison, H. L. and Wang, S. C. Physiology and pharmacology of vomiting. Pharmacol Rev 5:193–230, 1953.
7. Braunwald, E., Bloodwell, R. D., Goldberg, L. I., and Morrow, A. G. Studies on digitalis. IV. Observations in man on the effects of digitalis preparations in

the contractility of the non-failing heart and on total vascular resistance. J Clin Invest 40:52–59, 1961.

8. Brooker, G. and Jelliffe, R. W. Serum cardiac glycoside assay based upon displacement of ^{3}H-ouabain from Na-K-ATPase. Circulation 45:20–36, 1972.

9. Butler, V. P., Jr., Schmidt, D. H., Smith, T. W., Haber, E., Raynor, B. D., and DeMartini, P. Effects of sheep digoxin-specific antibodies and their Fab fragments on digoxin pharmacokinetics in dogs. J Clin Invest 59:345–359, 1977.

10. Caldwell, J. H., Bush, C. A., and Greenberger, N. J. Interruption of the enterohepatic circulation of digitoxin by cholestyramine. II. Effect on metabolic disposition of tritium-labeled digitoxin and cardiac systolic intervals in man. J Clin Invest 50:2638–2644, 1971.

11. Cattell, M. and Gold, H. The influence of digitalis glycosides on the force of contraction of mammalian cardiac muscle. J Pharmacol Exp Ther 62:116–135, 1938.

12. Christian, H. A. Digitalis therapy: Satisfactory effects in cardiac cases with a regular pulse-rate. Am J Med Sci 157:593–602, 1919.

13. Chung, E. K. Principles of Cardiac Arrhythmias. Baltimore: Williams & Wilkins, 1971.

14. Curd, J., Smith, T. W., Jaton, J. C., and Haber, E. The isolation of digoxin-specific antibody and its use in reversing the effects of digoxin. Proc Natl Acad Sci USA 68:2401–2406, 1971.

15. Dreifus, L. S., McKnight, E. H., Katz, M., and Likoff, W. Digitalis intolerance. Geriatrics 18:494–502, 1963.

16. Dudel, J. and Trautwein, W. Elektrophysiologishe Messungen zur Strophanthinwirkung am Herzmuskel. Naunyn Schmicdebergs Arch Pharmakol 232:393–407, 1958.

17. Eddleman, E. E., Jr., Willis, K., Greve, M. J., and Heyer, H. E. The effect of digitoxin on the apparent stroke volume, posteroanterior cardiac diameter, and the cardiac cycle in normal subjects as studied by the electrokymograph. Am Heart J 41:161–181, 1951.

18. Gillis, R. A., Raines, A., Sohn, Y. J., Levitt, B., and Standaert, F. G. Neuroexcitatory effects of digitalis and their role in the development of cardiac arrhythmias. J Pharmacol Exp Ther 183:154–168, 1972.

19. Harrison, T. R., Calhoun, J. A., and Turley, F. C. Congestive heart failure. II. The effect of digitalis on the dyspnea and on the ventilation of ambulatory patients with regular cardiac rhythm. Arch Intern Med 48:1203–1216, 1931.

20. Hoffman, B. F. and Singer, D. H. Effects of digitalis on electrical activity of cardiac fibers. Progr Cardiovasc Dis 7:226–260, 1964.

21. Hurwitz, N. and Wade, O. L. Intensive hospital monitoring of adverse reactions to drugs. Br Med J 1:531–536, 1969.

22. Moe, G. K. and Farah, A. E. Digitalis and allied cardiac glycosides. In: The Pharmacological Basis of Therapeutics, L. S. Goodman and A. Gilman, eds. New York: Macmillan, 1970, pp. 677–708.

23. Romero, J. C., Hoobler, S. W., and Kozak, T. J. Effect of anti-renin on blood pressure of rabbits with experimental renin hypertension. Am J Physiol 225:810–817, 1973.

24. Sanyal, P. H. and Saunders, P. R. Action of ouabain upon normal and hypodynamic myocardium. Proc Soc Exp Biol Med 95:156–157, 1957.

25. Schmidt, D. H. and Butler, V. P., Jr. Immunological protection against digoxin toxicity. J Clin Invest 50:866–871, 1971.

26. Schmidt, D. H. and Butler, V. P., Jr. Reversal of digoxin toxicity with specific antibodies. J Clin Invest 50:1738–1744, 1971.
27. Selden, R., Klein, M. D., and Smith, T. W. Plasma concentration and urinary excretion kinetics of acetyl strophanthidin. Circulation 47:744–751, 1973.
28. Selden, R. and Smith, T. W. Ouabain pharmacokinetics in dog and man: Determination by radioimmunoassay. Circulation 45:1176–1182, 1972.
29. Smith, T. W. Ouabain-specific antibodies: Immunochemical properties and reversal of Na$^+$,K$^+$-activated adenosine triphosphatase inhibition. J Clin Invest 51:1583–1593, 1972.
30. Smith, T. W. Radioimmunoassay for serum digoxin concentration: Methodology and clinical experience. J Pharmacol Exp Ther 175:352–360, 1970.
31. Smith, T. W., Butler, V. P., Jr., and Haber, E. Characterization of antibodies of high affinity and specificity for the digitalis glycoside digoxin. Biochemistry 9:331–337, 1970.
32. Smith, T. W., Butler, V. P., Jr., and Haber, E. Determination of therapeutic and toxic serum digoxin concentrations by radioimmunoassay. N Engl J Med 281:1212–1216, 1969.
33. Smith, T. W. and Haber, E. Digitalis. Boston: Little, Brown, 1974.
34. Smith, T. W. and Haber, E. Medical progress. Digitalis. N Engl J Med 289:945–952, 1010–1015, 1063–1072, 1125–1129, 1973.
35. Smith, T. W., Haber, E., Yeatman, L., and Butler, V. P., Jr. Reversal of advanced digoxin intoxication with Fab fragments of digoxin-specific antibodies. N Engl J Med 294:797–800, 1976.
36. Smith, T. W. and Kaplan, E. Radioimmunoassay of cardiac glycosides. In Cardiovascular Nuclear Medicine, H. W. Strauss, B. Pitt, and A. E. James, eds. St. Louis: Mosby, 1974.
37. Spiegelberg, H. L. and Weigle, W. O. The catabolism of homologous and heterologous 7S gamma globulin fragments. J Exp Med 121:323–338, 1965.
38. Waldmann, T. A. and Strober, W. Metabolism of immunoglobulins. Progr Allergy 13:1, 1969.
39. Wiggers, C. J. and Stimson, B. Studies on cardiodynamic action of drugs. III. The mechanism of cardiac stimulation by digitalis and G-strophanthin. J Pharmacol Exp Ther 30:251–269, 1927.
40. Wochner, R. D., Strober, W., and Waldmann, T. A. The role of kidney in the catabolism of Bence Jones proteins and immunoglobulin fragments. J Exp Med 126:207–221, 1967.

CHAPTER 22

UNLOADING THE FAILING HEART

JAY N. COHN

The concept that drugs that reduce the resistance to left ventricular ejection may improve the circulation in low-flow states is not a new one. Cournand, Richards, and their associates, early in their experience with cardiac catheterization, observed that injection of quinidine raised cardiac output in patients with heart failure (9). They attributed this response to the vasodilator effect of the drug. Nickerson and his colleagues demonstrated that peripheral dilation induced by blockade of the sympathetic nervous system improved blood flow and survival in experimental shock (10). Although the response to drugs such as Dibenzyline was dramatic in some of their experiments, they attributed it to the peripheral action of the blockade and failed to focus on the cardiac response to the reduced resistance. The latter could have been the major factor in the improved circulatory function in these experiments.

FRANK-STARLING MECHANISM

Studies in the 1960s demonstrated an increase in cardiac output when patients with heart failure were treated with antihypertensive drugs (5). The beneficial response to these agents was attributed to the prevalent notion that the failing heart was operating on a descending limb of its Frank-Starling curve so that a reduction in filling pressure would increase cardiac output. This explanation seemed appropriate because the Starling curve then served as the major descriptive tool for evaluating cardiac pump function. Subsequently, however, it became increasingly apparent that a descending limb of the Starling curve probably did not exist except in the preterminal phase of severe heart failure. Although these observations should have stimulated immediate interest in redefining the factors that control shifts in the Starling curve, efforts were delayed.

During the 1960s invasive monitoring of acutely ill cardiac patients became widespread. Our group became interested in the hemodynamics of shock and pump failure. We defined cardiogenic shock as a state of low cardiac output associated with an inappropriately elevated ventricular filling pressure. Our major goal was to improve left ventricular function. With the Frank-Starling curve as our guide to ventricular performance, we found ourselves attempting to alter cardiac output either by changing ventricular volume or by administering inotropic drugs (6).

Indeed, an increase in cardiac output with an unchanged or reduced end-diastolic ventricular pressure was comfortably defined as an increase in contractility that could be achieved only by administration of an inotropic agent. Thus, a wide number of inotropic drugs were employed. Some proved to be more reliable than others in generating improved left ventricular function. The physiological basis for attempts to alter resistance to outflow was available, but no one put the concept to work in the clinical or experimental situation.

OUTFLOW RESISTANCE MECHANISM

The problem was being attacked from another direction. Studies on isolated heart muscle demonstrated the importance of loading on myocardial contraction. Force-velocity relations made it clear that the lower the load placed on the heart muscle at the onset of shortening the greater the velocity and extent of shortening. However, the importance of "afterload" on the intact heart was discounted, largely because numerous studies suggested that the left ventricle could adjust to sizable alterations in outflow resistance and maintain a normal stroke volume and end-diastolic pressure (Anrep effect, "homeometric autoregulation") (11). Clinical studies did suggest, however, that the response to an increase in outflow resistance might distinguish a normal from an abnormal left ventricle. When resistance was increased with vasoconstrictor drugs such as angiotensin, or with other constrictor stimuli such as isometric hand grip, patients with significant heart disease responded to these interventions with a lowering of stroke volume or with a lesser rise in stroke work than did patients with normal hearts. These observations made the conclusion inescapable that, in terms of pump function, the outflow resistance was an important determinant of ventricular performance.

In translating isolated muscle studies to the intact ventricle, an attempt was made to utilize the same terminology. Thus, afterload (which is simply a weight in the isolated muscle bath) became defined in the intact heart as the myocardial wall tension or stress during ejection. The problem with this concept in the intact circulation is twofold: 1) the heart in part generates its own "load" by the amount of blood it ejects with each stroke, and 2) the load is continuously changing during ejection. Although afterload therefore became a very complex variable, it was often viewed as synonymous with arterial pressure. The error of this oversimplification is obvious. Ventricular volume is an important determinant of wall tension, and the amount that the muscle shortens during systole (stroke volume) influences afterload during ejection. Therefore, a dilated heart with a small stroke volume has a much higher afterload than a small heart with a large stroke volume, even though aortic pressure may be identical. The implication of these concepts is that in order to separate out the role of the peripheral circulation on the performance of the left ventricle as a pump, the term afterload should be discarded and replaced by a measurement that describes the load imposed on the heart by the periphery. Outflow resistance and impedance are appropriate terms.

An additional problem that has inhibited full understanding of the response of the heart to vasoconstrictor and vasodilator drugs has been the concept of cardiac work or stroke work. It has been traditional to calculate the external work of the heart as the product of stroke volume or cardiac output and mean ejection pressure. Since work implies energy utilization, it became all too easy for investigators and clinicians to assume that the greater the work the heart performed the more oxygen it consumed. This easy assumption that work and oxygen consumption were synonymous was challenged when it became generally accepted that volume work was somewhat less costly in terms of energy than pressure work. A full understanding of the significance of oxygen consumption and its relation to stroke volume awaited a more precise description of the determinants of myocardial oxygen consumption. Studies performed in the 1960s made it apparent that the pressure in the left ventricle, its radius during ejection, and the velocity with which its fiber shortened were far more important as determinants of oxygen consumption than was the amount of stroke volume it ejected (12). Indeed, the energy cost of fiber shortening itself (Fenn effect) is very low. Until this concept became generally accepted, it was widely felt that any intervention that increased stroke volume or cardiac output would consume energy.

CLINICAL HEART FAILURE

Our initial attempts to define the response to reduction in outflow resistance in heart failure were in patients with hypertensive heart disease. Heart failure in these patients was well known to respond clinically to acute reduction in blood pressure by antihypertensive agents. Therefore we were not surprised that infusion of sodium nitroprusside in patients with severe hypertension and heart failure caused a sharp rise in stroke volume and cardiac output. However, the agent failed to increase cardiac output in hypertensive patients whose blood pressures were as high but who were not in heart failure, even though the drop in blood pressure was comparable. This differential response to the vasodilator drug seemed to fit very well with the observations of others that vasoconstrictor drugs reduced cardiac output in patients with heart failure but not in those with normal ventricular function. We were therefore attracted to the practical implications of the idea that outflow resistance was much more of a determinant of left ventricular performance in the abnormal heart than in the normal heart (2).

We tested this hypothesis in the clinical setting of heart failure in the absence of hypertension. We selected for our first experiment a patient with acute myocardial infarction who was in pulmonary edema with a left ventricular end-diastolic pressure of 40 mmHg. His arterial pressure was 140/90 and his cardiac index was 2.0 liter/min. We began an infusion of sodium nitroprusside very cautiously. As the drip rate was increased the left ventricular end-diastolic pressure fell precipitously; the decrease was greater than the modest fall in arterial pressure. The patient's breathing improved almost immediately; the cardiac output was then found to have increased by approximately 50%. It was clear that the high systemic vascular resistance, even though the blood pressure was normal, contributed importantly to the control of the level of the cardiac output. By reducing systemic vascular resistance, we improved left ventricular function and effected a marked reduction in left ventricular filling pressure and an increase in stroke volume and cardiac output. The failure of heart rate to increase even though blood pressure fell during the infusion of sodium nitroprusside was reassurance that the intervention was probably not having a deleterious effect on the oxygen consumption of the heart. Instead, it suggested that the increase in stroke volume was being accomplished while myocardial wall tension and oxygen consumption probably decreased. These studies indicated that a shift of the Frank-Starling curve upward and to the left is not necessarily synonymous with an increase in contractility; the shift may also be achieved by a reduction in outflow resistance.

Since inotropic agents had been the traditional drugs used for shifting the Frank-Starling curve, we compared the effectiveness of vasodilator and inotropic drugs. In a group of 12 patients with severe congestive heart failure, we compared the effects of intravenous infusion of sodium nitroprusside and dobutamine; the latter is a potent and relatively selective inotropic sympathomimetic agent. The rate of infusion of nitroprusside was adjusted to achieve an optimum hemodynamic effect; the dobutamine was infused at a rate of 10 μg/kg $\cdot$ min, a dose that usually produces an optimal effect (1). As shown in Figs. 1 and 2, the response of the cardiac output was quite similar to the two interventions; systemic vascular resistance and pulmonary vascular resistance were similarly reduced. As expected, arterial pressure fell slightly during infusion of nitroprusside and rose slightly during dobutamine infusion. Changes in heart rate were slight with both agents; pulmonary wedge pressure fell with both, but to a greater extent during nitroprusside infusion. Although myocardial oxygen consumption was not measured in these studies, the major determinants of oxygen consumption increased during dobutamine infusion and fell during nitroprusside infusion. Furthermore, similar studies in experimental infarcts in dogs have confirmed that dobutamine increases myocardial oxygen consumption whereas nitroprusside reduces it (7). Consequently, inotropic and vasodilator interventions seem to cause similar augmentation of left ventricular

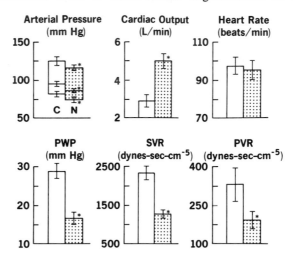

FIGURE 1   Response to nitroprusside infusion in 12 patients with severe heart failure. Arterial pressure falls slightly, but cardiac output is markedly augmented without a change in heart rate while pulmonary wedge pressure (PWP) and systemic (SVR) and pulmonary vascular resistance (PVR) fall. $^*p < 0.05$ compared with control. From Mikulic et al. (9a).

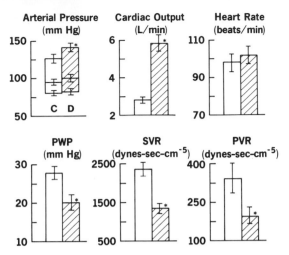

FIGURE 2 Response to dobutamine infusion in the same patients as in Fig. 1. Arterial pressure rises slightly along with a marked increase in cardiac output while PWP, SVR, and PVR all fall. $^{*}p < 0.05$ compared with control. From Mikulic et al. (9a).

performance. Inotropic drugs accomplish this effect by directly stimulating the heart to increase its force of contraction; as a result, reflexly constricted peripheral vessels relax. Vasodilator drugs primarily relax the resistance vessels, thus allowing the heart to empty better without augmenting its energy requirement.

If reduction of an elevated systemic vascular resistance can so improve left ventricular function when the heart is failing, why is the resistance elevated? Teleologically, one probably must go back to the basic design of the cardiovascular system, which appears to have been engineered to protect against trauma or volume loss. When cardiac output falls, a number of feedback mechanisms are activated to restore arterial pressure to previous levels. Some of these systems may respond acutely and others more chronically. They include the sympathetic nervous system, the renin-angiotensin system, other hormonal systems, renal retention of salt and water, and so on. An underresponsive system could result in uncontrolled hypotension, cerebral ischemia, and death, whereas an overresponsive system (if the heart were normal and could adjust to a wide range of resistances) would ensure protection of vital organs. Thus, a fail-safe overresponsive negative feedback system would be appropriate, except when the fall in cardiac output results from left ventricular disease. In this instance, the negative feedback becomes a positive feedback since every increment in outflow resistance may further decrease the performance of the pump. Pharmacological interruption of this vicious cycle may thus restore the circulation to a new, more satisfactory steady state.

SITES OF ACTION OF VASODILATOR DRUGS

The use of vasodilator agents in treating heart failure has broad therapeutic implications. Drugs that were previously utilized only for reducing systemic blood pressure in patients with hypertension are now being used to reduce systemic resistance, even though systemic hypertension is not present. However, much remains to be learned about how and where these agents exert their effects. For example, as indicated in Table 1, some of these agents may act on the systemic and pulmonary arterial circulation as well as the systemic venous bed. Differences in regional vascular effects of individual drugs will influence the regional distribution of cardiac output. One drug differs from another in the degree of reflex sympathetic discharge that accompanies the vasodilator effect, thereby shaping the overall hemodynamic response.

The most dramatic effects of vasodilator agents probably result from the reduction of systemic vascular impedance. This reduction accounts for the increase in left ventricular stroke volume, and is most pronounced in patients with mitral insufficiency. The pulmonary vascular effects of most of the drugs are not as prominent as the systemic vascular effects, although attempts to use vasodilator drugs in the management of cor pulmonale are now in progress.

The relative arterial and venous effects of different vasodilators may vary considerably. Since the arterial bed is the major factor in left ventricular outflow resistance, whereas the venous bed is the major determinant of peripheral blood volume, an arterial dilator would be expected predominantly to increase cardiac output in heart failure, whereas a venodilator would be expected to reduce ventricular filling pressure.

TABLE 1 Physiological effects of vasodilator drugs in heart failure

---

Reduced aortic and systemic vascular impedance
    Increased left ventricular ejection fraction
    Increased effective stroke volume
      Mitral regurgitation
      Septal defect
      Aortic insufficiency
    Reduced left ventricular wall tension
    Increased subendocardial blood flow (?)
    Reduced pulmonary capillary pressure

Reduced pulmonary vascular impedance
    Increased right ventricular ejection fraction (?)
    Increased effective stroke volume
      Tricuspid regurgitation
      Septal defect
    Arterial hypoxemia
    Increased "central blood volume"

Increased systemic venous compliance
    Reduced ventricular end-diastolic volume
    Reduced pulmonary capillary pressure

Reduced regional vascular resistance
    Direct effect versus reflex effect
    Varying redistribution of blood flow

Reflex sympathoadrenal discharge
    Increased heart rate
    Vasoconstriction

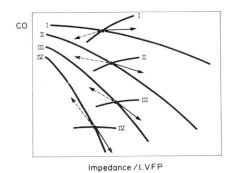

Impedance / LVFP

FIGURE 3 Preload and impedance in control of cardiac performance. Frank-Starling preload curves, numbered at the right, showing progressively more severe impairment of left ventricular function (I–IV) are superimposed on impedance curves, numbered at the left, also showing progressive impairment of function (I–IV). Most interventions alter both preload and impedance, so the effect on cardiac output (CO) is represented by the resultant of the two curves. From Cohn and Franciosa (4). Reprinted, by permission, from the New England Journal of Medicine (297:28, 1977).

In a particular patient, a decrease in ventricular filling pressure would be expected to reduce cardiac output in accordance with the Frank-Starling relationship. Also, a reduction in outflow resistance might increase output, the magnitude of the increase being related to the slope of the patient's outflow resistance curve. Analysis of the response in an individual patient can be carried out by superimposing these two families of curves, as shown in Fig. 3. Segments of the Frank-Starling curves from the most normal (I) to the most abnormal (IV) ventricular function are superimposed on outflow resistance curves, also arranged from the most normal (I) to the most abnormal (IV). A pure Starling effect would cause cardiac output to change along the Frank-Starling curve as filling pressure falls, so that a large fall might occur in a more normal heart (I) but only a slight fall in a more abnormal heart (IV). A pure outflow resistance effect would cause output to change along that line as resistance falls, a small increase of output in the more normal situation (I) and a large increase in severe heart disease (IV). The dashed lines with arrows in Fig. 3 indicate the response that would be anticipated to a drug that dilates both arterial and venous vessels. Output changes would be the result of these two independent influences.

Table 2 lists the vasodilator drugs that are available for clinical use. Some are for intravenous use only and are reserved for the patient in acute heart failure in the intensive care unit. Oral agents have attracted attention because of their potential use for the continued treatment of chronic congestive heart failure.

Hydralazine appears to be a pure arteriolar dilator (8). Pulmonary wedge pressure does not fall as much as it does with sodium nitroprusside, whereas the increase in cardiac output is slightly greater than that observed during infusion of sodium nitroprusside. The nitrates also exert some arterial dilating effect. However, because their effect on the venous capacitance vessels appears to predominate, they produce a more marked reduction in ventricular filling pressure than in outflow resistance. Accordingly, the increase in cardiac output is less marked than that elicited by nitroprusside or hydralazine. Prazosin, a vasodilator that seems to act, at least in part, by alpha adrenergic blockade, appears to exert a relatively balanced effect on the arterial and venous systems. A similar effect can be achieved by combining nitrates with hydrazaline (Fig. 4). The hemodynamic response to prazosin is characterized by both a reduction in ventricular filling pressure and a rise in cardiac output.

A mystery that remains unsolved is the lack of tachycardia in response to vasodilation. Even with prominent reductions in blood pressure during intravenous or oral administration of these drugs, patients with heart failure rarely demonstrate much of an increase in heart rate. The simplest explanation for this paradoxical response is that some portion of the sympathetic reflex arc is depressed. Either the afferent limb is not stimulated because the rising stroke volume counterbalances the fall in mean arterial pressure at the carotid baroreceptor, or perhaps norepinephrine is depleted from nerve endings of the heart.

THE PLACE OF VASODILATOR THERAPY

Whether the hemodynamic response to these agents will persist during chronic administration of the drugs is as yet conjectural. Long-term regulation of ventricular

TABLE 2 Vasodilator agents that
may be useful in heart failure

Intravenous use

Clinically available
1. Sodium nitroprusside
2. Diazoxide
3. Hydralazine
4. Phentolamine
5. Trimethaphan
6. Isoproterenol

Investigational
1. Prostaglandin A_1
2. Converting enzyme inhibitor

Oral use

Clinically available
1. Nitrates
2. Hydralazine
3. Prazosin
4. Dibenzyline

Investigational
1. Minoxidil
2. Guancydine
3. Trimazosin
4. Labetalol
5. Prostaglandins
6. Converting enzyme inhibitor
7. Salbutamol

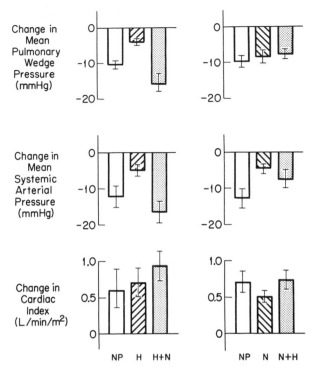

FIGURE 4 Hemodynamic effects of hydralazine (H), isosorbide dinitrate (N), and their combination (H + N and N + H) compared with the effect of nitroprusside (NP) in patients with heart failure. The combination mimics the effect of nitroprusside, whereas hydralazine and nitrate alone do not.

filling pressure should depend on the status of intravascular volume. Therefore, diuresis would tend to reduce filling pressure and oliguria to raise it. The renal response to these drugs may be at least as important as their venous effects in determining the long-term status of cardiac filling.

Perhaps of even more importance in applying this form of therapy is the question of whether it merely relieves symptoms or alters the natural history of congestive heart failure. Consideration must be given to the possibility that a persistent increase in outflow resistance plays an important role in the progressive nature of congestive heart failure. Until now, vasodilator agents have been used almost exclusively in subjects who have remained symptomatic despite traditional therapy. Whether early intervention with vasodilator drugs might arrest the progress of the disease and prevent the cardiac dilation that characterizes intractable heart failure is a subject that needs further exploration.

REFERENCES

1. Akhtar, N., Mikulic, E., Cohn, J. N., and Chaudhry, M. H. Hemodynamic effect of dobutamine in patients with severe heart failure. Am J Cardiol 36:202–205, 1975.

2. Cohn, J. N. Blood pressure and cardiac performance. Am J Med 55:351–361, 1973.
3. Cohn, J. N. and Franciosa, J. A. Selection of vasodilator, inotropic or combined therapy for the management of heart failure. Am J Med, in press.
4. Cohn, J. N. and Franciosa, J. A. Vasodilator therapy of cardiac failure. N Engl J Med 297:27–31, 1977.
5. Cohn, J. N., Liptak, T. E., and Freis, E. D. Hemodynamic effects of guanethidine in man. Circ Res 12:298–307, 1963.
6. Cohn, J. N. and Luria, M. H. Studies in clinical shock and hypotension. The value of bedside hemodynamic observations. J Am Med Assoc 190:891–896, 1964.
7. Franciosa, J. A., Notargiacomo, A. V., and Cohn, J. N. Comparative haemodynamic effects of vasodilator and inotropic agents in experimental myocardial infarction. Cardiovasc Res, in press.
8. Franciosa, J. A., Pierpont, G., and Cohn, J. N. Hemodynamic improvement after oral hydralazine in left ventricular failure: A comparison with nitroprusside infusion in 16 patients. Ann Intern Med 86:388–393, 1977.
9. Harvey, R. M., Ferrer, M. I., Cathcard, R. T., Richards, D. W., and Cournand, A. Some effects of digoxin upon the heart and circulation in man. Digoxin in left ventricular failure. Am J Med 7:439–453, 1949.
9a. Mikulic, E., Cohn, J. N., and Franciosa, J. A. Comparative hemodynamic effects of inotropic and vasodilator drugs in severe heart failure. Circulation 56:528–533, 1977.
10. Nickerson, M. and Gouris, J. T. Blockade of sympathetic vasoconstriction in the treatment of shock. J Trauma 2:399–411, 1962.
11. Sarnoff, S. F. and Mitchell, J. H. The control of the function of the heart. In: Handbook of Physiology: Circulation. W. F. Hamilton, ed. Washington, D.C.: American Physiological Society, 1962, vol. 1, pp. 480–532.
12. Sonnenblick, E. H., Ross, J., Jr., and Braunwald, E. Oxygen consumption of the heart. Am J Cardiol 22:328–336, 1968.

CHAPTER 23

SURGICAL INTERVENTION IN PATIENTS WITH MYOCARDIAL FAILURE

MORTIMER J. BUCKLEY

The role of the cardiac surgeon in relieving symptoms arising from failure of the myocardium has gradually evolved over the last 20 yr. Valvular replacement in patients with rheumatic valvular disease has proved beneficial. Similarly, elimination of shunts caused by congenital heart disease has often accomplished dramatic relief of congestive heart failure.

However, improvements in myocardial function after surgical intervention for complications of coronary artery disease have been more difficult to quantify. Resection of ventricular aneurysms often relieves symptoms of heart failure (3) and prolongs life (5). It is less certain that coronary arterial bypass at the time of ventricular aneurysm adds to longevity (5). Replacement of the mitral valve as treatment for rupture of a papillary muscle, both acute and chronic, sometimes affords dramatic relief (1).

Even more equivocal is the extent to which coronary arterial surgery improves myocardial function in left ventricular failure. The initial reports concerning coronary arterial revascularization with saphenous vein bypass grafts for patients in congestive heart failure revealed high mortality soon after operation and a poor prognosis for long-term survival. Subsequently, it was shown that those patients with active angina in whom episodes of severe congestive failure were associated with an increase in angina experienced the greatest postoperative improvement and the lowest mortality (7). This association of angina and episodic heart failure also suggested that ischemia of the myocardium accompanied each bout of increased congestive heart failure; improvement after surgery was attributed to better perfusion of the myocardium and to prevention of the recurrent ischemia.

CARDIOGENIC SHOCK AFTER MYOCARDIAL INFARCTION

The most severe type of congestive heart failure encountered by the cardiac surgeon is that of patients who suffer cardiogenic shock secondary to myocardial infarction. Our unit at the Massachusetts General Hospital sought to determine the role of circulatory assistance and cardiac surgery in the management of this disorder (2, 4, 6, 8).

Balloon Assist

Only patients who had no previous episode of congestive heart failure were included in the initial study. Each patient had a proved acute myocardial infarction. Myocardial failure was defined as a low-output state, characterized by 1) a cardiac index less than 2 liter/min $\cdot$ m^2 and 2) decreased compliance of the ventricle, as evidenced by pulmonary capillary wedge pressure or left ventricular end-diastolic pressure greater than 18 mmHg. In addition, these patients were usually hypotensive, with a mean arterial pressure of less than 65 mmHg.

The patients were treated with intra-aortic balloon assist and continued on this therapy for a period of hours to days. In 75% of these patients the hemodynamic state was markedly improved; moreover, 16% of patients treated with balloon assist survived. This outcome was a marked improvement over the usual 99% mortality in this group of patients.

Coronary arteriography and ventriculography were performed in these patients. All showed significant coronary artery occlusive disease. Some had reconstitution of blood flow through collateral vessels in the area of recent infarction, whereas in others the areas within the distribution of the recent infarction were avascular. In all patients, contractility was markedly diminished and the anterior apical area of the left ventricle was immobile; in most patients, inferior wall motion was also lost. The majority retained motion of the high lateral wall and contraction of the base.

Balloon Dependence
and Revascularization

All patients who failed to improve markedly on balloon assist died of low cardiac output. These were considered to be "balloon-dependent." Characteristically, this group consisted of patients who could not maintain a cardiac index greater than 2 liter/min $\cdot$ m^2, a filling pressure in the left ventricle or left atrium less than 18 mmHg, and a mean arterial pressure greater than 60 mmHg off the balloon. Recurrence of angina off the balloon also indicated balloon dependence. All of these balloon-dependent patients who were treated with medical therapy and balloon assistance alone went on to die, whether they were balloon-assisted for a few days or for as long as 3 wk. Although some could be weaned from the balloon, death resulted later because of a low cardiac output state or its complications.

Because of this inevitable mortality, surgical intervention was attempted early in their postinfarction course. An important guide to therapy was the state of the collateral circulation. Initial experience indicated that patients with avascular infarctions did not benefit from surgery unless they had a mechanical lesion such as a ventricular septal defect, mitral regurgitation associated with a ruptured papillary muscle, or ventricular aneurysm to be corrected. Accordingly, any patient without one of these mechanical defects was considered inoperable in the subsequent group. On the other hand, patients in whom the area of recent infarction had undergone revascularization by collateral vessels were considered to be surgical candidates. At present, 67 of these patients have undergone surgery. The rate of surgical survival is

53%. Of the 67 patients, 29 required mitral valve replacement and/or closure of a ventricular septal defect.

In the 38 patients who underwent revascularization per se, survival was 51%. In these patients, postoperative studies as late as 2 yr after surgery have shown some, but not full, improvement in contractility. Most of the patients have been restored to a New York Heart Association class II level of function. These studies have shown that mortality can be reduced and that clinical symptoms can be relieved. Two lines of evidence also suggest that myocardial function has improved: 1) these patients have not died of a low-output state, as would be expected from previous experience in similar patients who did not undergo surgery, and 2) angina has recurred in less than 10% of these patients, some of whom have now survived for 7 yr after surgery.

REVASCULARIZATION IN UNSTABLE ANGINA

The value of revascularization in improving myocardial function was further assessed in another group of patients, in whom evidence of resistant myocardial ischemia was associated with minimal changes in cardiac output but definite changes in myocardial compliance. These patients were categorized as having "persistent chest pain" when medical treatment with beta adrenergic blocking agents, vasodilators, and conventional medical therapy in the coronary care unit failed to relieve their pain. Most of these patients received at least 300 mg of propranolol (Inderal) a day and received vasodilators, either orally or intravenously. In patients whose pain could not be controlled at rest, balloon assistance was initiated.

Ninety-three patients with refractory pain at rest were included in this study. Balloon assistance relieved the pain completely in 95% of the patients and diminished it in all. Usually, patients whose pain persisted during circulatory assist also had angiographic evidence of severe vessel disease affecting either three vessels or the main left coronary artery. This group of 93 patients included 41 patients with recent myocardial infarction in whom extension of the infarction seemed likely; the others had severe unstable angina.

All patients were characterized hemodynamically and then underwent surgery. Those with recent acute infarction showed marked increases in pulmonary wedge pressure during each episode of pain. Ventriculograms showed that contractility was diminished in the area of recent infarction. More than 50% of the patients had increased pulmonary wedge pressures at rest.

At the time of surgery, complete revascularization was attempted. Mitral valve surgery and infarct resection were not necessary in any of these patients. The overall survival was 96%, with mortality occurring predominantly among the patients who had had recent infarctions. The perioperative infarction rate was 2%. Thus, the use of the circulatory assist device appeared to protect the myocardium during a critical period and allowed surgical intervention to be carried out with a lower mortality than is generally reported for comparable patients with unstable angina. Postoperative studies have shown a marked improvement in myocardial function in the patients who had unstable angina alone: myocardial contractility had been maintained and wedge pressures were not high in the early postoperative period. Clinical recurrent myocardial failure has not been observed in these patients, even in those who are now 4 yr past the operation.

PERSPECTIVE

The role of cardiac surgery in the management of patients who have myocardial failure centers about two problems. The first—myocardial failure related to mechanical defects such as mitral regurgitation and ventricular septal defects—has been well defined as surgically treatable. This is true even in patients who have these lesions as complications of coronary arterial disease. Less settled is the second—the role of surgery in the reversal of myocardial failure associated with poor ventricular function alone. Our studies and those at other centers have shown that benefit may result from coronary artery bypass surgery if recurrent myocardial failure is associated with 1) angina, 2) ST and T wave changes during pain, and 3) changes in ventricular compliance during pain, as evidenced by a rise in the pulmonary capillary wedge pressure or left ventricular end-diastolic pressure during the episode of pain.

Coronary revascularization alone in patients who have severe congestive failure related to scarring of the myocardium and destroyed muscle has produced poor results. Today, noninvasive studies, particularly stress thallium imaging, have demonstrated that the best relief of intermittent failure can be obtained in patients who show delayed and poor perfusion with thallium in areas of decreased contractility. After successful surgery, thallium studies have shown essentially normal perfusion of these segments.

The challenge to the cardiologist and the surgeon is then to determine, in the patient with congestive failure, how much of this decreased function is related to a reversible mechanical defect, to reversible myocardial ischemia, or to destroyed myocardium. Previous poor results with coronary surgery for myocardial failure have been related to inappropriate selection of patients who do not have reversible myocardial ischemia and to damage of the myocardium during the surgical procedure. Proper selection of patients and careful attention to myocardial protection during the entire operative period has led to marked improvement in the management of patients with myocardial failure.

REFERENCES

1. Austen, W. G., Sokol, D. M., DeSanctis, R. W., and Sanders, C. A. Surgical treatment of papillary-muscle rupture complicating myocardial infarction. N Engl J Med 278:1137–1141, 1968.
2. Buckley, M. J., Mundth, E. D., Daggett, W. M., Gold, H. K., Leinbach, R. C., and Austen, W. G. Surgical management of ventricular septal defects and mitral regurgitation complicating acute myocardial infarction. Ann Thorac Surg 16:598–609, 1973.
3. Cooley, D. A., Collins, H. A., Morris, G. C., Jr., and Chapman, D. W. Ventricular aneurysm after myocardial infarction. Surgical excision with use of temporary cardiopulmonary bypass. J Am Med Assoc 167:557–560, 1958.

4. Gold, H. K., Leinbach, R. C., Sanders, C. A., Buckley, M. J., Mundth, E. D., and Austen, W. G. Intra-aortic balloon pumping for control of recurrent myocardial ischemia. Circulation 47:1197–1203, 1973.
5. Loop, F. D., Effler, D. B., Navia, J. A., Sheldon, W. C., and Groves, L. K. Aneurysms of the left ventricle: Survival and results of a ten year surgical experience. Ann Surg 178:399–405, 1973.
6. Mundth, E. D., Buckley, M. J., Daggett, W. M., McEnany, M. T., Leinbach, R. C., Gold, H. K., and Austen, W. G. Intra-aortic balloon pump assistance and early surgery in cardiogenic shock. Adv Cardiol 15:159–167, 1975.
7. Mundth, E. D., Harthorne, J. W., Buckley, M. J., Dinsmore, R., and Austen, W. G. Direct coronary arterial revascularization: Treatment of cardiac failure associated with coronary artery disease. Arch Surg 103:529–534, 1971.
8. Mundth, E. D., Yurchak, P. M., Buckley, M. J., Leinbach, R. C., Kantrowitz, A., and Austen, W. G. Circulatory assistance and emergency direct coronary artery surgery for shock complicating acute myocardial infarction. N Engl J Med 283:1382–1384, 1970.

[?] [?] [?] [?] [?] [?] [?] [?] [?] [?] [?] [?]
[?] [?] [?] [?] [?] [?] [?] [?] [?] [?] [?]
[?] [?] [?] [?] [?] [?] [?] [?] [?]
[?] [?] [?] [?] [?] [?] [?] [?] [?]
[?] [?] [?] [?]
[?] [?] [?] [?] [?] [?] [?] [?] [?] [?] [?]
[?] [?] [?] [?] [?] [?] [?] [?]
[?] [?] [?] [?]
[?] [?] [?]

CHAPTER 24

MECHANICAL CIRCULATORY ASSISTANCE AND REPLACEMENT: AN EVOLVING PERSPECTIVE

JOHN C. NORMAN

The history of artificial organs, both as assist and replacement devices, is almost as ancient as human history. Long before Western civilization began its ascendancy, devices to replace portions of the body were being fashioned in Asia, Africa, India, and the Middle East. And there is no suggestion in available records that these modalities of treatment were considered to be unique for their times.

The idea of building devices to augment, simulate, or substitute for the function of the heart must have been weighed repeatedly over the ages. But not until four decades ago were studies initiated that would bring the idea to reality. At that time John Gibbon began studies of an artificial pump-oxygenator to bypass the heart and lungs. This temporary method of bypassing the heart and lungs proved successful in animals, and the first human patient underwent successful cardio-pulmonary bypass in 1953. By the late 1950s, cardiopulmonary bypass was widely used to support patients during intracardiac surgery. Also, workable intracardiac valves and blood vessel prostheses were being developed. These advances supported the view that methods of mechanical circulatory assistance and/or replacement might be feasible.

My objectives in this overview are to focus on three major devices for augmentation, simulation, and replacement of the failing circulation: 1) the intra-aortic balloon pump (IABP), 2) the intracorporeal partial artificial heart or abdominal left ventricular assist device (ALVAD), and 3) the total artificial heart. Many technical details will be omitted, even though many of the major innovations have been based on technological advances. ALVAD technology will be discussed in greater detail than either the IABP or the total artificial heart because of its current applications to profound postcardiotomy and postinfarction shock.

INTRA-AORTIC BALLOON PUMP

History

The first IABP was conceived, designed, assembled, and tested in a mock-circulatory loop during a single afternoon by Stephen R. Topaz, a young mechanical engineering graduate from Purdue, and Spiro Moulopoulos, a cardiologist from Athens working in Willem Kolff's laboratory at the Cleveland Clinic, in April 1961. Over the next 6-mo period, it was modified, improved, tested in 4 or 5 animals, and utilized in a postcatheterization resuscitative attempt on a patient of Mason Sones, then head of the cardiology and cineangiography departments. As with most laboratory gadgetry, this original IABP was used only a few times in terminal circumstances over the next 5 yr and there were no survivors. Its further development and testing were sponsored by the Artificial Heart Program of the National Heart Institute, beginning in 1966. Experimental and subsequently clinical units became available for limited clinical testing mainly through the efforts of the Artificial Heart Program Office working through contractual agreements with industry. By the late 1960s, a considerable literature had evolved. Aside from pilot clinical studies, however, the lag time from conception to widespread clinical utilization was approximately 10 yr. During 1976, however, more than 5000 patients with postcardiotomy circulatory insufficiency underwent IABP mechanical circulatory support in this country alone. An equal number of patients were treated with this device in other countries. IABP is now used to treat refractory ventricular dysrhythmias; to stabilize preinfarction or unstable angina, preoperatively; to support patients during visualization of coronary and ventricular anatomy in precarious clinical settings; and to treat postcardiotomy and postinfarction low-output or cardiogenic shock states. Most recently, we have used IABP as an adjunct in resuscitative measures following cardiac arrest of any etiology. The reported results of IABP for cardiogenic shock without additional surgery are shown in Table 1 (5).

Basic Considerations

Reduced to essentials, the intra-aortic balloon is an intravascular volume displacement device that enhances the existing circulation. The timing of inflation

TABLE 1 Reported results of intra-aortic balloon pumping for cardiogenic shock without additional surgery[a]

	Patients	
Source	Total no.	Survivors (%)
Dunkman	25	18
Scheidt	87	17
Lawrence	15	47
O'Rourke	30	36
Willerson	27	11
Hochberg	112	28
Lefemine	14	71
Texas Heart Institute	30	40
Total	340	Average 27

[a]Adapted from Lefemine et al. (5).

and deflation is precisely synchronized with the cardiac cycle. Inflation is achieved during diastole after the aortic valve closes, and deflation is synchronized with systole. The balloon and cable are constructed of antithrombogenic, biocompatible materials and are inserted preferably via the left or (less preferably) the right common femoral artery within a short segment prosthetic vascular graft that is anastomosed to the artery to allow temporary vascular access. The cable is attached to a portable pneumatic drive console, and the balloon is positioned in the descending thoracic aorta proximal to the origin of the left subclavian artery and above the origins of the renal arteries. Actuation of the balloon reduces left ventricular outflow impedance during systole, shifts the phase of the peak arterial pressure contour into diastole, and increases the cardiac output (by about 500–800 ml/min). In addition, coronary blood flow increases markedly during diastole, while there is a decrease in left ventricular diastolic volumes and pressures, in the volume of the left ventricular chamber, and in the tension and O_2 consumption of the ventricular wall. The performance of the right ventricle is indirectly improved by the balloon-induced decrease in left heart filling pressure.

Current Status

Over the last 3 yr, a Circulatory Support Service has evolved in our institution for the clinical care of critically ill postcardiotomy and postinfarction patients who require mechanical circulatory assistance (4). Monitoring is accomplished by introducing a Swan-Ganz catheter (flow-directed, quadruple-lumen) and measuring right atrial, pulmonary artery, and pulmonary capillary wedge pressures and cardiac output, using a thermodilution method. Pharmacological agents such as digitalis, propranolol, furosemide, isoproterenol, dopamine, nitroprusside, epinephrine, and levarterenol (norepinephrine) are used in conjunction with IABP according to the hemodynamic state, as judged from the heart rate, right and left heart filling pressures, cardiac output, urine output, and peripheral vascular resistance, and the estimated need for inotropic or chronotropic (beta) stimulation or blockade, vasoconstrictive (alpha) stimulation, vasodilation, or dopaminergic effects (alpha + renal vasodilation).

Our clinical experience with the intra-aortic balloon shows an increase in survival from 28.6% during a 3-mo period in 1975 to 62% during the first 6 mo of 1977, primarily in postcardiotomy patients who are at high risk. Our experience with the last 188 of a total of 300 who required intra-aortic balloon support is summarized in Table 2.

We have also formulated classification systems for monitoring these post-cardiotomy or cardiogenic shock patients during the period of support by an IABP. A score of 0–16 is determined by assigning values of 0–4 to increasing ranges of cardiac index, decreasing pulmonary capillary wedge pressures, decreasing systemic vascular resistances, and increasing urinary outputs; the values are then summed. Classification from A to C is based on plots of cardiac index against systemic vascular resistance at optimal preload levels (Fig. 1). The results indicate that a score of 10–16 and/or a classification of A is optimal (all survive). Twenty percent of class B patients expire, whereas a persistent score of 6, and/or a classification of

TABLE 2 Experience with intra-aortic balloon pumping patients after cardiotomy[a]

	1975 (October–December)	1976	1977 (January–June)
Total patients	14	108	66
Survival	4 (28.6%)	52 (48%)	41 (62%)
Nonsurvival	10 (71.4%)	56 (52%)	25 (38%)
Age	55 ± 8.87	54.14 ± 10.26	54.5 ± 9.8
Male	9 (64.3%)	86 (80%)	56 (85%)
Survival	4	44	40
Nonsurvival	5	42	16
Age	54 ± 9.2	54.7 ± 9.9	54.8 ± 9.6
Female	5 (35.7%)	22 (20%)	10 (15%)
Survival	0	8	2
Nonsurvival	5	14	8
Age	55.7 ± 9.4	52.2 ± 11.4	52.9 ± 11.2

[a]Data from the Texas Heart Institute.

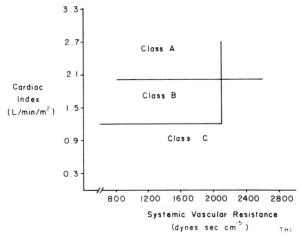

FIGURE 1 Scheme for classification of patients subjected to intra-aortic balloon pumping (IABP) after cardiotomy. Classifications are based on hemodynamic indices that can be measured intraoperatively or during the immediate postoperative period. (Class A) Cardiac index > 2.1 liter/min · m²; systemic vascular resistance < 2100 dyn · sec/cm⁵. Class A patients do not require continued IABP support, have the most favorable hemodynamic responses, and are at lowest risk. (Class B) Cardiac index ≤ 2.1 but > 1.2 liter/min · m²; systemic vascular resistance < 2100 dyn · sec/cm⁵. Class B patients require continued IABP support, have less favorable hemodynamic responses, and are at a higher risk. Because of the precarious condition of these patients, LVAD implantation could be considered in those in low class B who do not demonstrate marked improvement within 12–24 hr. (Class C) Cardiac index ≤ 2.1 liter/min · m²; systemic vascular resistance ≥ 2100 dyn · sec/cm⁵, or cardiac index ≤ 1.2 liter/min · m² independent of systemic vascular resistance. Class C patients have poor responses to combined pharmacological and mechanical support, are at highest risk, and should be considered as candidates for LVAD implantation. Mnemonic: "Rule of twos and ones (2's & 1's)," i.e., *2100* SVR (upper boundary, class B), *1.2* CI (lower boundary, class B), and *2.1* CI (upper boundary, class B). From Norman (8).

C during IABP support, is incompatible with survival and may be indicative of a need for more substantial circulatory support (10).

We now use IABP to provide circulatory assistance during shock and low-output states, preoperatively and postoperatively, and both prophylactically and therapeutically for serious left ventricular dysfunctions and/or impending infarction. The IABP-dependent patient remains a problem. Some of these patients have subsequently undergone cardiac transplantation, with good results (K. Reemtsma and D. Bregman, personal communication). A representative chest radiograph, showing an IABP in the descending thoracic aorta and the Swan-Ganz catheter in place, is shown in Fig. 2.

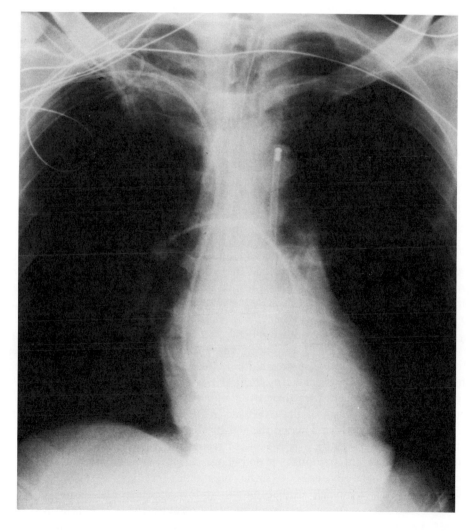

FIGURE 2 Intra-aortic balloon pump in situ in the thoracic aorta. From Norman (8).

LEFT VENTRICULAR ASSIST DEVICES
OR PARTIAL ARTIFICIAL HEARTS

History

In 1965, Miguel Serrato of the Head and Neck Clinic of the University of Texas Dental Branch in Houston was approached by William O'Bannon of Rice University's Department of Biomedical Engineering to help build an extracorporeal device that would pump blood from the left atrium to the thoracic aorta. The project was a joint effort by Baylor University Medical School and Rice University to develop a partial artificial heart. Serrato used a 75-W light bulb as a first approximation to form an impression in dental clay, which was duplicated in plaster of Paris to form a mold. From the mold, a rudimentary left ventricular assist device (LVAD) was cast in Lucite and the flexing bladder was covered with Dacron velour. O'Bannon completed the pneumatic drive console, and the unit was tested in six calves and used in a postcardiotomy resuscitation attempt by Michael DeBakey later that year. Design, testing, validation, experimental modification, and the first clinical trial took 6 mo. The first clinical unit was mounted extracorporeally between the third and fifth ribs after excision of the fourth rib. The same year, under the aegis of the National Institutes of Health, our efforts began in William Bernhard's laboratory at the Children's Hospital in Boston. Ten years of research and development elapsed before initial clinical trials were undertaken in accord with federal protocols and criteria (9).

Abdominal Left Ventricular Assist Device:
Concepts, Hypotheses, and Strategies

In considering the development and clinical application of any new device, therapy, or method, it would seem that from the outset the undertaking must have several positive aspects: 1) it must provide information not available by other means, 2) it must be an improvement over existing means, 3) it must be doable, and 4) it must satisfy some provable need.

Our clinical ALVAD or intracorporeal partial artificial heart is a mechanical analog of the left ventricle. It is undergoing initial clinical trials in humans in an attempt to reverse profound, postcardiotomy ventricular failure that is resistant to pharmacological and conventional mechanical (IABP) support. Results to date have shown that it is more effective than IABP support in humans. Comparisons of the hemodynamic effectiveness of the IABP and ALVAD are shown in Tables 3 and 4.

A major hypothesis underlying the use of this apparatus is that the reversibly depressed human left ventricle is capable of recovering if it can be totally unloaded ("put to rest") for an appropriate period (hours, days, or weeks). We attempted to accomplish this goal by using a single prosthetic ventricle that is capable of accepting the entire biologic cardiac output at low pressures (20–40 mmHg) and ejecting it into the systemic circulation at high pressures (80–150 mmHg) without damage to other vital organs or to the circulating blood and without causing infection or thrombotic or embolic phenomena.

We designed the device to be positioned in the abdomen through a median

TABLE 3 Comparison of effectiveness of intra-aortic balloon pumping and abdominal left ventricular assist device on left ventricular performance

Method	Left ventricular			
	dP/dt	Systolic pressure	Stroke work	$M\dot{V}O_2$
IABP[a]	1	9	20	13
ALVAD[a]	83	88	84	40
Effectiveness (IABP/ALVAD)	83	9.8	4.2	3.1

[a]Values are percentage decreases following actuation of IABP or ALVAD, experimentally and clinically.

sternotomy that is extended into the abdomen (12). This approach facilitates removal without reentering the thorax or mediastinum and avoids compromise of the pulmonary parenchyma.

An Intracorporeal Partial Artificial Heart System: Technical Summary

The ALVAD system consists of three major subsystems: 1) the left ventricular assist device, 2) a clinical drive console, and 3) a pneumatic pump monitor.

Abdominal Left Ventricular Assist Device

The ALVAD is a single-chambered, implantable blood pump that is actuated by an external pneumatic drive console. The pumping chamber is symmetrical about a central axis. It weighs 470 g, is 17 cm long, and has a maximum diameter of 6.3 cm with a displacement of 300 ml. The pumping chamber consists of a polyurethane bladder that collapses in three segments or lobes when pneumatic pressure is applied to the space between the bladder and titanium housing. Unidirectional flow is imparted by caged silicone rubber disk valves at the inflow and outflow orifices. The design stroke volume is 85 ml, and a stroke volume limiter system prevents overcollapse of the pumping bladder. Polyester fibrils (approximately 25 μm in length) coat all blood-contacting surfaces except the valve disks and the inflow and outflow grafts. These fibrils provide a matrix on which a unique bioderived blood-compatible surface develops—i.e., a pseudointima consisting of fibrin, platelets, white cells, and erythrocytes. Blood is received from the apex of the left ventricle through a semiflexible transdiaphragmatic inlet tube and ejected into the infrarenal abdominal aorta through a tightly woven low-porosity graft. A single pneumatic drive line penetrates the integument. Before beginning clinical trials in December 1975, we performed more than 20,000 hr of *in vivo* testing in acute and chronic experiments in dogs and calves. The results indicated that:

1. The ALVAD is hemodynamically effective in capturing the total cardiac output, is mechanically reliable, and does not damage the circulating blood.
2. The configuration is practical.
3. No untoward perturbation of cardiac function was demonstrable when inflow tubes were left in situ in the left ventricular apex over extended periods (up to 289 d).

TABLE 4 Comparison of intra-aortic balloon pumping and abdominal left ventricular assist devices in hemodynamics

Parameter[a]	IABP			ALVAD			Effectiveness (IABP/ALVAD)
	Off[b]	On[b]	Change (%)	Off[b]	On[b]	Change (%)	
HR	81 ± 2	80 ± 2	↓ 1	81 ± 2	79 ± 2	↓ 3	3.0
CI	1.49 ± 0.08	1.56 ± 0.09	↑ 5	1.49 ± 0.08	2.01 ± 0.15	↑ 35	7.0
AoP	68 ± 1.1	69 ± 2.2	↑ 1	68 ± 1.1	85 ± 1.8	↑ 25	25.0
PCW	20 ± 1.0	19 ± 1.0	↓ 5	20 ± 1.0	14 ± 1.0	↓ 30	6.0
RA	19.5 ± 1.0	18.5 ± 1.0	↓ 5	19.5 ± 1.0	17 ± 1.0	↓ 13	2.6
PA	28 ± 1.2	27 ± 1.2	↓ 4	28 ± 1.2	24 ± 1.1	↓ 14	3.5
PVR	859 ± 55	814 ± 59	↓ 5	859 ± 55	538 ± 28	↓ 37	7.4

[a]HR, heart rate; CI, cardiac index; AoP, mean aortic pressure; PCW, left heart filling pressure and right ventricular afterload; RA, right atrial pressure; PA, mean pulmonary artery pressure; PVR, pulmonary vascular resistance.
[b]Values are means ± SD; $n = 5$.

Clinical Drive Console

For actuation and control of the ALVAD, an external clinical drive console was developed and tested. It provides 1) pneumatic drive and control, 2) electronic logic, and 3) fail-safe mechanisms, which are desirable for clinical use. Fail-safe functions are also provided for: 1) electrocardiogram (ECG) interruption, 2) primary subsystem mechanical or electrical failure, 3) loss of external pneumatic power, and 4) loss of a-c line power. There are two modes of operation: 1) ECG-triggered counterpulsation, and 2) variable fixed-rate asynchronous pumping. There are two pneumatic subsystems. The primary subsystem will operate in either mode; the secondary subsystem provides drive pressure at adjustable fixed rates, should the primary system fail for any reason.

Pneumatic Pump Monitor

The pneumatic pump monitor (PPM) was developed for control and quantitation of ALVAD function. This device consists of a pneumatic isolation piston and cylinder in the pump drive line, a piston displacement transducer, a drive line pressure transducer, and an analog computer with digital display and analog outputs. By adjusting the isolation piston displacement, the pump stroke volume can be regulated to any percentage (20-100) of full capacity, thereby continuously avoiding pump bladder overcollapse and the possibility of denuding the developing pseudointima. The piston displacement and drive line pressure transducer signals are utilized to compute pump stroke volume. Flow rates in excess of 10 liter/min have been measured in experimental animals and rates up to six liter/min have been achieved in humans.

Approach to Selection of Patients

We have adopted the following approach in selecting patients for our initial clinical trials: 1) all adult patients undergoing intracardiac surgery are reviewed by members of our Circulatory Support Service; 2) all high-risk patients are monitored by clinical engineers during weaning from cardiopulmonary bypass in anticipation of difficulties; 3) all patients experiencing difficulties are given pharmacological support according to an institutional and federal protocol; those not responding then undergo conventional mechanical (IABP) circulatory support; 4) those patients not responding to combined pharmacological and IABP support over a 2-hr period are considered as possible candidates for ALVAD implantation; and 5) thereafter, informed consent for ALVAD implantation is obtained from the patient's relatives and tape-recorded in the presence of a patient advocate, a chaplain, and representatives of the administration.

Criteria for Implantation
after Cardiopulmonary Bypass

All adult patients undergoing cardiopulmonary bypass are weaned from bypass in stepwise fashion by decreasing the arterial flow while the volume is concurrently replaced from the arterial reservoir; the objective is to achieve a mean aortic pressure > 70 mmHg without bypass. If this goal is not accomplished, pharmacological agents (Ca^{2+}, digitalis, dopamine, norepinephrine, epinephrine, etc.) are administered. If these measures prove unsuccessful, partial cardiopulmonary bypass is reinstituted and augmented with IABP, after which cardiopulmonary bypass is gradually withdrawn. If the mean aortic pressure cannot be maintained $> 65-70$ mmHg in the presence of continued pharmacological and IABP support, during and after bypass withdrawal, the patient becomes a candidate for ALVAD.

Methods of Clinical Implantation

Before implanting the device, partial cardiopulmonary bypass is reinstituted; all pharmacological agents are stopped and the IABP pump and cable are removed from the left common femoral artery. The median sternotomy is extended to and beyond the umbilicus and the infrarenal abdominal aorta is widely exposed, particular attention being paid to meticulous hemostasis (the patient is totally heparinized). A low-porosity woven graft (preclotted with fresh donor blood) is anastomosed end-to-side to the infrarenal abdominal aorta, and a small aperture is fashioned in the left hemidiaphragmatic leaf to accept the inlet tube of the pump. Concomitantly, moderate systemic hypothermia ($30°C$) is reinduced and total cardiopulmonary bypass is reinstituted.

The heart is elevated and a full-thickness circular segment of the left ventricular apex is removed with a cylindrical coring knife. A sewing ring is attached to the left ventricular apex, using 12-14 full-thickness mattress sutures reinforced with Teflon pledgets. The pump outlet graft is attached to the ALVAD outlet with a quick-connect fitting. After the pneumatic drive line has been exteriorized through a stab wound just above the left iliac crest in the midaxillary line, the pump is positioned intracorporeally along the left flank. The inlet tube is passed from the abdomen through the aperture in the left hemidiaphragmatic leaf and inserted into the left ventricular apex (within the sewing ring), and the left ventricular apex sewing ring is secured to the inlet tube. Residual air in the biologic-prosthetic system is evacuated from the ascending aorta, the left ventricle, and the ALVAD outlet graft. An abdominal film of the ALVAD in situ during mechanical systole is shown in Fig. 3.

Discontinuation of Cardiopulmonary Bypass and Actuation of the Blood Pump

ALVAD pumping is initiated with a single, asynchronous stroke while the outlet graft is cross-clamped. Any residual air within the pump is expelled and evacuated by aspirating the outlet graft. This process is repeated and the outlet graft cross clamp is then removed. Because of low systemic venous return during concomitant, continued cardiopulmonary bypass, low-rate (30-40 beats per minute) asynchronous pumping without vacuum assistance is then utilized for the initiation of ALVAD support. As cardiopulmonary bypass flow is reduced, systemic venous return increases. The ALVAD synchronous pumping rate is increased until it approximates the patient's rate to ensure that the pump captures the complete left ventricular output by maximally unloading the left ventricle. This unloading minimizes left ventricular wall tension and work while the ALVAD improves the systemic and coronary circulation. Asynchronous pumping is also effective during recurrent ventricular dysrhythmias, including ventricular fibrillation; for instance,

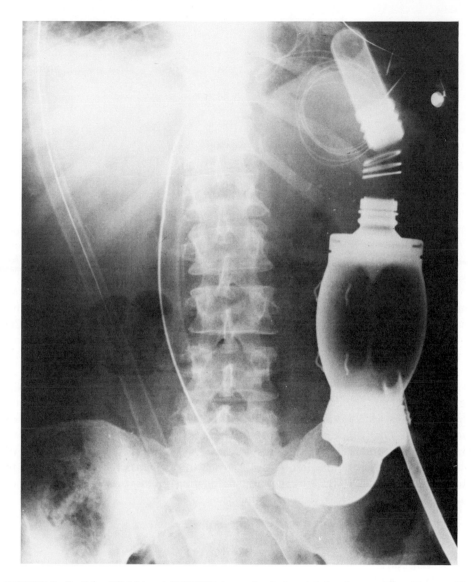

FIGURE 3 Partial artificial heart (ALVAD) in mechanical systole in a human. From Norman (8).

during multiple clinical episodes of ventricular fibrillation persisting up to 10 min, ALVAD pump outputs have varied between 2.4 and 3.4 liter/min, and systemic arterial pressures have been maintained in humans between 85/50 and 130/80 mmHg (Fig. 4). Flows up to 6.5 liter/min have been achieved during synchronous ALVAD pumping in humans.

After the biologic heart rate and rhythm have stabilized, synchronous pumping is utilized. This pumping mode decreases the impedance to left ventricular ejection and achieves maximal ALVAD-generated aortic pressure during diastole, which

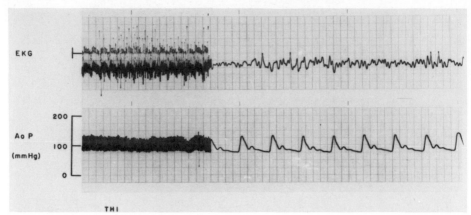

FIGURE 4 Electrocardiogram and aortic pressure (AoP) 20 min after ALVAD implantation, during an episode of spontaneous ventricular fibrillation. Continued asynchronous ALVAD pumping results in maintenance of AoP at 130/75 mmHg with an ALVAD flow of 3.2 liter/min and an ALVAD stroke volume of 55 ml/beat. The patient defibrillated internally shortly thereafter. From Norman (8).

improves systemic and coronary perfusion. Synchronous pumping is most effective during normal sinus rhythms at a rate of 60–120 beats per minute. Should ECG synchronization be lost, the ECG interrupt detector of the drive console automatically converts to fixed-rate asynchronous pumping.

Functional State of the Right Ventricle during ALVAD Pumping

In patients with severely depressed postcardiotomy left ventricular failure that warrants ALVAD implantation, the outputs of the two ventricles are equal. However, intracorporeal left ventricular assist devices can eject only the volume of blood received through the left ventricle from the right heart. Our experience to date suggests that LVADs achieve optimal function in the presence of intact, or only moderately depressed, right heart function.

Quantitative Indices of Left Ventricular Recovery after ALVAD Implantation

During these initial ALVAD clinical trials, we have documented progressive decreases in biologic left ventricular ejection delay time (EDT)—the interval following interruption of ALVAD pumping required for left ventricular filling and ejection and concomitant progressive decreases in QRS duration (electric recovery). Nearly linear increases in the magnitude of biologic left ventricular pressure, flow, and work generation (mechanical recovery) in humans have also been recorded. Representative data obtained during brief intervals of interrupted ALVAD pumping in humans are summarized in Fig. 5.

Methods of Weaning

In the patient with tenuous circulation following left ventricular recovery, abrupt permanent cessation of ALVAD pumping can result in an increase in left ventricular end-diastolic pressure (LVEDP) and a decrease in cardiac output (CO). On the other hand, a gradual reduction of ALVAD pumping at 4–6-hr intervals maintains LVEDP and CO at preweaning levels. We are currently evaluating three interrelated weaning methods that depend on a gradual reduction in either ALVAD pumping rate or stroke volume.

ALVAD Removal

Following ventricular recovery and stabilization, the patient is returned to the operating room and the abdominal incision is reopened. The inner and outer inlet grafts just beneath the diaphragm and the outlet graft at the infrarenal abdominal aorta are occluded with vascular clamps. The outer proximal graft is opened and the inner graft is divided and oversewn. The outlet graft is divided between vascular clamps and oversewn. The pneumatic drive line is divided intraabdominally and the pump is removed.

To date, we have had experience with ALVAD in 13 patients ranging in age from 46 to 68 yr (6, 7, 11). Except for one nonsurgical patient in cardiogenic shock, the others had undergone aortic or mitral valve replacement for rheumatic

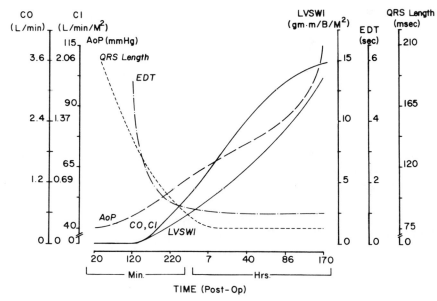

FIGURE 5 Composite analysis of physiological data obtained over a 6-d period of ALVAD pumping in a human during brief interruptions of prosthetic support. Mechanical ventricular recovery is demonstrated by progressive increases in arterial pressure (AoP) from 40 to 155 mmHg, cardiac output (CO) from 0 to 3.6 liter/min, cardiac index (CI) from 0 to 2.06 liter/min · m², and left ventricular stroke work index (LVSWI) from 0 to 14 g · m/beat · m². The ejection delay time (EDT) decreased from more than 6 sec to less than 1 sec. Electric ventricular recovery is demonstrated by decreases in QRS durations from 206 to 76 msec. These data indicate that the profoundly depressed human left ventricle, initially incapable of ejection, can recover if totally unloaded with support of the systemic circulation by partial artificial heart pumping over periods of up to 1 wk. From Norman (8).

valvular disease or aortocoronary bypass grafting. During ALVAD support, the flow ranged from 3.0 to 6.5 liter/min. The duration of ALVAD support ranged from 1 to 140 hr. We succeeded in removing the pump and weaning 2 patients from ALVAD assistance (after 128 and 140 hr of assistance, respectively). It should be noted that each of the patients was considered to be desperately ill and unlikely to survive. Although we have not yet succeeded in achieving long-term survival, the preliminary trials in irretrievable patients appear promising.

TOTAL ARTIFICIAL HEART

History

Unlike the IABP and LVADs, which were conceived in laboratories, total artificial hearts were first mentioned in a science fiction article published nearly 60 yr ago. Flint (3) described his version of implantation of a total artificial heart in a human as follows.

> It was of silver, shaped like a flattened egg, and a trifle smaller than that laboring, human blood pump. To it was attached a pair of long, flexible silver pipes, which led to "Billie" knew not where. And near one extremity, the egg was provided duplicate sources, in vest pocket size, of power for operating [this] mechanical heart. The electricity worked the air pumps, which in turn supplied the little silver egg . . . implanted in the patient . . . with both pressure and vacuum, while doubtless the artificial organ itself housed a valve system which did the rest. The regulating device kept the blood circulating at the proper rate. The surgeon seemed satisfied with it all . . . .

In 1937 in Moscow, Vladimir Petrovich Demikhov devised a compact apparatus consisting of two adjacent membrane pumps that performed the functions of both ventricles of the canine heart after their removal. Nothing more was done until 1957, when Peter F. Salisbury of the Institute of Medical Research, Cedars of Lebanon Hospital, Los Angeles, combined several theoretical possibilities for supplementation of bodily functions for prolonged periods by factitious means and suggested that an artificial heart could be developed. At the same time, S. P. McCabe exhibited an implantable heart made of polyvinyl chloride and noted that such devices might be powered by external electromagnets rather than by a fluid. The following year, B. Kusserow, T. Akutsu, and W. J. Kolff reported on their initial experiments regarding a permanent indwelling intracorporeal blood pump, which would substitute for cardiac function (a right ventricular assist device from the University of Vermont, which antedated Serrato's and O'Bannon's work by nearly a decade) and permanent substitutes for both valves and hearts (total artificial heart).

State of the Art

It has now been demonstrated that total artificial hearts actuated by transcutaneous, external pneumatic drive lines can assume the total circulatory demands of large experimental animals for periods up to 6 mo; e.g., in 1976

Kazuhiko Atsumi at the University of Tokyo maintained a goat for 100 d with a total artificial heart. Emil Bücherl has recorded nearly similar experiences in calves at the Free University in West Berlin. William Pierce and the group at Penn State-Hershey Medical Center have calves living between $1\frac{1}{2}$ and 2 mo; Yukihiko Nose's experience at Cleveland Clinic documents a 145-d survival; and 185-d survivals have been achieved by Willem Kolff and Don Olsen at the University of Utah.

A Scenario

It is not difficult to extrapolate from current institutional and federal guidelines for the use of intracorporeal LVADs and partial artificial hearts to guidelines for the use of a total artificial heart in humans. An example may help to identify a hypothetical candidate. The hypothetical patient under consideration is a 54-yr-old male with a previous history of multiple myocardial infarctions associated with episodes of ventricular automaticity. Coronary artery arteriography and left ventriculography reveal major critical occlusions of the right, left anterior descending, and obtuse marginal branches of the circumflex coronary arteries and a large ventricular aneurysm containing thrombus. The decision is made for surgical therapy.

After left ventricular aneurysmectomy and double reversed saphenous vein aortocoronary bypassing procedures, difficulty is encountered in weaning the patient from cardiopulmonary bypass. Extensive aortobilateral iliac occlusive disease prevents insertion of an intra-aortic balloon, and the presence of multiple proximal ascending aortic saphenous vein graft anastomoses and the arterial perfusion cannula in a short ascending aortic segment preclude antegrade insertion of an intra-aortic balloon into the ascending aorta. An intracorporeal LVAD is implanted, allowing the patient to return to the recovery room.

However, over the next month, multiple attempts to wean the patient from the intracorporeal LVAD are unsuccessful. The situation appears to be preterminal. A possible solution could then be elective, unhurried transplantation or, if no donor is available, implantation of a total mechanical heart in order to prolong the period during which a suitable donor can be found.

This sequence of events is not farfetched. In fact, there is a precedent. In 1969, Denton Cooley and Domingo Liotta implanted an externally actuated pneumatically driven total mechanical heart into the mediastinum of a preterminal patient. The device sustained the patient for approximately 64 hr. Figure 6 shows a chest film of this patient with a total artificial heart in situ. A biologic heart transplant was then performed. The patient died 36 hr later. The ethical, moral, and legal issues that resulted were without precedent, and the litigations reached the U.S. Supreme Court in late 1974. Dismissal of the case against Drs. Cooley and Liotta was upheld (2).

SUMMARY

Mechanical support of the failing circulation is emerging as a useful adjunct in the care of critically ill patients with circulatory insufficiency. Clinical use of the intra-aortic balloon pump is now widespread, and its use is increasing in pre- and postoperative, pre- and postinfarction settings of low cardiac output or cardiogenic shock and cardiac arrest.

Intracorporeal partial artificial hearts (ALVADs) are now undergoing initial clinical trials. They are more effective hemodynamically than the IABP, do not require an intact ECG signal for activation, and can maintain circulation in the presence of ventricular fibrillation. So far, 13 preterminal post cardiotomy patients have undergone implantation of this device, and we have found that the profoundly depressed left ventricle, initially incapable of ejection, can recover if totally supported for a period of 1 wk. These devices are prototypes of longer-lived

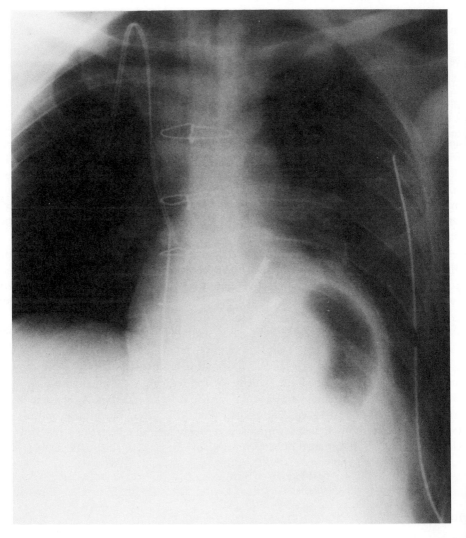

FIGURE 6 Total artificial heart in a human. Three of the four prosthetic valves are visible. From Norman (8).

TABLE 5 Mechanical circulatory support and/or replacement: State of the art

Condition	IABP[a]	PAH/LVAD[b]	TAH[c]
A. Postcardiotomy low-output syndrome	++++	++	0
B. Postinfarction cardiogenic shock	++	±	0
C. Prophylactic Left main lesions Ventricular dysrhythmias	+++	0	0
D. Cardiac arrest	+	0	0
E. Chronic left ventricular failure (atherosclerotic-cardiomyopathic)	0	+	0
F. Pretransplant	+	±	+

[a]IABP, intra-aortic balloon pumping.
[b]PAH/LVAD, partial artificial heart/left ventricular assist device.
[c]TAH, total artificial heart.

electrically actuated devices, now in the early experimental stages. The development of the total artificial heart continues, suggesting that it will ultimately be feasible as a bridge or an alternative to transplantation (Table 5). The remaining tasks are not insurmountable and the rewards are substantial (1).

REFERENCES

1. Annas, G. J. Allocation of artificial hearts in the year 2002: Minerva vs. National Health Agency. Am J Law Med 3:59–76, 1977.
2. Curran, W. J. Law-medicine notes. The first mechanical heart transplant: Informed consent and experimentation. N Engl J Med 291:1015–1025, 1974.
3. Flint, H. E. The devolutionist. Argosy 75:2, July 1921.
4. Hibbs, C. W., Edmonds, C. H., Slogoff, S., and Norman, J. C. Circulatory support service: A new paradigm in intensive care. In: Eighth Annual Conference on Advanced Medical Systems, the Third Century, Chevy Chase, Md., Society of Advanced Medical Systems, 1977, vol. 1, p. 15.
5. Lefemine, A. A., Kosowsky, B., Madoff, I., Black, H., and Lewis, M. Results and complications of intraaortic balloon pumping in surgical and medical patients. Am J Cardiol 40:416–420, 1977.
6. Norman, J. C. An intracorporeal (abdominal) left ventricular assist device (ALVAD). XXX: Clinical readiness and initial trials in man. Cardiovasc Dis (Tex Heart Inst) 3(3):249–288, 1976.
7. Norman, J. C. Intracorporeal partial artificial hearts: Initial results in ten patients. Artificial Organs 1(1):41–52, 1977.
8. Norman, J. C. Mechanical circulatory assistance. Cardiovasc Dis (Tex Heart Inst) 4(4):444–464, 1977.
9. Norman, J. C. and Bernhard, W. F. Criteria, protocols and reporting forms for initial left ventricular assist device clinical trials (special supplement). Cardiovasc Dis (Tex Heart Inst) 2(4):438–458, 1976.
10. Norman, J. C., Cooley, D. A., Igo, S. R., Hibbs, C. W., Johnson, M. D., Bennett, J. G., Fuqua, J. M., Trono, R., and Edmonds, C. H. Prognostic indices for survival during post-cardiotomy intraaortic balloon pumping: Methods of

scoring (0–16) and classification (A–C) with implications for left ventricular assist device utilization. J Thorac Cardiovasc Surg 74(5):709–720, 1977.

11. Norman, J. C., Fuqua, J. M., Bennett, J. G., Trono, R., Hibbs, C. W., Edmonds, C. H., Igo, S. R., and Cooley, D. A. An intracorporeal (abdominal) left ventricular assist device (ALVAD): Initial clinical trials, LX. Arch Surg 112:1442–1451, 1977.

12. Norman, J. C., Whalen, R. L., Daly, B. D. T., Migliore, J., and Huffman, F. N. An implantable abdominal left ventricular assist device (ALVAD). Clin Res 20:855, 1972.

CHAPTER 25

CURRENT STATUS OF CARDIAC TRANSPLANTATION

EDWARD B. STINSON

Cardiac transplantation in a human was first performed in December 1967. Subsequently, 346 heart transplant procedures have been performed in 338 recipients by 66 teams in 22 countries throughout the world. Of these patients 77 are living, and 1 is surviving nearly 9 yr after transplantation. The initial enthusiasm with which the clinical advent of cardiac transplantation was received and the subsequent disenchantment because of the generally low survival rates can be inferred from the graph shown in Fig. 1.

At Stanford University Medical Center an active program in clinical heart transplantation was begun in January 1968 and has been maintained at a steadily increasing level since that time. This program was predicated on nearly a decade of experimental research in the canine model; during this preclinical phase surgical techniques were standardized, diagnosis and control of acute cardiac graft rejection were investigated, physiological aspects of the transplanted, denervated heart were examined, and, most importantly, long-term survival was achieved. This review describes our clinical experience with the selection of appropriate recipients for cardiac replacement, principles of early and late postoperative management, function of the transplanted human heart, and long-term postoperative survival and rehabilitation.

RECIPIENT SELECTION

Stringent selection criteria have been developed to identify the potential recipients who are most likely to benefit from operation. It is self-evident that the primary criterion is the presence of advanced cardiac disease, associated with severe disability, irremediable by ordinary forms of medical or surgical therapy. A complete cardiovascular evaluation, in some cases including endomyocardial biopsy, is performed in order to exclude treatable causes of disease. Factors that contraindicate orthotopic cardiac transplantation include excessive elevation of pulmonary vascular resistance above 8-10 Wood units (a necessary consideration inasmuch as a normal donor right ventricle is limited in its ability to increase acutely its external workload), any active infection, diabetes mellitus requiring

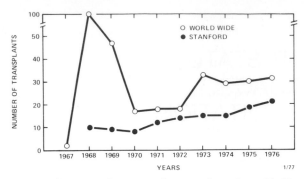

FIGURE 1 Number of cardiac transplant procedures performed worldwide and at Stanford University Medical Center, 1967–1976.

insulin, age greater than 55 yr, any systemic disorder that would separately limit survival or predispose to excessive postoperative morbidity, and unresolved pulmonary infarction. The latter contraindication is related to our experience with 19 patients who presented clinical and/or radiographic evidence of pulmonary embolism at the time of transplantation, 32% of whom died postoperatively because of infection in the area of involved pulmonary parenchyma. A psychosocial evaluation is also important because of the direct correlation of psychosocial stability and a history of medical compliance with the probability of postoperative rehabilitation in surviving patients. Because of the stringency of these criteria, only approximately 15-20% of patients initially screened as potential recipients are officially selected for transplantation. It should be recognized, however, that these restraints reflect in large part the current state of the art in organ transplantation, especially the need for generalized and indefinite immunosuppression with its attendant hazards, and they are subject to modification with future developments in selective control of the immune response.

At present, 80% of patients accepted for transplantation undergo operation, while the remainder die before a suitable donor becomes available. The extremely limited prognosis of accepted recipients is illustrated by the latter patients, whose average survival after selection is 55 d. Such patients do not, of course, constitute a control group, but they do serve to illustrate the severity of cardiac disease in patients selected for transplantation.

The classification of primary disease etiology in the 129 patients included in our series is shown in Table 1. The most common category has been advanced

TABLE 1 Recipient diagnosis

Category	No. of patients
Coronary artery disease	77
Idiopathic cardiomyopathy	48
Posttraumatic aneurysm	1
Valve disease with cardiomyopathy	3
Total	129

coronary artery disease associated with global left ventricular dysfunction unamenable to standard aortocoronary bypass and ventricular reconstructive techniques. The next most common category includes patients with idiopathic cardiomyopathy. The latter patients have been younger than those with coronary artery disease (39 compared with 46 yr), and in recent years they have constituted an increasingly greater proportion of patients undergoing transplantation.

OPERATIVE TECHNIQUES

Matching of donors and recipients for cardiac transplantation is based on straightforward considerations, including reasonable comparability of body mass, ABO blood group compatibility, and the absence of a positive lymphocyte crossmatch (cytotoxic effect of recipient serum on donor lymphocytes). Histocompatibility (HLA) typing is not currently utilized for donor-recipient matching because of the lack of reliable correlations based on HLA typing alone. It is expected, however, that future refinements in the definition of immunologic determinants of allograft rejection will render such assays clinically important.

Operative techniques for orthotopic heart transplantation have not changed significantly since their original successful formulation in the laboratory and subsequent minor modification for clinical application (3). Protection of the cardiac graft between the time of excision from the donor and the time of implantation in the recipient is achieved by simple hypothermia alone, induced by immersion in cold 0.9% saline at 3–4°C. Recently, however, efforts have been made to procure hearts from distant donors, and in these cases ischemia intervals of 2–3 hr are required. Hearts procured in this fashion have been preserved by core hypothermia produced by flushing the coronary vasculature with Sack's solution, a hyperkalemic electrolyte solution similar to many types of hypothermic cardioplegia solutions currently in use for routine cardiac operations (4). Donor hearts thus preserved for 2–3 hr have functioned satisfactorily with positive myocardial inotropic support, but detailed hemodynamic observations are lacking. It should be noted, however, that in nearly all cases temporary myocardial inotropic support is provided for the first three postoperative days because of temporary depression of donor cardiac output (5); otherwise, the early postoperative care of cardiac recipients differs little from that of routine cardiac surgical patients, except for the institution of immunosuppression.

REJECTION AND IMMUNOSUPPRESSION

The heart, like other solid organ allografts, is subject to host immune responses that result in acute but reversible rejection episodes in most cases during the first few postoperative weeks. During the first 2 mo after transplantation, the average frequency of diagnosed rejection episodes is 1 per 34 patient days; after this interval the risk of acute rejection decreases markedly to a level of 1 episode per 325 patient-days. Nevertheless, because of the indefinite risk of acute graft rejection, immunosuppression, augmented transiently during acute rejection episodes, is required. We have utilized a triple immunosuppressive protocol that incorporates corticosteroids, azathioprine, and antihuman antithymocyte globulin produced in rabbits immunized against human thymocytes (1). The latter biologic agent is employed routinely only during the first $1\frac{1}{2}$ wk after transplantation, but it may be reinstituted for additional short courses as a treatment for acute graft rejection. Its administration is individualized on the basis of circulating levels of rabbit globulin, as measured by radioimmunoassay. Such measurements make it possible to determine the kinetics of rabbit globulin disposition in individual recipients and thus the doses necessary to achieve therapeutic levels, as defined by depression of the thymus-dependent subpopulation of peripheral lymphocytes (T lymphocytes) to a range of 10% of normal or less during the first several postoperative weeks.

Clearly, the key to successful negotiation of the critical first 2-3 mo after transplantation is early, sensitive diagnosis of impending graft rejection episodes. The most useful indices for diagnosis of cardiac rejection include auscultation for the detection of abnormal diastolic heart sounds (a clue to changes in ventricular compliance that accompany the rejection process), the standard electrocardiogram (diagnostic features include a generalized decrease in QRS voltage and atrial arrhythmias), and, in recent years, percutaneous transvenous endomyocardial biopsy and immunologic monitoring by measurement of circulating levels of T lymphocytes. The goal of management during the early postoperative period is appropriately timed institution of augmented immunosuppressive measures before the development of irreversible morphological changes in the graft. The typical pathological features of acute cardiac rejection are similar to those encountered with other solid organ allografts; they include subendocardial and interstitial infiltration with mononuclear cells, interstitial edema, and, in cases of severe rejection, irreversible changes such as myocyte degeneration (myocytolysis) and replacement fibrosis. Except for the latter changes, the histological abnormalities associated with acute rejection are fully reversible.

Graft endomyocardial biopsy has proved to be a highly valuable diagnostic tool because it provides objective histological assessment of graft status and can be performed safely on a serial basis. The technique for endomyocardial biopsy is simple. By using the Seldinger technique for percutaneous introduction of the biopsy forceps into the right internal jugular vein under local anesthesia, the donor right ventricular endomyocardium can be sampled repetitively. After percutaneous insertion, the biopsy forceps is guided under fluoroscopic control into the region of the right ventricular apex, and a 2-3-mm specimen is removed with the biting jaws of the instrument. Altogether, more than 1200 endomyocardial biopsies have been performed within the context of the transplantation program without serious morbidity or mortality. Minor complications have included atrial arrhythmias and pneumothorax (0.2%). Because of the safety of this procedure and the highly valuable information it provides, current protocols include routine biopsy at 5-7-d intervals during the first 8 wk after transplantation or immediately on suspicion of rejection as evidenced by clinical or electrocardiographic findings; after treatment of rejection episodes for the purpose of monitoring the histological response to therapy; and at the annual evaluation of long-term survivors. In addition to providing information about the morphological expression of immune responses to the cardiac graft, endomyocardial biopsy constitutes a standard for comparison with other potentially useful indices of rejection.

One such index, which was recently evaluated and promises a high degree of sensitivity for the early diagnosis of rejection, is the circulating level of peripheral T lymphocytes (the subpopulation of lymphocytes considered primarily responsible for allograft injury). Typically, levels of T lymphocytes diminish rapidly during routine postoperative administration of antithymocyte globulin and are less than 10% of normal by 3–6 d after transplantation. The onset of subsequent rejection episodes, which have been confirmed by biopsy, is heralded by increases in circulating T lymphocyte levels ($r = 0.93$; $p < 0.001$). Thus, immunosuppression may be augmented during early stages of activation of the efferent limb of the immune response, as manifested by rises in T lymphocyte levels, before the determination of severe graft damage. Diagnosis of impending allograft rejection by immunologic monitoring is still being studied, but experience with the assay described above indicates that even more refined techniques may be developed that will virtually eliminate acute rejection after transplantation.

Once diagnosed, episodes of acute cardiac rejection are treated by reinstitution of antithymocyte globulin, usually in combination with high-dose pulses (1 g/d) of a corticosteroid preparation such as methylprednisolone, and anticoagulation with heparin for 5–7 d (heparin is given because of microthrombosis in the coronary vasculature during acute rejection). In cases of rejection classified as mild on the basis of histological and clinical criteria, the antirejection therapy may be limited to the use of antithymocyte globulin alone, at doses that are individually modulated according to the kinetics of disposition; this is preferable because of the cumulative infectious and metabolic toxicity of corticosteroids.

Nearly all (95%) early postoperative acute rejection episodes can be successfully reversed by the measures described above, but the frequency of attendant infectious complications is high. The magnitude of this problem is indicated in Table 2, where the infections encountered in our series are summarized according to the type of etiologic agent. A total of 392 infections in the 129 recipients have been diagnosed; opportunistic pathogens and mixed infections have been common. More pertinent to the practical implications for postoperative management is the fact that 75% of long-term survivors have sustained one or more potentially fatal infections. These considerations show the importance of aggressive diagnosis and treatment of infection in the immunocompromised cardiac recipient in order to achieve long-term

TABLE 2 Recipient infections

Agent	No. of infections	No. of patients
Bacterial	226	90
Fungal	47	42
Nocardia	23	18
Viral	77	63
Protozoan	19	18
Total	392	

survival. Surveillance for infection is maintained at a high level during the first 3 postoperative months, during which infectious episodes occur at a rate of 1 per 49 patient-days. After the first postoperative year, the overall rate of serious infection decreases to 1 episode per 455 patient-days.

LATE POSTOPERATIVE MANAGEMENT

At present, approximately 85% of patients are discharged from the hospital after cardiac transplantation at our center. After discharge, recipients may still sustain graft rejection or infection, but, as noted above, these occur with a greatly decreased frequency after the early postoperative period. An additional complication that emerged during our early experience with cardiac transplantation, however, was a phenomenon that we termed accelerated graft atherosclerosis (2). This was a seemingly accelerated form of coronary arteriosclerosis caused by myointimal proliferation, associated fibrosis, and subsequent atherosclerotic degeneration. It was postulated to derive primarily from immunologically mediated injury of the donor coronary arterial endothelium; repeated cyclically, the resultant reparative process led to occlusive lesions of the major coronary arteries, the consequences of which included myocardial infarction, sudden death, and ischemic dysfunction with congestive heart failure.

In 1970 a prophylactic regimen directed toward intermediate steps in the formulated pathogenesis of accelerated donor coronary atherosclerosis was developed. It included chronic treatment with an oral anticoagulant (warfarin sodium) and a platelet antagonist (dipyridamole), as well as more strict control of serum lipid levels and maintenance of ideal body weight. This protocol reduced the incidence of graft atherosclerosis from nearly 100% at 3 yr after transplantation to about 20% and thus removed this complication as an apparently inevitable barrier to long-term survival. Its continuing occurrence in a minority of patients, however, is an indication for annual coronary arteriographic study of long-term recipients. Detection of this process is considered an indication for elective retransplantation in recipients without other complicating factors.

During the first several months after transplantation the appearance of lesions of accelerated coronary arteriosclerosis is predominantly proliferative, as illustrated in Fig. 2. Subsequently, infiltration or in situ production of lipids leads to an atheromatous lesion that is virtually indistinguishable on a morphological basis from native, spontaneously occurring atherosclerosis, as shown in Fig. 3. The arteriographic appearance of graft atherosclerosis is demonstrated in Fig. 4. Although luminal narrowing appears to be discrete (stenotic lesion in the proximal left anterior descending coronary artery and complete occlusion of the circumflex coronary artery in Fig. 4), the disease process is diffuse and precludes aortocoronary bypass grafting. Graft replacement is therefore the only realistic alternative, and it has been attempted twice for this complication in our series, once successfully.

Another indication for cardiac retransplantation is intractable recurrent acute rejection in the early postoperative period. This maneuver is considered for any recipient in whom control of the acute rejection process cannot be achieved, as documented by repeated graft biopsy, and in whom active infectious complications

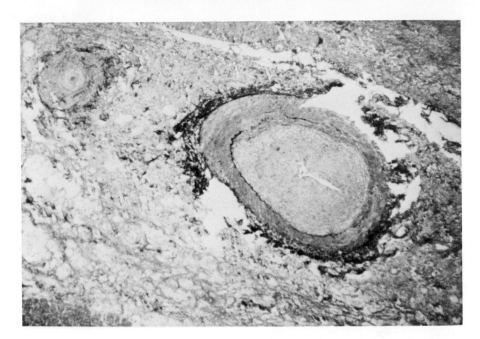

FIGURE 2 Cross section of the atrioventricular nodal artery removed from the graft of a patient who died several months after transplantation because of recurrent, acute rejection. Nearly total luminal obliteration is present, caused by proliferation of the intimal layer. The immediate cause of death in this case was a Stokes-Adams attack.

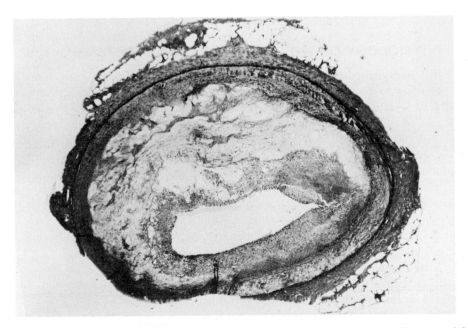

FIGURE 3 Cross section of the left anterior descending coronary artery in a graft recovered 2 yr postoperatively after death from myocardial infarction. Luminal narrowing results from an eccentric atheromatous plaque containing lipid. From Stinson et al. (5a).

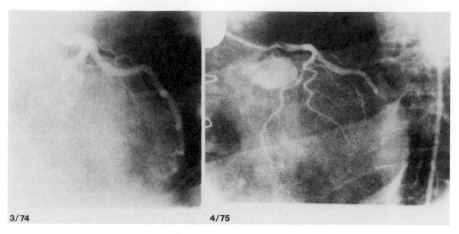

3/74   4/75

FIGURE 4   Selective left coronary arteriogram (right panel) obtained 2 yr postoperatively in a patient who developed accelerated donor coronary atherosclerosis. High-grade stenosis of the left anterior descending coronary artery and occlusion of the circumflex artery are evident.

are not present. Four patients have undergone reoperation for this reason, three successfully. This experience has documented both the feasibility and the value of cardiac retransplantation in selected cases. Retransplantation should be considered a realistic strategy in any patient with irreversible graft failure who is free from active infection.

PHYSIOLOGY OF THE TRANSPLANTED HEART

The transplanted heart is anatomically denervated at the time of operation, and its responses to physiological maneuvers or cardioactive drugs are characteristic of a denervated state. In no recipient, studied up through 7 yr after operation, has evidence of efferent autonomic reinnervation been identified. Persistent denervation, however, although associated with atypical responses to physiological interventions or cardioactive drugs that exert an influence through neural pathways, does not result in any important overall cardiovascular impairment. Electrophysiological studies have documented that pacemaker and conduction system functions in the transplanted heart are normal, as assessed by sinus node recovery times, conduction intervals (AH and HV), and atrioventricular nodal refractory periods. Beta receptors remain intact, as illustrated by responses to norepinephrine and isoproterenol and the effects of competitive blockade with propranolol.

Virtually all patients in our series who have survived 1 yr or more after transplantation have returned to New York Heart Association functional class I status. Cardiac catheterization studies performed one or more years postoperatively have documented normal or nearly normal function of the transplanted heart under resting conditions (6). The response of the transplanted heart to muscular exertion is characteristic of the denervated state, consisting of a slow, gradual increase in heart rate and cardiac output, both of which eventually reach normal or nearly normal levels for the amount of work performed during sustained exercise. The absolute level of cardiac output both at rest and during exercise, however, is in the lower range of normal, although the slope of the regression of cardiac output on oxygen consumption ("exercise factor") is identical to the normal value. The Frank-Starling mechanism is an important feature in augmenting stroke volume during the early stages of exercise. Other intrinsic mechanisms of the human myocardium, such as dependence on preload and afterload, as well as inotropic responses to changes in cardiac frequency remain intact. Studies in progress indicate that during sustained exertion the transplanted heart exhibits marked increases in contractile state that are heavily dependent on circulating levels of catecholamines. Hypersensitivity of the transplanted heart to beta receptor agonists, however, has not been documented. These studies have confirmed that intrinsic myocardial mechanisms, in combination with circulating catecholamine support, are sufficient to support ordinary physical activity.

LONG-TERM SURVIVAL

Postoperative survival rates, calculated by the actuarial method for the entire series of 129 patients, are 55, 47, 38, 30, and 27% at 1, 2, 3, 4, and 5 yr postoperatively. Standard errors for these survival rates do not exceed 5.5%. Fifty-two patients are currently living, 9 more than 5 yr after cardiac transplantation. Current expectations for survival after transplantation, however, are more accurately described by the survival experience of 63 consecutive patients who have undergone operation since October 1973, when immunosuppressive treatment with antithymocyte globulin of rabbit origin and transvenous endomyocardial biopsy for diagnosis of acute graft rejection were routinely incorporated into the program. Survival rates at 1, 2, and 3 yr postoperatively for these patients are 68, 62, and 59% (Fig. 5). A projection of these data, based on subsequent interval attrition rates, indicates an expectation for 5-yr survival after cardiac transplantation at present in the range 40–50%. Patients undergoing transplantation after failure of previous cardiac operations to provide therapeutic benefit have even higher 1-yr

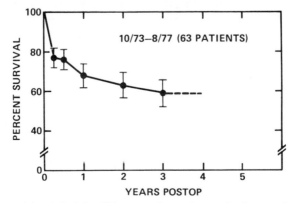

FIGURE 5 Postoperative survival in 63 consecutive patients who have undergone transplantation since October 1973.

survival rates, around 80%. The reasons for this phenomenon are not yet well defined, but this observation shows the potential usefulness of heart replacement for patients in whom ordinary forms of therapy have been exhausted.

Just as important as survival rates after transplantation is the quality of life of the patients undergoing this procedure. Rehabilitation may be defined simply as the restoration of physical and psychosocial capacity to a level at which the patient has the option to return to employment or to an activity of choice. Fifty-nine patients in our total series have survived for at least 1 yr after transplantation. On the basis of the definition of rehabilitation stated above, 90% of these patients have achieved rehabilitation at that time interval and the majority have returned to active employment.

CONCLUSION

Experience in cardiac transplantation at Stanford University Medical Center has documented that in carefully selected recipients biologic replacement of the heart not only extends longevity in patients with terminal cardiac disease, but also provides genuine rehabilitation. The success rates currently achieved are comparable or superior to those generally reported for renal transplantation from unrelated donors. The primary feature restricting more widespread application of cardiac transplantation as a therapeutic modality is the necessity for long-term generalized immunosuppression with its associated complications.

Cardiac transplantation remains a highly complex and challenging project. Despite the problems involved, however, worthwhile clinical results have been achieved. At present, the expectation for survival for at least 1 yr after transplantation is 67%, and 90% of long-term survivors have been rehabilitated. Studies of the function of the transplanted human heart have confirmed that although a denervated state persists, intrinsic myocardial mechanisms are sufficient to support the stresses of ordinary physical activity.

REFERENCES

1. Bieber, C. P., Lydick, E., Griepp, R. B., David, L. A., Oyer, P. E., and Stinson, E. B. Radioimmune assay of heterologous serum gamma globulin in patients receiving antihuman thymocyte globulin. Transplantation 20(5):393–398, 1975.
2. Griepp, R. B., Stinson, E. B., Bieber, C. P., Reitz, B. A., Copeland, J. G., Oyer, P. E., and Shumway, N. E. Control of graft arteriosclerosis in human heart transplant recipients. Surgery 81(3):262–269, 1977.
3. Lower, R. R. and Shumway, N. E. Studies on orthotopic homotransplantation of the canine heart. Surg Forum 11:18–19, 1960.
4. Reitz, B. A., Brody, W. R., Hickey, P. R., and Michaels, L. L. Protection of the heart for twenty-four hours with intracellular (high K$^+$) solution and hypothermia. Surg Forum 25:149–151, 1975.
5. Stinson, E. B., Caves, P. K., Griepp, R. B., Oyer, P. E., Rider, A. K., and Shumway, N. E. Hemodynamic observations in the early period after human heart transplantation. J Thor Cardiovasc Surg 69(2):264–270, 1975.
5a. Stinson, E. B., Griepp, R. B., Doug, E., Jr., and Shumway, N. E. Results of human heart transplantation Stanford University. Transplant. Proc 3(1):337–342, 1971.
6. Stinson, E. B., Griepp, R. B., Schroeder, J. S., Doug, E., Jr., and Shumway, N. E. Hemodynamic observations one and two years after cardiac transplantation in man. Circulation 45:1183–1194, 1972.

INDEX